Library of
Davidson College

VIRGINIA IN FOREIGN AFFAIRS, 1933-1941

Rorin Morse Platt

Visiting Assistant Professor of History
at
The University of Tennessee at Chattanooga

UNIVERSITY
PRESS OF
AMERICA

Lanham • New York • London

327.73
P719v

Copyright © 1991 by

University Press of America®, Inc.
4720 Boston Way
Lanham, Maryland 20706

3 Henrietta Street
London WC2E 8LU England

All rights reserved
Printed in the United States of America
British Cataloging in Publication Information Available

Library of Congress Cataloging-in-Publication Data
Platt, Rorin Morse.
Virginia in foreign affairs, 1933-1941 / by Rorin Morse Platt.
p. cm.
Includes bibliographical references and index.
1. United States—Foreign relations—1933-1945—Public opinion.
2. Public opinion—Virginia. I. Title.
E806.P57   1991
327.73'009'043—dc20   90–28401 CIP

ISBN 0–8191–7803–9 (cloth : alk. paper)

 The paper used in this publication meets the minimum requirements of
American National Standard for Information Sciences—Permanence
of Paper for Printed Library Materials, ANSI Z39.48–1984.

DEDICATION

TO

DR. WAYNE S. COLE,

The quintessential scholar, teacher, and gentleman.

ACKNOWLEDGEMENTS

I am eternally indebted to my dissertation advisor, Dr. Wayne S. Cole, Professor of History at the University of Maryland at College Park, to whom this study is dedicated. Dr. Cole guided the progress of this manuscript from beginning to end. He provided the author with invaluable criticism and advice. Professor Cole is the quintessential scholar, teacher, and gentleman.

I would also like to thank Dr. George H. Callcott, Professor of History at the University of Maryland at College Park, for being a second reader. He posed many excellent questions and made numerous helpful suggestions.

Pulitzer prize-winning editor and historian, Virginius Dabney, provided the author with many important insights into the critical issues of the Roosevelt era. His prominent role as an "opinion-maker" is well-documented in this study. I am most appreciative of his kindness, patience, and courtesy.

I am most grateful to the staffs of those libraries and repositories who assisted me in researching this work. I am especially indebted to the patient, knowledgeable, and courteous staffs at the Virginia State Library, the Virginia Historical Society, the University of Virginia Library, and the Manuscript Room of the Library of Congress.

Two Hearst Travel grants from the History Department of the University of Maryland made possible my research in a number of the manuscript collections consulted in this study.

I owe special gratitude to Muffin Kennedy, Connie P. Looney, and Mary Cleveland of The University of Tennessee at Chattanooga, who spent countless hours preparing and typing this book.

I would also like to express my sincere thanks to Amanda Marrion who typed the manuscript in its original form as a dissertation at the University of Maryland.

This book would not have been possible without the invaluable assistance, encouragement, and inspiration of Dr. and Mrs. John B. Catlett and especially Jane. Words cannot express my gratitude.

I am also indebted to my father, who provided me with constant support throughout my academic career.

Rorin Morse Platt

Richmond, Virginia
Chattanooga, Tennessee
November, 1990

CONTENTS

Foreword		vi
Preface		vii
List of Maps		xii
Chapter I	From Old Dominion to New Dominion: The Coming of Internationalism in the Cavalier State	1
Part I	Virginia, the New Deal, and Foreign Affairs in the Roosevelt Era	21
Chapter II	Depression, Roosevelt, and the New Deal in Virginia	21
Chapter III	The New Dominion in the Community of Nations	41
Chapter IV	Markets Beyond the Chesapeake: Virginia and Reciprocal Trade	63
Chapter V	Virginia is a Good Neighbor	79
Part II	Virginia and American Foreign Policy Before Pearl Harbor	111
Chapter VI	World War II: Virginia's Cornucopia	111
Chapter VII	Cavalier Neutrality	123
Chapter VIII	Virginia's Road to Pearl Harbor: The Triumph of Internationalism	153
Chapter IX	Conclusion	225
Bibliography		229
Index		249

FOREWORD

Rorin Platt has done a scholarly and well-written study of sentiment among Virginians concerning issues of foreign import in the years immediately preceding the entry of the United States into World War II. He has surveyed the question from every angle, scanned the pertinent documents and studied prevailing trends with a discerning eye.

The reluctance of Virginians and other Americans to be drawn into the war when the fighting began in Europe kept this country out of it at first. Despite Virginia's Anglo-Saxon heritage and its instinctive aversion to such a monster as Adolf Hitler, the Old Dominion was predominantly isolationist in the middle and late 1930s. But Britain's valiant defense in the face of Hermann Goering's roaring bombers caused a good many citizens of the state to modify their views. Then came Pearl Harbor, and Virginians and all other Americans made their united decision on that fateful Sunday afternoon to fight for survival.

Mr. Platt has put the whole problem of Virginia's attitude toward the war into proper perspective. He has canvassed the field and studied the views of all classes of Virginia citizens. He has examined those views in their economic, cultural, political and ideological aspects. The result is an important and illuminating study.

Virginius Dabney

PREFACE

Recent scholarship has argued that the South has not been consistently internationalist during much of the twentieth-century. Southern support for American intervention in the First and Second World Wars was based on economic self-interest, the blood tie to Great Britain, a martial tradition, and loyalty to the Democratic Party. Southern internationalism began to decline, however, as the South became more industrialized, protectionist-minded, less dependent on its cotton and tobacco exports, more Republican, and reluctant to intervene economically and militarily on behalf of non-Western states.[1]

While Virginia was overwhelmingly populated by native-born people of Anglo-Saxon heritage proud of their martial tradition and disdainful of the party of Lincoln, that tribe of Cavaliers had waged war against their English cousins more than once and had voted for Herbert Hoover in 1928. Nonetheless, Virginia's support for a more internationalist foreign policy during the Roosevelt era was also based on those economic, cultural, and political factors. The forces that played the most significant role in influencing those sentiments were, however, ideological, economic, and cultural.

This book is primarily an effort to describe the foreign policy sentiments of Virginians during the pre-Pearl Harbor Roosevelt era[2] and to examine the forces that helped shape those sentiments. It, furthermore, attempts to discern which political, ideological, cultural, and economic bases influenced the views of Virginians on four major foreign policy issues of that period: League of Nations and World Court membership, reciprocal trade,

---

[1] For accounts critical of the theme of "Southern internationalism," see Paul Seabury, The Waning of Southern 'Internationalism' (Princeton: Center of International Studies, 1957); Alexander DeConde, "The South and Isolationism," Journal of Southern History 24(1958): 332-46; Charles O. Lerche, Jr., The Uncertain South: Its Changing Patterns of Politics in Foreign Policy (Chicago: Quadrangle Books, 1964), pp. 34-57; Alfred O. Hero, Jr., The Southerner and World Affairs (Baton Rouge: Louisiana State University Press, 1965), p. 547; and George C. Herring and Gary R. Hess, "Regionalism and Foreign Policy: The Dying Myth of Southern Internationalism," Southern Studies Fall (1981): 247-77.

[2] For the most recent scholarly and comprehensive study of Franklin D. Roosevelt's foreign policy, see Robert Dallek, Franklin D. Roosevelt and American Foreign Policy, 1932-1945 (New York: Oxford University Press, 1979).

the Good Neighbor policy, and interventionism. While this study has not ignored the foreign policy opinions of Virginia's "common people," it has concentrated on the views of those politicians, churchmen, journalists, educators, businessmen, and labor leaders (i.e. "opinion-makers") who helped shape and guide the state's foreign policy views.

This state study of foreign affairs has attempted to fill the void in the history of Virginia's reaction to the major foreign policy issues of the pre-Pearl Harbor Roosevelt era. Heretofore, relatively few scholarly accounts have been written about Virginia's role during the era of the Second World War. This work also reiterated the importance of state studies of foreign policy. Most significantly, it has reenforced the argument that the foreign policy sentiments of Southerners (in this case, Virginians) were largely internationalist during that seminal period of modern history.

None of the major foreign policy issues examined in this study originated in the Commonwealth of Virginia. All of them had national or international origins. Consequently, few state studies of foreign policy during the Roosevelt era exist.[3] Nonetheless, America's embrace of internationalism

---

[3]Those state studies that helped serve as models for this book include: John C. Crighton, Missouri and World War One: A Study in Public Opinion (Columbia: University of Missouri Studies, 1947); Christopher C. Gibbs The Great Silent Majority: Missouri's Resistance to World War I (Columbia: University of Missouri Press, 1988); George C. Callcott, "Maryland's World War II" in Maryland and America: 1940 to 1980 (Baltimore and London: The Johns Hopkins University Press, 1985), pp. 29-58; C. Calvin Smith, War and Wartime Changes: The Transformation of Arkansas, 1940-1945 (Fayetteville, Ar.: University of Arkansas Press, 1986). In his historiographical piece, "Virginia in the Twentieth Century: Recent Interpretations," The Virginia Magazine of History and Biography 94(1986): 131-60, Ronald L. Heinemann argued that until recently, historians paid little attention to events and people of twentieth-century Virginia. Heinemann noted that while much has been written on Virginia political history during the past twenty years, the influence of the Second World War on Virginia has gone largely unnoticed. The impact of that "seminal event of the modern period" on the state, Heinemann contended, "demands a major treatise." Heinemann neglected, however, to mention Jonathan J. Wolfe's unpublished Ph.D. dissertation, "Virginia in World War II" (University of Virginia, 1971). Wolfe's monograph did not focus on the foreign policy views of Virginians during the war. Instead, it examined political, economic, and social developments in the state between 1940 and 1946. Wolfe described the political struggle between the conservative Byrd organization and the New Deal Democrats led by then Governor James H. Price. He paid particular

did have origins in the cultural backgrounds, political loyalties, economic changes, and struggles between the noninterventionists and interventionists in Virginia and throughout the states of the union.

A state's experiences can be representative of the country as a whole. Maryland historian George C. Callcott has argued: "As often as not, events and problems express themselves more intensely, and their outcomes are more clear, in a single state than in a national compromise that results when all states act collectively."⁴ That certainly was true in Virginia. The Old Dominion's accelerated pace of urbanization, industrialization, and modernization coincided with the strengthening of internationalist, interventionist forces in American society. That was also true of other states of the union. The growing industrialization and urbanization of the United States weakened the rural and small town bases for isolationism not only in Virginia, but throughout most of the country. The declining strength of Britain and France, the Axis challenges to peace, and changes in modern warfare propelled the United States into a more internationalist foreign policy.⁵ This study attempts to show how Virginia's experiences during the

___

attention to the political career and governorship of Colgate W. Darden, Jr. (1942-46), a conservative with considerable "political acumen" and "independence of action." Wolfe argued that Virginians disdained isolation and vigorously supported Roosevelt's interventionist foreign policy. The Second World War, Wolfe maintained, brought great economic change and prosperity to the Old Dominion. Federal monies helped pull Virginia out of the Great Depression. The salaries of federal government employees living in Virginia stimulated the state's economy. Newly-constructed defense plants provided thousands of Virginians with jobs. The war itself greatly accelerated Virginia's already-existing manufacturing and commercial concerns; it made the state's embrace of urbanization and industrialization irreversible. Race relations deteriorated during the war; that set the stage for later changes in Virginia. Yet the prosperity brought by the war cushioned social change in the state. After 1945, Virginians were convinced that the war had vindicated their value system. They saw themselves--the heirs of Washington and Jefferson--as the chief defenders of democracy against the evils of totalitarianism. Wolfe concluded that Virginians derived from World War II cogent reasons to support the United Nations.

⁴Callcott, Maryland and America, p. xi.

⁵Wayne S. Cole, Roosevelt and the Isolationists, 1932-45 (Lincoln, Nebraska and London, England: University of Nebraska Press, 1983), pp. 13-14. In this authoritative account of Roosevelt's policies and actions toward the isolationists, Cole argued that isolationism declined as its agricultural

pre-Pearl Harbor Roosevelt era contribute to an understanding of the national experience during those years. It describes America's embrace of internationalism working itself out in the cities, towns, and farms of the Old Dominion.

It should be stated at the outset that this book does not examine Virginia's attitudes concerning the Sino-Japanese war in East Asia. The focus of this study's treatment of interventionism pertains almost exclusively to Europe and American aid-to-Britain from 1939 through 1941. Most Virginians agreed with Roosevelt that the greatest threat to American national security and world peace came from Nazi Germany, not militarist Japan. Many Virginians believed that Hitler would attack the United States after conquering Britain. Few, if any, Virginians foresaw a Japanese attack on America. An overwhelming majority of Virginians also concurred with FDR's view that the security and survival of Britain and France were more important to American interests than was the fate of China. Virginians were linked to Britain by blood, language, religion, and economic and political values. The concerns of Christian missionaries notwithstanding, the same could not be said of their relationship with the Chinese. Finally, Virginians also agreed with Roosevelt that the United States should avoid a military confrontation in Asia so as to preserve American military power in the event of war with the Axis powers. (FDR's undeclared naval war against German submarines in the Atlantic did not extend to the Pacific.)[6]

This book is organized both topically and chronologically. Chapter one states the thesis and provides an overview of this study. The second chapter discusses the impact of the Great Depression on Virginia, popular acceptance of the New Deal's relief measures, and the strained relationship between the Roosevelt administration and Senators Carter Glass and Harry F. Byrd. Chapter three examines Virginians' views on United States' membership in the League of Nations and World Court. The fourth chapter studies the response of Virginia's political, economic, and press elites to the reciprocal trade agreements program. Chapter five describes the level of support the Good Neighbor policy enjoyed in the Old Dominion. The sixth chapter

---

bases succumbed to the growing industrialization, modernization, and urbanization of the United States. America's embrace of internationalism was due to those domestic influences as well as the external factors of repeated challenges from the Axis powers (and later the Soviet Union), the decline of Britain and France, and the scientific and technological advances of modern warfare (e.g. atomic weaponry), which made the "continentalist" concept of "fortress America" obsolete.

[6]Ibid., p. 239.

analyzes the economic benefits an increasingly industrialized and urbanized Virginia received as a result of American rearmament before and during the Second World War. Chapter seven studies Virginians' views on American neutrality during most of the 1930s. The eighth chapter examines Virginia's embrace of interventionism, with particular emphasis on aid-to-Britain. Chapter nine, the final chapter, seeks to draw some solid conclusions from the questions raised in this manuscript.

Hopefully, this study will encourage future scholarly examinations of Virginia's response to the major foreign policy issues of the twentieth-century. Much work needs to be done to fill the gap in the history of the commonwealth during the modern era. Additionally, historians might consider thoroughly reevaluating the whole question of southern internationalism during much of this century. If Virginia's experience was more than an aberration, then an abundance of evidence awaits the curious scholar.

LIST OF MAPS

Virginia's Nine Congressional Districts, 1941   3

Post-World War II Virginia   4

CHAPTER I

FROM OLD DOMINION TO NEW DOMINION:
THE COMING OF INTERNATIONALISM IN THE CAVALIER STATE

Because of domestic and external forces beyond the control of President Franklin D. Roosevelt, the United States turned away from isolationism even before the Japanese attack on Pearl Harbor. That was even more true in the Commonwealth of Virginia than in much of the rest of the country. During the pre-Pearl Harbor Roosevelt era, the overwhelming majority of Virginians embraced FDR's internationalist foreign policies for primarily ideological, national security, economic, and cultural reasons. In the Old Dominion, foreign policy positions came from the "top-down," not from the "bottom-up." The "leadership elite" formulated foreign policy attitudes, which filtered down to the grass roots level. Yet, most "common" Virginians agreed with the foreign policy views of those "opinion-makers." Most Virginians shared a common outlook and consensus world view that went beyond deference.

During the turbulent 1930s and early 1940s, world-wide depression and totalitarian aggression shook the foundations of the Western world. At home, FDR's New Deal program proved unable to restore economic prosperity. Abroad, Fascist Italy, Nazi Germany, and militarist Japan embarked on aggression and even war in Africa, Europe, and Asia, respectively. Civil war in Spain pitted Nationalists and Fascists against liberals, anarchists, Socialists, and Communists. In September, 1938, in Munich, Britain and France capitulated to Hitler's demands over Sudetenland, the German-speaking region of Czechoslovakia. Less than one-half year later, London and Paris paid a price for their appeasement of Hitler; Germany seized the rump of the Czech state. In August, 1939, Moscow and Berlin signed a nonaggression pact that enabled Hitler to invade Poland on September 1. Britain and France honored their treaty obligations to Warsaw and declared war on Germany on September 3, thus plunging Europe into war for the second time in the twentieth-century. By late summer, 1940, after the fall of France and during the "Battle of Britain," heated debate in the United States pitted interventionists against noninterventionists. American efforts to supply Britain with war material led the United States into a "shooting war" with German submarines in the Atlantic and pushed the country closer to actual war.

In response to those challenges, Virginians enthusiastically supported Roosevelt's policies of international cooperation, economic reciprocity, the "good neighbor," discretionary neutrality, and ultimately, interventionism. Most influential Virginians endorsed American cooperation with the League of Nations and United States membership in the World Court in the interests of international cooperation and world peace. They eagerly embraced the reciprocal trade program of Secretary of State Cordell Hull. Most Virginians believed that economic reciprocity would open additional markets for the state's exports and bring economic prosperity to the commonwealth. Influential Virginians were confident that increased trade, expanding markets, stronger hemispheric security, and a revitalized Monroe Doctrine would result from the Good Neighbor policy with Latin America. During the pre-World War II period, Virginians supported congressional neutrality legislation as well as greater presidential discretion over arms embargoes as the best ways for America to stay of European wars. After war broke out in Europe in September, 1939, Virginians quickly endorsed FDR's call for an end to the arms embargo, the extension of cash-and-carry, and aid-to-Britain. Their support for aid-short-of-war was based on their firm belief that Hitler threatened American liberty, democracy, neutrality, freedom of the seas, world markets, national security, and the survival of their English brethren. Imbued with a strong martial tradition, thousands of Virginians volunteered to fight for their country.

Unlike the "isolationist" states of the Midwest, the Old Dominion is part of the Atlantic Seaboard. Virginia is the farthest north of the southern states. West Virginia and Maryland form the state's northern border. Maryland and the District of Columbia lie to the northeast and the Atlantic Ocean to the east. North Carolina and Tennessee border Virginia on the south and Kentucky and West Virginia on the west. Modern Virginia has a surface area of 40,817 square miles, including 1,037 square miles of inland waters, excluding the 1,511 square miles of the Chesapeake Bay within the state's jurisdiction. It ranks 36th in size among the states. Virginia has 112 miles of Atlantic coastline and 230 miles of coastline on the Chesapeake Bay.[1]

Virginia's five major geographic regions include the tidewater, the piedmont, the Blue Ridge, the Valley of Virginia, and the Allegheny Mountains. Tidewater is Virginia's sandy coastal plain between the Atlantic Ocean and the fall line, an imaginary line that runs from north to south and intersects the rivers of eastern Virginia at the points where they are no longer navigable. The Potomac, Rappahannock, York, and James rivers divide the state's northern tidewater into narrow peninsulas. The Northern Neck is the peninsula between the Potomac and Rappahannock rivers. The land between the Rappahannock and York rivers is called the Middle Peninsula or Middle Neck. The Peninsula refers to the land between the York and James rivers. The Tidewater also includes the Eastern Shore, that portion of Virginia and

---

[1]Emily J. Salmon, ed. A Hornbook of Virginia History, 3rd edit. (Richmond: Virginia State Library, 1983), p. 5.

Congressional Directory

VIRGINIA
(9 districts)

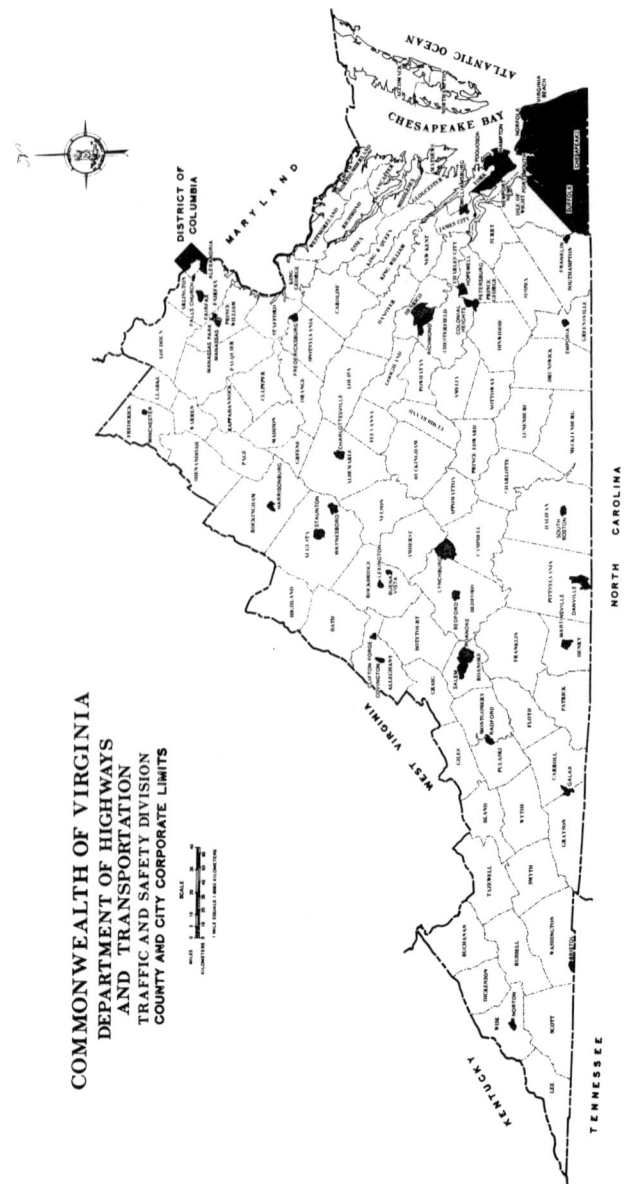

FROM OLD DOMINION TO NEW DOMINION 5

Maryland between the Chesapeake Bay and the Atlantic Ocean.[2]

The Piedmont refers to that area of rolling hills between the fall line and the Blue Ridge Mountains. The Blue Ridge Mountains are located west of the piedmont and stretch northeast to southwest; they form the easternmost range of the Allegheny Mountains. The Valley of Virginia is situated immediately west of the Blue Ridge and consists of a series of river valleys. The Shenandoah River, the northernmost valley, flows north from Augusta County to Harpers Ferry, West Virginia, where it meets the Potomac River. The James and Roanoke rivers and their tributaries run through the central portion of the Valley, from northern Rockbridge County to Roanoke County. The New River and Clinch and Holston rivers flow westward into the Ohio River and drain the southernmost part of the valley, southwest of the city of Roanoke. The Allegheny Mountains are located west of the Valley and form part of the Appalachian system. They run along the Virginia-West Virginia border and in the extreme southwestern counties of the Old Dominion.[3]

Three other, less easily defined geographic areas of Virginia include: Southside, Southwest Virginia, and Northern Virginia. Southside refers to that area of tidewater and piedmont located between the James River and the Virginia-North Carolina boundary and east of the Blue Ridge Mountains. Southwest Virginia is that region south of Roanoke and west of the Blue Ridge. Northern Virginia refers to those Virginia cities and counties located within an approximate 30 mile radius of Washington, D.C.[4]

During the Roosevelt presidency, two-thirds of Virginia's population lived on farms or in towns of 2,500 or less. In 1930, the state's population was 2,421,851 (20th nationally). Virginia was a culturally-homogeneous, deferential, politically-cohesive, socially-stable state. Between 1933 and 1941, Virginia's eleven-man congressional delegation remained solidly Democratic. The commonwealth's political elite practiced noblesse oblige, civility, honor, and fiscal restraint. An oligarchy controlled state government, but it was honest, frugal, and conservative.[5]

---

[2]Ibid., pp.3-4.

[3]Ibid., p. 4.

[4]Ibid., pp. 4-5.

[5]Ronald L. Heinemann, Depression and New Deal in Virginia: The Enduring Dominion (Charlottesville: University Press of Virginia, 1983), pp. 1-2,8; V. O. Key, Jr., Southern Politics In State and Nation (New York:

Throughout the pre-Pearl Harbor Roosevelt era, the overwhelming majority of Virginians were protestant. Southern Baptists constituted the largest religious denomination; Methodists came in second. Most Virginians were native-born whites with Anglo-Saxon or Scotch-Irish heritage. Twenty-seven percent of the state's population was black. Virginia was a traditional, aristocratic society of planters, farmers, miners, industrialists, businessmen, lawyers, doctors, teachers, and housewives. The Old Dominion was mostly a rural state, but its economy was diversified and balanced between agriculture, manufacturing, and trade. The presence of a major ocean port and proximity to the federal government in Washington also helped balance the state's economy. Major industries included tobacco, textiles, coal, timber, fishing, education, and state and federal government. Tobacco was the chief agricultural export and cash crop, followed by apples, peanuts, wheat, potatoes, and corn. Dairy and livestock farming was also important to the state's farm economy. More than 192,000 farmers lived in Virginia.[6]

Virginia was hard hit by the Great Depression, but suffered less than most other states because of its balanced economy, political conservatism, and spirit of traditionalism. Consequently, federal spending programs played a less influential role in Virginia than in other states. Labor strikes, growing urban unemployment, mine closings, sporadic rioting and violence, falling tobacco and wheat prices, and drought struck the Old Dominion. In response to that crisis, Governor John Garland Pollard--with the advice of Senator Harry F. Byrd--cut state expenditures and salaries, preserved a balanced budget, transferred the county highway system to state control, and continued the pay-as-you-go policy for road construction. Those fiscally conservative policies protected Virginians from a burdensome state debt and softened the impact of the depression on the commonwealth. By the late 1930s, Richmond had become the fastest growing industrial center in the county. Virginia's agriculture was also showing a good recovery. Even the "Roosevelt recession" of 1937-38 had a more limited impact on the state than on the rest of the country. Virginia's 3.1% jobless rate in 1937-38 was one of the lowest in the

---

Vintage Books, 1949), pp. 10-11, 19-20, 27-28.

[6]Howard Odum, <u>Southern Regions of the United States</u> (Chapel Hill: The University of North Carolina Press, 1936), pp. 91, 140-42; Oscar Handlin, <u>The American People in the Twentieth Century</u> (Cambridge: Harvard University Press, 1954), pp. 83-84; Howard Odum and Harry E. Moore, <u>American Regionalism: A Cultural-Historical Approach to National Integration</u> (New York: Henry Holt and Company, 1938), pp. 520, 535-36; Heinemann, <u>Depression and New Deal</u>, pp. 1-2, 8-10, 107.

United States.[7]

Most Virginians approved of the New Deal despite their traditional self-reliance. Roosevelt's emergency relief programs benefitted thousands of Virginians. Yet the electorate continued to support Senators Byrd and Glass, both vigorous critics of the president's programs. Senator Byrd embraced Roosevelt's balanced budget and states rights platform in the 1932 presidential election. He also supported--albeit temporarily--the National Industrial Recovery Act (NIRA), despite its dubious constitutionality. But he broke with the president in 1933 over the Agricultural Adjustment Act, which gave the secretary of agriculture unprecedented power. Roosevelt's deficit spending for public works programs and the growing bureaucratization of government alienated Byrd even more. Unlike Byrd, conservative Senator Carter Glass opposed the New Deal from the beginning. The senior senator from Virginia was particularly outraged by Roosevelt's "court-packing plan" by which liberal, pro-New Deal justices could be added to the United States Supreme Court. He attacked the president's decision to devalue the dollar and abandon the gold standard. Both senators opposed the Federal Emergency Relief Administration (FERA), the Works Progress Administration (WPA), the Public Works Administration (PWA), and other New Deal measures that brought jobs to the state.[8]

Roosevelt's efforts to purge conservatives from the Democratic Party in the South and Virginia and replace them with New Dealers backfired. His attempt to place a progressive judge on the federal bench, despite opposition from Glass and Byrd failed miserably. By 1938, Roosevelt had largely abandoned his domestic reform agenda and worked hard to gain southern congressional support for his foreign policy. A year later, even Glass and the president were reconciled. There was no tacit understanding or "deal" made between Roosevelt and Virginia's two senators. Glass and Byrd did not embrace FDR's aid-to-Britain policy in return for the president's abandonment of the New Deal in Virginia. Roosevelt simply lost his battle for reform but won the war for his increasingly interventionist policies. Senators Glass and Byrd--like their fellow Virginians--supported Roosevelt's internationalist policies for primarily ideological, national security, economic, and cultural reasons.[9]

---

[7]Heinemann, Depression and New Deal, pp. ix-x, 1-20, 169-78.

[8]Ibid., pp. ix, 44-47, 55, 58, 89, 137-40, 145-47.

[9]Ibid., pp. 147-52.

Warren F. Kuehl, a noted authority on internationalism, wrote: "As a foreign policy, it [internationalism] has usually been discussed as the antithesis of isolationism, and in that sense it has involved a definite commitment or political entanglement through multinational treaties or governmental membership in international organizations."[10] Kuehl also maintained: "The idea of distinct political entities, representing different cultures but related through formal bodies such as a League of Nations or world court, has remained at the core of political internationalist thought."[11] Indeed, throughout much of the pre-Pearl Harbor Roosevelt era, American internationalists advocated United States membership in the League of Nations and World Court; they also supported reciprocal trade agreements, the Good Neighbor policy, discretionary neutrality, and aid to Britain and France during the Second World War.[12]

Wayne S. Cole, the leading authority on Roosevelt and the isolationists, has argued that in the 1930s most Americans were isolationists. As adherents of America's traditional foreign policy, they did not want to sever economic relations with the rest of the world, but did oppose intervention in European wars, "entangling alliances" such as United States membership in the League of Nations and World Court, and Roosevelt's aid-short-of-war policies. Those "noninterventionists" were not pacifists; they supported military preparations for continental defense in the Western Hemisphere, but opposed military preparations designed for American involvement in foreign wars, particularly in Europe. Fearing that a large navy would facilitate intervention overseas, they generally opposed big naval appropriations. They favored air power preparations designed for continental defense. As unilateralists, the noninterventionists "guarded American sovereignty and freedom of action." According to Cole, "They wanted to leave Americans free to determine when, where, how, and whether the United States should involve itself abroad." American isolationists believed in the power of example; they argued that the United States could more effectively lead the world by strengthening

---

[10] Warren F. Kuehl, "Internationalism," in Encyclopedia of American Foreign Policy, ed. Alexander DeConde (New York: Scribner's, 1978), vol. 2, p. 443.

[11] Warren F. Kuehl, "Internationalists," in Biographical Dictionary of Internationalists, ed. Warren F. Kuehl (Westport, Conn. and London: Greenwood Press, 1983), p. ix.

[12] For a summary of Roosevelt's thinking on internationalism, see Warren F. Kuehl, "Internationalism and Peace," in Franklin D. Roosevelt: His Life and Times, An Encyclopedic View, eds. Otis L. Graham, Jr., and Meghan Robinson Wander (Boston: G. K. Hall & Co., 1985), pp. 205-208.

democracy, freedom, and prosperity at home than it could through involvement in foreign alliances and wars. They did not want the United States to be the "world's policeman" or to rebuild the world in an American image. Consequently, they supported the neutrality legislation of the 1930s, the Johnson Act (1934), and the Nye Committee investigation of the munitions industry (1934-36).[13]

During the 1930s, most of the leading isolationists were not conservatives; many were more liberal than Roosevelt. Many feared that America's involvement in foreign wars would destroy the New Deal's reforms at home and jeopardize the very freedoms they were supposed to defend. While in sympathy with Roosevelt's domestic progressivism, they favored restraining the president, the military, big business, and financiers as they operated in foreign affairs. The overwhelming majority of the isolationists were not pro-Nazi, pro-fascist, or pro-Axis. They did, however, oppose Roosevelt's aid-short-of-war policies, which they believed would lead to American involvement in the European war. The isolationists lost both their majority status and battle against Roosevelt's interventionist policies by the autumn of 1940, when most Americans--in support of the president's foreign

---

[13] Wayne S. Cole, "Isolationism," in Franklin D. Roosevelt: His Life and Times, and Encyclopedic View, eds. Otis L. Graham, Jr., and Meghan Robinson Wander (Boston: G. K. Hall & Co., 1985), pp. 211-13; Wayne S. Cole, Roosevelt and the Isolationists, 1932-45 (Lincoln, Nebraska and London: University of Nebraska Press, 1983), pp. 6-14. For the best scholarly historical definition of isolationism, see Albert K. Weinberg, "The Historical Meaning of the American Doctrine of Isolation," American Political Science Review 34(1940): 539-47. For a scholarly treatment of the subject during the twentieth-century, see Selig Adler, The Isolationist Impulse: Its Twentieth Century Reaction (London and New York: Abelard-Schuman, Ltd., 1957). See also Alexander DeConde, "On Twentieth-Century Isolationism," in Isolation and Security: Ideas and Interests in Twentieth-Century American Foreign Policy, ed. Alexander DeConde (Durham, N.C.: Duke University Press, 1957, pp. 3-32. Manfred Jonas provided a succinct summary of America's isolationist heritage and the evolution from isolationism to internationalism in "Isolationism," in the Encyclopedia of American Foreign Policy, ed. Alexander DeConde (New York: Scribner's, 1978), vol. 2, pp. 496-506. In Isolationism in America, 1935-1941 (Ithaca, N.Y.: Cornell University Press, 1966), Jonas analyzed the isolationism of the late 1930s, which combined the traditional notion of non-entanglement and unilateralism with the strong pacifist sentiments of that period. (ibid., pp. 23-24, 71, 98-99, 169). Also see Thomas G. Paterson, "Isolationism Revisited," The Nation 209 (1969): 166-69.

policy--believed it was more important for the United States to assure a British victory over the Axis powers than to keep out of the war.[14]

President Roosevelt concentrated on domestic economic and political affairs during his first term in office. He did not press for American membership in the League of Nations. The United States Senate never voted for American membership in that international body. During the 1930s, membership in the league was not a major issue. Public support for the league was very weak at that time. Nonetheless, Southerners continued to revere the name of the Virginia-born Woodrow Wilson, the chief architect of the league's covenant. According to a 1937 Gallup Poll, 44 percent of Southerners polled favored American membership in the league; that was the strongest support recorded in any region of the country. Many influential Virginians advocated international cooperation, American membership in the league, or at least collaboration with it. They believed that many of the league's failures (including World War II) were the result of America's refusal to join it. Many contended that American entry into that body would make it a more effective instrument of world peace; states would be less likely to defy the league if the United States were a member. Still, a number of Virginians remained disillusioned over the league's failure to halt aggression, end war, and make the world "safe for democracy." Even the league's supporters perceived it as weak and ineffective in the face of fascist aggression during the 1930s.[15]

In 1935, Roosevelt proposed to make the United States a member of the World Court. The president's half-hearted fight for the proposal resulted in the Senate's rejection of the treaty. Most southern Democratic senators supported the court resolution. Virginia's senators voted for adherence to the court every time. The Wilsonian legacy, influential support for international cooperation, and the past efforts of former Senator Claude A. Swanson, a leading advocate of the court, strongly influenced Virginians' support for the proposal. Most Virginians simply did not believe that American adherence would--in any way--compromise national sovereignty or security. Instead, they maintained that United States membership in the court would reduce the

---

[14] Cole, "Isolationism," pp. 211-13; Cole, Roosevelt and the Isolationists, pp. 6-14.

[15] George C. Herring and Gary R. Hess, "Regionalism and Foreign Policy: The Dying Myth of Southern Internationalism," Southern Studies Fall (1981), p. 256; Interview with Virginius Dabney, November 28, 1986, Richmond, Virginia.

chances of a world war.[16]

Primarily a producer of raw materials, the South had suffered from the Smoot-Hawley tariff of 1930 that restricted foreign imports and led to retaliation against American exports. The South exported 50-60% of its cotton, 40% of its tobacco, and 33% of its rice. That need for access to overseas markets helped explain the South's support for economic reciprocity and its alarm over Hitler's European war, which closed many of its traditional markets. The Great Depression, the European war, and Japan's reduction of its cotton imports led to the collapse of the foreign market. As a chief tobacco exporter, Virginia was particularly affected. In the fall of 1939, the British, the South's major buyer, withdrew from the bright leaf market due to government restrictions designed to conserve foreign exchange. Only the Commodity Credit Corporation's purchase of 360,000 pounds of tobacco on behalf of the British companies, saved the tobacco market from collapse. As a traditional supporter of low tariffs, the South was quick to embrace the reciprocal trade program of Secretary of State Cordell Hull, himself a Democrat and a Southerner. Hull's policy was designed to lower trade barriers and expand foreign markets for goods, including the South's cotton and tobacco. A 1938 Gallup Poll indicated that 92% of all Southerners supported reciprocal trade agreements; 94.8% of southern congressmen also supported Hull's program. Despite some opposition from southern textile and sugar manufacturers, the overwhelming majority of the South's elected representatives consistently voted for economic reciprocity. Virginia's support for reciprocal trade, Carter Glass, notwithstanding, was also economically-motivated. The high tariffs of the 1930s hurt the state's exports. Hull's policies created more markets for Virginia's tobacco.[17]

While the United States was reluctant to entangle itself in European affairs, it did, however, broaden its relationship with Latin America. The

---

[16] George L. Grassmuck, Sectional Biases In Congress on Foreign Policy (Baltimore: The Johns Hopkins Press, 1951), pp. 83-84, 88, 154; Interview with Dabney, November 28, 1986; Congressional Directory, 74th Congress, 1st sess., January, 1935, pp. 145-146, Congressional Record, 74th Congress, 1st sess., 1935, 79:1146-47.

[17] Virginius Dabney, "The South Looks Abroad," Foreign Affairs 19 (1940), pp. 172-176; Virginius Dabney, Below the Potomac: A Book About the New South (Port Washington, N.Y.: Kennikat Press, 1969), pp. 273-82; Key, Southern Politics, p. 353; Alexander DeConde, "The South and Isolationism," Journal of Southern History 24(1958), p. 339; Herring and Hess, "Regionalism and Foreign Policy," p. 256.

Good Neighbor policy President Herbert Hoover initiated in 1929-33 proved to be most prescient in light of America's battle with Hitler a decade later. The decision to forsake military intervention in Latin America produced improved relations that, in turn, provided the United States with much needed markets during the depression and friendly neighbors during World War II. The war strengthened hemispheric security and ties between the United States and Latin America. The Good Neighbor policy also manifested itself in increased trade and cultural relations between the "Colossus of the North" and its southern neighbors. Despite religious differences and trade competition, the South developed increased cultural and educational awareness of Latin America. Many schools introduced Spanish language courses and Latin American history into their curricula. Latin America scholars visited Richmond as part of a cultural exchange program. The Southern Council on International Relations endorsed the "Good Neighbor" policy at is annual "The South in International Affairs" conferences in 1940 and 1941. Most Virginians supported FDR's policy because they believed it would bring increased trade and prosperity to the commonwealth. They also contended that it would bolster American security in the Western Hemisphere and invigorate the Monroe Doctrine.[18]

The Second World War helped the South's economy expand at an unprecedented rate. Exports increased over 250%. The war provided more jobs per capita in the South than in any other part of the country. Virginia, with its fifty military and naval installations, gained economically from Roosevelt's military buildup during the pre-Pearl Harbor period. The Old Dominion was a chief beneficiary of the more than $10 billion the federal government poured into the South for defense production. In 1941, Virginia was among the top ten states receiving army and navy contracts. Munition and powder plants sprang up throughout the state.[19] Not surprisingly, the state's congressional delegation consistently supported defense appropriations. Residents of the Hampton Roads area, a strategically-located shipbuilding and military and naval center, were directly affected by the great defense boom. But their support for FDR's rearmament program and aid-to-Britain policies was based on the same fear shared by other Virginians: the Axis powers threatened American security, democracy, markets, and kindred across the

---

[18] Interview with Dabney, November 28, 1986; Bryce Wood, The Making of the Good Neighbor Policy (New York and London: Columbia University Press, 1961), p. 159; Marian D. Irish, "Foreign Policy and the South," The Journal of Politics X(1948), pp. 315-18.

[19] Irish, "Foreign Policy and the South," pp. 308-15. See also Jonathan J. Wolfe, "Virginia in World War II" (Ph.D. diss., University of Virginia, 1971), pp. 139-94, 196.

Atlantic.[20]

During the inter-war period, most Virginians saw no reason for the United States to involve itself in Europe's bloody conflicts. They remembered only too well the senseless slaughter of the First World War. Despite America's costly intervention, peace and democracy had not prevailed in postwar Europe. Anti-war and pro-neutrality sentiment existed throughout the commonwealth. Nonetheless, most of the state's political elite considered themselves internationalists. A majority of them advocated greater presidential discretion over arms embargoes. Even before the 1938 Anschluss and throughout the late 1930s, a majority of Southerners (including Virginians) were considerably more convinced than Americans in other parts of the country that there would be another major European war and that the United States could not or should not keep out of it. They were the least inclined of any Americans to agree that Britain and France should have appeased Hitler at Munich rather than go to war for the defense of Czechoslovakia.[21]

Perhaps the most crucial litmus test for the South's (and Virginia's) support for FDR's internationalist foreign policies was the issue of American aid-to-Britain during the pre-Pearl Harbor period. Its unhappiness with Roosevelt's domestic policies, notwithstanding, the South was the most internationalist, interventionist, belligerent, and pro-British section of the country on the eve of America's entry into the Second World War.[22] A May,

---

[20] In The Waning of Southern 'Internationalism' (Princeton: Center of International Studies, 1957), p. 15, Paul Seabury maintained that the South, attached to its European roots with its conservative values and institutions, considered Hitler a threat to its traditional way of life. More importantly, the Germans threatened the British-dominated market of which the South had so important a stake. Seabury concluded: "The articulate Southerner saw Nazi aggression as a dagger thrust at the heart of this system." (ibid.).

[21] Alfred O. Hero, Jr., The Southerner and World Affairs (Baton Rouge: Louisiana State University Press, 1965), pp. 92, 94; Interview with Dabney, November 28, 1986.

[22] William L. Langer and S. Everett Gleason, The Challenge to Isolation, 1937-1940 (New York: Harper & Brothers Publishers, 1952; 1964), p. 225; Dabney, "The South Looks Abroad," pp. 171, 177-78, Dabney, Below the Potomac, pp. 272- 285-88; Interview with Dabney, November 28, 1986. Dabney attributed the South's (and Virginia's) strong interventionist sentiments to: its large Anglo-Saxon population, the paucity of foreign-born,

1941, Gallup Poll revealed that the South was more willing than any other region of the country to declare war on Germany.[23] A Gallup Poll of early

---

German, or Italian-Americans in the South, Southern cotton and tobacco farmers' dependence on British markets, England's sympathy with the Confederacy, the South's martial tradition, the incompatibility of George Mason's Bill of Rights with totalitarianism, and hatred of Hitler. See also John Temple Graves, "The Fighting South," Virginia Quarterly Review 18 (1942): 60-61, 68. Graves, a Southern journalist, argued that "it is not the existence of an Anglo-Saxon tradition which explains the Southern position in this war so much as it is the non-existence of a Germanic tradition. . . . the South's greater belligerency today comes not of ties with any country across the sea but a lack of ties" (ibid., p. 68). See also Graves' The Fighting South (New York: G. P. Putnam's Sons, 1943), pp. 5, 13-18. Samuel Lubell agreed with Graves in The Future of American Politics, 2nd edit., rev. (Garden City, N.Y.: Doubleday & Company, Inc., 1956), p. 141; C. Vann Woodward, The Burden of Southern History, rev. edit.(Baton Rouge and London: Louisiana State University Press, 1960; 1968), p. 194; George B. Tindall, The Emergence of the New South, 1913-1945 (Baton Rouge: Louisiana State University, 1967), pp. 687-88, 691. Tindall wrote that the South's support for a vigorous foreign policy was due to its identification with the British, German conquests that had jeopardized cotton and tobacco trade with Europe and Britain, few German, Italian, or Irish elements that had formed an anti-British or isolationist nuclei in other areas, Southern history having bred a psychology of danger and defense, and the South's military-patriotic tradition. Also see DeConde, "The South and Isolationism," pp. 332-33; Wayne S. Cole, "America First and the South, 1940-1941,"Journal of Southern History 22 (1956): 36-47. Southern support for Roosevelt's interventionist policies, Cole concluded, was due to is large Anglo-Saxon population, proud military tradition, loyal Democratic constituency, dependence on foreign markets, desire for increased economic prosperity (which a war might bring), protection of home and hearth, and its belief that the war was a struggle between the forces of good versus evil. The most recent study of the South and foreign affairs, Tennant S. McWilliams' The New South Faces the World: Foreign Affairs and the Southern Sense of Self, 1877-1950 (Baton Rouge: Louisiana State University Press, 1988) traced the evolution of the New South's foreign policy sentiments from the isolationism of the postbellum era to the internationalism of the Cold War period. McWilliams' neo-revisionist work argued that the South's embrace of expansionism and internationalism was a symptom of deep-seated sectional insecurities. Southern support for Wilsonianism continued throughout the 1920s and 1930s and culminated in the South's belligerent anti-Communism during the post-World War II era.

[23] Irish, "Foreign Policy and the South," p. 312.

October, 1941, indicated that 88% of all Southerners believed it more important that Germany be defeated than for the United States to keep out of the war.[24]

Between 1933 and 1941, southern congressmen were less supportive of "isolationism" and neutrality than were their colleagues from other parts of the country. Political scientist Paul Seabury has written: "The South's legislative role . . . furnished the bedrock of support without which United States policy might well have been paralyzed in the European crisis, or at least far more irresolute that it was."[25] Southern historian George B. Tindall maintained that the South's legislative role "furnished . . . the cement that bound together a divided party." In 1941, Senator Glass favored "doing every thing possible, to bring about the downfall of Hitler and his gang." He declared that American ships should "blow hell out of" any Nazi U-boats they encountered. Glass was "in the vanguard" of the congressional battle for aid-to-Britain.[26] Despite their opposition to many of his economic and social programs, southern congressmen provided Roosevelt with overwhelming support for aid-short-of-war policies. Southern political scientist V.O. Key, Jr., observed that on 34 of 76 roll call votes dealing with foreign policy during the late 1930s and early 1940s, Southerners (including Virginians) provided more solid support for FDR's policies than other Democrats or Republicans.[27] Ninety-eight percent of southern Democrats in Congress supported the

---

[24] George Gallup, The Gallup Poll: Public Opinion, 1935-1971, vol. I (New York: Random House, 1972), pp. 300-301.

[25] Robert A. Dahl, Congress and Foreign Policy (New York: Harcourt, Brace and Co., 1950), p. 192; Seabury, Waning of southern 'Internationalism,' p. 2.

[26] Tindall, Emergence of the New South, pp. 687, 691; Wolfe, "Virginia in World War II, pp. 211-12.

[27] Irish, "Foreign Policy and the South," pp. 306-26; Key, Southern Politics, pp. 352-54; Irving Howard, "The Influence of Southern Senators on American Foreign Policy from 1939 to 1950" (Ph.D. diss., University of Wisconsin, 1955); Elmo Roberds, "The South and United States Foreign Policy, 1933-1952" (Ph.D. diss., University of Chicago, 1955); DeConde, "The South and Isolationism," pp. 340-41; Charles O. Lerche, Jr., The Uncertain South: Its Changing Patterns of Politics in Foreign Policy (Chicago: Quadrangle Books, 1964), p. 48.

president's national defense and military assistance to the Allies measures.[28] Southerners furnished the strongest support of any region of the country for the Neutrality Act of 1939, which repealed the arms embargo and extended cash-and-carry, the Burke-Wadsworth Selective Service Act (1940) and the Draft Extension Act (1941), the Lend-Lease Act (1941), the Ship Seizure Bill (1941), and repeal of the Neutrality Act (1941). In October, 1939, twenty of the sixty-three Senate votes for repeal of the arms embargo came from the South; only Senator Robert Reynolds, the controversial isolationist from North Carolina, opposed it. In the House of Representatives, 110 Southerners voted against a motion to retain the arms embargo, and only 8 voted for. In September, 1940, the South led all other regions of the United States in congressional support of the selective service act. Southerners voted 103 to 3 in favor of the bill in the House and 28 to 2 in favor of it in the Senate. The extension of the draft passed by only one vote in 1941; again, southern support was overwhelming and critical. In March, 1941, 120 Southerners in the House voted for Lend-Lease and only 5 opposed it. In the Senate, 29 Southerners supported it and only Reynolds voted against it. Lend-Lease would not have passed without those southern votes. Again, the "solid Democratic South" provided the president with the crucial backing he needed in order to proceed with his aid-to-Britain policies.[29]

From 1933 through 1938, foreign policy issues were largely down-played in most congressional and presidential elections throughout the country. Foreign policy reemerged as an important issue in the 1940 election. Both presidential candidates, Wendell L. Willkie and Franklin D. Roosevelt, were committed to an internationalist foreign policy. Nevertheless, neither supported American military intervention (i.e. troops) in the European conflict. Most isolationists probably voted for Willkie, and most interventionists voted for FDR, though many conservative Republican businessmen voted against him. Neither party provided the electorate with clear foreign policy alternatives (as was generally the case throughout American history). Due to equivocation on foreign policy issues during the campaign, the election results did not constitute a clear mandate on foreign policy. Nonetheless, Roosevelt's victory assured him of another term in which

---

[28] Key, Southern Politics, pp. 353-54; Howard, "Influence of Southern Senators," pp. 30-43, 51-52, 62, 129, 157.

[29] Lerche, Uncertain South, p. 38; DeConde, "The South and Isolationism," pp. 341-42; Herring and Hess, "Regionalism and Foreign Policy," pp. 257-58.

to battle both the isolationists at home and the Axis powers abroad.[30]

There was little disagreement over foreign policy issues in Virginia during the 1940 election. Roosevelt's interventionist policies found favor with a solid majority of Virginians of diverse political, economic, ethnic, religious, and occupational backgrounds throughout the commonwealth. Virginia's farmers, workers, teachers, editors, businessmen, clergy, professionals, Democrats, conservatives, liberals, New Dealers, and Byrd organization regulars stood united in their support of the president. Despite their growing disillusionment with his New Deal programs and opposition to a third term, many Virginians considered FDR's foreign policy experience essential to American security during the world war. The state's congressional delegation was more likely to fault the Roosevelt administration's failure to halt defense plants strikes than to criticize its increasingly risky interventionist policies.[31]

Public pressure groups played major roles in the foreign policy debates of 1940-41. They served as important, albeit inexact, barometers of public opinion. The two most influential groups in Virginia were William Allen White's Committee to Defend America by Aiding the Allies and the militant Fight for Freedom Committee. Most Virginians agreed with the aid-short-of-war views of the White Committee, although the Fight for Freedom Committee was much larger and better organized. Senator Glass served as its honorary national chairman. The America First Committee, the country's leading noninterventionist organization, found little support in the South, and especially in Virginia. Chapters were organized in Richmond, Norfolk, and Roanoke, but they were small and ineffective. The American First Committee had virtually died out in the South by late 1941, when it has reached its highest degree of support in the North and Middle West.[32]

---

[30] See pp. 383-405 in Cole's _Roosevelt and the Isolationists_ for an excellent discussion of the 1940 election campaign in which isolationism versus interventionism and a third term for FDR were major issues.

[31] Interview with Dabney, November 28, 1986.

[32] Cole, "American First and the South," pp. 36-47. The best analyses of sources of isolationist support include Ralph H. Smuckler, "The Regions of Isolation, _The American Political Science Review_ 47 (1953), pp. 386-401. Smuckler wrote: "The absence of isolationist strength in the South and Southwest [found in this study] was in striking contrast to its presence in states of the North." (ibid., p. 397). See also Leroy N. Rieselbach, _The Roots of Isolationism: Congressional Voting and Presidential Leadership in Foreign Policy_ (Indianapolis: Bobbs-Merrill Company, 1966); Jonas, _Isolationism in_

In the autumn of 1940, after the fall of France and during the Battle of Britain, isolationism reached its lowest level of popularity in the Old Dominion. Stirred by Britain's plight, Virginians had become considerably more militant. The eminent historian and Pulitzer prize-winning editor of the Richmond Times-Dispatch, Virginius Dabney, argued that the South stood squarely against the Axis tyranny. He asserted that the South supported aid-to-Britain even if it meant American entry into the European war. Dabney maintained that the war made the United States realize its "intimate relationship to the rest of the world."[83] As early as May, 1940, he wrote:

> This country is entering a new era. It is an era in which the isolationist congressman of the Middle West and Far West have been almost wholly discredited, for no proof is required to demonstrate that the United States is drastically affected by what has happened, and is happening, on the plains of France and Flanders. Mere incantations to the effect that we ought to let Europe go hang, and to mind our own business, no longer impress any informed person as sensible. We still must keep out of the war, but we cannot possibly claim that the outcome of the war makes no difference to us. It makes an enormous difference.[34]

Virginia's proud military traditions certainly influenced the foreign policy views of its citizens. Lexington was the home of the Virginia Military Institute (VMI), the "West Point of the South." Army Chief of Staff General George Catlett Marshall and General George S. Patton attended the celebrated academy. Virginia was the birthplace of some of the country's greatest generals and war heroes: George Washington, Robert E. Lee, and Thomas J. "Stonewall" Jackson. The Old Dominion would achieve similar distinction during the Second World War. Virginians eagerly volunteered for

---

America, p. 22; and Samuel Lubell, "Who Votes Isolationist and Why," Harper's Magazine 202(April 1951): 29-36.

[33] Dabney, "South Looks Abroad," pp. 171, 187.

[34] Richmond Times-Dispatch, May 20, 1940, p. 10; Dabney to Rorin M. Platt, December 7, 1986, (Letter in author's possession.); Wolfe, "Virginia in World War II," p. 211. Wolfe wrote: "Virginians were as incapable of indifference toward international affairs as toward race relations. They had long rejected Isolationism of the mid-western stamp and all its Republican supporters. Virginians generally also had little use for pacifism. In fact, people in the Old Dominion usually exhibited bellicosity in many situations and were interventionists. They revered military virtues and military leaders. These traits were clearly demonstrated in the early 1940s." (ibid.)

the armed forces. Many were honored for their bravery; thousands fell in battle in service to their country. The South led the country in voluntary enlistments in the armed services even before the draft became law.[35]

While relatively few foreign-born, Roman Catholic, German, Italian, and Irish-Americans lived in the state during the pre-Pearl Harbor period, Virginians of those backgrounds were not in vocal opposition to Roosevelt's foreign policies by early 1941. The commonwealth's overwhelmingly white, protestant, Anglo-Saxon population was strongly pro-British and interventionist. Even the state's black editors supported interventionism and contended that blacks should enjoy the right to serve their country in all branches of the armed forces. Virginia's tiny Jewish community was also part of that foreign policy consensus.[36]

Unquestionably, most Virginians perceived Hitler as a dangerous threat to Western civilization, Christianity, democracy, and the national security interests of the United States. They believed that Hitler's war violated American neutrality and freedom of the seas. It also closed European markets for Virginia's exports and threatened to destroy Great Britain, the mother of parliaments. Consequently, they supported any means necessary--rearmament, aid-to-Britain, and even war itself--to protect their economic interests, save their ancestral homeland, and preserve their most fundamental political ideals. As heirs of those Virginians who built the republic, they did not shrink from their duty to defend the world's greatest bastion of liberty from the legions of tyranny.

---

[35] Louis D. Rubin, Jr., Virginia: A History (New York and London: W. W. Norton & Co., 1984), p. 174; Irish, "Foreign Policy and the South," p. 312; Graves, "Fighting South," p. 61; Graves, Fighting South, p. 5.

[36] Wolfe, "Virginia in World War II," pp. 211-12.

PART I

VIRGINIA, THE NEW DEAL, AND FOREIGN AFFAIRS IN THE ROOSEVELT ERA

CHAPTER II

DEPRESSION, ROOSEVELT, AND THE NEW DEAL IN VIRGINIA

Virginius Dabney was certainly correct when he wrote that "The hard-pressed citizens of the commonwealth ... came through the depression with fewer scars, both material and psychological, than were suffered by the people of most other states." He credited that to the efficient management of the state's relief agencies and the traditional self-reliance of Virginia's citizenry. "At all events," Dabney concluded, "the Old Dominion emerged from the ordeal in relatively good shape, with her agriculture showing a good recovery and her industry ahead."[1]

Most historians accept that characterization of Virginia during the 1930s.[2] The impact of the Great Depression and New Deal on Virginia was indeed softened by the state's balanced economy, political conservatism, and spirit of traditionalism. While the New Deal's relief and reform measures affected the lives of thousands of Virginians, the enduring effects of its program were minimal; Virginia remained anything but a modern, progressive state.[3] Like many other states, however, Virginia faced unprecedented

---

[1] Virginius Dabney, Virginia: The New Dominion (Charlottesville: University Press of Virginia, 1971), p. 506.

[2] Ronald L. Heinemann, Depression and New Deal in Virginia: The Enduring Dominion (Charlottesville: University Press of Virginia, 1983), pp. ix-x; Matthew Page Andrews, Virginia: The Old Dominion (Garden City, N.Y.: Doubleday, Doran & Company, Inc., 1937), pp. 583-84, 588-90; Louis D. Rubin, Jr., Virginia: A History (New York and London: W. W. Norton & Company, 1984), pp. 169-71.

[3] Heinemann, Depression and New Deal, pp. ix-x, 183-90; Robert F. Hunter, "Virginia and the New Deal," in The New Deal: The State and Local Levels, eds. John Braeman, Robert H. Bremner, and David Brody (Columbus, Ohio: Ohio State University Press, 1975), pp. 103-36. Hunter agreed with Heinemann that due to its balanced economy, Virginia was less affected by the depression than were other states and that helped to reduce the influence

economic and social turmoil during the 1930s. Labor unrest, unemployment, plummeting incomes, bankruptcies, mine closings, occasional violence, reduced crop and coal production, declining industrial output, a halving of exports, falling tobacco and wheat prices, and drought plagued the Old Dominion. In early 1932, with the blessing of Senator Harry F. Byrd,[4] Governor John Garland Pollard, also a fiscal conservative, cut state expenditures and salaries (including his own), maintained a balanced budget, transferred the county highway system to state control, and preserved the pay-as-you-go policy for

---

of federal spending programs in the state. The federal government's farm programs were not suited for Virginia's agriculture. Urban relief affected fewer in Virginia than in more urbanized states. Consequently, Hunter wrote, "The New Deal had little to offer that would meet Virginia's social and economic needs." (ibid.).

[4]Most biographical accounts of Byrd's political career are rather sympathetic. See James R. Sweeney, "Harry Byrd: Vanished Policies and Enduring Principles," The Virginia Quarterly Review 52(1976): 596-612. "No Virginian of the 20th century," Sweeney wrote, "has left so deep an imprint on the politics of the Old Dominion as did Senator Harry F. Byrd, Sr. . . . While some Virginians regarded the aristocratic Byrd as a symbol of reaction, others saw in him the essence of all that was good in Virginia: honor, conviction, courage, and a selfless dedication to the public weal . . . . [Byrd] is remembered not only as the preeminent figure in Virginia politics but also as a leading conservative Democrat in the United States Senate." (ibid., p. 596). A majority of Virginians admired, respected, and even loved Senator Byrd, a descendant of one of Virginia's oldest and most prominent families. An honest politician well-respected by his Senate colleagues, Byrd once refused to accept $200,000 in federal soil-conservation payments to which he was legally entitled, because he had himself voted for the law under which the payment was made. See Rubin, Virginia, p. 173, and William S. White, "Meet the Honorable Harry (the Rare) Byrd," Reader's Digest 82(1963); 205-12. For accounts of Byrd's early political career, see Robert T. Hawkes, "The Emergence of a Leader: Harry Flood Byrd, Governor of Virginia, 1926-1930," Virginia Magazine of History and Biography 82(1974): 259-81. Hawkes wrote that Byrd's governorship (1926-30) exemplified his lifelong philosophy of efficiency and economy and "would be the most significant and progressive administration in twentieth-century Virginia." (ibid., pp. 281, 259-60). See also Hawkes's "The Career of Harry Flood Byrd, Sr., To 1933" (Ph.D. diss., University of Virginia, 1975). A political conservative throughout his career, Byrd's limited government and fiscally responsible views appealed to a majority of Virginia's voters (ibid., pp. ii-iii). A look at Byrd's first few years as senator under the New Deal can be found in Joe B. Tarter's "Freshman Senator Harry F. Byrd: 1933-1934" (M.A. thesis, University of Virginia, 1972).

DEPRESSION, ROOSEVELT, AND THE NEW DEAL IN VIRGINIA

road construction.[5] As a result of those draconian measures, Virginians escaped an insurmountable state debt and suffered less than most of their fellow Americans. By the end of the decade, Richmond had become the country's fastest growing industrial center. Despite the "Roosevelt recession" of 1937-38, few Virginians faced unemployment; even the state's agricultural sector experienced prosperity.[6]

In the 1932 presidential election, Virginians supported Franklin D. Roosevelt[7] by a more than two-to-one margin. While some Virginians gave early favorite-son support to Senator Byrd,[8] most Democrats enthusiastically

---

[5]See John L. Hopewell, "John Garland Pollard: A Progressive in the Byrd Machine," in The Governors of Virginia, 1860-1978, eds. Edward Younger and James T. Moore (Charlottesville: University Press of Virginia, 1982), pp. 247-60. As governor, Pollard supported balanced budgets and stable taxes. He embraced Byrd's program and "never wavered from it." Hopewell believed that Pollard's success in achieving reforms was largely due to his compromising and cooperation with the Byrd organization. (ibid., pp. 253, 259-60). Also see Hopewell's "An Outsider Looking In: John Garland Pollard and Machine Politics in 20th Century Virginia" (Ph.D. diss., University of Virginia, 1976); Heinemann, Depression and New Deal, pp. 13-18.

[6]Heinemann, Depression and New Deal, pp. 3-20, 170; Hopewell, "John Garland Pollard," pp. 253, 259; Rubin, Virginia, pp. 169-71.

[7]For the most comprehensive study and best biography of FDR, see Frank Freidel's four volume work: Franklin D. Roosevelt (Boston: Little, Brown and Company, 1952-73). A good single-volume treatment of Roosevelt is James MacGregor Burns, Roosevelt: The Lion and Fox (New York: Harcourt, Brace, and Company, 1956). Burns wrote that FDR was more like a fox than a lion; he was more likely to manipulate politicians than confront them. Roosevelt's shrewd tactics, political accommodations, and failure to make full use of his leadership abilities, Burns concluded, undermined the president's reform agenda. See also Friedel's F.D.R. and the South (Baton Rouge: Louisiana State University Press, 1965). That is the best work available on the New Deal and the South.

[8]For authoritative accounts of Byrd's unsuccessful 1932 quest for the presidency, see Brent Tarter, "A Flier on the National Scene: Harry F. Byrd's Favorite-Son Presidential Candidacy of 1932," Virginia Magazine of History and Biography 82(1974): 282-305, and Ronald L. Heinemann, "Harry Byrd for President: The 1932 Campaign," Virginia Cavalcade 25(1975): 28-37.

embraced their party's nominee who ran on a balanced budget, reduced government spending, and states' rights platform.[9] That public support for Roosevelt continued throughout his presidency.[10] Most Virginians endorsed the New Deal's[11] reforms despite their conservative beliefs, and gave even greater support to Senators Glass and Byrd, both strong opponents of the president's policies.[12]

---

[9] Heinemann, Depression and New Deal, pp. 44-45.

[10] Ibid., pp. ix, 44-51; Rubin Virginia, pp. 170-71.

[11] For the best survey of political perspectives and New Deal policies during the 1930s, see William E. Leuchtenburg's Franklin D. Roosevelt and the New Deal, 1932-1940 (New York, Evanston, Ill., and London: Harper & Row Publishers, 1963). Leuchtenburg saw the New Deal as an unfinished social revolution that benefitted farmers and workers, but left behind the urban poor, sharecroppers, and blacks. A more critical appraisal of Roosevelt and the New Deal can be found in Paul Conkin's The New Deal (New York: Harlan Davidson, 1967; 1975). Conkin argued that Roosevelt lacked great leadership qualities and a definite economic policy. Despite the New Deal's efforts to end the depression, poverty and unemployment persisted. Historiographical essays on the New Deal are offered in Alonzo Hamby's The New Deal: Analysis & Interpretation (New York and London: Longman, 1981). For the New Deal's affect on the states, see James T. Patterson, "The New Deal and the States," American Historical Review 73(1967): 70-84. Patterson maintained that the New Deal did help change the states. Many states centralized services, increased taxes, embraced progressive labor laws, and increased relief spending. (ibid., p. 84). See also Freidel, F.D.R. and the South. Freidel wrote that without the South, Roosevelt's 1932 election victory, the enactment of the New Deal's programs, and aid-to-Britain would not have been possible. (ibid., pp. 2, 33, 46). Southern congressmen supported the New Deal because of party loyalty and the economic assistance it brought to their constituents. (ibid., pp. 53-54).

[12] Heinemann, Depression and the New Deal, p. ix; Robert F. Hunter, "Carter Glass, Harry Byrd, and the New Deal, 1932-1936," Virginia Social Sciences Journal 4(1969): 91-103. Hunter saw Virginians' support for Byrd, Glass, as well as FDR, as a paradox. (ibid., p. 91), a "manifestation of a desire for a balance of power in Washington; a qualified endorsement of the social and economic reforms of Roosevelt, with the safety factor of watchdogs of the treasury like Glass and Byrd to keep them from going too far or costing too much." (ibid., p. 102).

DEPRESSION, ROOSEVELT, AND THE NEW DEAL IN VIRGINIA 25

In 1933, Governor Pollard appointed Byrd to the Senate seat vacated by then Senator Claude A. Swanson, whom FDR had chosen as his secretary of the navy. Byrd supported Roosevelt for president after his own nomination had died on the floor of the 1932 Democratic convention. During the Hundred Days he continued that support until faced with the Agricultural Adjustment Act and still more deficit spending for public works programs. Byrd then joined his colleague Senator Glass[13] in opposing the National Industrial Recovery Act[14] and other domestic programs.[15] Despite being offered the secretaryship of the treasury under Roosevelt, Glass became,

---

[13] Biographies of Glass are generally overly-sympathetic or incomplete. See Alfred C. Koeniger, "'Unreconstructed Rebel': The Political Thought and Senate Career of Carter Glass, 1929-1936" (Ph.D. diss., Vanderbilt University, 1980). Koeniger portrayed Glass as a courageous, crafty, calculating statesman whose conservatism in the 1930s sprang from the same factors that had made him a reformer during the Progressive era. Glass's sympathies were with the business-oriented middle class whose individualism he associated with the early American republic. (ibid., pp. iii-v). See also James E. Palmer, Jr., Carter Glass: Unrecognized Rebel (Roanoke, Va.: Institute of American Biography, 1938), Rixey Smith (Glass's secretary) and Norman Beasley, Carter Glass: A Biography (New York and Toronto: Longmans, Green and Co., 1939), and Harry E. Poindexter, "From Copy Desk to Congress: The Precongressional Career of Carter Glass," (Ph.D. diss., University of Virginia, 1966).

[14] See Ronald L. Heinemann's "Blue Eagle or Black Buzzard? The National Recovery Administration in Virginia," Virginia Magazine of History and Biography 89(1981): 90-100. The NRA was initially accepted in Virginia where workers benefited from the most minimal wage and hour standards, Heinemann argued. But its liabilities outweighed its assets: "too many codes, too many bureaucrats, too little muscle, and too little trust" compounded with persistent unemployment and no prospect of prosperity fueled criticism of the NRA throughout the state. (ibid.).

[15] Heinemann, Depression and New Deal, pp. 46-47, 107-8, 137-40; Rubin, Virginia, pp. 170-171; Hunter, "Glass, Byrd, and the New Deal," p. 91. Hunter wrote that Glass and Byrd were considered "key figures in the conservative coalition in opposition to nearly everything Franklin D. Roosevelt represented." (ibid).

instead, an outspoken foe of New Deal liberalism in Virginia.[16] Glass warned that "Roosevelt is driving this country to destruction faster than it has ever moved before. Congress is giving this inexperienced man greater power than that possessed by Mussolini and Stalin, put together."[17]

Throughout Roosevelt's presidency, both of Virginia's senators consistently opposed the New Deal's domestic reforms as destructive of constitutional government. Glass and Byrd voted against relief programs, farm bills, labor reforms, housing legislation, the Social Security Act, progressive taxation, and even FDR's executive appointments. Leading all of his fellow Democrats in the Senate, Glass voted against Roosevelt's major domestic programs 81 percent of the time. Byrd opposed 65 percent of the president's legislation.[18]

The significance of Virginia's two senators' opposition to the New Deal extended far beyond the Senate floor where they cast their votes. It permeated the very heart and soul of Virginia politics. Historian Allen Moger has written that "Virginia's reputation for political and economic conservatism is usually attributed to some of the state's able leaders of recent years. But both the leaders and their policies," Moger concluded, "are largely the result of Virginia history and tradition. . . . Conservatism and tradition have both played a part in Virginia life and government, a fact that largely explains the state's reputation for dignity, honesty, and efficiency in government. . . . It has prevented too rapid change and has saved the commonwealth from political and fiscal extremes."[19] Conservative Democratic Virginia was described by a foremost political scientist as a "political museum piece," controlled by an honorable, efficient, pro-business, oligarchy headed by Senator Byrd.[20] With its "tightly articulated hierarchy of power," "competent management," and "restricted electorate," the so-called "Byrd machine" dominated Virginia's politics for most of the twentieth-century. Due to its power and influence, on the average only 11.5 percent of eligible voters voted in the state's Democratic primaries between 1925 and 1945. Thus a

---

[16] Heinemann, Depression and New Deal, pp. 45, 47, 55-6, 58, 138-40, 145-46; Friedel, F.D.R. and the South, pp. 46, 49, 55, 61, 77, 93.

[17] Heinemann, Depression and New Deal, p. 47.

[18] Ibid., pp. 139-140.

[19] Allen Moger, "Virginia's Conservative Political Heritage," South Atlantic Quarterly 50(1951), p. 318.

[20] Key, Southern Politics, p. 19

DEPRESSION, ROOSEVELT, AND THE NEW DEAL IN VIRGINIA

smaller proportion of Virginia's potential electorate voted for governor than in any other southern state.[21] The organization's honesty, efficiency, low tax and good roads policies, however, gained it popular support; the anti-organization opposition remained weak and lost the major political battles of the 1930s.[22] Historian James T. Patterson described the entrenched Byrd organization as a "formidable barrier to systematic patronage;" it was "invulnerable to threats of loss of patronage." Senator Byrd's supporters were able to get their share of federal jobs without backing New Deal reforms.[23]

A solid majority of Virginia's congressional delegation epitomized the Byrd organization's philosophy during the New Deal era. Most supported pro-business, low taxation, anti-labor union, limited government (including social services), fiscally responsible policies. (That included Congressmen Otis Bland, Thomas Burch, Colgate Darden, Patrick H. Drewry, A. Willis Robertson, and Howard Smith. Representative Andrew J. Montague voted with Byrd and Glass only half the time.)[24] That was no less true of George C. Peery, Virginia's governor from 1934-38, and an important figure in the Byrd organization. As the state's chief executive, Peery provided "steady, conservative leadership that continued Byrd's philosophy and programs,

---

[21] Ibid., p. 20; For the finest analytical study of Virginia's political system and politics under the Byrd organization, see J. Harvie Wilkinson, III's <u>Harry Byrd and the Changing Face of Virginia Politics, 1945-1966</u> (Charlottesville: University Press of Virginia, 1968). Wilkinson, now a federal judge, explained how urbanization, the Republican Party, the black vote, and "massive resistance" helped undermine the Byrd organization. See also Jack Bass and Walter DeVries, <u>The Transformation of Southern Politics: Social Change and Political Consequences, Since 1945</u> (New York: Basic Books, Inc., 1976), pp. 339-40.

[22] Key, Southern Politics, pp. 19-21, 26-34; Rubin, <u>Virginia, pp. 171-73.</u>

[23] James T. Patterson, <u>The New Deal and the States: Federalism in Transition</u> (Princeton: Princeton University Press, 1964), pp. 171-72.

[24] Key, Southern Politics, pp. 19, 26-27; Heinemann, <u>Depression and New Deal</u>, pp. 140-41.

reinforced Byrd's opposition to the New Deal, and allowed the new senator the freedom to shift much of his attention to national affairs."[25]

As governor, Peery supported a balanced budget, fiscal integrity, and pay-as-you-go. Opposed to deficit financing and a burgeoning bureaucracy, Peery believed that greater government efficiency and individual initiative provided the best solutions to the problems of the depression.[26] At the same time, Peery embraced significant reforms such as unemployment insurance, enactment of a trial justice system, and the appropriation of Virginia's first funds for direct relief. During Peery's administration, the 1934 deficit of more than $2 million was converted into a projected surplus of over $5 million in 1938. The state's bonded indebtedness decreased from $20,009,535 to $16,866,455 during his term of office. Despite Virginia's return to economic health, little was spent on education or welfare. Historian Joseph A. Fry wrote that "This unbending conservatism and devotion to pay-as-you-go had led Peery and the organization to sacrifice human priorities at the alter of fiscal orthodoxy."[27] Fry maintained that Peery's response to the depression "mirrored that of the organization, and his administration embodied the philosophical tenets that have dominated twentieth-century Virginia government: efficiency, pay-as-you-go, suspicion of national spending, and hostility to the growing federal bureaucracy."[28]

The New Deal did, however, have its share of influential advocates in Virginia. They included former governor Westmoreland Davis, Assistant Secretary of State R. Walton Moore, Secretary of the Navy Claude A. Swanson, secretary of the Democratic state committee Martin Hutchinson, publisher of the Bristol Herald-Courier, Charles Harkrader, future governor James H. Price, Congressmen Clifton A. Woodrum from the sixth district, and John W. Flannagan, Jr., of the "Fighting Ninth" district. A member of the powerful House Appropriations Committee, Woodrum voted for (and often

---

[25] Joseph A. Fry, "George C. Peery: Byrd Regular and Depression Governor," in The Governors of Virginia, 1860-1978, eds. Edward Younger and James T. Moore (Charlottesville: University Press of Virginia, 1982), p. 261.

[26] Joseph A. Fry, "The Organization in Control: George Campbell Peery, Governor of Virginia, 1934-1938," Virginia Magazine of History and Biography 82(1974): 306-30; Joseph A. Fry, "George Campbell Peery: Conservative Son of Old Virginia" (M.A. thesis, University of Virginia, 1970).

[27] Fry, "George C. Peery: Byrd Regular," p. 273.

[28] Ibid., p. 274.

DEPRESSION, ROOSEVELT, AND THE NEW DEAL IN VIRGINIA

engineered passage on the House floor) almost all of Roosevelt's domestic programs through 1936. Publisher of the Portsmouth Star, Norman Hamilton, served the second district in Congress until defeated in 1938 by the organization candidate, Colgate Darden.[29]

Strong feelings for and against the New Deal persisted throughout Roosevelt's first term. By mid-1935, the Pulitzer prize-winning historian and editor of the Richmond News-Leader, Douglas Southall Freeman had turned against the president. In his June 24, 1935, letter to his publisher John Stewart Bryan, Freeman wrote:

> I hope I have not gone too far in criticizing the latest antics of His Excellency, the President. That demagogic message in which he tried to steal the thunder of Huey Long was a little more than I could stand. The President seems to have given himself over to the left wing New Dealers, and apparently he has embraced the full philosophy of Sister Perkins. I do not deny that there are good arguments for the high taxation of very large fortunes, and I tried to put both sides of the case in the third editorial of June 20th; but as I interpret Mr. Roosevelt's policy, he would carry this business of confiscatory taxation to the point where he would make it a crime for anyone to be thrifty enough to bequeath to the next generation enough money to maintain a family tradition. When he does that, it seems to me he destroys conservatism. Perhaps that is exactly what he wants to do.... We have never had within the whole of modern history a democracy that did not have in it some of the evidence of aristocracy, which aristocracy had in part to be sustained by inherited wealth. He is therefore, not merely destroying family life, but he is taking from democracy one of its few stabilizing and intelligent elements. It is a dark situation and one

---

[29] Heinemann, Depression and New Deal, pp. 140-141; James E. Sargent, "Clifton A. Woodrum of Virginia: A Southern Progressive in Congress, 1923-1945," Virginia Magazine of History and Biography 89(1981): 341-64; James E. Sargent, "Woodrum's Economy Bloc: The Attack on Roosevelt's WPA, 1937-1939," Virginia Magazine of History and Biography 92(1985), p. 176; Alvin Hall, "Politics and Patronage: Virginia's Senators and the Roosevelt Purges of 1938," Virginia Magazine of History and Biography 82(1974), pp. 332-33.

against which I think we should, cost what it may, [oppose]. I am sure you are of that mind."[30]

Carter Glass's criticism of the New Deal was decidedly more blunt. In his October 5, 1936, letter to Harry F. Byrd, he wrote: "I hate the New Deal just as much as I ever did and have not the remotest idea of making any speeches for it."[31] Glass's awkward stance during the 1936 election was best reflected in his October 15, 1936, letter to his secretary, Mr. J. W. Rixey Smith, in which he wrote that he "intended to support the President for reelection, notwithstanding my unalterable opposition to those New Deal measures which I regarded as unconstitutional and which the Courts have decided to be unconstitutional."[32] Glass did indeed endorse FDR's reelection bid in the 1936 Virginia Democratic party platform (which he wrote in its entirety). At the same time, that leading critic of Roosevelt's administration adamantly declined to speak on behalf of the president's candidacy despite the urgings of Democratic National Chairman James A. Farley. At the request of the Thomas Jefferson Memorial Foundation, Glass did, however, introduce Roosevelt at Monticello on Independence Day. He praised Roosevelt's "courage and patience" and noted that the president "professes the humanitarianism and the love of the plain people which Thomas Jefferson manifested." That "good-will" between the president and the senator was short-lived. In his July 17, 1936, remarks at the Patrick Henry bicentennial ceremonies in Ashland, Glass said that if Patrick Henry were alive today he would have resisted the New Deal's tyranny just as he had fought the misrule of George III. Glass later denied that he had attacked Roosevelt, but rather blamed the New Deal on Congress and reaffirmed that his vote would be cast for the president in November.[33]

---

[30] Douglas S. Freeman to John Stewart Bryan, June 24, 1935, Douglas Southall Freeman Papers, Library of Congress, Washington, D.C.

[31] Glass to Harry F. Byrd, October 5, 1936, Harry F. Byrd Papers, University of Virginia Library, Charlottesville, Virginia.

[32] Glass to J.W.R. Smith, October 15, 1936, Glass to Wilber A. Myers, October 6, 1936, Carter Glass Papers, University of Virginia Library, Charlottesville, Virginia.

[33] Alfred C. Koeniger, "The Politics of Independence: Carter Glass and the Election of 1936," South Atlantic Quarterly 80(1981), pp. 95, 101-103.

DEPRESSION, ROOSEVELT, AND THE NEW DEAL IN VIRGINIA

Harry F. Byrd disliked the New Deal as much as Glass, yet unlike his senior colleague he did make a series of last-minute speeches for Roosevelt.[34] The popular, moderate New Dealer, Lt. Governor James H. Price, was certainly more effusive in his support for FDR's reelection. In his July 25, 1936, letter to the president, Price wrote that he was "taking advantage of this opportunity to tell you that old Virginia will be found in the forefront of Democratic States in the approaching general election regardless of the attitudes of some people we know. We are confidently looking forward to your triumphant re-election and the perpetuation of your programs for a more abundant life.[35]

As early as mid-1935, Secretary of the Navy Claude A. Swanson indicated his support for Roosevelt's reelection. In his June 20, 1935, letter to the president, Swanson included a June 19 Richmond Times-Dispatch clipping which stated that a "Roosevelt-for-President Club" had been established in Charlottesville and Albermarle County. Swanson told FDR that "This is very pleasing indeed to me." "It is specially gratifying," he wrote, "that the resolution which was adopted unanimously, at the home of Jefferson, resolves that this club will do all possible to uphold you and your Administration."[36] In his June 24, 1935, reply, Roosevelt told Swanson that he was "delighted that these Virginia Counties have started the ball rolling." "I hope," the president said, "it will be copied in other Counties."[37]

The 1936 election results confirmed the ambiguity in Virginia politics. Both Senator Glass and President Roosevelt won reelection overwhelmingly. Roosevelt received 234,980 votes (70.2%); Glass got 244,518 votes (91.7%), his biggest win ever in a Senate race. Approximately 75,000 citizens who voted for either Roosevelt or Landon did not bother to vote in the senatorial race; of those who did, however, 95 percent voted for Glass and only 5 percent supported his Republican challenger, George Rohlsen. Still, the

---

[34] Ibid., p. 106.

[35] James H. Price to Franklin D. Roosevelt, July 25, 1936, President's Personal File 3743, Franklin D. Roosevelt Papers, Franklin D. Roosevelt Library, Hyde Park, N.Y.

[36] Claude A. Swanson to Roosevelt, June 20, 1935, President's Personal File 2610, Roosevelt Papers.

[37] Roosevelt to Swanson, June 24, 1935, President's Personal File 2610, Roosevelt Papers.

acerbic critic of the New Deal received 8,538 votes more than FDR in Virginia, without even campaigning.[38] Undoubtedly, Glass lost votes because of his opposition to the New Deal and his behavior during the campaign (e.g. the Ashland speech). Yet, despite some disaffection in the electorate, Glass retained a solid bedrock of support, especially in Southside Virginia and the Shenandoah Valley.[39]

Virginia's New Dealers scored a major upset the following year when their candidate--Lt. Governor James H. Price--was elected governor. Price, a fervent supporter of Roosevelt's policies, shattered the Byrd organization's hegemony over Virginia politics for the first time in almost a decade. Realizing that it would be difficult to defeat him, the Byrd machine finally supported the popular independent in order to avoid embarrassment; some organization stalwarts and young insurgents even tried to ride Price's campaign coattails. The new governor's popularity was achieved in virtual defiance of the organization. Indeed, Price's candidacy for governor, historian Alvin L. Hall wrote, "became the focal point of opposition to Byrd and Glass." An "anomaly in twentieth-century Virginia politics . . . [Price] became governor without the initial blessings of Senator Harry F. Byrd during a period when Byrd's control of state politics was virtually unchallenged." Price defeated his Democratic primary challenger, Vivian Page of Norfolk, by the largest majority in the history of the primary in Virginia, carrying every city and county in the state. In the general election, Price's Republican opponent J. Powell Royall, won only two southwestern counties.[40]

Price's upset victory did not usher in a golden age for the New Deal in Virginia. Despite his widespread popularity and fealty to fiscal conservatism and a balanced budget, Governor Price was unable to get his progressive legislation through the Byrd machine-dominated General Assembly. Price's

---

[38] Hunter, "Glass, Byrd, and the New Deal," p. 102; Koeniger, "Politics of Independence," p. 105.

[39] Koeniger, "Politics of Independence," pp. 105-106.

[40] Alvin L. Hall, "James H. Price and Virginia Politics, 1878 to 1943" (Ph.D. diss., University of Virginia, 1970); Alvin L. Hall, "James Hubert Price: New Dealer in the Old Dominion," in The Governors of Virginia, 1860-1978, eds. Edward Younger and James T. Moore (Charlottesville: University Press of Virginia, 1982), pp. 277, 280; Wilkinson, Harry Byrd and the Changing Face, p. 8; Rubin, Virginia, p. 171; Carl J. Vipperman, "The Coattail Campaign: James H. Price and the Election of 1937 in Virginia," in Essays in History (Charlottesville: History Club, University of Virginia) 8(1962-63), pp. 47, 50, 59-60.

DEPRESSION, ROOSEVELT, AND THE NEW DEAL IN VIRGINIA 33

naivete, lack of political skill, and dismissal of E. R. Combs, the powerful chairman of the state Compensation Commission Board and chief of staff of the Byrd organization, antagonized machine regulars. Worse, it undermined passage of popular proposals such as old-age assistance legislation, additional funding for public education, reduction of the poll tax, and legislative redistricting. Price's failure to punish his political enemies, challenge Senator Byrd's control of the Democratic party, and build his own political machine weakened the hand of the anti-organization forces and New Dealers in the state. Senator Byrd's public statements, notwithstanding, his organization's attacks on the reform-minded governor also contributed to the latter's legislative failures. Concerned with its self-preservation, fearful that Price would run against Byrd in the 1940 Senate primary, and convinced that the Price faction was sowing discord and partisanship with the state Democratic party, the Byrd organization buried Price's progressive proposals.[41]

The climax of Price's unsuccessful tenure as governor came in the summer of 1938 when he backed Roosevelt's unsuccessful attempt to appoint Floyd H. Roberts of Bristol as U.S. District Judge for the Western District of Virginia.[42] Price's recommendation of and support for the progressive judge was a direct challenge to both Byrd and Glass who successfully opposed the nomination via "senatorial courtesy." It furthermore worsened the governor's relations with organization leaders and weakened his public support. Most importantly, it constituted a major setback for Roosevelt, the New Deal, and the anti-organization forces in the state.[43]

The Judge Roberts affair was an example of FDR's failed efforts to discipline, undermine, and even purge conservatives from the Democratic Party of Virginia. Fearing that southern conservatives might gain control of

---

[41] Wilkinson, Harry Byrd and the Changing Face, p. 8; Vipperman, "Coattail Campaign," pp. 60-61; John Syrett, "Ambiguous Politics: James Price's First Months as Governor of Virginia," Virginia Magazine of History and Biography 94(1986), pp. 454, 476; John Syrett, "The Politics of Preservation: The Organization Destroys Governor James H. Price's Administration," Virginia Magazine of History and Biography 97(1989), pp. 437-38; Hall, "J. H. Price: New Dealer, "pp. 277, 283, 286-88.

[42] Roosevelt to Glass, July 6, 1938, Glass Papers; Hall, "J. H. Price: New Dealer," p. 285.

[43] Hall, "J. H. Price: New Dealer," p. 285; Koeniger, "Unconstructed Rebel," pp. 229-30.

the Democratic National Convention in 1940, Roosevelt tried to replace many of them with his own supporters.[44] The already strained relationship between Roosevelt and Virginia's two senators needed no further stimulus.[45] Virginia's ruling class was well aware of FDR's attempt to remake their Democratic party in his own image. In his July 12, 1938, letter to John Stewart Bryan, Douglas S. Freeman wrote: "[FDR] certainly is doing everything in his power to disrupt the South politically. I wonder if he is doing this deliberately with an eye to the realignment of conservatives and liberals."[46]

Certainly Glass and Byrd were none too happy that the president would nominate a New Dealer to the federal bench in their own state. But Glass was even more incensed that in ignoring his and Byrd's preferences for the vacant judgeship, Roosevelt would also violate the time-honored custom of "senatorial courtesy" (i.e. the president would withdraw his nominee if the senators from his state found him to be personally or politically offensive). Glass and Byrd also believed that FDR undermined and even transferred their control over federal patronage in the state to Governor Price. Despite his denials, Roosevelt never satisfactorily convinced Virginia's two senators that Price enjoyed no such veto power. In fact, FDR officially justified his selection of Roberts as an attack on "senatorial courtesy," which he believed to be an abuse of power. Ultimately, the Senate's prerogative and the Byrd machine prevailed; the Senate Judiciary Committee rejected Roberts by a 15-3 margin; the full Senate voted 72-9 against the president's nominee. Most significantly, the people of Virginia were not happy with their president's behavior; in the 1938 congressional elections Byrd' Democrats scored impressive victories, including Colgate Darden's win over New Dealer Norman Hamilton in the second district. Disaffection with Roosevelt's "court-packing" scheme in 1937 and his attempted "purges" the following year spelled the death knell for the liberal faction in Virginia's Democratic Party.[47]

---

[44] Hall, "Politics and Patronage," pp. 331-50; Heinemann, Depression and New Deal, pp. 147-52. The Judge Roberts affair proved James M. Burns wrong when he said FDR was too cautious to challenge the Byrd organization. See Burns's Roosevelt, pp. 378-80.

[45] Interview with Virginius Dabney, Richmond, Virginia, November 28, 1986.

[46] Freeman to John Stewart Bryan, July 12, 1938, Freeman Papers.

[47] Hall, "Politics and Patronage," pp. 331-50; Senator Glass's press release of February 9, 1939, James E. Palmer, Jr., "The 'Unreconstructed Rebel' Strikes Back," pp. 1-14 (February 1939), in a folder of addresses given by Glass, Glass Papers; Franklin D. Roosevelt, The Public Papers and Addresses

DEPRESSION, ROOSEVELT, AND THE NEW DEAL IN VIRGINIA

As early as 1937, even Congressman Woodrum began to advocate policies out of line with those of the president. Woodrum called for greater fiscal responsibility, cutbacks in government expenditures, reductions in the bureaucracy, and streamlining of the Works Progress Administration (WPA). The congressman became the leading House Democratic spokesman for the "Economy Bloc." Still, Woodrum continued to defend Roosevelt and was one of the first members of the House to support the infamous "court-packing" bill. (John W. Flannagan, Jr., was the only other Virginia congressman to endorse it).[48] In his February 5, 1937, memo for the press, Woodrum wrote:

> The suggestions of the President should appeal to citizens who are interested in seeing an administration of the judicial branch of the government that functions with despatch [sic] and that is responsive to the changing times. The proposed bill calls for no constitutional change and no departure from our fundamental system of government, but advocates the plain, simple proposition that controversial questions should be settled quickly and by judges of mental and physical ability to cope with important problems.[49]

Woodrum again defended FDR in his March 30, 1937, House speech in which he credited the president for leading the country out of the depression and back to economic recovery. (At the same time, Woodrum called on Congress to start cutting the cost of government and work toward a balanced budget.)[50] In his May 8, 1937, speech to the Young Democrats of Lynchburg (Glass's hometown), Woodrum again defended Roosevelt, calling him the Democratic Party's "valiant standard-bearer." He also said that the United States was much better off in 1937 than during previous Republican administrations. Roosevelt's economic recovery program had done such a good job restoring the country's prosperity, Woodrum concluded, that the time had come for the federal government to withdraw "as rapidly as possible"

---

of Franklin D. Roosevelt, 8:126-33.

[48] Sargent, "Woodrum's Economy Bloc," pp. 177-80; Virginia Democrat Magazine, (February 1937), Clifton A. Woodrum Papers, Roanoke Public Library, Roanoke, Virginia, Roanoke Times, February 14, 1937, pp. 1, 2, May 9, 1937, pp. 1, 2.

[49] Woodrum's February 5, 1937, memo for the press, Woodrum Papers.

[50] Roanoke World-News, March 30, 1937, pp. 1, 7; Richmond Times-Dispatch, March 31, 1937, p. 13.

from the field of relief and allow the states and localities able to do so, to resume their normal burdens and functions.[51] In his July 6, 1938, speech at the Institute of Public Affairs at the University of Virginia, Woodrum paid tribute to Roosevelt, calling him "the greatest liberal-thinking Democrat produced in the last half century."[52]

After his close reelection win in 1938, Woodrum began to attack the New Deal through the WPA, the important administration jobs relief program, without directly criticizing the president. The WPA offered little benefit to Woodrum's constituency and to most Virginians. Woodrum's Appropriation Committee's investigation of the subversive influences of the left-wing, Communist-backed Workers' Alliance of America (WAA)--which had thousands of members with WPA jobs--further damaged Roosevelt's New Deal. The congressman's attacks on the WPA resulted in a Fiscal Year (FY) 1940 Relief Act that reduced funding, wages, and jobs in the controversial program. The WAA's leadership was further outraged by Woodrum's leading role in the "Economy Bloc;" WPA cuts were labeled, "Woodrumed." The outbreak of war in 1939 fueled congressional sentiment to increase defense expenditures. The House Appropriations Committee's report on hearings for the FY 1940 Relief Act justified reductions in WPA expenditures by arguing that over the 1.1 million persons beyond the WPA's 2.7 million beneficiaries would be employed by the armed services or other government defense work.[53]

The New Deal's reform agenda had waned even before war erupted in Europe. Roosevelt's "court-packing" plan, southern purges, and the 1937-38 recession produced widespread dissatisfaction with his administration. In the 1938 congressional elections, Republicans won 81 new seats in the House and 8 in the Senate. Congress had not passed any major reform bill since the Fair Labor Standards Act of 1938. The war had concentrated Congress's attention to defense preparation, not social or economic reform. Roosevelt's Justice Department prosecuted fewer anti-trust violations by 1940 in the interest of accelerating defense production. After the United States entered in the war in 1941, anti-trust prosecutions virtually ceased. During the war, Congress and the administration even abolished the Civilian Conservation

---

[51] Woodrum's May 8, 1937, speech to the Young Democrats of Lynchburg, Woodrum Papers.

[52] Richmond News-Leader, July 6, 1938, p. 1; New York Times, July 7, 1938, p. 5.

[53] Roanoke Times, November 20, 1938, pp. 33, 40; Sargent, "Woodrum's Economy Bloc," pp. 175, 181-85, 196-98, 201.

DEPRESSION, ROOSEVELT, AND THE NEW DEAL IN VIRGINIA

Corps (CCC), the National Youth Administration (NYA), and the WPA. Other non-defense expenditures were sharply reduced as well. Businessmen took government positions once filled by New Dealers.[54]

Due to those changing circumstances, Roosevelt was forced to abandon reform in the South in exchange for southern congressional support for his increasingly interventionist foreign policy.[55] FDR unilaterally ended his patronage fight with Senator Glass as early as 1938. Thereafter, Roosevelt concentrated his energies on securing Virginia's congressional delegation's support for his foreign policy. Historian Alfred C. Koeniger wrote that "With war approaching in Europe and national elections pending in 1940, he [FDR] would not further damage the prestige of his administration on patronage fights he could not win. The purge was over; Roosevelt the lion again became Roosevelt the fox."[56] Indirect steps toward reconciliation between Glass and Roosevelt began as early as the winter of 1939. In his February 9, 1939, letter to the president's secretary Stephen Early, Douglas S. Freeman wrote:

> Confidentially, I am very much disturbed over the row between the President and Senator Glass, and cannot see how anything is to be gained by pressing the fight. The effect on Virginia will be definitely to divide the President's followers here and, what doubtless concerns him more, to put into the background the many issues of State advancement that call for united action. The economic betterment of Virginia in the larger spiritual implications of the New Deal cannot be attained if we have a split over a question that can, I think, be settled amicably.

---

[54] Richard Polenberg, War and Society: The United States, 1941-1945, (Philadelphia: Lippicott, 1972), pp. 74, 77-79, 83, 90-91.

[55] Paul Seabury, The Waning of Southern 'Internationalism', (Princeton: Center of International Studies, 1957), pp. 16, 27. Seabury wrote that "The coming of the war in 1939 evoked an almost 100 percent Southern legislative support for the Roosevelt administration and for the Western democracies, and a regional willingness to use military means, if necessary, to prevent German domination of the European continent and of Britain. (ibid., p. 27).

[56] Alfred C. Koeniger, "The New Deal and the States: Roosevelt versus the Byrd Organization in Virginia," Journal of American History 68(1982), pp. 876-77, 891; Koeniger, "Unconstructed Rebel," pp. 229-30.

Freeman asked Early to show the president his letter and enclosed his News-Leader editorial concerning the matter.[57]

Roosevelt took the first concrete steps toward reconciliation with Glass later that year. The president inquired--through others--whether Glass would object to the appointment of James E. Heath, a prominent attorney, staunch New Dealer, and old friend of the senator, as collector of customs for the commonwealth. Glass sent word back to the White House that the appointment would not be objectionable to him. When FDR learned of the senator's bout with bronchitis, he and his wife Eleanor were the first to send him flowers and a get-well message. The president was deeply moved that Glass would leave his sick bed to attend the special session of Congress he had called on September 21, 1939, to consider revision of the neutrality bill. Roosevelt was even more impressed with the senator's statement that his appeal to Congress for repeal of the arms embargo was the "best speech he ever made." FDR invited Glass to the White House just a few hours after his address. Roosevelt was said to have slapped the 81 year old Virginian on the back and said: "Well, it took a war to get us together again. I hope it will take an earthquake to separate us!" During their meeting, FDR and Glass discussed neutrality law revision and the latter's contention that Richmond should stay clear of federal affairs and Washington should keep out of the commonwealth's concerns. Rapprochement between Roosevelt and Glass did more than neutralize the reformist faction in the Democratic Party of Virginia. Born of a mutual concern for the survival of Britain and America's security interests, it facilitated, and even strengthened Virginia's wholehearted support for Roosevelt's aid-to-Britain policy.[58]

There is no evidence to suggest that Glass embraced repeal of the arms embargo in exchange for FDR's promise to abandon his purges and reform efforts in the Old Dominion. Glass loathed Hitler, Nazism, and fascist aggression. His support for aid-to-Britain was based on his principled belief that Roosevelt's policies were in the best interests of his state, his country,

---

[57] D. S. Freeman to Stephen Early, February 9, 1939, Freeman Papers; Koeniger, "Unreconstructed Rebel," p. 230.

[58] Richmond Times-Dispatch, September 29, 1939, pp. 1, 9; Alexandria Gazette, October 2, 1939, p. 4; Koeniger, "New Deal and the States," pp. 891-93; Robert A. Divine, The Illusion of Neutrality, (Chicago: University of Chicago Press, 1962), p. 307.

DEPRESSION, ROOSEVELT, AND THE NEW DEAL IN VIRGINIA

and democracy. It is unlikely that Glass would have abandoned his most cherished beliefs under any circumstances.[59]

Still, by the end of 1939, the political chasm between the national Democratic party and Virginia's political establishment remained. In his November 24, 1939, letter to David K. E. Bruce, Senator Byrd wrote:

> I think it would be extremely inadvisable to have my name considered for the Presidency. I have no inclination whatever to be a candidate, and secondly, in view of the situation existing in the Democratic Party I can see no possibility of success. I have opposed so many of the major New Deal policies that my nomination would be, in fact, a repudiation of quite a substantial part of what the Democratic Party has claimed as worthwhile achievements under the New Deal.[60]

---

[59] Interview with Dabney, November 28, 1986. Few Virginians were as close to the state's political elite as was Dabney. The Richmond Times-Dispatch editor and celebrated historian, denied knowledge of any "deal" allegedly made between FDR and Virginia's two senators. Seabury, Waning of Southern 'Internationalism', p. 16. Seabury wrote that "It is difficult to gauge, even at our distance in time, the extent to which Roosevelt's abandonment of reform in the South was a conscious quid pro quo for conservative Southern support in foreign policy matters. Certainly there was a strange coincidence in the administration's abandonment of legislative measures deeply antagonistic to Southern interests (such as a federal anti-lynching bill in 1938) and the nearly unanimous support it received from the South on foreign policy." (ibid.).

[60] Byrd to David K. E. Bruce, November 24, 1939, Byrd Papers.

CHAPTER III

THE NEW DOMINION IN THE COMMUNITY OF NATIONS

During the Roosevelt administration, many influential Virginians supported collective security, international cooperation, American membership in the League of Nations (or at least collaboration with it), and adherence to the Protocols of the Permanent Court of International Justice as essential steps towards achieving world peace. The prominent role of the state's political elite in espousing Wilsonian causes was indicative of that Virginia-born president's pervasive influence in the South (and Virginia) more than a decade after his death. The league's advocates attributed the lack of world peace and stability to America's failure to join that international body in 1920. According to public opinion surveys and southern newspapers during the 1930s, Southerners, including Virginians, were more supportive of United States membership in the League of Nations and World Court than other regional groups. Still, during the pre-Pearl Harbor Roosevelt era, a majority of Americans, including Southerners, did not support collective security and American membership in the league. A 1937 public opinion poll revealed that only 44 percent of Southerners polled (higher than other regional groups) approved of America's entry into the league. Opponents of the league cited its failure to halt aggression and feared America's membership would entangle it in European wars and conflicts. By the end of the 1930s, many Virginians no longer believed that the league was an effective instrument of world peace. The United States never joined the league; in 1935, it failed also to accept the court proposal.[1]

---

[1] See Richard N. Current, "The United States and 'Collective Security': Notes on the History of an Idea," in Isolation and Security: Ideas and Interests in Twentieth-Century American Foreign Policy, ed. Alexander DeConde (Durham, N.C.: Duke University Press, 1957), pp. 33, 47-48. Current defined collective security as "cooperative action among the [sovereign] nations of the world to enforce peace." See also Richard N. Current, "Consequences of the Kellogg Pact," in Issues and Conflicts: Studies in Twentieth-Century American Diplomacy, ed. George L. Anderson (Lawrence, Ks.: University of Kansas Press, 1959), p. 221. Collective security has never been precisely defined; in fact, it has enjoyed different meanings, some even contradictory. Also see Roland N. Stromberg, Collective Security and American Foreign Policy: From the League of Nations to NATO (New York: Frederick A. Praeger, 1963), p. 230. Stromberg wrote that collective security had been discredited during much of the twentieth-century. Roland N. Stromberg, "The Ideas of Collective Security," Journal of the History of

Cognizant of public opinion and the exigencies of the depression, President Roosevelt did not publicly advocate American membership in the League of Nations. Nor did he attempt to maneuver the country into the league. He did, however, support cooperation with it in the interests of world peace. In early 1935, FDR urged Senate approval of the Protocols of the Permanent Court of International Justice. On January 29, 1935, the vote on American adherence to the World Court proposal fell seven votes short of the required two-thirds majority. Southern senators provided 18 of the 52 votes in favor of the protocols. Senators Glass and Byrd of Virginia voted for the proposal. Only 5 of the 36 votes against came from southern senators. Senator Kenneth McKellar of Tennessee was detained and did not vote; had he been present, however, he would have voted in favor. Two other senators from the South did not vote as well. The Senate's rejection of the World Court at that time was further evidence of the strength of isolationist sentiment in America. Reflecting the isolationist mood of the country, Congress passed a series of neutrality bills during Roosevelt's administration. [2]

Ideas 17(1956), p. 250. See Manfred Jonas, "The United States and the Failure of Collective Security in the 1930s," in Twentieth-Century American Foreign Policy, eds. John Braeman, Robert H. Bremner, and David Brody (Columbus, Oh.: Ohio State University Press, 1971), pp. 292-93. Current argued that the consequences of the Kellogg-Briand Pact (1928), which renounced war as "an instrument of national policy," "provided a philosophical basis for much of the 'interventionist' thinking of the 1930s . . . [and] furnished arguments for the Roosevelt program of aid to the Allies after 1939 and contributed much to the policies that led to Pearl Harbor." See Current, "Consequences of the Kellogg Pact," pp. 210, 226-27. Alfred O. Hero, Jr., The Southerner and World Affairs (Baton Rouge: Louisiana State University Press, 1965), p. 223; George C. Herring and Gary R. Hess, "Regionalism and Foreign Policy: The Dying Myth of Southern Internationalism," Southern Studies, Fall (1981), p. 256. A June 9, 1941, Gallup Poll indicated that only 51% of all Americans believed that the United States should join a league of nations after the European war had ended; 52% of Southerners polled felt that way. See George Gallup, The Gallup Poll: Public Opinion, 1935-1971, (New York: Random House, 1972), Vol. I, p. 283. Gallup Polls on Virginians' views on this and other foreign policy issues discussed in this study do not exist.

[2] See Robert Dallek, Franklin D. Roosevelt and American Foreign Policy, 1932-1945, (New York: Oxford University Press, 1979), pp. 11-12, 17, 19, 69, 70-71, 95-96, 110, 120. FDR abandoned his early Wilsonianism and support for the league in 1932 due to pressure from the isolationist publisher William Randolph Hearst. (ibid., p. 19). See also William E. Leuchtenburg, Franklin D. Roosevelt and the New Deal, 1932-1940, (New York: Harper & Row

Virginians feared little from America's adherence to the World Court protocols; a majority supported it.³ Senator Claude A. Swanson, a staunch Wilsonian, vigorously defended both the League of Nations and the World Court.⁴ He had led the Senate fight for American adherence to the protocols

---

Publishers, 1963), pp. 10, 198-99, 215-17. Gary B. Ostrower argued that "neither the Hoover nor Roosevelt Administrations ever really had a League policy at all." Roosevelt's ambivalence toward Geneva was influenced by the fear of war, the New Deal's economic nationalism, and the strength of isolationist opinion. FDR and Hull's internationalist sentiments never materialized into a coherent policy of collective security. See Ostrower's Collective Insecurity: The United States and the League of Nations during the Early Thirties (Lewisburg, Pa.: Bucknell University Press, 1979), pp. 199, 203, 205-206. For a critical account of the Senate's rejection of the World Court see Denna F. Fleming, The United States and the World Court, 1920-1966, rev. edit. (New York: Russell & Russell, 1945; 1968). Fleming argued that the defeat was partly due to "lax management," weak organization, and timid behavior on the part of the court's friends, especially on the Senate Foreign Relations Committee. (ibid. pp. 41, 60, 62, 131, 133-36, 138-39). In "The Roosevelt Administration and the World Court Defeat, 1935," The Historian 40 (1978): 463-78, Robert D. Accinelli maintained that the January 29, 1935, Senate vote against the World Court resolution was primarily due to FDR and his pro-court allies' failure to provide "bolder and more alert leadership." Roosevelt feared that Senate cooperation on domestic legislation might not be forthcoming if he made an all-out effort on behalf of the court. See also Gilbert N. Kahn, "Presidential Passivity on a Nonsalient Issue: President Franklin D. Roosevelt and the 1935 World Court Fight," Diplomatic History 4 (1980): 137-160. Kahn agreed with Accinelli that the "overly cautious" FDR did little to get the Senate's approval for the court proposal. George L. Grassmuch, Sectional Biases In Congress On Foreign Policy (Baltimore: The Johns Hopkins Press, 1951), pp. 83-84, 88; Congressional Directory, 74th Congress, 1st sess., January, 1935, pp. 145-46; Congressional Record, 74th Congress, 1st sess., 1936, 79: 1146-47; Interview with Virginius Dabney, Richmond, Virginia, November 28, 1986; Jonas, "U.S.and the Failure of Collective Security," pp. 241-93; Stromberg, Collective Security, pp. 238-39, 245.

³Grassmuck, Sectional Biases, p. 84; Interview with Dabney, November 28, 1986.

⁴Denna F. Fleming, The United States and the League of Nations, 1918-1920 (New York: G. P. Putnam's Sons, 1932), pp. 241-44. Senator Swanson's July 14, 1919, opening speech on the Senate's proposed ratification of the League of Nations filled ten pages of the Congressional Record. He argued

long before Roosevelt entered the White House.⁵ Like many of his fellow Virginians, Swanson did not believe that America's membership in the World Court would undermine its self-interests or sovereignty. The court adjudicated international legal disputes; it lacked the power to enforce its decisions. Most Virginians, including Swanson, saw American adherence to the protocols a step closer to Woodrow Wilson's vision of world peace and international justice. In any event, during the pre-Pearl Harbor period, United States membership in both the league and the court was not a major, nor even a minor issue in any political campaign in the state.⁶

Virginia's earliest support for American involvement in the community of nations can be traced back to the efforts of Senator Swanson and his colleague, Carter Glass. Swanson, Democratic minority leader of the Foreign Relations Committee from 1923 to 1933, introduced a resolution proposing adherence to the World Court on the Harding-Hughes terms in the spring of 1924.⁷ In December, 1925, he urged reconsideration of the court question and continued to lead the court fight in both the Foreign Relations

---

that honor, prudence, self interest, and national prestige demanded United States participation in the league and sanction of the treaty ending the war. Swanson was most prescient when he said that the First World War proved that incalculable and widespread destruction was likely to result from failure of collective action in an international crisis. See also Henry C. Ferrell, Jr., Claude A. Swanson of Virginia: A Political Biography (Lexington: The University Press of Kentucky, 1985). Ferrell wrote that Swanson urged Wilson to soften his opposition to the Lodge reservations, but the president refused. "A leading representative of the Senate group adhering to the principles of Woodrow Wilson," Swanson continued to support the leadership of his fellow Virginian behind the scenes (though absent from) of the 1920 Democratic National convention in San Francisco. (ibid., pp. 123-26. 131, 181).

⁵Fleming, The United States and the World Court, pp. 41, 60, 62, 131, 135; Ferrell, Swanson, pp. 175-77.

⁶Interview with Dabney, November 28, 1986.

⁷James E. Palmer, Jr., Carter Glass: Unreconstructed Rebel (Roanoke, Va: Institute of American Biography, 1938), p. 240; Grassmuck, Sectional Biases, p. 72; Fleming, The United States and World Organizations, p. 242; Thomas N. Guinsburg, The Pursuit of Isolationism in the United States Senate from Versailles to Pearl Harbor (New York: Garland Press, 1981), pp. 85-86; Herring and Hess, "Regionalism," p. 255.

THE NEW DOMINION IN THE COMMUNITY OF NATIONS 45

Committee and on the floor of the Senate.[8] Swanson also wrote the fifth reservation to the protocol and incorporated it into the resolution of adherence. It stated that the United States would not be bound by an advisory opinion unless it had joined in requesting it. Due to pressure from anti-court senators who wanted more protection for the United States, Swanson offered a tougher substitute reservation on January 23, 1926. That expanded fifth reservation was written with the assistance of John Bassett Moore of Columbia University, himself a judge on the court. It stated that the court could not "without the consent of the United States entertain any request for an advisory opinion touching any dispute or question in which the United States has or claims an interest." Both President Calvin Coolidge and the Wilsonian Democrats accepted the reservation.[9]

Swanson volunteered to lead the Democrats in the fight for approval of the Root formula.[10] It provided that the United States could indicate its opposition to any League of Nations advisory request to the World Court. If overridden by league members, it could then withdraw without discredit. Both Swanson and Secretary of State Henry L. Stimson publicly endorsed the Root formula in early September, 1929. Due to the depression and congressional elections, President Herbert Hoover decided to delay submitting the protocols until December, 1930. In March, 1931, Swanson called for consideration of the proposal, but failed by one vote to get it out of the Foreign Relations Committee.[11] In December, 1931, Hoover and Stimson asked Swanson to be a delegate at the World Disarmament Conference in Geneva. Swanson's decision to accept did not indicate his abandonment of

---

[8] Ferrell, Swanson, pp. 175-76.

[9] Guinsburg, Pursuit of Isolationism, pp. 104-105; Fleming, The United States and World Organizations, pp. 242, 251; Ferrell, Swanson, pp. 176-77.

[10] The Root formula was named for Elihu Root, former secretary of war, secretary of state, United States senator, member of the Permanent Court of Arbitration at The Hague, president of the Carnegie Endowment for International Peace, Nobel prize recipient, member of the committee of jurists at The Hague, which devised the Permanent Court of International Justice, and United States delegate to the Washington Conference on Limitation of Armaments. As a member of the commission to revise the World Court Statute, he devised a formula to facilitate American entry. See "Elihu Root," in the Encyclopedia of American History, 6th edit, eds. Richard B. Morris and Jeffrey B. Morris (New York: Harper & Row, Publishers, 1953; 1982), p. 1142.

[11] Ferrell, Swanson, p. 177.

the court issue. In his December 29, 1931, letter to Governor John Garland Pollard, he wrote: "You have probably noticed that action on the World Court has been put off until legislation affecting domestic problems has been handled. You may rest assured that this matter will be pushed to the utmost."[12]

Senator Swanson was still in Geneva when the Foreign Relations Committee finally moved for reconsideration of the World Court proposal in March, 1932. Even then, he advised Senator Joseph T. Robinson in guiding the resolution through the committee. In his December 12, 1932, letter to Governor Pollard, Swanson wrote that he was "doing everything possible to have the World Court matter disposed of during the present session of Congress." The senator assured Pollard that the matter had his "earnest attention and best efforts."[13]

The depression, unsettled conditions in Europe and Asia, and the caution of Senator Key Pittman, the minority leader of the committee in Swanson's absence, undercut further action on the protocols.[14] Even Swanson realized that the time was not ripe for a vote on the proposal. In his January 6, 1933, letter to Douglas S. Freeman, he wrote: "I am an earnest advocate of the United States entering the World Court, under the Root Formula, and as soon as possible." Swanson indicated, however, that the resolution stood a better chance of passage during the next session of Congress. He told Freeman that while he agreed with him that "it would be best to dispose of the matter at this session," many feared that if favorable action were taken then France and other debtor states would ask the World Court to allow them to settle their debts through separate negotiations on the ability to pay. Swanson promised that he would reach a "more definite conclusion" after conferring with President-elect Roosevelt. He wrote: "I am very desirous of getting the matter behind us and will take advantage of the first opportunity to secure favorable action. I am deeply interested, and there is nothing I can do that I will not do."[15] Swanson soon left the Senate to serve as Roosevelt's secretary of the navy.

---

[12] Swanson to John G. Pollard, December 29, 1931, John G. Pollard Executive Papers, Virginia State Library, Richmond, Virginia.

[13] Swanson to Pollard, December 12, 1932, Pollard Papers.

[14] Ferrell, Swanson, p. 177.

[15] Swanson to Douglas S. Freeman, January 6, 1933, Douglas S. Freeman Papers, Library of Congress, Washington, D.C.

THE NEW DOMINION IN THE COMMUNITY OF NATIONS   47

Perhaps no man in the Commonwealth of Virginia epitomized the Wilsonian legacy better than Carter Glass. The outspoken newspaper publisher and "Father of the Federal Reserve System," served in the Wilson cabinet as secretary of the treasury. Glass's devotion to the twenty-seventh president was legendary. In 1922, he had opposed the Four-Power Pact[16] simply because some of its supporters had voted against Wilson's League of Nations.[17] On January 17, 1936, he bitterly denounced Senator Gerald P. Nye for his accusation that Wilson "falsified" about his knowledge of the Allied secret treaties before the Versailles conference in 1919. Glass also attacked Nye for having suggested that Wilson was compelled by the "house of Morgan" (i.e. Wall Street) to drag the United States into the First World War. Glass told his fellow senators that: "I resent it [that accusation], as every American citizen who knew Woodrow Wilson would resent it, as an infamous libel, whether suggested or whether directly made." During his speech, the senior senator from Virginia banged his desk so hard that his hand bled.[18]

In August, 1919, Glass submitted to President Wilson a detailed treasury report explaining the extent to which failure to ratify the Versailles treaty was "impeding" American business interests. In his February 9, 1920, letter to Wilson, he agreed with the chief executive that acquiescence to Senator Henry Cabot Lodge's treaty reservations would constitute betrayal of both the Democratic party and the president himself. In his May 28, 1920, letter to Glass, Wilson thanked the senator for sending him a copy of the Virginia Democratic party platform that supported the League of Nations. (Glass wrote the platform himself.) In his November 3, 1921, letter to John Stewart Bryan, Glass wrote that "Had the United States gone into the League of Nations the world would have disarmed long ago and we would have security against war for many years to come, if not forever." On Armistice Day, 1923, Glass praised Wilson for his achievements as president, most notably, his League of Nations. Glass said: "If the League of Nations as you conceived it has done well without the aid or countenance of this powerful republic, of what inestimable value to civilization it would have been in these

---

[16] The Four-Power Treaty, signed on December 13, 1921, stipulated that the United States, Britain, France, and Japan respect one another's possessions in the Pacific and refer future disputes in that region to a joint conference.

[17] Palmer, Carter Glass, pp. 166, 178-79, 314.

[18] The provisions of the Allies' secret treaties ran counter to Wilsonian principles. Glass's January 17, 1936, speech to the Senate, Carter Glass Papers, University of Virginia Library, Charlottesville, Virginia; Herring and Hess, "Regionalism," p. 256.

fateful years had we not withheld our sympathy and deserted our allies of the great war."[19]

Senator Glass was no less devoted to the World Court. Between 1923-35, he answered hundreds of constituents' letters imploring him to support their position on this matter. In one such letter to Adolph Lewisohn, Glass wrote: "I doubt if you could be more in favor of our joining the World Court than I; but the men in the U.S. Senate who favor in whole the isolation which Mr. Hughes advocates in part seem determined to block all progress in the direction of effective international cooperation." In his December 14, 1931, reply to Mrs. L. H. Price, secretary of the Lynchburg branch of the American Association of University Women, Glass wrote: "I am heartily in favor of the adherence of this country to the World Court and you may rest assured I will do everything I can to have the question acted upon favorably at an early date." Glass assured Governor Pollard in his January 2, 1934, letter that he saw "no reason why the General Assembly of Virginia should not, if it pleases, ask the Senate of the United States to ratify the World Court Treaty." "It is my expectation," the senator wrote, "to vote for ratification, should we ever reach the question in the Senate."[20]

On the eve of the historic Senate vote on the court, Glass was polled as an "enthusiastic" supporter of the resolution. Glass reiterated his support to his constituents just days before casting his vote. On January 29, 1935, the senator was finally given the opportunity to vote for American adherence to the court. After the Senate rejected the protocols, Glass blamed its defeat on Roosevelt's bitterest antagonists and expressed his dismay most vividly in his February 9, 1935, letter to Dr. R. E. Blackwell, president of Randolph-Macon College. Glass wrote: "I was much distressed at the defeat of the World Court proposition in the Senate. I do not think this would have happened had some of those who affect to be in favor of the World Court

---

[19] Glass to Woodrow Wilson, August 13, 1919, Glass to Wilson, February 9, 1920, Wilson to Glass, May 28, 1920, Glass to John Stewart Bryan, November 3, 1921, Glass's November 11, 1923, Armistice Day speech, Glass Papers.

[20] Glass to Adolph Lewisohn, February 14, 1925, Glass to L. H. Price, December 14, 1931, Glass Papers; Glass to John G. Pollard, January 2, 1934, Pollard Papers.

THE NEW DOMINION IN THE COMMUNITY OF NATIONS 49

been somewhat more aggressive. However, Father Coughlin, Huey Long and the Hearst newspapers scared some Senators."[21]

After filling Swanson's vacant Senate seat in 1933, Harry F. Byrd laid to rest rumors that he did not support the World Court. In his September 29, 1933, reply to Douglas S. Freeman's inquiry on that subject, Byrd wrote:

> I cannot imagine how the rumor got abroad that I am opposed or indifferent to the World Court. The World Court, as you know, has not been under direct consideration by the Senate, and I have not been requested to express myself one way or the other in regard to the matter. I can say to you, however, that I expect to vote for American adherence to the World Court when the matter is presented to the Senate.[22]

A few months later, Byrd reiterated his support in another letter to Freeman. His January 2, 1934, letter to Governor Pollard was no less supportive of the court. "I have seen Senator Glass," Byrd wrote the governor, "and he expects to vote for adherence of this country to the World Court with appending reservations, and I shall do the same." The junior senator also saw "no reason" why the General Assembly should not pass a resolution asking the United State Senate to ratify the treaties for adherence.[23]

Senator Byrd was also labeled an "enthusiastic" adherent of the protocols before the long-awaited Senate vote. Despite his many differences with Roosevelt, he did not hesitate to cast his vote in favor of the court. After the Senate rejected the treaty, Byrd suggested to Virginius Dabney that he write an editorial stating that during Roosevelt's three great legislative crises, both Virginia senators stood squarely behind him. He reminded Dabney that he and Glass had used their influence and votes in backing FDR

---

[21] Edgar B. Nixon, ed., Franklin D. Roosevelt and Foreign Affairs, vol. 2 (Cambridge: The Belknap Press of Harvard University Press, 1969) pp. 353-54; Glass to Roberta Wellford, January 5, 1935, Glass to Cornelia S. Adair, January 16, 1935, Glass to James W. Gordon, January 10, 1935, Glass to Kermit P. Flora, January 28, 1935, Glass to R. E. Blackwell, February 9, 1935, Glass Papers; Palmer, Carter Glass, p. 241; Guinsburg, Pursuit of Isolationism, pp. 164, 166.

[22] Freeman to Harry F. Byrd, December 19, 1933, Byrd to Freeman, September 29, 1933, Freeman Papers.

[23] Byrd to Freeman, December 27, 1933, Freeman Papers; Pollard to Byrd, December 31, 1933, Byrd to Pollard, January 2, 1934, Pollard Papers.

on his veto of the Economy Bill, the World Court vote, and adoption of the McCarren Amendment. At the same time, he noted that "The so-called progressives and radicals in the Senate, who have proclaimed their admiration for the President, in each of these instances voted against him." Byrd concluded that while he had "no apologies whatever" to make for his attitude on "any public question," he did not wish the "thought to prevail" that he and Glass were opposed to "everything the President desires."[24]

Prominent Virginians in federal service shared their elected representatives' enthusiasm for a larger role for the United States in world affairs. Diplomat Alexander Wilbourne Weddell's internationalist sympathies were well-known. Early in 1933, Esther Everett Lape, member in charge of the American Foundation, wrote Weddell requesting that he ask Senator Swanson to make a motion in the Senate to consider the World Court treaties. In his reply Weddell asked Lape to write him again in the future when Congress was more likely to consider the protocols. (Despite his sympathy for the court, Weddell had been preoccupied with his candidacy to the ambassadorship of Argentina. He also realized that Congress was faced with Roosevelt's domestic legislation and probably would not reconvene before the first of the year.) Nearly nineteen months after Senate confirmation of his ambassadorship, Ann C. Voigt of the League of Nations Association's membership department, wrote Weddell and expressed her pleasure that he had joined her organization.[25]

The Virginian who played the most important role in drafting the final World Court resolution was Assistant Secretary of State R. Walton Moore, former head of the state bar association. In September, 1934, Moore, along with his close friend, Secretary of State Cordell Hull, and Assistant Secretary Francis B. Sayre, gained Roosevelt's approval to present a resolution favoring American adherence to the court at the next session of Congress. Hull instructed Moore and Sayre to draw up the necessary legislation. On December 28, 1934, Roosevelt gave them the final go-ahead and permission to contact Key Pittman, chairman of the Senate Foreign Relations Committee. Moore later attributed the court defeat to the lax efforts of those close to the

---

[24] Nixon, *Franklin D. Roosevelt*, pp. 353-54; Byrd to Virginius Dabney, February 28, 1935, Executive folder A, p. 435, Harry F. Byrd Papers, University of Virginia Library, Charlottesville, Virginia.

[25] Esther Everett Lape to Alexander Wilbourne Weddell, January 3, 1933, Weddell to Lape, June 21, 1933, Anne C. Voigt to Weddell, December 28, 1934, Alexander Wilbourne Weddell Papers, Virginia Historical Society, Richmond, Virginia.

THE NEW DOMINION IN THE COMMUNITY OF NATIONS 51

president who had given certain senators the impression that FDR was indifferent on the issue.[26]

On the state level, the World Court issue was very much alive during the administration of Governor John Garland Pollard. In the winter of 1930, Pollard informed Everett Colby of the New York-based National World Court Committee that he approved of American adherence to the court. In his July 10, 1931, reply to the chairman of the committee, John O'Ryan, the governor wrote: "I fully agree with you that our country ought to support prompt ratification of the Protocols, which is now before the Senate. I am deeply interested in the subject." Later that year, Pollard wrote Senator Swanson that he hoped that "something can be done in the interest of the World Court" before the senator left for the Geneva disarmament conference.[27]

Pollard continued to pressure Swanson to act on the court issue during the following year. In his December 9, 1932, letter to Swanson, the governor wrote: "I am writing to express the hope that you may see your way clear to use your influence to settle the World Court issue at this session of Congress." The senator assured Pollard that he was "doing everything possible to have the World Court matter disposed of during the present session of Congress." Swanson wrote that the matter had his "earnest attention and best efforts."[28]

In early 1934, upon the urging of Esther Lape and the approval of Senators Glass and Byrd, Governor Pollard recommended to Virginia's General Assembly that it pass a resolution asking the United States Senate to ratify the three World Court treaties. (Pollard initially hesitated because as the outgoing chief executive, he felt this best left to his successor.) The

---

[26] Cordell Hull, <u>The Memoirs of Cordell Hull</u> (New York: The Macmillan Co., 1948), p. 388; Wayne S. Cole, <u>Roosevelt and the Isolationists, 1932-45</u>, (Lincoln, Nebraska and London: University of Nebraska Press, 1983), p. 124.

[27] Everett Colby to Pollard, February 17, 1930, Pollard to Colby, n.d., John O'Ryan to Pollard, July 9, 1931, Pollard to O'Ryan, July 10, 1931, Pollard to Swanson, December 22, 1931, Pollard Papers.

[28] Lape to Pollard, December 8, 1932, Pollard to Lape, December 9, 1932, Pollard to Swanson, December 9, 1932, Lape to Pollard, December 17, 1932, Pollard to Lape, December 19, 1932, Swanson to Pollard, December 12, 1932, Pollard Papers.

General Assembly honored the governor's wish during its January, 1934, session.[29]

The state's leading newspapers were also strongly in favor of American membership in both the League of Nations and the World Court. Virginia's most respected editors, Douglas S. Freeman and Virginius Dabney, played a key role in shaping public opinion on those issues. Much of their thinking on America's role in the world was influenced by their publisher, John Stewart Bryan. Born in 1871 of a prominent industrialist and publisher, Bryan succeeded his father in running the Richmond News-Leader and Richmond Times-Dispatch. Educated at the University of Virginia and the Harvard Law School, Bryan served his city, state, and country in various capacities: rector of the University of Virginia, president of the College of William and Mary, president of the American Newspaper Publishers Association, delegate to several Democratic national conventions, prominent Episcopal layman, member of the internationalist Century Club, and member of the War Council of the Young Men's Christian Association. (This position took him to the Paris Peace Conference in 1919). Bryan's support for American entry into the First World War and his enthusiastic embrace of Wilson's peace program were clearly reflected in the editorial pages of both the News-Leader and the Times-Dispatch, both Democratic papers with a statewide circulation.[30]

In his unpublished biography of Bryan, Douglas S. Freeman portrayed his subject as a fervent admirer of Wilson and defender of the League of Nations. Freeman wrote that Bryan "had been sustained in spirit throughout the war by the hope that out of it would come a new world order, an international organization strong enough to enforce peace." Freeman maintained that "To no cause did he [Bryan] give himself with more of prayer, of faith and of effort." Bryan was convinced that "The covenant of the League of Nations, though recognized as defective or dubious in some respects, seemed in very truth to be a new covenant of man and ideals." According to Freeman, Bryan was outraged that "cynical" men like Henry

---

[29] Lape to Pollard, December 13, 1933, Pollard to Lape, December 15, 1933, Lape to Pollard, December 19, 1933, Pollard to Glass, December 31, 1933, Pollard to Byrd, December 31, 1933, Glass to Pollard, January 2, 1934, Byrd to Pollard, January 2, 1934, Draft Resolution for the Virginia State Legislature, January, 1934, Pollard Papers.

[30] Harold L. Fowler, "John Stewart Bryan," in the Dictionary of American Biography, supplement three, 1941-1945, ed. Edward T. James (New York: Charles Scribner's Sons, 1973), pp. 115-16; clipping from the Baltimore Sun, July 1, 1934, "Scrapbook, 1934-35," John Stewart Bryan Papers, Virginia Historical Society, Richmond, Virginia.

Cabot Lodge could oppose the League on the basis of "petty politics" and "jealousy and hatred of Woodrow Wilson." Freeman concluded that "Opposition to the League seemed to him [Bryan] almost profanation."[31]

During much of his editorship of the News-Leader, the Johns Hopkins-trained Freeman served as a member and trustee of both the Rockefeller Foundation and the Carnegie Endowment for International Peace. Freeman's internationalist affiliations and admiration for Bryan strongly influenced his thinking on the league and the court. The News-Leader frequently urged the United States government to support the league and its use of sanctions against Japanese and Italian aggression during the 1930s. Freeman's editorials also argued that the United States shared some of the blame for the world's problems for not having joined the league in 1920. In its February 27, 1933, editorial, the News-Leader asserted that "By refusing to join, the United States have a heavy responsibility at the bar of history for keeping the league from being a full success. We must not make it a failure by refusing to cooperate." By 1936, the News-Leader admitted that it was "futile to hope for America's early adherence to the league of nations." But even after the Munich crisis in September, 1938, it still held that "the principle on which it [the League] was founded in 1919 still offers the best hope of saving the world from self-destruction."[32]

Freeman's sympathies for the World Court and his desire to see early Senate ratification of the protocols were clearly reflected in his correspondence with Senators Swanson, Glass, Byrd, and Thomas J. Walsh of Montana.[33] Those sentiments were also expressed in Freeman's lengthy editorials. In its January 17, 1935, editorial, the News-Leader argued for American adherence, asserting that such action would result in a necessary revision of the freedom of the seas doctrine. Freeman strongly believed that

---

[31] Douglas S. Freeman, John Stewart Bryan: A Biography (New York: Charles Scribner's Sons, 1947), pp. 24-25, not published for sale, Douglas S. Freeman Papers, Virginia Historical Society, Richmond, Virginia.

[32] Biographical sketch of Freeman, Freeman Papers; Richmond News-Leader, February 27, 1933, p. 8, February 28, 1933, p. 8, March 14, 1933, p. 8, October 29, 1935, p. 8, November 7, 1935, p. 10, February 24, 1936, p. 8, September 16, 1938, p. 10, January 2, 1939, pp. 2, 12.

[33] Freeman to Swanson, January 4, 1933, Freeman to Swanson, January 7, 1933, Freeman to Thomas J. Walsh, January 11, 1933, Walsh to Freeman, January 14, 1933, Freeman to Walsh, January 16, 1933, Freeman to Walsh, January 23, 1933, Walsh to Freeman, January 25, 1933, Freeman to Glass, December 8, 1933, Freeman to Byrd, December 8, 1933, Freeman Papers.

a broader definition of contraband would reduce the chances of the United States getting involved in another war. (That would allow oil, cotton, and scrap iron to be included among the "implements of war.") After the Senate rejected the court proposal, the News-Leader chided the opposition senators for having taken themselves and their prerogatives too seriously.[34]

Virginius Dabney's internationalist sympathies originated with his father, a history professor at the University of Virginia. Richard Heath Dabney was a life-long personal friend and fraternity brother of Woodrow Wilson. He made speeches on behalf of the League of Nations throughout the state. While Virginius Dabney conceded that the League of Nations and World Court were not major nor even minor issues during the 1930s, the fact that Wilson had been a Virginian influenced those concerned with those matters.[35]

Dabney's distress that the United States had not entered the league manifested itself in numerous editorials he wrote during the pre-Pearl Harbor period. The Times-Dispatch's editor believed that America's entry into the league would make it a more effective instrument of world peace. He also felt that nations would be less likely to defy the league if the United States was a member. Dabney credited the league's mediation efforts for having averted war between France and Germany over the Saar controversy. The Times-Dispatch's appraisal of the league's handling of sanctions against Italy in 1935 was more ambiguous. Its August 29, 1935, editorial labeled the league "impotent" for having failed to levy sanctions against Italy. It maintained that French opposition to the sanctions weakened the chances of avoiding war between Ethiopia and Italy. The paper's attitude changed, however, after the league did indeed threaten economic embargoes against the Italians one month later. Once again, the Times-Dispatch praised the league's actions for having prevented war. The threat of sanctions alone had enhanced the league's prestige. The Times-Dispatch encouraged the United States to cooperate with the league in applying sanctions against Italy. That could best be done, it argued, through congressional revision of the Neutrality Act. The paper described the League of Nations and World Court as the "hope of mankind." The Times-Dispatch also reiterated its support for American membership in those two world bodies. Only international

---

[34] Richmond News-Leader, January 17, 1935, p.8, January 31, 1935, p. 8.

[35] Interview with Dabney, November 28, 1986.

organization and United States participation, it warned, could stop aggression and prevent another European war.³⁶

Joining a chorus of condemnation world-wide, the Times-Dispatch pilloried the infamous Hoare-Laval proposal. In its December 20, 1935, editorial the paper stated that the Anglo-French territorial concessions to Benito Mussolini's regime had stabbed the newly revitalized league in the back. A few months later, the paper once again credited the league for having spared the world another war. The Times-Dispatch asserted that despite its deficiencies, the league had successfully negotiated a peaceful solution to the Ethiopian conflict and had prevented war between Germany and France over Rhineland. Ten days later, the paper embraced a French proposal for an international police force under the aegis of the league.³⁷

Within the space of nearly two years, the Times-Dispatch's assessment of the league had once again changed. In its February 24, 1938, editorial it described the league as "largely impotent." Without benefit of Germany, Japan, Italy, and the United States as members, the league gave "little promise of useful and effective service to the cause of peace." The editorial went on to castigate the United States for not having joined the league during Wilson's administration, thereby lending its "immense prestige and power" to the cause of peace and "international collective action." The absence of America helped create a "moribund" league unable to halt Japanese aggression in Manchuria and China, the Italian conquest of Ethiopia, Germany's re-occupation of Rhineland, and German-Italian intervention in the Spanish Civil War. The Times-Dispatch repeated those views later that year and the next. It added that an American presence during the post-World War I period would have resulted in revision of the Versailles treaty and a softening of the Allies' vengeful policies against Germany which led to the rise of Adolph Hitler.³⁸

On the eve of the Munich debacle, the Times-Dispatch maintained that the United States shared part of the blame for the likely dismemberment of

---

³⁶Richmond Times-Dispatch, November 29, 1934, p. 6, December 3, 1934, p. 6, December 12, 1934, p. 8, December 12, 1934, p. 8, August 29, 1935, p. 8, September 28, 1935, p. 6, November 11, 1935 p. 6, November 11, 1935, p. 6.

³⁷Ibid., December 20, 1935, p. 18, March 31, 1936, p. 10, April 10, 1936, p. 16.

³⁸Ibid., February 24, 1938, p. 8, May 15, 1938, p. 2, September 26, 1938, p. 8, December 10, 1939, p. 2.

Czechoslovakia. The United States helped draft the Versailles treaty, which gave birth to that eastern European state, but refused to help carry out that settlement through membership in the league. The editorial further blamed the Johnson Act (which forbade United States loans to countries defaulting on their war debts), the protectionist Smoot-Hawley tariff, and the neutrality acts for exacerbating the world-wide economic crisis and giving notice to the British and French that they could expect no help from America in the event they went to war to defend democracy. The Times-Dispatch concluded that while the British and French betrayal of the Czechs was indeed contemptible, American policies for the preceding eighteen years had not only helped make the rise of dictators inevitable, but made those two democracies' resistance to fascist aggression more difficult. Still, Virginia's leading newspaper wanted no part in Europe's wars. In December, 1939, it opposed the league's invitation to the United States for cooperation in providing Finland with relief after the Soviet invasion. The paper feared that America's assistance might lead to its involvement in another European war.[39]

The Times-Dispatch's position on the World Court issue also fluctuated. Its editorials reflected the general public's disinterest in the matter during the depths of the depression. Economic problems and suspicion of Europe precluded the paper's active support for United States membership. Later in 1934, that attitude changed as international tensions heated up and the Senate prepared to vote on the court resolution. The Times-Dispatch strongly recommended American membership in the court as necessary for the maintenance of world peace. In its January 31, 1935, editorial the paper described the court defeat as "a tragedy not only for this country but for the world." Still, the paper held hopes for eventual American adherence.[40]

The less influential weeklies and dailies (all Democratic) throughout the state did not hold a consensus view on American membership in the League of Nations. Little opposition could be found, however, to United States adherence to the World Court. As was the case with the News-Leader and the Times-Dispatch, the less prestigious papers' editorial views were affected by volatile political and economic happenings world-wide. Consequently, their editorial positions also fluctuated over the years. A majority of those newspapers believed that the United States' failure to join

---

[39] Ibid., September 26, 1938, p. 8, September 29, 1938, p. 12, December 14, 1939, p. 2.

[40] Ibid., March 25, 1934, p. 2, December 3, 1934, p. 6, January 11, 1935, p. 12, September 26, 1938, p. 8, January 31, 1935, p. 8, November 11, 1935, p. 6.

the league in 1920 contributed to that body's inability to halt aggression and maintain world peace. They agreed with the Times-Dispatch and the News-Leader that without American participation in the league, it would remain "impotent."[41] Most of those papers did not advocate United States membership during the pre-Pearl Harbor period. Several did, nonetheless, urge American cooperation with Geneva.[42] A few editors praised the league's role in averting war between Hungary and Yugoslavia. In 1935, many editorials supported its sanctions against Italy. Some editors even favored a world police force to implement the league's policies.[43] The league remained the hope of civilization.[44] Even before the September, 1938, sell-out at Munich, however, editorial opinion had changed. The press no longer perceived the failure-ridden league as at least a worthy humanitarian body and useful world forum.[45]

Editorial support for American participation in the World Court remained consistent throughout Roosevelt's first term. The Alexandria Gazette, "America's Oldest Daily," embraced the court when most Virginians were more concerned with surviving the depression.[46] Other papers revealed their pro-court sympathies well after the Hundred Days. Virginia's

---

[41] Daily Progress (Charlottesville), November 19, 1934, p. 4, January 31, 1935, p. 4, April 22, 1935, p. 4, December 13, 1937, p. 4, February 25, 1938, p. 4, May 14, 1938, p. 4; Danville Register, August 7, 1935, p. 4, August 21, 1935, p. 4; Alexandria Gazette, April 16, 1935, p. 4, December 28, 1935, p. 4, May 8, 1936, p. 4, October 4, 1937, p. 4; Roanoke Times, May 4, 1936, p. 6, May 6, 1936, p. 6, July 9, 1939, p. 6; Norfolk Ledger-Dispatch, December 14, 1937, p. 10.

[42] Norfolk Ledger-Dispatch, December 29, 1933, p. 8, October 9, 1935, p. 10; Alexandria Gazette, October 14, 1937, p. 4.

[43] Alexandria Gazette, December 17, 1934, p. 4; Daily Progress (Charlottesville), September 27, 1935, p. 4, December 13, 1937, p. 4; Danville Register, October 9, 1935, p. 4, March 31, 1935, p. 6, December 28, 1935, p. 4, Norfolk Ledger-Dispatch, December 31, 1935, p. 10, June 2, 1937, p. 10.

[44] Alexandria Gazette, April 16, 1935, p. 4, October 4, 1937, p.4; Danville Register, September 14, 1937, p. 4.

[45] Norfolk Ledger-Dispatch, July 6, 1935, p. 6, August 16, 1935, p. 8, August 21, 1935, p. 6; Alexandria Gazette, October 3, 1938, p. 4; Danville Register, September 22, 1938, p. 4.

[46] Alexandria Gazette, January 13, 1933, p. 4.

newspapers treated the court matter as a bi-partisan issue. They believed Roosevelt's assurance that United States membership in the court would not harm American sovereignty, but rather further the cause of world peace. After the Senate's rejection of the court protocols, the Norfolk Ledger-Dispatch wrote that Virginians who supported the resolution "must take what comfort they can from the reflection that both Virginia Senators voted for it."[47]

Despite the general lack of public interest in the league and court matters, a significant minority of Virginians, representing a variety of professional, vocational, and religious affiliations, expressed their opinions on America's role in the community of nations.[48] Many exerted pressure on their elected representatives via letters, resolutions, and petitions.[49] Advocates of American adherence to the World Court believed that United States membership would help insure world peace. They included members of: the Richmond Peace Council, the Young Women's Christian Association, the state bar association, the Virginia League of Women Voters, the Richmond League of Women Voters, chambers of commerce, the American Association of University Women, university presidents and administrators, college students, judges, and protestant ministers.[50] Opponents feared America's

---

[47]Ibid., January 13, 1933, p. 4; Roanoke Times, January 17, 1935, p. 6; Norfolk Ledger-Dispatch, January 17, 1935, p. 8, January 30, 1935, p. 6, January 5, 1936, p. 6.

[48]A Round Table meeting on "The Relation of the United States With the League of Nations" was held during the July 2-15, 1933, session of the Institute of Public Affairs at the University of Virginia. See The University of Virginia News Letter, June 15, 1933, p. 1.

[49]For example, see Dr. Lough's suggestion that the Richmond Peace Council's chairman write Virginia's senators asking their support for the World Court. Minutes of the January 8, 1935, meeting of the Richmond Peace Council. Richmond Peace Council Papers, James Branch Cabell Library, Virginia Commonwealth University, Richmond, Virginia.

[50]Ibid.; At its April 6, 1934, meeting, the Richmond Peace Council went on record favoring the World Court treaties and requesting that Senators Robinson and Pittman lend their support in bringing the protocols out of committee so that the Senate could ratify them before adjournment. Minutes of the April 6, 1934, meeting of the Richmond Peace Council, Richmond Peace Council Papers. Mrs. John H. Davis, et al., (representing the ladies of the Lynchburg Young Women's Christian Association) to Glass, n.d.; membership of the YWCA, Newport News, to Glass, January 23, 1935, James

involvement would entangle it in Europe's controversies. They were fewer in number and generally did not represent specific organizations.[51]

Protestant opinion generally favored America's cooperation with the league in the interest of world peace. Citing what they considered the anachronism of absolute national sovereignty and the need for international justice, many protestants also supported American adherence to the court. Baptist editorialists, intellectuals, and ministers were the most vocal. They blamed the breakdown of world peace on their country's failure to join the league and the court. Many supported the league's sanctions against Italy in 1936 and were sympathetic to the idea of an international police force to carry out its decisions.[52] For the most part, Methodist, Presbyterian, Quaker, and Brethren editors and ministers agreed. Dr. Beverly D. Tucker, rector of historic St. Paul's Episcopal Church, Richmond, a wealthy and influential congregation, asserted that the World Court and League of Nations were "the most effective means yet devised for settling international disputes in a pacific manner." He rejected the notion that the league was a failure because it failed to halt Italian and Japanese aggression. Tucker maintained: "The United States should lend to the League all possible cooperation in its effort to settle international disputes by peaceful means." He concluded that: "The essential task . . . is not the creation of an international police, but the

---

W. Gordon to Glass, January 8, 1935, Roberta Welford to Glass, January 3, 1935, Welford to Glass, January 17, 1935, Cornelia S. Adair to Glass, January 14, 1935, W. S. Harney (representing the membership of the Norfolk Association of Commerce) to Glass, January 7, 1935, Mrs. Walter S. Chisholm (representing the membership of the Charlottesville branch of the American Association of University Women) to Glass, February 16, 1932, Ilena M. Bailey (representing the membership of the Blacksburg branch of the American Association of University Women) to Glass, March 25, 1935, Julian A. Burruss to Glass, February 1, 1932, R. E. Blackwell to Glass, February 8, 1935, Emmet M. Frazer to Glass, January 22, 1935, membership of the International Relations Club, State Teachers College, Fredericksburg, to Glass January 18, 1935, James H. Ricks to Glass, February 8, 1935, H. D. Brown, Jr., (representing the Lynchburg Ministerial Association) to Glass, February 6, 1935, Kermit P. Flora (representing the Student Ministers at Bridgewater College) to Glass, January 17, 1935, Glass Papers.

[51] A. C. Black to Glass, January 20, 1935, L. W. Carpenter to Glass, January 28, 1935, Glass Papers.

[52] Religious Herald, January 9, 1936, p. 3, February 3, 1938, p. 10, March 17, 1938, p. 10, September 8, 1938, p. 10, December 28, 1939, pp. 4-5, December 18, 1941, pp. 4-5, October 26, 1933, p. 3.

transformation of national policies sufficiently to make possible the granting of comprehensive jurisdiction to the League of Nations.[53]

Virginia's small Roman Catholic population was less expressive on those international issues. The Catholic press was, however, isolationist-oriented and critical of the league and court. The Virginia Catholic newspaper, the official organ of the Richmond diocese, castigated Italian aggression against Christian Ethiopia. But at the same time, Catholic opinion feared American involvement with those world organizations would jeopardize United States sovereignty and divert attention from pressing economic problems at home.[54]

Black editorial opinion focused almost exclusively on the League of Nation's role in the Italian-Ethiopian conflict of 1935-36. Virginia's blacks identified racially with the Ethiopians and stood steadfastly behind their struggle to maintain their sovereignty. Norfolk's Journal and Guide, a long-established black newspaper, praised the league's condemnation of Italian aggression and application of sanctions. That support weakened, however, after sanctions proved ineffective and the proposed Hoare-Laval territorial concessions were revealed. Britain's role in the Geneva negotiations were perceived as an effort to protect its empire rather than an attempt to save Ethiopia's independence. The Journal's disillusionment with the league was manifestly clear after its recognition of Italy's conquest and ejection of Haile Selassie's government from its ranks. Thereafter, the newspaper portrayed the league as ineffective and impotent. The league's failure to halt aggression in Europe, Asia, and especially Africa had made it unworthy of those high

---

[53] Richmond Christian Advocate, November 9, 1939, p. 11; Virginia Methodist Advocate, April 25, 1940, p. 10, July 11, 1940, p. 10; H. D. Brown, Jr., to Glass, February 6, 1935, Glass Papers; Presbyterian of the South and Presbyterian Standard, November 6, 1935, pp. 3-5, November 3, 1937, pp. 2-3, December 24, 1941, p. 2; January 19, 1935, telegram from Edward F. Raiford, clerk, the Virginia quarterly meeting of the Religious Society of Friends (Quakers) to Glass, Kermit P. Flora to Glass, January 17, 1935, Glass Papers; transcript of Richmond Peace Councils radio address "Interviews for Peace," over WRVA, November 10, 1936, pp. 6-9, Richmond Peace Council Papers.

[54] See George Q. Flynn, Roosevelt and Romanism: Catholics and American Diplomacy, 1937-1945 (Westport, Conn. and London, England: Greenwood Press, 1976), pp. 7-8; Virginia Catholic, January, 1933, p. 14, February, 1935, p. 10, September, 1935, pp. 8-9, 26.

ideals which set it into motion after the First World War. The Journal viewed the World Court as no more effective than the league.[55]

"America's Oldest Colored Weekly," the Richmond Planet, also empathized with the Ethiopians and bitterly denounced Mussolini as a "rapist" and "power crazed Whop." The Planet's tone was far more radical than that of the Journal. (One of the Planet's leading columnists, Donald Burke, was a self-proclaimed Communist whose condemnations of American and European "imperialism" and praise for the Soviet Union were standard fare.) In its July 13, 1935, editorial the Planet blamed the "Imperialistic governments of England, France and the United States," the "League of Nations," as well as Italy for the "attempted rape of Abyssinia." The paper's editorials strongly denounced the Roosevelt administration's "cowardice," "hypocrisy,""policy of neutrality," and "studied indifference" to the plight of Ethiopia. It asserted that Wilson's League of Nations and "self-determination for weaker peoples, a world free for democracy, a war to outlaw war [were] all . . . pushed into oblivion with the aid and consent of a man [i.e. FDR] Wilson honored with high office . . . and who was supposed to share his ideals and aspirations for a world free from the horror of war." The Planet argued that the league's economic sanctions against Italy were not enough; it urged that military, oil, and scrap iron embargoes be applied as well. In the absence of league-imposed military sanctions, the paper exhorted the United States and other nations to sell the Ethiopians the weapons and munitions they required. The Planet's October 12, 1935, editorial criticized America's "hypocritical" "neutrality" (i.e. arms embargo), which put "the strong and aggressive nation and the weak and outraged nation on the same footing." The paper concluded that the league's failure to thwart Mussolini's imperial designs on Ethiopia had led it to the "junkpile" of history.[56]

By the time the Second World War had begun, even the most loyal of Virginia's advocates of American cooperation with the league had become disillusioned. The league's impotence and lack of credibility were all too

---

[55] Journal and Guide (Norfolk), July 27, 1935, p. 8, August 17, 1935, p. 8, September 21, 1935, p. 8, October 16, 1937, p. 8, October 12, 1935, p. 8, November 2, 1935, p. 8, December 21, 1935, p. 8, January 25, 1936, p. 8, January 9, 1937, p. 8, January 9, 1937, p. 8, August 21, 1937, p. 8, June 5, 1937, p. 8, August 21, 1937, p. 8, October 16, 1937, p. 8, March 5, 1938, p. 8, May 28, 1938, p. 8, August 21, 1937, p. 8.

[56] Richmond Planet, July 13, 1935, p. 12, July 27, 1935, p. 12, September 7, 1935, p. 12, October 12, 1935, p. 12, November 9, 1935, p. 12, December 14, 1935, p. 12, December 28, 1935, p. 12, May 9, 1936, p. 12, May 16, 1936, p. 12.

apparent to many Virginians. Woodrow Wilson's instruments for preserving world peace proved unable to halt the march of extremist ideologies, imperialism, and war. Most Virginians shared their leadership elite's disappointment over the failures of Wilsonianism. They believed that much of the world's problems could be attributed to America's failure to join the League of Nations and World Court. The outbreak of another European war focused their attention on keeping out of the conflict rather than on international cooperation.

CHAPTER IV

MARKETS BEYOND THE CHESAPEAKE: VIRGINIA AND RECIPROCAL TRADE

In 1934, few Virginians noticed the passage of the Reciprocal Trade Agreements Act. Four years later, a Gallup Poll indicated that while 92 percent of Southerners polled supported the reciprocal trade program, only one-half of them were aware of efforts to implement that policy. Nevertheless, important opinion-makers in Congress and the press supported that landmark legislation as a significant step toward free trade and expanding markets for the state's agricultural and industrial producers. With the exception of Senator Carter Glass, Virginia's congressional delegation voted for reciprocal trade. Most legislators accepted Representative A. Willis Robertson's view that economic reciprocity would reduce many trade restrictions on Virginia's exports and increase its volume of trade with the rest of the world. A majority of the commonwealth's newspaper editors, especially Douglas S. Freeman, commented favorably on Secretary of State Cordell Hull's trade program. They believed that lower tariffs and fewer trade restrictions would mitigate the effects of the depression, help restore prosperity to Virginia, and further the interests of world peace.[1]

During the post-World War I era, high tariffs, quotas, sanitary regulations, foreign exchange controls, and other restrictive devices helped create a decline in world trade. The Great Depression further reduced the volume of America's foreign trade. Manufacturers, northern and western farmers, and economic nationalists in the Roosevelt administration opposed efforts to liberalize the country's tariff policies on a reciprocal basis. Many farmers believed that reciprocal trade policies would undermine domestic farm prices, benefit eastern industry at their expense, and violate the Constitution (via a delegation of congressional power to the president). Business realized that reciprocity would weaken protectionism. Economic nationalists feared liberalization could eliminate import quotas, prohibit bilateral barter agreements, and legitimize most-favored-nation clauses. Secretary of State Hull, the leading champion of trade liberalization in FDR's cabinet, argued that economic reciprocity would stimulate the American economy through an increase in exports. During the 1932 presidential campaign, Roosevelt supported Hull's reciprocal trade program. Due to

---

[1]Dabney, "The South Looks Abroad," p. 174; Dabney, Below the Potomac, p. 275; Interview with Virginius Dabney, Richmond, Virginia, November 28, 1986.

opposition from many industrialists and farmers, however, he compromised his position by the end of the campaign. After Roosevelt entered the White House in 1933, Agricultural Adjustment Administration director George Peek and brainstruster Raymond Moley vigorously opposed Hull's program. By early 1934, however, the president finally reembraced his secretary of state's low tariff and internationalist principles. Peek's resignation in November, 1935, and the departure of Moley wounded the economic nationalist bloc in the Roosevelt administration. [2]

Secretary Hull, a veteran Wilsonian from Tennessee and an authority on tariffs, was the chief architect of the Reciprocal Trade Agreements Act. That legislation was designed to lower trade barriers, increase American exports to other countries, and help maintain world peace. It authorized the president to negotiate bilateral trade agreements with foreign states. Under the act the chief executive was empowered to increase or reduce existing tariff duties by as much as 50 percent on a reciprocal basis; those agreements also included most-favored-nation clauses. Hull was convinced that excessive trade barriers such as high tariffs provoked cycles of economic retaliation, exacerbated economic rivalries, and often led to war. As a leading tobacco exporter, Virginia suffered from the highly restrictive Smoot-Hawley tariff of 1930. That Republican-sponsored tariff kept many foreign goods out of the country and led to retaliation against the state's agricultural exports. In 1934, a number of leading Virginians believed that Hull's reciprocal trade program

---

[2]Grace L. Beckett, The Reciprocal Trade Agreements Program (New York: Columbia University Press, 1941), pp. 15-16; Arthur W. Schatz, "The Reciprocal Trade Agreements Program and the 'Farm Vote' 1934-1940," Agricultural History 46(1972): 498-514; Cole, Roosevelt and the Isolationists, pp. 95-112; Robert F. Smith, "Reciprocity," in Encyclopedia of American Foreign Policy, ed. Alexander DeConde (New York: Charles Scribner's Sons, 1978), pp. 867, 878; Hull, Memoirs, pp. 172, 352; William R. Allen, "The International Trade Philosophy of Cordell Hull, 1907-1933," American Economic Review 43 (1953), pp. 103-104, 106, 108, 114, 116; William R. Allen, "Cordell Hull and the Defense of the Trade Agreements Program, 1934-1940," in Isolation and Security: Ideas and Interests in Twentieth-century American Foreign Policy, ed. Alexander DeConde (Durham, N.C.: Duke University Press, 1957), pp. 107-32; Donald F. Drummond, "Cordell Hull," in An Uncertain Tradition: American Secretaries of State in the Twentieth-Century, ed. Norman A. Graebner (Westport, Conn.: Greenwood Press Publishers, 1980), pp. 184-209; Dallek, Franklin D. Roosevelt and American Foreign Policy, pp. 19-20, 38, 48-49, 84, 92-93; Leuchtenburg, Franklin D. Roosevelt and the New Deal, pp. 200, 203-205.

would reverse the harsh tariff policies of previous administrations.[3]

Virginia's senior senator, Carter Glass, supported tariff reduction throughout his career. He did not, however, support the Reciprocal Trade Agreements Act of 1934, nor did he vote for its extension in 1937 and 1940. Glass maintained that Secretary Hull's program was an unconstitutional delegation of congressional authority to the executive branch. Furthermore, he did not believe it would significantly reduce tariff rates. In his August 3, 1936, letter to Hull, Glass wrote that he was unhappy that the Democratic party, with a Democratic president, and a two-thirds majority in both houses of Congress had "not repealed or radically modified" the "Smoot Hawley high protective tariff act." He also asserted that while Hull was his first choice to draft and enforce tariff legislation, he nevertheless believed that "the levying of taxes, whether tariff or internal," was "a function for Congress and not for executive officials." Glass concluded: "If this is not sound Democracy, essential to representative government, I have misread the principles and practices of the Democratic party since its foundation."[4]

In January, 1940, Senator Glass was especially concerned about Britain's embargo on American tobacco, which violated their 1938 reciprocal trade agreement with the United States. The senator alerted Secretary Hull

---

[3] Hull, Memoirs, pp. 84, 172, 352. See Julius W. Pratt's sympathetic biography of Roosevelt's secretary of state, Cordell Hull, 1933-1944 (New York: Cooper Square, 1964), pp. xi-xii, 29-30. See also Allen, "Trade Philosophy," pp. 101-116; Allen, "Cordell Hull," pp. 107-32; Drummond, "Cordell Hull," pp. 184-209; The Southern Planter, August, 1938, pp. 4, 13; Beckett, Reciprocal Trade Agreements, p. 16. For a favorable account of the background and evolution of the Roosevelt-Hull reciprocal trade program, see Henry J. Tasca, The Reciprocal Trade Policy of the United States: A Study in Trade Philosophy (Philadelphia: University of Pennsylvania Press, London: Oxford University Press, 1938); Smith, "Reciprocity," p. 878; Adler, Uncertain Giant, pp. 118-19; Dallek, Franklin D. Roosevelt and American Foreign Policy, pp. 84, 92-93, 122-23; Leuchtenburg, Franklin D. Roosevelt and the New Deal, pp. 203-205.

[4] Interview with Virginius Dabney, Richmond, Virginia, November 28, 1986; Richmond Times-Dispatch, June 6, 1934, p. 8; Congressional Record, 73rd Congress, 2nd sess., 1934, 78: 10395; Ibid., 75th Congress, 1st sess., 1937, 81: 1612; Ibid., 76th Congress, 3rd sess., 1940, 86: 4105; Carter Glass to Thomas P. Brockway, n.d., Cordell Hull to Glass, July 28, 1936, Glass to Hull, August 3, 1936, James F. Byrnes to Glass, February 21, 1940, Carter Glass Papers, University of Virginia Library, Charlottesville, Virginia.

to the serious harm facing Virginia tobacco growers unless the embargo was lifted. He also sent Hull the Virginia General Assembly's joint resolution urging Britain's removal of its embargo on American tobacco. The secretary assured the senator that the State Department was doing all it could to convince the British government to modify its policy. Hull, State Department counselor R. Walton Moore, and Under Secretary of State Sumner Welles strongly appealed to the British government to modify its embargo on American agricultural products, especially tobacco. Hull warned the British of "rising resentment" against its policy within the United States.[5]

Senator Harry F. Byrd "heartily" agreed with President Roosevelt on tariff reduction. In May, 1934, he argued that embargoes, restrictions, and trade barriers such as the Fordney and Smoot-Hawley tariffs reduced American exports and were the "prime cause[s] of the world-wide depression." The senator maintained that their "removal or modification" were "necessary step[s] to end the depression," revive the country's foreign trade, and restore prosperity. Unlike his senior colleague, however, he supported the reciprocal trade agreement program in 1934 and voted for its extension in 1937 and 1940. Byrd argued that unlike the heads of state in many other countries the president lacked the authority to enter into trade agreements and tariff revision quickly and effectively, without congressional approval. The senator asserted that by virtue of its lengthy debates, procrastination, "log-rolling,"and kowtowing to the "pressure of organized minorities," Congress was "incapable of making tariff adjustments required in the negotiation of reciprocal trade agreements." Byrd maintained that those very impediments to swift congressional action on trade matters were largely "responsible for the iniquitous trade barriers" that had been enacted in previous administrations. He reasoned that "It would be utterly impossible for Congress to act with sufficient unanimity or dispatch to make changes required in the negotiation of commercial treaties." The senator further argued that "If we agree that reciprocal commercial treaties are necessary, there is no other course but to grant the President the authority requested."[6]

---

[5]Glass to Hull, January 22, 1940, Glass to Hull January 23, 1940, Hull to Glass, January 30, 1940, File Numbers 641.116/2570, 641.116/2574, United States Department of State, Central Decimal File, National Archives, Washington, D.C.; United States, Department of State, Foreign Relations of the United States: Diplomatic Papers, 1940, 3: 89-102.

[6]Interview with Dabney, November 28, 1986. See Senator Byrd's record of Senate roll-call votes, Box 349, pp. 386-90, Senator Byrd's press release of May 21, 1934, Harry F. Byrd Papers, University of Virginia Library, Charlottesville, Virginia.

As the operator of the world's largest, privately-owned apple orchards and representative of powerful agricultural constituencies within the state, Senator Byrd was vitally concerned with the depressed state of farm exports. In a letter to Secretary Hull in the spring of 1933, he wrote, "As President of the Eastern Apple Growers Association I am very anxious to see that apples are included in any reciprocal treaties that are made with other nations. . . . The success of the apple industry is absolutely dependent upon our apple exports." Hull's reply assured the senator that his concerns were "well known" to the State Department and other government agencies involved in trade negotiations.[7]

Senator Byrd blamed America's high tariff walls for the drastic reduction in the country's agricultural exports. High tariffs led to foreign retaliation against American agriculture. European and Latin American governments severely restricted--via tariffs and embargoes--the purchase of American farmers' surplus crops. In a press release in May, 1934, Byrd pointed out that foreign retaliation was responsible for the drastic reduction in Virginia's great dark tobacco and apple exports. Seventy percent of Virginia's dark tobacco and twenty to twenty-five percent of the country's apple production normally were exported. The senator argued that foreign trade restrictions on tobacco, as well as on wheat, cotton, apples, and other agricultural commodities threatened American farmers with "disaster." He warned that millions of farmers faced going out of business unless markets could be secured for their surpluses. Byrd noted that as a result of the Smoot-Hawley tariff, even Britain, traditionally a low tariff country and America's largest market for apples, had become protectionist. The senator was convinced that to revive foreign trade, sell surplus goods abroad, and preserve its agriculture, the United States had to increase imports by reducing its tariff rates. He believed that those objectives could best be achieved "through the negotiation of reciprocal treaties with foreign nations, with executive authority to offer the inducement of more favorable duties."[8]

After enactment of the 1934 Reciprocal Trade Agreements Act, Senator Byrd continued to urge the State Department to negotiate and implement reciprocal agreements favorable to Virginia's apple growers. Virginia's junior senator was especially concerned about British and French discrimination against American apple exporters. In a letter to Secretary Hull

---

[7]Dabney, *Virginia*, p. 480; Byrd to Hull, April 13, 1933, Hull to Byrd, April 19, 1933, File Number 611.0031/456, Department of State, Central Decimal File.

[8]Senator Byrd's press release of May 21, 1934, Byrd Papers.

in 1936 he pointed out that European--and particularly British and French--tariffs and restrictions on American apples had almost completely ruined a market for one-sixth of the country's apple crop. Byrd enclosed a letter from Carroll R. Miller, secretary of the Appalachian Apples organization, that described the apple exporters' plight, and asked the senator to call upon Hull "to open active negotiations at once to have removed (or very materially reduced) the high tariffs and restrictions imposed, especially by England and France, on United States apples sent into those countries." Miller urged the State Department to "work through 'favored nation' or other channels open to them." Byrd wrote Hull that he agreed with Miller and hoped that "something can be done to relieve the present restrictions in England and France." In his reply Hull assured the senator that the State Department was aware of high European duties and other trade restrictions on American fruits, and was "making special efforts in negotiating trade agreements to provide improved access to foreign markets for our [America's] agricultural and other export products."[9]

Four years later Senator Byrd was no less concerned with the severe consequences of Britain's embargo on American tobacco. In January, 1940, the senator conveyed his displeasure over the embargo to Secretary Hull. Byrd also sent the secretary the Danville Chamber of Commerce's resolution protesting Britain's embargo, which it asserted would "cause great loss and distress" to Virginia's tobacco farmers. The resolution noted that Britain's actions violated its reciprocal trade agreement with the United States. Hull assured Byrd that "every effort" would be made "to obtain modification of the British policies."[10]

In an address to a joint meeting of the civic clubs of Danville in March, Byrd (whose mother owned a tobacco farm) said that "The first and most important problem of the growers of tobacco is to have lifted the embargo that has been placed by the United Kingdom against the importation of American tobacco." The senator also noted that Britain's twenty-year accord to purchase tobacco from Turkey and Greece was a violation of its reciprocal trade agreements with the United States. He told his audience that he had asked the senators from all tobacco-producing states to join him in a "strong protest to the State Department so that our government will insist that any

---

[9] Byrd to Hull, January 11, 1936, Hull to Byrd, January 23, 1939, Byrd to Hull, May 6, 1936, and enclosure, Hull to Byrd, May 21, 1936, File Numbers 611.0031/2187-88, Department of State, Central Decimal File.

[10] Byrd's January 19, 1940, telegram to Hull, Byrd to Hull, January 23, 1940, Hull to Byrd, January 30, 1940, File Numbers 641.116/2566, 647.116/2571, Department of State, Central Decimal File.

contracts with other nations for purchases in violation of the trade agreements be cancelled." He also insisted that it was "certainly not fair or reasonable" during the British embargo for the United States government to permit the exportation of tobacco seed to foreign countries for cultivation of crops in direct competition with American tobacco exporters. British manufacturers bought American tobacco seed, at little cost, grew a substitute tobacco, and competed against United States tobacco exports. Byrd urged American tobacco growers to pressure Congress to pass--once again--his bill that prohibited such exportation. (Roosevelt had vetoed the original bill.) On June 5, 1940, Byrd's measure became law after passing both houses of Congress; that time Roosevelt allowed the bill to become law without his signature. Two days later the senator said that he was "hopeful" that the statute "will in some measure, at least, alleviate the difficult conditions which have arisen in the tobacco growing sections of Virginia and other tobacco growing states."[11]

Virginia's most enthusiastic advocate of Hull's reciprocal trade program was Representative A. Willis Robertson of the seventh district, which included many of the state's largest apple orchards. He served in the Virginia state senate for ten years before winning a House seat in 1932. During his fourteen years as a Democratic congressman, Robertson served on the tariff subcommittee of the powerful Ways and Means Committee. That subcommittee held hearings on the resolution to continue the reciprocal trade agreements program. While on the committee, Robertson frequently maintained that reciprocal trade was a viable alternative to war.[12]

Congressman Robertson's unqualified support for the Reciprocal Trade Agreements Act was also reflected in his correspondence with Secretary Hull

---

[11] Byrd's March 13, 1940, speech to the joint meeting of the civic clubs of Danville, Virginia; Byrd's June 7, 1940, statement for the press, Byrd Papers.

[12] Biographical sketch of A. Willis Robertson, A. Willis Robertson Papers, Earl Gregg Swem Library, College of William and Mary, Williamsburg, Virginia; Robertson to Harry F. Byrd, Jr., May 22, 1936, Byrd Papers; Robertson to Hull, January 14, 1939, Hull to Robertson, July 31, 1939, Representative Robertson's press release of December 12, 1939, Robertson Papers; Robertson to Douglas S. Freeman, January 25, 1940, Robertson to Freeman, January 29, 1940, Robertson to Freeman, February 1, 1940, Robertson to Freeman, February 15, 1940, Robertson to Freeman, February 21, 1940, Robertson to Freeman, August 28, 1940, Douglas S. Freeman Papers, Library of Congress, Washington, D.C. In 1946, upon the death of Carter Glass, Robertson entered the Senate where he served until 1966.

and Under Secretary Sumner Welles. In a letter to Hull in August, 1939, Robertson wrote that he was "more and more impressed" with the secretary's "thought that international trade on a further and fairer basis is not only the best road to world peace but perhaps the only road." The congressman also implied that the chances of war would not diminish unless Germany was able to secure freer access to essential raw materials and more favorable markets for its finished products. In November, 1939, he wrote Welles: "Personally, I am not only committed to this [reciprocal trade] program, but I believe in it and do not wish to see the Administration give ground to the isolationists who have no program to offer in lieu of world trade except one that must ultimately come to rest upon a general price-fixing program, which does not fit into my scheme of a representative Democracy."[13]

Three weeks later, Robertson reiterated his backing for economic reciprocity in a letter to Hull. The congressman also enclosed a clipping from a Northern Virginia Daily editorial that endorsed his stand on continuation of Hull's reciprocal trade program. He also attached a copy of his December 12, 1939, press release concerning reciprocity that also appeared in the Daily. Robertson's statement expressed "unqualified support" for Hull's policies. It asserted that the final congressional decision on whether to continue the reciprocal trade program "would indicate the attitude this Nation would take toward the establishment of permanent and lasting peace at the conclusion of the present war in Europe." Robertson maintained that "the world must work out some program of international trade on a mutually beneficial basis or else remain an armed camp with no prospect of any permanent peace." He concluded that the absence of peace would mean "nothing else than financial chaos, revolution and the spread of totalitarian government until civilization as we know it has been utterly destroyed." The congressman asked Hull if he thought the Democratic National Committee "could find appropriate means" of disseminating the Daily's editorial.[14]

In his reply, Hull thanked Robertson for his letter and enclosures and wrote that it would be "highly desirable" to circulate his statement. The secretary assured the congressman that he would forward the contents of his letter to the committee. Hull also wrote that he was "deeply grateful" for Robertson's "continued support of the trade agreements program." He

---

[13] Robertson to Hull, August 2, 1939, Robertson to Sumner Welles, November 24, 1939, Robertson Papers.

[14] Clipping from the Northern Virginia Daily, December 13, 1939, folder 6, Box 1, Robertson's press release of December 12, 1939, Robertson to Hull, December 14, 1939, Robertson Papers.

concluded: "Your courageous attitude is an inspiration to me."[15]

During the 1940 debate over extension of the reciprocal trade program, Robertson also corresponded with editor Douglas S. Freeman. In a letter to Freeman, the congressman wrote: "Evidence so far presented to our Committee is overwhelming to the effect that the net results of the Reciprocal Trade Agreement Program have been beneficial to our country while working no real hardship on any particular group." Over the course of the following month, Robertson kept Freeman informed of his committee's hearings concerning extension of the trade program. He also sent him copies of those hearings, an index to them, and his committee's majority report. The congressman informed Freeman that Republican committee members' attacks on his defense of reciprocal trade took "the nature of a tribute to the damage" he had done to their argument that the effects of Hull's program, and not the Smoot-Hawley tariffs, had been "injurious to the country."[16]

Later that year, Robertson urged Freeman to write an editorial on the reciprocal trade program once it reached the House. The congressmen contended that the "Hull Trade Agreement Program" was "really the heart of our foreign policy, which is that we can't expect the friendship and cooperation of nations with whom we are unwilling to deal on a fair basis." He also criticized Senator Charles L. McNary's argument that the effects of the trade agreement program were "all injurious to domestic agriculture."[17]

Economic reciprocity came slowly for Virginia's apple growers. As early as 1936, Congressman Robertson expressed concern to the State Department over foreign discrimination and bans on American apple exports. In a 1940 letter to Assistant Secretary of State Henry F. Grady, he blamed the drop in Virginia's apple exports on Canadian competition and the absence of British purchases that previous winter due to the war. Robertson expressed hope that the government--via import quotas--would protect the state's apple growers from "war-time dumping." In his reply, Grady assured the congressman that the State Department was very concerned about the plight

---

[15] Hull to Robertson, December 18, 1939, Robertson Papers.

[16] Robertson to Freeman, January 25, 1940, Robertson to Freeman, January 29, 1940, Robertson to Freeman, February 1, 1940, Robertson to Freeman, February 3, 1940, Robertson to Freeman, February 15, 1940, Robertson to Freeman, February 21, 1940, Freeman Papers.

[17] Robertson to Freeman, August 28, 1940, Freeman Papers.

of the American apple industry and hoped to help remedy that situation.[18]

In the summer of 1940, Robertson reiterated his fear to Secretary Hull that Canadian apples would flood the American markets. Hull promised the congressman that the State Department and the Committee for Reciprocity Information were paying close attention to the domestic apple situation. The secretary acknowledged that while foreign trade barriers had reduced the number of American exports, including apples, "every effort" had been made since 1934 under the reciprocal trade agreements program "to restore and expand" America's foreign markets through the "reciprocal reduction of excessive trade barriers and the removal and prevention of discriminatory trade practices."[19]

Despite his sympathy for Britain's wartime plight, Robertson was no less alarmed over the British embargo on American tobacco. In January, 1940, he sent Secretary Hull the Danville Chamber of Commerce's resolution deploring Britain's embargo. On January 24, 1940, Congressman Thomas G. Burch sent Hull the same resolution and wrote that the matter was of "vital importance" to a majority of his constituents; he "earnestly" requested that the State Department give "serious thought and study to the situation." Representative Patrick H. Drewry also wrote Secretary Hull about the embargo and enclosed copies of his constituents' protests against Britain's policy. Hull sent Robertson, Burch, and Drewry the same assurances on the subject he had provided Secretary Glass and Byrd.[20]

Editorial opinion in the Old Dominion stood solidly behind Hull's trade policies. Foremost among Virginia editors who championed the reciprocal trade cause was Douglas S. Freeman of the Richmond News-Leader. Freeman kept in regular contact with the State Department and Representative Robertson on that issue. He frequently provided the

---

[18] Robertson to Harry F. Byrd, Jr., May 22, 1936, Byrd Papers; Robertson to Henry L. Grady, April 4, 1940, Grady to Robertson, April 12, 1940, Robertson to Grady, April 16, 1940, Robertson Papers.

[19] Robertson to Hull, n.d., Hull to Robertson, September 4, 1940, Robertson Papers.

[20] Robertson to Hull, January 23, 1940, Robertson to A. A. Booth, January 23, 1940, Robertson to Charles I. Keyt, January 30, 1940, Hull to Robertson, January 30, 1940, Robertson Papers; Thomas G. Burch to Hull, January 24, 1940, Hull to Burch, January 30, 1940, Patrick H. Drewry to Hull, January 25, 1940, Hull to Drewry, February 5, 1940, File Numbers 641.116/2576, 641.116/2577, Department of State, Central Decimal File.

congressman with moral support during the hearings on extension of the reciprocal trade program. In his August 19, 1940, letter to Robertson, Freeman offered editorial support for his re-election campaign. The editor concluded that in his judgment the congressman was "rendering the most useful service of any member of the Virginia House delegation."[21]

Freeman used his editorship of the News-Leader as a bully pulpit for economic reciprocity. As early as March 30, 1934, the News-Leader endorsed Hull's trade liberalization policy as a "definite retreat from the policy of trade-isolation" and "extreme economic nationalism." It argued that reciprocal trade agreements would promote lower tariffs and reduce the possibility for war. The paper was particularly pleased that the United States signed reciprocal trade agreements with Canada and the United Kingdom. Its February 23, 1938, editorial maintained that "Our gain through better access to British markets may render this country more sympathetic to closer relations with the British Commonwealth of Nations." The News-Leader also supported Hull's plan to establish an economic trade bloc for major democracies and lesser nations. It reasoned that peace might prevail if the totalitarian states found it was in their interest to join that league and abandon economic rivalry.[22]

---

[21] Freeman to George S. Messersmith, July 12, 1938, Messersmith to Freeman, July 13, 1938, Freeman to Robertson, January 27, 1940, Freeman to Robertson, January 30, 1940, Freeman to Robertson, February 2, 1940, Freeman to Robertson, February 5, 1940, Freeman to Robertson, February 22, 1940, Freeman to Robertson, August 19, 1940, Freeman Papers.

[22] Richmond News-Leader, March 30, 1934, p. 8, December 4, 1935, p. 8. A March 16, 1938, Gallup Poll revealed that 73% of Americans polled approved of Secretary's Hull policy of seeking a reciprocal trade agreement with Great Britain. See Gallup, The Gallup Poll, pp. 93-94. Arthur W. Schatz, "The Anglo-American Trade Agreement and Cordell Hull's Search for Peace, 1936-1938, "Journal of American History 57 (1970): 85-103. According to Schatz, Hull believed that an Anglo-American trade agreement would lower tariff barriers, lessen economic rivalries, revive the world economy, and reduce the chances of war. Also see Richard N. Kottman, Reciprocity and the North Atlantic Triangle, 1932-1938, (Ithaca, N.Y.: Cornell University Press, 1968). Kottman argued that the 1935 United States-Canada reciprocal trade agreement made possible the strengthening of Anglo-American relations that culminated in the 1938 United States-United Kingdom accord. (ibid., p. 10). Richmond News-Leader, February 23, 1938, p. 8.

In December, 1939, Freeman's editorials urged the Senate to extend the reciprocal trade program for another three years. The News-Leader argued that "were we to abandon the Trade Agreements upon their expiration, how could we hope to have our expressions of good will, our loud acclaim of Pan-Americanism, regarded otherwise than as mere sales talk?" Its March 28, 1940, editorial concurred with Senators Glass and Byrd's opposition to a "crippling amendment" requiring Senate ratification of all reciprocal trade agreements. The paper concluded that "If now America turns away from this wise policy of trade agreements, we may expect new walls to be raised against this country's exports."[23]

Other leading newspapers throughout the state shared the News-Leader's view that the Reciprocal Trade Agreements Act and its 1937 and 1940 extensions were in the best economic and national security interests of Virginia and the country. The press was supremely confident that economic reciprocity would bring freer trade, lower tariffs, increased exports, expanding markets, a revival of America's foreign trade, greater international cooperation (especially among the democracies), prosperity, and peace to a troubled world. Senator Glass, notwithstanding, they did not believe that Hull's policy was an unconstitutional delegation of congressional power to the executive branch of government.[24]

In its November 29, 1939, editorial, the Richmond Times-Dispatch credited the reciprocal trade agreements program with the rise in farm exports from $662,000,000 in 1932 to $828,000,000 in 1938. As early as December 9, 1936, the Daily Progress (Charlottesville) noted a "material increase" in the volume of America's foreign trade since the enactment of the reciprocal trade act. Thirteen months later, the paper asserted that Hull's program was the chief factor in the $1.5 billion increase in the value of America's international trade. During the first eleven months of 1937, sales to countries with which the United States had reciprocal treaties, increased 43.3%, while sales with non-agreement countries increased only 31.3%. The Daily Progress maintained that reciprocity benefitted not only those engaged in the manufacture and sale of exported products, but the thousands of workers in other industries involved in the preparation and transportation of the products as well. The paper concluded that reciprocity was "a healthful

---

[23] Richmond News-Leader, December 4, 1939, p. 10, January 26, 1940, p. 10, March 28, 1940, p. 10.

[24] Richmond Times-Dispatch, April 30, 1934, p. 8, May 14, 1934, p. 8, June 6, 1934, p. 8, March 1, 1935, p. 16, November 14, 1935, p. 12, November 19, 1935, p. 8, November 22, 1937, p. 8.

MARKETS BEYOND THE CHESAPEAKE 75

stimulus to domestic economy as a whole."[25]

In its January, 1939, issue the Norfolk and Western Magazine (the official publication of the Norfolk and Western Railway) applauded the United States-United Kingdom reciprocal trade agreement and asserted that it and the other seventeen agreements already negotiated would "greatly stimulate" foreign purchases of American raw materials and manufactured goods, and thereby "promote needed security and international peace." The Southern Planter, an influential agricultural journal, was no less supportive of Hull's liberal trade policies.[26]

Virginia's editors were particularly sanguine about the beneficial effect reciprocal trade would have on the state's depressed tobacco and apple industries. Between 1939 and 1941, newspapers throughout the commonwealth expressed concern over the losses Virginia's farmers sustained as a result of Britain's embargo on American tobacco and apples. Numerous editorials argued that Hull's policies would open new markets for tobacco and apple producers's surpluses. In its February 27, 1940, editorial, the Alexandria Gazette emphasized how crucial the reciprocal trade program was for the state's tobacco, apple, textile, lumber, and wood pulp exporters who were largely dependent on foreign markets. The paper concluded that Hull's trade policy constituted one of his "most outstanding" accomplishments. It denounced Republican efforts to require senatorial approval of reciprocal agreements and maintained that "Few states will benefit more than Virginia from the international trade agreements negotiated by Secretary of State Hull." In its February 25, 1937, editorial the Danville Register, the leading daily in the heart of southside Virginia's tobacco country, cited the reciprocal trade program as "One of the most important, if least publicized, achievements of the Roosevelt administration."[27]

---

[25] Richmond Times-Dispatch, November 29, 1939, p. 10, March 25, 1941, p. 8; Daily Progress (Charlottesville), May 5, 1934, p. 4, June 15, 1934, p. 4, May 14, 1936, p. 4, August 19, 1936, p. 4, November 4, 1936, p. 4, December 9, 1936, p. 4, January 25, 1937, p. 4, January 10, 1938, p. 4, July 28, 1939, p. 4, September 8, 1938, p. 4.

[26] Norfolk and Western Magazine, January, 1939, pp. 8-9; The Southern Planter, March 1934, p. 20, September, 1935, p. 16, September, 1936, p. 16, July, 1940, p. 10.

[27] Norfolk Ledger-Dispatch, March 6, 1934, p. 6, March 30, 1934, p. 8, May 2, 1934, p. 6, June 7, 1934, p. 8, November 19, 1935, p. 10, January 25, 1937, p. 10, November 20, 1937, p. 6, December 16, 1937, p. 10; Roanoke Times,

Most historians generally have concluded that the reciprocal trade program was not wholly successful because it did not go far enough. A majority of America's foreign trade was transacted with countries with which it had signed reciprocal trade agreements. America's share of world trade had definitely increased as a result of reciprocal trade. Hull's program liberalized the movement of goods by reducing some trade barriers. It also prevented further significant reductions in trade, helped remove some discriminatory tariff treatment, and precluded additional restrictions on America's foreign trade. In sum, America's volume of foreign trade would have been much less without reciprocal trade agreements. Nonetheless, economic reciprocity had not significantly increased either imports or exports. Many tariff barriers were left untouched. Currencies remained unstabilized. Economic recovery certainly was not uniform throughout the world. Hull's policies tended to benefit American rather than world economic interests. Despite the celebrated Anglo-American trade agreement of 1938, Britain's imperial preference system of tariffs remained substantially in place throughout World War II. Neither did that accord create genuine cooperation, harmony, and unity between London and Washington. The Second World War did that. Most importantly, the Anglo-American agreement and the entire system of economic reciprocity failed to prevent the European war.[28]

Nevertheless, Virginians' support for reciprocal trade never wavered during the Roosevelt administration. As late as the president's fourth term, important politicians credited Hull's trade policies for reductions in tariffs and the increase in America's foreign trade. Between 1934 and 1945, the United States signed reciprocal trade agreements with twenty-seven countries and tariff rates were reduced on the average by 44% of their base rate. In his September 5, 1944, address to the joint membership of the Rotary and Kiwanis Clubs in Richmond, Congressman Clifton A. Woodrum repeated

---

June 14, 1934, p. 6, October 8, 1936, p. 6, November 29, 1936, p. 6; Danville Register, May 1, 1936, p. 6, February 25, 1937, p. 6, April 7, 1940, p. 6, April 14, 1940, p. 6, June 12, 1941, p. 4; Alexandria Gazette, January 30, 1935, p. 4, September 17, 1935, p. 4, October 28, 1939, p. 4, February 27, 1940, p. 4, March 11, 1940, p. 4; The Commonwealth, October, 1939, p. 36.

[28] Tasca, Reciprocal Trade Policy, pp. 269, 277, 284; Smith, "Reciprocity," p. 878; Beckett, Reciprocal Trade Agreements, pp. 111-13; Grace L. Beckett, "Effect of the Reciprocal Trade Agreements upon the Foreign Trade of the United States," Quarterly Journal of Economics 54 (1940): 80-94; Allen, "Cordell Hull," pp. 128-32; Dallek, Franklin D. Roosevelt and American Foreign Policy, pp. 92-93; Schatz, "Anglo-American Trade Agreement," p. 103; Kottman, Reciprocity, pp. 272-75.

Hull's standard argument that excessive trade barriers and economic rivalries often led to war. The congressman asserted:

> Under the leadership of Secretary Hull, we had, up to the present world conflict, since 1934, made notable progress in building the framework of trade treaties with the principal nations of the earth and more particularly our South American neighbors.

Woodrum observed that more than 65 percent of America's foreign trade had been carried on with those twenty-seven countries with which it had signed reciprocal trade agreements since 1934. Britain and Canada, respectively, had been the largest and second largest customers for American exports. Historians, notwithstanding, the people of the Old Dominion judged economic reciprocity an unqualified success. They agreed with the commonwealth's leadership elite that Hull's trade program was essential to the state's economic well-being and continued prosperity.[29]

---

[29] Smith, "Reciprocity," p. 878; Clifton A. Woodrum's September 5, 1944, address before the joint membership of the Rotary and Kiwanis clubs in Richmond, Virginia, Clifton A. Woodrum Papers, Roanoke Public Library, Roanoke, Virginia.

CHAPTER V
VIRGINIA IS A GOOD NEIGHBOR

Most Virginians paid little attention to Franklin D. Roosevelt's Latin American policies. There were, however, a significant number of influential diplomats, politicians, editors, educators, and Roman Catholics throughout the state who endorsed Roosevelt's Good Neighbor policy. Those Virginians believed that the interests of their state and nation were best served through a noninterventionist policy in Latin America. They were confident that increased trade, expanding markets, stronger hemispheric security, and a revitalized Monroe Doctrine would result from a noncoercive relationship with their southern neighbors. That need for better relations between the United States and Latin America became ever clearer to Virginians as Nazi penetration of the Western Hemisphere increased and war clouds appeared over Europe once more.[1] Well before the Pearl Harbor attack, the policy of the "good neighbor" had borne fruit. America's respect for Latin American sovereignty, its rejection of military intervention, its restoration of the traditional de facto recognition policy, its promotion of educational and cultural exchanges, and its reciprocal trade program resulted in friendly cooperation between the two Americas. Most importantly, those improved relations fostered a multilateral defense of the peace and security of the Western Hemisphere.[2]

For most of its history United States relations with Latin America had been less than harmonious. The cornerstone of that relationship was the Monroe Doctrine of 1823. Fearful of European designs on the New World and committed to American dominance over Latin American markets, President James Monroe warned the Quadruple Alliance against further

---

[1]Interview with Virginius Dabney, Richmond, Virginia, November 28, 1986.

[2]Bryce Wood, The Making of the Good Neighbor Policy (New York and London: Columbia University Press, 1961). According to Wood, the Good Neighbor policy meant that the United States would abandon both military intervention and political interference in Latin America. It also encouraged economic reciprocity and supported cooperative hemispheric defense. Wood maintained that Latin American instability had never posed a genuine security threat to the United States; most American intervention had been mistaken overreaction. (ibid., p. 159). See also Langer and Gleason, Challenge to Isolation, pp. 40-42.

colonization and intervention in the Western Hemisphere. He also promised that the United States would not intervene in European wars or alliances. The original intent of that message was perverted in 1904 when the Roosevelt Corollary based American intervention in Latin America on the pretext of preventing European states from forcibly collecting their debts there. President William Howard Taft's "Dollar Diplomacy," designed to protect and promote American commercial interests, also used the Monroe Doctrine as an instrument of United States intervention in Latin America. Many Latin Americans perceived the Monroe Doctrine as a vehicle to further American economic interests in their countries. Consequently, anti-Yankee sentiment increasingly prevailed throughout much of Latin America.[3]

America's "retreat from imperialism" in the Western Hemisphere began during Calvin Coolidge's presidency and continued throughout Herbert Hoover's administration. In November, 1928, before his inauguration, Hoover made a good-will tour of the Latin American republics. After entering the White House in 1929, he pursued a nonpartisan policy of nonintervention, peace, and understanding with Latin America. Hoover helped Chile and Peru settle the Tacna-Arica territorial dispute, and ordered the withdrawal of United States marines from Nicaragua. His secretary of state, Henry L. Stimson, sanctioned the Clark Memorandum (1930), which repudiated the use of the Roosevelt Corollary to justify intervention in Latin America. The traditional de facto recognition policy was also restored for most of Latin America. As a result of Hoover's efforts relations between the United States and Latin America improved greatly and Pan-American solidarity was strengthened. Despite Latin American antipathy for the Smoot-Hawley tariff of 1930, Hoover's Good Neighbor policy did much to lessen Latin American fears of United States imperialism and laid the seeds for further cooperation and good-will during Roosevelt's administration and the Second World War.[4]

Franklin D. Roosevelt continued and expanded Hoover's policy of nonintervention and cooperation in Latin America. In his inaugural address of March 4, 1933, and his April 12 Pan American Day speech, Roosevelt gave the Good Neighbor Policy its name and declared his steadfast support for equality, sovereignty, cooperation, and economic reciprocity among the countries of the Western Hemisphere. In December, 1933, at the

---

[3] See Dexter Perkins, A History of the Monroe Doctrine, rev. ed., (Boston: Houghton Mifflin, 1963), for a detailed examination of the Monroe Doctrine.

[4] For a comprehensive analysis of the origin of the Good Neighbor policy and Hoover's Latin American policies, see Alexander DeConde, Herbert Hoover's Latin American Policy (Stanford, Calif.: Stanford University Press, 1951).

Montevideo conference, Secretary of State Cordell Hull renounced armed intervention. In May, 1934, the United States and Cuba signed a treaty that abrogated the Platt Amendment. In August, 1934, the last United States marines left Haiti. Despite pressure throughout 1935 from American Catholics, Roosevelt refused to intervene against the Mexican government's persecution of the Roman Catholic Church. In 1936, the United States forfeited its right to intervene in Panama. During the 1936 Buenos Aires conference, the American states transformed the Monroe Doctrine from a unilateral declaration into a multilateral pact. In 1938, the State Department acquiesced in Mexican expropriation of the properties of American oil companies after insisting on adequate compensation. Also in 1938, FDR approved of the establishment of a Standing Liaison Committee made up of the Undersecretary of State, the Army Chief of Staff, and the Chief of Naval Operations. It was designed to counter growing fascist and Nazi propaganda and commercial advances in Latin America. The commission attempted to facilitate American arms sales to Latin America and increase United States military representation there. At the Pan-American conference in December of that year, the United States and the Latin American republics signed the Declaration of Lima, which stated that they would act independently to defend the principles of continental solidarity against outside aggression should their peace, security, or territorial integrity be threatened. At the same time, FDR asked Congress to expand the Export-Import Bank's lending authority (i.e. capital) by one-half billion dollars to finance Latin America's surplus exports. In his April 14, 1939, Pan American Day address, Roosevelt promised that the United States would defend the integrity of the Western Hemisphere and provide Latin American states with sufficient economic support for them to eschew commercial relations with the Axis powers. At a September, 1939, meeting in Panama the Latin American states unanimously agreed to common rules of neutrality, established the Inter-American Financial and Economic Advisory Commission to support monetary stability and compensate for loss of European trade through greater hemispheric exchange, and adopted the United States-sponsored Declaration of Panama, which established a "neutrality zone" extending some 300 miles from each countries' shores. The declaration called for a multilateral defense of that zone from "hostile act[s] by non-American belligerent nation[s]." After the fall of France, delegates to the July, 1940, Havana conference accepted a "no transfer" principle that would set up a "collective trusteeship" over any European possession in the Western Hemisphere threatened with transfer to Axis ownership.[5]

---

[5]The Platt Amendment (1901) gave the United States the right to intervene in Cuba's domestic and foreign affairs. Cuba incorporated the United States' quasi-protectorate status into its constitution. The finest comprehensive study of FDR's Latin American policies is Irwin F. Gellman,

Secretary of State Cordell Hull's reciprocal trade program was an integral component of the Good Neighbor policy. The secretary believed that economic reciprocity would gain markets, good-will, and cooperation for the United States in Latin America.⁶ During 1935 alone, the State Department concluded agreements with Brazil, Columbia, Haiti, and Honduras, and had begun negotiations with nine other Latin American states.⁷ Nonetheless, as late as 1939, significantly lower trade barriers and substantive economic recovery had yet to materialize fully in Latin America.⁸

One of the more effective advocates of Roosevelt's Latin American policies was a Virginian named Alexander Wilbourne Weddell. As United States ambassador to Argentina from 1933-39, Weddell played a major part in implementing the Good Neighbor policy. He played a decisive role in ending the Chaco War between Paraguay and Bolivia. Due to his efforts,

---

Good Neighbor Diplomacy: United States Policies in Latin America, 1933-1945 (Baltimore and London: Johns Hopkins University Press, 1979). Gellman argued that the Good Neighbor policy rejected American military intervention designed to protect mere economic interests in Latin America; it did, nonetheless, support intervention when vital strategic interests were at stake. (ibid., pp. 1-2, 92, 104, 155, 227). See also Edward O. Guerrant, Roosevelt's Good Neighbor Policy (Albuquerque: University of New Mexico Press, 1950), p. 172. In the Memoirs of Cordell Hull (New York: Macmillan Co., 1948), vol. 2, p. 1139, the secretary of state wrote that the United States' pursuit of the Good Neighbor policy paid off after the Japanese attack on Pearl Harbor because the Latin American republics rallied to its side. See also Dallek, Franklin D. Roosevelt and American Foreign Policy, pp. 38-39, 63, 122-24, 128, 175-77, 234; Langer and Gleason, Challenge to Isolationism, pp. 40-42, 132-34; Leuchtenberg, Franklin D. Roosevelt and the New Deal, pp. 207-209, 306.

⁶Pratt, Cordell Hull, pp. xi-xii, 29-30; Selig Adler, The Uncertain Giant, 1921-1941: American Foreign Policy between the Wars (New York: Macmillan, 1965), pp. 118-120.

⁷Dallek, Franklin D. Roosevelt and American Foreign Policy, pp. 122-23; Adler, Uncertain Giant, p. 119.

⁸For a critical, Marxist account of American reciprocity with Latin America, see Dick Steward, Trade and Hemisphere: The Good Neighbor Policy and Reciprocal Trade (Columbia: University of Missouri Press, 1975). Steward maintained that "American economic diplomacy primarily enhanced the self-interests of the United States. It did not promote real economic recovery in Latin America." (ibid., pp. viii-ix).

relations between the United States and Argentina gradually improved. After years of hostility, both countries signed a sanitary convention in 1935 (which the Senate failed to ratify), and a trade agreement in 1941. Born in 1876 in Richmond, the son of the rector of the historic St. John's Episcopal Church, Weddell studied law at George Washington University, but quickly grew dissatisfied and left school for consular service in Denmark. Weddell served with the Foreign Service in Zanzibar, Italy, Athens, Cairo, Calcutta, and Mexico City. After serving as ambassador to Argentina, Weddell accepted the ambassadorship to Spain, where he served from 1939-42. Throughout much of his life, Weddell and his wife, Virginia Chase Steedman, a wealthy St. Louis widow of Virginian ancestry, played prominent roles in the philanthropic, cultural, and social life of the commonwealth. The Weddells were intimate with many of the leading diplomatic, political, and social figures of that era.[9]

Throughout the Roosevelt administration, Weddell enjoyed a cordial relationship with the president and identified with his noblesse oblige and humanitarianism. Well into the New Deal, Weddell expressed confidence in Roosevelt. In October, 1935, he wrote a friend: "I still believe that President Roosevelt is going to continue to be found on the side of Right and on the right side." Four years later, Weddell defended the president and wrote that "Roosevelt will be recognized as the greatest humanitarian who ever sat in the White House." He concluded "that the final result of his [FDR's] attitude, his policies, and his ideals has been to save the capitalistic system." Despite his support of the president, Weddell managed to preserve his friendship with conservative Democrats such as Glass, Byrd, and Freeman.[10]

In the spring of 1933, Weddell hoped to be named ambassador to Greece where he had served years before. But Roosevelt needed the talents of the veteran, Spanish-speaking diplomat to improve relations with

---

[9]"Biographical sketch of Alexander Wilbourne Weddell," Description and Guide Index to Selected Manuscript Accessions Since 1981 (Richmond: Virginia Historical Society, 1985), pp. 1-6; "Biography of Alexander W. Weddell," Alexander Wilbourne Weddell Papers, Virginia Historical Society, Richmond, Virginia; K. Richmond Temple, "Alexander Weddell: Virginian in Diplomatic Service," Virginia Cavalcade 34 (1984): 22-39; Harold F. Peterson, "Alexander Wilbourne Weddell," in the Dictionary of American Biography, supplement four, 1946-50, eds. John Garraty and Edward T. James (New York: Charles Scribner's Sons, 1974), pp. 863-64.

[10]Weddell to Bradford H. Walker, October 28, 1935, Weddell to S. Pinkney Tucker, January 19, 1939, Weddell to Douglas S. Freeman, September 26, 1936, Weddell Papers.

Argentina, a leading Latin American republic and persistent antagonist of the United States. As a loyal Democrat, patriot, and sincere adherent of the Good Neighbor policy, Weddell felt obligated to oblige the president. Roosevelt did not overlook the fact that Weddell was wealthy enough to assume the expensive social requirements in Buenos Aires, Latin America's most Europeanized capital.[11]

Virginia's congressional delegation also endorsed Roosevelt's Latin American policies. They wholeheartedly promoted Weddell for the ambassadorship to Argentina. Senator Claude A. Swanson, a long-time foe of United States military intervention in Latin America, assured Weddell that he would "aid" him in securing an ambassadorship "in every possible way." Glass sent Hull a "strong endorsement" of Weddell's nomination and wrote President Roosevelt a letter on March 10, 1933, recommending him for a high diplomatic post. The senator praised Weddell's ability and dedication and concluded that "no single appointment you [Roosevelt] could make would give us [Virginians] greater satisfaction than that of Mr. Weddell." Byrd spoke to Postmaster General James A. Farley on behalf of Weddell and urged Glass to see Roosevelt directly on the matter. On March 23 Byrd wrote Weddell that: "I have never endorsed any one with greater satisfaction than I have you because of your supreme qualifications for the position." In his March 27 letter to Weddell, Byrd wrote that he had discussed his appointment to Buenos Aires with Hull that morning. On May 5 Roosevelt assured the senator that Weddell's appointment would be sent to the Senate on May 9. In his May 8 telegram to Weddell, Byrd wrote that he would arrange for immediate confirmation and included his congratulations. Congressman Andrew Jackson Montague also recommended Weddell to the president and praised his fellow Virginian as "a competent and highminded diplomat." The Senate confirmed Weddell's appointment to Argentina on the afternoon of May 31, 1933.[12]

Pan-American supporters throughout the United States also enthusiastically endorsed Roosevelt's choice for the ambassadorship to Argentina. John L. Merrill, president of the Pan-American Society, wrote that "we rejoice that the United States is to be represented by you in

---

[11] Interview with Virginius Dabney, November 28, 1986, Richmond, Virginia; Temple, "Weddell," pp. 22, 32.

[12] Ferrell, <u>Swanson</u>, pp. 180-81; Claude A. Swanson to Weddell, January 16, 1933, Byrd to Weddell, March 7, 1933, Glass to Roosevelt, March 10, 1933, Byrd to Weddell, March 23, 1933, Byrd to Weddell, March 27, 1933, Byrd to Weddell, May 8, 1933, Andrew Jackson Montague to Roosevelt, April 5, 1933, Byrd to Weddell, May 31, 1933, Weddell Papers.

Argentina." Harry T. Collins, professor of Latin America relations at the University of Pennsylvania and director of the Wharton School of Finance and Commerce, praised the new ambassador's 1933 speech to the Pan American Society in New York City. He wrote that Weddell's address represented the "new spirit of diplomacy in American affairs." Collins, an authority on international trade and a member of the society, concluded that Weddell's views fostered better relations between Argentina and the United States.[13]

In his highly acclaimed Pan American Society speech, Weddell expressed his sincere desire for better understanding and trade relations between the United States and its sister republics to the south. He emphasized the high priority President Roosevelt placed on "a new diplomacy, of a new ideal in the relations of states, of a foreign service not solely concerned with promoting our own interests." Weddell criticized the old, cynical diplomacy of "crass materialism" and "unenlightened selfishness." He asserted that in its relations with Latin America the United States wanted "no big brother attitude, no paternalistic attitude, but a neighborly and exact reciprocity." The ambassador urged a "jettisoning of prejudices, a jettisoning of any feelings of imagined superiority and an avoidance of that inordinate affection for certain nations which is so often accompanied by dislike of others." Weddell concluded that it was of "vital importance to every nation of this continent that the various governments, individually, take, without further delay, such action as may be possible to reduce all unnecessary and artificial barriers and restrictions which now hamper the healthy flow of trade between the peoples of the American republics." In the following months he reiterated the necessity for better understanding between the North American and the Ibero-American.[14]

Weddell's first official assignment in carrying out FDR's Latin American policies came in November, 1933, when he served as a delegate to the Seventh International Conference of the American States at Montevideo, Uruguay. The ambassador played a supportive role in helping Secretary of State Hull gain the confidence of the Latin American delegates. Weddell and

---

[13] Silvia C. Leao to Weddell, June 20, 1933, Weddell to Leao, June 21, 1933, John L. Merrill to Weddell, July 24, 1933, Harry T. Collins to Weddell, September 19, 1933, Clark Stearns to Weddell, March 20, 1937, Weddell Papers.

[14] Weddell's August 15, 1933, remarks before the Pan American Society, New York City, Weddell to George W. Hinman, Jr., September 25, 1933; Weddell to Harry T. Collins, October 5, 1933, Weddell Papers; New York Times, August 16, 1933.

Hull supported the protocol that stated: "no state has the right to intervene in the internal or external affairs of another." Renunciation of armed intervention in the affairs of another American state became the foundation of Roosevelt's Good Neighbor policy. Later Hull congratulated the ambassador for his "fine work" at the conference and his "splendid efficiency" as America's representative to Argentina.[15]

Ambassador Weddell's most notable achievement came in 1935 at the Buenos Aires peace talks between Bolivia and Paraguay. Those two landlocked countries had fought for three years over the disputed Chaco Boreal, which was located between the Paraguay River and the Andes. On June 9, 1935, when negotiations between the two republics seemed on the verge of failure, Weddell personally intervened to keep the conversations in progress. New York Times correspondent John W. White credited Weddell with pushing the belligerents toward a cease-fire and saving the peace talks. Four days later, Bolivia and Paraguay signed an armistice agreement. Bolivia awarded Weddell the Grand Cross of the Condor of the Andes for his role in ending the bloody Chaco War. The director general of the Pan American Union, prominent Virginians, and State Department officials expressed their gratitude to Weddell for his contribution to the cause of peace in the Western Hemisphere. In November, 1935, President Roosevelt wrote to Weddell:

> The disturbed condition of world affairs during the year which is coming to a close has caused a measurable increase in your labors in protecting American interests, and I appreciate the distinguished service which you have rendered in this connection. I am grateful for the thorough manner in which you have kept me informed of developments abroad, and the counsel which you have supplied has been of great value to me.[16]

During his six years as ambassador to Argentina, Weddell fought a determined, albeit not wholly successful, battle to conclude a trade agreement

---

[15] Adler, Uncertain Giant, pp. 106, 111; Cordell Hull to Weddell, April 7, 1934, Weddell Papers.

[16] Robert A. Divine, The Illusion of Neutrality (Chicago: University of Chicago Press, 1962), pp. 31-32; Richmond News-Leader, June 12, 1935, p. 1; Temple, "Alexander Weddell," p. 36; Weddell to Edmund Randolph Williams, June 29, 1935, Weddell to Bradford H. Walker, October 28, 1935, Weddell to Douglas Gordon, July 11, 1935, L. S. Rowe to Weddell, June 13, 1935, John Stewart Bryan to Weddell, July 10, 1935, Weddell to Bryan, August 5, 1935, Edward N. Calisch to Weddell, July 22, 1935, Franklin D. Roosevelt to Weddell, November 27, 1935, Weddell Papers.

and sanitary convention between Buenos Aires and Washington. Argentina suffered an unfavorable balance of trade with the United States; it imported far too many American manufactured goods and failed to sell enough of its agricultural products in return. Buenos Aires believed that a trade agreement would remedy that problem and improve overall relations with the United States as well.[17]

President Roosevelt shared that Argentinian perspective. In a White House conversation with Weddell on July 8, 1933, FDR emphasized "developing and strengthening" America's "mutual trade relations" with Argentina. Roosevelt told Weddell that the United States government should help that country sell its goods to America. He recognized that "A reciprocal treaty might be difficult to carry out;" the two countries were--to an extent-- in agricultural competition with each other. Nevertheless, Roosevelt told Weddell that he wanted him to support the idea of a trade agreement upon his return to Buenos Aires. Weddell believed that such an agreement would create "a wave of good feelings as would affect my whole tenure." He considered FDR's "new gospel" to be "revolutionary."[18]

Weddell was well aware that the trade issue was a leading obstacle to improved relations between the United States and Argentina. In September, 1933, he wrote to Undersecretary of State William Phillips,

> Again, in the event of failure to conclude a satisfactory reciprocal trade agreement between the two countries [United States and Argentina], an atmosphere of ill will may arise requiring much patience and tact to keep within reasonable bounds.

Weddell was also cognizant of the benefits the United States would reap from such an argument. In a letter to Secretary Hull in 1935 he argued that the Argentine government was unstable and anxious to loosen its close economic ties with Britain. Weddell maintained that the opposition party in Argentina and its press allies would continue to exploit that instability unless the Argentine Cabinet signed a commercial agreement with the United States. He concluded that a trade agreement would greatly improve relations between the two countries.[19]

---

[17]Temple, "Alexander Weddell," pp. 32, 36.

[18]Memorandum of Weddell's conversation with Roosevelt, July 8, 1933, Weddell Papers.

[19]Weddell to William Phillips, September 22, 1933, Weddell to Cordell Hull, February 24, 1935, Weddell Papers.

Toward the end of 1935, Weddell informed Assistant Secretary of State Sumner Welles that despite an increase in United States trade with Argentina during the previous year, Britain remained Buenos Aires' biggest buyer. The United States, he wrote, was a poor second, even though its purchase of Argentine products had more than doubled over the past year. Weddell attributed the British advantage to the absence of a trade agreement between the United States and Argentina and the fact that the British, unlike the Americans, were given the official exchange rate. He also informed the assistant secretary that Argentina was eager to sign such an agreement with the United States. Weddell believed that an agreement should be signed as soon as possible because the Good Neighbor policy needed concrete results. More than a year and a half later, he reiterated that view in a telegram to Secretary of State Hull:

> The Argentine attitude of the moment seems more favorable toward giving us better treatment than it has been for some time and I note signs of a willingness to do more provided they have some assurances of a trade agreement being negotiated in the near future. . . . Were the Embassy accordingly to assure the Argentines that trade negotiations would begin shortly or within some specific period, I feel that we should be able to secure better exchange treatment, if not entire relief from the present discrimination. And if possible a strong intimation of our hope would be helpful.

In his September 3, 1937, reply Hull wrote that "if deliberations now in progress (partly owing to your telegram) result in an affirmative decision by policy-making officials it will be possible to announce trade agreement negotiations with Argentina within the very near future." Later that year Weddell assured Welles that he was still exerting pressure on Buenos Aires to end its exchange discrimination against the United States.[20]

Six months after he had resigned as ambassador to Argentina, Weddell remained confident that despite opposition from domestic protectionist forces a trade agreement would eventually be concluded. He wrote that he was "happy in the thought that this difficult obstacle and problem in our relations

---

[20] Weddell to Sumner Welles, November 29, 1935, Weddell to Welles, January 30, 1936, Weddell Papers; United States, Department of State, Foreign Relations of the United States: Diplomatic Papers, 1937, 5: 213-14; Weddell to Welles, November 9, 1937, Weddell Papers.

with Argentina is on the way to solution and renewal." A trade agreement between the two countries was finally signed on October 14, 1941.[21]

The United States Department of Agriculture's ban on imported Argentine meat from areas infested with foot-and-mouth disease further exacerbated relations between the two countries. Beef was Argentina's chief export, and Buenos Aires viewed the embargo as a protectionist measure. Ambassador Weddell strongly urged the Senate to ratify the sanitary convention that the United States and Argentina signed on May 24, 1935. That agreement called for the signatories to cooperate on methods to prevent the introduction and spread of infectious and contagious plant and animal diseases and of insect pests into each other's territory. Under the treaty, neither government could prohibit the importation of agricultural or meat products from uninfected regions, but could ban them from areas that were contaminated. The convention did not apply to live animals or to duties on either animals or plant or animal products. The embargo on imported Argentine animals remained intact.[22]

In numerous letters and conversations with President Roosevelt and members of the Senate, Ambassador Weddell emphasized how the treaty's ratification would benefit both the United States and Argentina. In his January 17, 1935, conversation with the president, he argued that the convention would not harm American cattle interests. Weddell asserted that the treaty "would immensely strengthen our [America's] general position in Argentina" and bolster their government as well. In a letter to Harry F. Byrd early in 1936, Weddell asked the junior senator to vote for the convention and persuade Senator Glass to support it as well. The ambassador wrote that passage of the treaty was in the interests of good relations between the two countries and would constitute an act of "simple justice." Byrd promised to vote for the convention and speak to Glass about it as well.[23]

---

[21] Weddell to S. Pinkney Tuck, September 6, 1939, Weddell Papers; Temple, "Alexander Weddell," p. 36; Richmond Times-Dispatch, October 13, 1941, p. 6.

[22] Temple, "Alexander Weddell," pp. 32, 36; Department of State, Foreign Relations, 1935, 4: 296-99; Hull to Key Pittman, August 20, 1935, Weddell Papers.

[23] Memorandum of Weddell's conversation with Roosevelt, January 17, 1935, Weddell to Byrd, January 28, 1936, Byrd to Weddell, February 13, 1936, Weddell to Byrd, March 4, 1936, Weddell to Hull, March 4, 1936, Weddell Papers.

Nearly a year later, Weddell expressed concern over rising opposition to ratification of the treaty. He wrote Douglas Freeman:

> Such ratification would be an act of bald justice to this country. To pillory Argentina before the world as having foot and mouth disease throughout its vast territory, as we do today, is unjust and unfriendly.

Weddell reiterated Hull's argument that failure to ratify the convention "would be taken as notice that this Government does not intend to deal fairly or frankly in trade matters. We cannot afford to carry such a reputation." Despite mounting opposition in the Senate, Weddell continued--rather discreetly at times--to push for ratification.[24] Just weeks before his resignation as ambassador, he continued to lobby members of the Senate for their votes. In letters and conversations with Secretary Hull and Senators Charles L. McNary, John Overton, Millard Tydings, Arthur Capper, and Key Pittman, Weddell mentioned Glass and Byrd's consistent support for the convention. The ambassador's efforts were to no avail; due to domestic opposition, the Senate never approved the treaty.[25]

Trade problems with Argentina were not the only major concern for the Roosevelt administration during Weddell's tenure as ambassador. President Roosevelt was especially worried about increased Nazi-fascist activity in Latin America, particularly in areas heavily populated with Germans and Italians. Realizing the need for a collective security system in the absence of unilateral military intervention, the president pushed for a special meeting of the American states to deal with that problem. On December 1, 1936, the Inter-American Conference for the Maintenance of Peace met in Buenos Aires. The delegates adopted a strong renunciation of intervention in the affairs of any state. Most importantly, they endorsed a declaration of solidarity that called for consultation whenever the peace of the Western Hemisphere was threatened. While the conference did not embrace collective security for the New World, it did continentalize the Monroe Doctrine. Weddell's efforts to strengthen hemispheric unity at Buenos Aires did not go unnoticed. After the conference ended, Secretary Hull offered his "heartiest congratulations on [Weddell's] . . . splendid work." The secretary wrote that Weddell's "fine

---

[24] Weddell to Douglas S. Freeman, January 15, 1937, Douglas S. Freeman Papers, Library of Congress, Washington, D.C.; Weddell to Hull, March 12, 1937, Weddell Papers.

[25] Weddell to Hull, January 24, 1939, memorandum of Weddell's conversation with Charles L. McNary, John Overton, Millard Tydings, Arthur Capper, and Key Pittman, March 11, 1939, Weddell Papers; Temple, "Alexander Weddell," p. 36.

cooperation and able assistance contributed greatly to the success of the Conference." Hull concluded that it was "a source of much satisfaction" to himself and other members of the United States delegation to have had "the benefit of . . . [Weddell's] wise counsel and advice on the many subjects which we had under discussion."[26]

Weddell shared Roosevelt's apprehension over German and Italian activity in Latin America. In November, 1937, he wrote Sumner Welles describing the growing fascist movement in Argentina. The ambassador contended that fascism appealed to many in the military and among the country's large number of Italian and German residents. He believed it unlikely, however, that the fascists would come to power unless there was trouble over the Argentine Congress' ratification of their presidential elections. Weddell did not expect that to happen. Less than a year later the ambassador reiterated his concern over "the presence and strength of Italian and German propaganda" in Latin America in a letter to Douglas S. Freeman. He informed the Richmond News-Leader editor that German groups regularly displayed Adolph Hitler's portrait and paraded in swastika armbands. Weddell urged Freeman to emphasize the "gravity" of the situation to his fellow trustees at the Carnegie Endowment for International Peace and the Rockefeller Foundation. He implied that the Carnegie Endowment should provide more assistance to countries such as Argentina that were "facing the brunt of the attacks against democratic institutions."[27]

On numerous occasions, Weddell enlisted Freeman's assistance in urging the Rockefeller Foundation financially to assist cultural and educational projects aimed at strengthening ties between the United States and Argentina. Weddell specifically encouraged the foundation to subsidize scholarships for Argentines wishing to study library science, journalism, higher English, literature, drama, and architecture in the United States. Weddell firmly believed that those Argentines given the opportunity to study in the United States would return to their country as "active propagandist[s] in favour of better relations between the two countries."[28]

---

[26] Adler, Uncertain Giant, pp. 113-14; Hull to Weddell, January 18, 1937, Weddell Papers.

[27] Weddell to Welles, November 17, 1937, Weddell Papers; Weddell to Freeman, April 14, 1938, Freeman Papers.

[28] Weddell to Freeman, September 23, 1937, Weddell to Freeman, November 27, 1937, Weddell to Freeman, July 27, 1938, Weddell to Freeman, December 1, 1938, Freeman Papers.

Despite Weddell's ongoing efforts to draw Argentina closer to the United States, relations between the two countries remained tense. In December, 1938, at the International Conference of American States in Lima, Argentina opposed American support for mutual consultation in the event of external threats to hemispheric security. Buenos Aires resented American dominance in the Pan American Union. America's friendship with Brazil, Argentina's traditional foe, further contributed to Argentina's deep-seated anti-Americanism. Economic rivalry with the United States, and the growing fascist movement in Argentina did nothing to build confidence between the two republics. Argentine opposition to genuine defense cooperation resulted in the conference's adoption of a watered-down version of hemispheric consultation. The Argentine Foreign Minister Carlos Saavedra Lama played no small role in efforts to weaken America's influence in Lima and at other Pan American conferences. Nevertheless, Ambassador Weddell maintained cordial relations with him and other Argentine authorities from the president on down, throughout his tenure in Buenos Aires.[29]

At the time of his resignation as ambassador to Argentina in March, 1939, Weddell was admired and respected by many throughout Latin America. The ambassador's sympathetic portrait of his host country, Introduction to Argentina, gained him many admirers. Weddell praised the Argentines' heritage and patriotism. He described the Argentine people as "courteous and sober-minded." Through his book he hoped to eliminate misconceptions that Argentines and Americans held of one another and bring them closer together. In that volume, Argentine President Roberto Ortiz testified to "the widespread feeling" that Weddell was "the American Ambassador who has been closest to us." In his December 14, 1939, letter to the Virginia Museum of Fine Arts concerning its exhibition of Argentine art, Don Felipe A. Espil, Argentine ambassador to the United States, wrote:

> For what has been done in this field in order to make Argentina known and understood by the people of the United States, my country is indebted, more perhaps than to any other living American, to a distinguished son of Virginia: The Honorable Alexander Wilbourne Weddell.

Espil praised Weddell's "charming and inspiring book" and credited "his enlightened initiative" that made possible "the hospitality extended by the Virginia Museum of Fine Arts to a representative group of Argentine paintings and sculpture." The Argentine ambassador concluded:

---

[29] Adler, Uncertain Giant, pp. 115-16; Temple, "Alexander Weddell," p. 36; Weddell to Byrd, July 27, 1936, Weddell Papers.

The artistic creations of a country are the best exponents of its psychology and its temperament. In this regard no better surroundings could have been found in the United States for this display of our national art, then the historical capital of Virginia, rightly known in Argentina for its tradition of generosity, hospitality, and friendliness.[30]

Ambassador Weddell well understood his many positive contributions toward implementation of Roosevelt's Latin American policies. Nevertheless, he credited the president for the success of the Good Neighbor policy. In 1935, he wrote that since FDR entered the White House and especially after Secretary Hull's Latin American tour, "the feeling of respect, confidence and friendliness in South American countries toward the United States has been stronger than at any time in our history."[81] Weddell was so pleased with Roosevelt's 1937 "Constitution Day" speech and sanguine about relations between the two Americas that he suggested to the president that all of his formal addresses be translated in advance into Spanish and Portuguese and given to Latin American newspapers and other media outlets. Weddell assured Roosevelt that "everything" he said received "wide attention in Latin America, certainly in Argentina."[32]

Even after assuming the ambassadorship to Spain, Weddell retained a firm belief in the Good Neighbor policy. In a speech before the American Chamber of Commerce in Spain, he concurred with Roosevelt that the "policy of the Good Neighbor" must be reciprocal, not unilateral. "In a word," he said, "the good neighbor policy is not a one-way street, nor is it an arrangement under which brickbats may be continuously given in exchange for boguets!" The ambassador pointed out that international crises in the past had often arisen out of the fact that governments have pursued "unenlightened selfishness" and not the "policy of the Good Neighbor." Weddell asserted that "good will between nations is only won and retained by equitable dealings in which both parties to transactions gain something. Mutual profit is an axiom of business." He concluded that "Statesmen who

---

[30]Temple, "Alexander Weddell," p. 36; See Alexander Wilbourne Weddell, Introduction to Argentina (New York: The Greystone Press, 1939); Don Felipe A. Espil to the Virginia Museum of Fine Arts, printed in the Richmond News-Leader, December 14, 1939.

[31]Weddell to Hudson Strode, October 21, 1935, Weddell Papers.

[32]Weddell to Roosevelt, September 30, 1937, Roosevelt to Weddell, October 12, 1937, Weddell Papers.

drive too sharp a bargain not alone alienate nations but plant the seed of discord."[33]

Those sentiments were shared by another diplomat from Virginia, Benjamin Muse, a veteran foreign service officer, liberal state senator, gentleman farmer, journalist, author, civil rights activist, and Republican candidate for governor in 1941. Muse served as counselor of the United States delegation to the Seventh International Conference of American States at Montevideo in November, 1933. A North Carolinian by birth, Muse attended Trinity college (now Duke University) and the George Washington University. During the First World War, he served in the British Army. In 1920 he entered the diplomatic service and rose from clerk to first secretary of the embassy. After Roosevelt's inauguration, Muse toured Argentina, Paraguay, Uruguay, and Brazil, where he had spent much of his diplomatic career. He was a staunch advocate of Roosevelt's Good Neighbor policy. He broke with the president, however, over his court-packing plan and became a Republican in 1939.[34]

At the Montevideo Conference, Muse was part of an American delegation that included five fellow Virginians: Mrs. Cordell Hull, wife of the secretary of state, Alexander W. Weddell, ambassador to Argentina and delegate to the conference, Hugh Cummings, Jr., special assistant to Hull, and John Stewart Bryan, Jr., assistant secretary to the delegation. Muse noted that "very unusual participation of Virginians in the United States Delegation" in his July 7, 1934, remarks concerning the conference before the round table on "The Good Neighbor Policy with Latin America" at the Institute of Public Affairs, at the University of Virginia in Charlottesville.[35]

---

[33] Weddell's January, 1940, (n.d.), remarks before the American Chamber of Commerce in Barcelona, Spain, Weddell Papers.

[34] "Benjamin Muse," in Contemporary Authors: A Bio-Bibliographical Guide To Current Authors And Their Works, eds. James M. Ethridge and Barbara Kopala (Detroit: Gale Research Co., 1967;1977), vols. 1-4, 1st revision, p. 699; Biographical sketch of Benjamin Muse, clipping from the Richmond Times-Dispatch, September 28, 1941, Benjamin Muse Papers, Duke University Library, Durham, North Carolina.

[35] Muse's July 7, 1934, remarks before the Round Table on "The Good Neighbor Policy with Latin America," Institute of Public Affairs, University of Virginia, Charlottesville, Virginia, Benjamin Muse Papers, University of Virginia Library, Charlottesville, Virginia.

In his talk before the round table, Muse vigorously defended Roosevelt's Latin American policies. He specifically praised Hull's efforts at Montevideo to end the Chaco War and to encourage lower tariffs. Muse noted a "new spirit of sympathy and understanding" in the United States' relationship with Latin America after Roosevelt entered the White House. He asserted that those improved relations reached a "very high point" at the Montevideo Conference and culminated in the abrogation of the Platt Amendment. The diplomat conceded, however, that the conference had not "satisfactorily" resolved the issue of intervention. He maintained that it had "never been satisfactorily met at any conference or under any national administration." Muse concluded that the provisions on intervention in the conference's protocol were "vague." "There is nothing in the terms of the convention," he observed, "which would prevent the landing of United States Marines to evacuate American citizens who might be in danger."[36]

According to Muse, "the greatest value" of the Montevideo meeting rested in the "sheer fact" that it took place at all. He characterized that meeting as a "great and friendly assembly" that signaled the American republics' "common interests," "common purposes," and "growing spirit of unity." Muse believed that the good-will that pervaded the conference was "of a nature to give encouragement to every friend of harmony and cooperation in the Americas." He acknowledged, however, the "resentment" certain Latin American states held against the United States for its "high tariff wall." Nevertheless, Muse asserted that the "outstanding achievement" of the conference as far as "concrete results" were concerned, was the resolution on Economic, Commercial and Tariff Policy. Originally known as the "Hull Plan," it was based on tariff reduction through international agreement. Muse noted that Hull's proposal was later incorporated into the Reciprocal Trade Agreements Act of 1934.[37] He concluded that Hull's "tireless" efforts to end the Chaco War and his "frank and forthright" approach to the tariff problem were "major factors in creating the notable atmosphere of good will at Montevideo." To those efforts he added Hull's "public assurances and interpretations of the Good Neighbor Policy," especially the United States' renunciation of military intervention in Latin America.[38]

Support for closer ties between the United States and Latin America also extended into the armed forces. The most notable representative of that

---

[36] Ibid.

[37] Ibid.

[38] Ibid.

opinion was Chief of Staff and General of the Army, George Catlett Marshall. Born in Pennsylvania, but widely related in Virginia, he as the most famous graduate of the Virginia Military Institute serving during the World War II era. Marshall was stationed in Washington, D.C. during the war but retired to Leesburg, Virginia, after serving as secretary of state and secretary of defense in the Truman administration. [39]

On December 17, 1940, General Marshall told a meeting of the National Aeronautic Association in Washington that he was happy to participate in their celebration of Pan-American Aviation Day. He cited that event as further evidence of closer cooperation and understanding between the United States and Latin America. Marshall said that it gave added emphasis to the importance "of our mutual program for hemispheric defense." The general argued that aviation was probably the "most effective factor" in drawing the American republics closer together. He also asserted that "Aviation will undoubtedly be one of the most effective factors in an active defense of this Hemisphere against intrusions from abroad." Marshall maintained that the "Caribbean theatre, the great crossroads of Pan-American relationships is not only the critical area of our defense but geographically, it is an ideal center for the conduct of our air defense." He concluded that it was "in the air that our most intimate relationship with all of Latin America will be maintained." Four weeks later, Marshall's address to the Fourth Annual Pan-American Conference in Washington emphasized how "urgent, how vital" was the "necessity for cooperative action by all of the republics of this hemisphere" in keeping war out of the Western Hemisphere. [40]

The Old Dominion's elected representatives generally supported Roosevelt's trade policies with the Latin American states. They were especially concerned with obtaining fairer treatment for the state's agricultural exporters. Senator Glass, a rock-ribbed advocate of lower tariffs who doubted the constitutionality of the Reciprocal Trade Agreements Act, referred complaints concerning Argentina's restriction on Virginia exports to the State Department. In his October 19, 1935, telegram to Cordell Hull, Senator Byrd, a strong advocate of reciprocal trade, urged the secretary to recommend to Roosevelt a reduction in the import duty on Argentine grapes

---

[39] The authoritative biography of Marshall is Forrest C. Pogue's George C. Marshall, 4 vols. (New York: Viking, 1963-87); Dabney, Virginia, p. 512.

[40] George C. Marshall's December 17, 1940, remarks before the National Aeronautic Association, Washington, D.C., Marshall's January 14, 1941, address to the Fourth Annual Pan American Conference, Washington, D.C., George C. Marshall Papers, George C. Marshall Research Library, Lexington, Virginia.

in return for a reduction in the Argentine import duty on American fruit. Byrd wrote that the United States would have the "advantage" from such an arrangement. Hull assured the senator that his request was "receiving careful consideration."[41]

In the fall of 1939, Congressman A. Willis Robertson, another firm adherent of reciprocal trade, also urged the Department of Agriculture and the Department of State to establish more equitable trade relations with Latin America. He was especially concerned that unless a fairer commercial agreement could be reached, Argentine apples would flood the American market and compete unfairly with his apple-growing district. The European war had already reduced Virginia's export of apples to Britain and France. Robertson was no less concerned that a new trade agreement would lower American duties on imported Argentine turkeys. The congressman feared that would have an adverse effect on the state's turkey farmers. Secretary Hull forwarded the congressman's letters to the Committee for Reciprocity Information.[42]

On October 30, 1939, Byrd, Robertson, and ten other congressmen, expressed concern over the proposed trade agreement with Argentina to Assistant Secretary of State Henry F. Grady. They strongly opposed further reductions in America's duties and supported a lowering of Argentina's excessive trade restrictions on American apple and pear exports. On November 13, 1939, Grady promised Robertson that "every effort" would be made "to obtain the most favorable treatment possible" for American apples, pears, and other exports in the trade negotiations with Argentina. In his November 22, 1939, response to Robertson, Acting Secretary of State Sumner Welles assured him that domestic turkey interests would receive "thorough consideration" in the proposed trade agreement with Argentina. Six months later, Robertson questioned the "advisability" of negotiating such an agreement until the United States government could "better appraise the

---

[41] Fred E. Willman to Glass, November 6, 1939, Glass's November 9, 1939, note to the State Department, Sumner Welles to Glass, November 21, 1939, Byrd's October 19, 1935, telegram to Hull, Hull to Byrd, October 31, 1935, File Numbers 611.3531/1272, 611.3551/1272, 611.3531/1272, 611.3531/362, United States Department of State, Central Decimal File, National Archives, Washington, D.C.; Byrd to Weddell, February 13, 1936, Weddell Papers.

[42] A. Willis Robertson to Hull, September 8, 1939, Hull to Robertson, September 16, 1939, Robertson to Hull, September 18, 1939, Henry A. Wallace to Robertson, November 18, 1939, Robertson to Henry F. Grady, November 16, 1939, A. Willis Robertson Papers, Earl Gregg Swem Library, College of William and Mary, Williamsburg, Virginia.

impact of the European War" on American agriculture. In his April, 1940, correspondence with Douglas S. Freeman, he noted that foot and mouth disease had recently appeared in Patagonia, which had been the only area in Argentina free of the disease. Robertson wrote Freeman that he opposed a resumption of trade negotiations until a plan could be designed that allowed "substantial importations from the Argentine that would not be harmful to our domestic agriculture."[43]

Byrd and Robertson also supported efforts to strengthen solidarity in the Western Hemisphere and protect it from external threats. In his January 10, 1939, letter to Secretary Hull, Robertson congratulated him on his "splendid achievements at Lima." On June 17, 1940, Byrd voted for the Monroe Doctrine Act of 1940, which incorporated Roosevelt's "no-transfer" declaration.[44]

Virginia's governor James H. Price lent moral support for Pan-Americanism and the Good Neighbor policy on the state level. In March, 1941, his executive assistant, W. M. Kemper, promised Rafael Gimenez, the Pan American League's Virginia state director, that either the governor or his representative would be "very glad" to welcome the league's student division's annual convention to Richmond on April 5, 1941. On September 20, 1941, Price told a Lansing, Michigan audience that "social, cultural, and spiritual strands" were needed "to hold the peoples as well as the nations of the Western Hemisphere together in peace and true friendship." He asserted that Pan-Americanism should be regarded as "a process of thought and a code of procedure designed to bind the American republics in closer social and cultural bonds as well as economic and joint-defense ties." Price maintained that "Closer relations between the Americas. . . must . . . be predicated on a sound foundation built of mutual respect, confidence and understanding."[45]

---

[43] Byrd, et al., to Grady, October 30, 1939, File Number 611.3531/1252, Department of State, Central Decimal File; Grady to Robertson, November 13, 1939, Welles to Robertson, November 22, 1939, Robertson Papers; Robertson to Freeman, April 5, 1940, Robertson to Freeman, April 9, 1940, Freeman Papers.

[44] Robertson to Hull, January 10, 1939, Hull to Robertson, January 13, 1939, Robertson Papers; See Senator Byrd's record of Senate roll-call votes, Box 349, Harry F. Byrd Papers, University of Virginia Library, Charlottesville, Virginia.

[45] W. M. Kemper to Rafael Gimenez, March 31, 1941, James H. Price's September 20, 1941, speech on "National Unity," Lansing, Michigan, James H. Price Executive Papers, Virginia State Library, Richmond, Virginia.

The state's premier conservative editorialist, Douglas S. Freeman, actively promoted closer relations between the United States and Latin America. He encouraged better understanding throughout the Americas through his many personal and professional associations. In the pages of the Richmond News-Leader, the editor forcefully attacked "Dollar Diplomacy" and military intervention in Latin America. Freeman was also an admirer of Alexander W. Weddell and welcomed his accession to the ambassadorship in Buenos Aires.[46]

Freeman encouraged the State Department and the Rockefeller Foundation to sponsor more programs designed to draw Latin America closer to the United States. In letters to Assistant Secretary of State George S. Messersmith and Ambassador Weddell, he commended the idea of a system of awards honoring the distinguished service of Latin American journalists. Freeman wrote that "there is today nothing on the Western Hemisphere more important." He also lent his approval for a $10,000 Rockefeller Foundation Grant to the Foreign Policy Association to aid in establishing a Latin American information service. Freeman considered that proposal "fundamentally sound." He agreed with the foundation's Raymond B. Fosdick that more work needed to be done in the fields of library science development and the teaching of English in Latin America.[47]

A strong advocate of better trade relations with Latin America, Freeman vigorously supported early Senate approval of the United States-Argentina sanitary convention. He considered it "iniquitous" that nearly four years after the treaty had been signed, the Senate had not yet approved it. Freeman assured Weddell that he intended to begin an active campaign in support of ratification as soon as the treaty came up for discussion before the Senate committee. In his May 19, 1939, editorial in the News-Leader, he argued that failure to sanction the convention weakened America's efforts to become a

---

[46] Weddell to Freeman, July 29, 1933, Freeman to Weddell, August 1, 1933, Dr. and Mrs. Freeman to Mr. and Mrs. Weddell, August 19, 1933, Freeman Papers; Richmond News-Leader, November 11, 1933, p. 8, December 29, 1933, p. 8.

[47] Freeman to Weddell, December 22, 1937, Freeman to George S. Messersmith, August 4, 1938, Freeman to Weddell, August 5, 1938, Fletcher Warren to Freeman, August 5, 1938, Freeman to Raymond B. Fosdick, October 19, 1938, Fosdick to Freeman, October 26, 1938, Douglas S. Freeman Diary, December 7, 1938, Sydnor H. Walker to Freeman, May 24, 1939, Freeman to Walker, May 30, 1939, Walker to Freeman, June 1, 1939, Fosdick to Freeman, October 31, 1940, Freeman to Fosdick, November 1, 1940, Freeman Papers.

"good neighbor." The editor applauded the State Department's purchase of a small quantity of canned Argentine beef for the navy. When the Senate then undid that sale in a rider to an appropriations' bill, Freeman asked: "What chance . . . is there to win Argentinian friendship in the face of these persistent and unreasoning restraints? 'Good neighbor?' Well may Argentina laugh at the unctuous phrase." Freeman sent the editorial to Assistant Secretary Messersmith with his "best regards and as a contribution to the good fight you are making." The secretary gave the editorial to Hull. In his April 6, 1940, letter to A. Willis Robertson, Freeman conceded that while the congressman might be "right" about the trade agreement with Argentina, the "prospect of any importation of Argentine cattle" under the sanitary convention was "negligible."[48]

Freeman also shared Weddell and Roosevelt's concern with Nazi-fascist penetration of the Western Hemisphere. In his April 23, 1938, letter to Weddell, he assured the ambassador that both the Carnegie Endowment for International Peace and the new Rockefeller Foundation-funded world wide radio service were "alive to the situation." Freeman believed that the radio service's programs for Latin America should be supplemented with "some strong and positive Pan American propaganda by short wave radio." He was also convinced of the need for "better connection" between the press services of the United States and the newspapers of Latin America. Freeman wrote: "The whole situation is one that concerns me very deeply." He worried that Brazil and perhaps other Latin American countries would serve as bases for fascism in the Western Hemisphere. Freeman asked Weddell to keep him informed on the situation so that he could "communicate intelligently" with his colleagues on the boards of the Rockefeller and Carnegie foundations.[49]

Throughout the Roosevelt administration, other Virginia newspaper editors also supported the president's Latin American policies. Most papers regarded the Good Neighbor policy as a rational approach to Latin America. Many editors believed it implemented the Monroe Doctrine. They maintained that United States military intervention in Latin America could

---

[48] Freeman to Weddell, January 23, 1937, Freeman Papers; Weddell to Francis B. Sayre, March 18, 1939, Weddell Papers; Richmond News-Leader, March 10, 1939, p. 10, May 19, 1939, p. 8; Freeman to Messersmith, May 20, 1939, Messersmith to Freeman, May 22, 1939, File Number 611.355/201, Department of State, Central Decimal File, and in Freeman Papers; Messersmith's May 22 note to Hull, File Number 611.355/201, Department of State, Central Decimal File; Freeman to Robertson, April 6, 1940, Freeman Papers.

[49] Freeman to Weddell, April 23, 1938, Freeman Papers.

only be justified in conjunction with Pan American consultation and cooperation. The Platt Amendment, Roosevelt Corollary, and "Dollar Diplomacy" were viewed as relics of the past. The Norfolk Ledger-Dispatch supported abrogation of the Platt Amendment. The paper did not believe that the Monroe Doctrine and the Good Neighbor policy were incompatible. It maintained that how Latin American republics governed themselves was not an American affair. The Ledger-Dispatch did not, however, believe that the Good Neighbor policy precluded the United States' right to intervene in Latin America under all circumstances. It argued that by virtue of the Monroe Doctrine the United States could still unilaterally remove any European or Asian base or colony in Latin America with or without the latter's consent. Still, the Ledger-Dispatch approved of the 1936 treaty with Panama. It emphasized that while the United States had surrendered its guardianship over that republic, it still had the right to protect the Panama Canal. The paper argued that the new treaty protected American interests in the canal and "serves notice to Latin America that the 'good neighbor' policy is not a matter of mere words." In its December 10, 1938, editorial the paper concluded:

> Properly and helpfully and with great ability, the Roosevelt Administration has gone far in its 'good neighbor' policy. But it has not gone, and will not go, so far as to weaken the hands-off warning of the Monroe Doctrine.[50]

In 1933, Virginia's newspapers applauded the announced withdrawal of United States marines from Nicaragua and Haiti. The press justified America's original military intervention in those two countries as necessary and altruistic, not imperialistic. They maintained, however, that the removal of those troops promoted cooperation and better business relations with Latin America.[51]

---

[50] Richmond News-Leader, November 11, 1933, p. 8, December 29, 1933, p. 8, February 22, 1939, p. 10, April 17, 1939, p. 10; Richmond Times-Dispatch, December 12, 1939, p. 8, June 5, 1940, p. 10, June 22, 1941, p. 6, July 31, 1941, p. 10; Norfolk Ledger-Dispatch, December 29, 1933, p. 8, June 1, 1934, p. 8, March 7, 1935, p. 6, December 13, 1937, p. 6, October 22, 1938, p. 6, December 10, 1938, p. 6, July 30, 1940, p. 6; Alexandria Gazette, January 4, 1934, p. 4, April 7, 1939, p. 4; Danville Register, May 17, 1933, p. 4, September 8, 1940, p. 4; Daily Progress (Charlottesville), November 9, 1936, p. 4.

[51] Richmond Times-Dispatch, January 3, 1933, p. 6, August 9, 1933, p. 6; Alexandria Gazette, February 7, 1933, p. 4; Norfolk Ledger-Dispatch, August 9, 1933, p. 8.

Virginia's newspapers were more ambivalent about military intervention in the case of Cuba. In 1933-34, Cuba experienced considerable instability and threats of revolution; American intervention was a real possibility. The Virginia press denounced the dictatorial, oppressive rule of Cuban President Gerado Machado and lamented the overthrow of his pro-American successor, Carlos Manuel de Cespedes. Numerous editorials urged the Roosevelt administration to avoid military intervention unless--as a last resort-- American lives and property were threatened. They considered the dispatch of United States warships to Cuba as a wise precautionary gesture and applauded Ambassador Welles' mediation efforts. The newspaper argued, however, that a hasty American military response would be unwise and set back efforts to improve economic and diplomatic relations between the United States and Latin America. The press maintained that Roosevelt could hardly afford to engage American marines on foreign soil with a depression at home and new crises evolving in Europe and Asia. Nevertheless, Virginia's editors believed that by virtue of the Monroe Doctrine and even the notorious Platt Amendment the United States had the right to maintain order so close to its shores. The restoration of order in Cuba a year later made it easier for most editors to support the 1934 Cuban-American treaty that effectively repealed the Platt Amendment. [52]

In 1938, the possibility of armed intervention reappeared after the Mexican government expropriated American oil properties. Mutual hostility and suspicion had characterized relations between the United States and Mexico since the Mexican Constitution of 1917 won adoption. The Roosevelt administration realized that armed intervention would severely damage much of the good-will that had been built up through the Good Neighbor policy. Most Virginia editors agreed; a repetition of America's 1913 incursion into Mexico would disrupt trade, encourage Nazi-fascist elements in Latin America, and weaken hemispheric defense. They urged the United States

---

[52] Richmond News-Leader, April 27, 1933, p. 8, August 14, 1933, p. 8, September 7, 1933, p. 8; Richmond Times-Dispatch, February 10, 1933, p. 8, August 9, 1933, p. 6, August 11, 1933, p. 8, August 14, 1933, p. 6, September 7, 1933, p. 6, September 11, 1933, p. 6, November 10, 1933, p. 12, May 31, 1934, p. 8; Norfolk Ledger-Dispatch, August 8, 1933, p. 8, August 10, 1933, p. 8, August 12, 1933, p. 8, August 14, 1933, p. 8, August 17, 1933, p. 8, August 30, 1933, p. 8, September 7, 1933, p. 8, September 9, 1933, p. 8, September 12, 1933, p. 8, September 13, 1933, p. 8; Alexandria Gazette, February 27, 1933, p. 4, April 21, 1933, p. 4, May 3, 1933, p. 4, August 18, 1933, p. 4, September 20, 1933, p. 4; Danville Register, May 31, 1934, p. 4; Daily Progress (Charlottesville), March 6, 1933, p. 4, August 9, 1933, p. 4, August 16, 1933, p. 4, September 7, 1933, p. 4, May 31, 1934, p. 4; Roanoke Times, May 6, 1933, p. 6, January 25, 1934, p. 6, December 3, 1940, p. 6.

government to negotiate for a just settlement of the losses. In its October 31, 1938, editorial, the Daily Progress (Charlottesville) argued that:

> With business recovery gradually getting under way, we do need the good will and trade of Mexico. But more than that, it is for our best interests that we perpetuate a Mexican government that is sympathetic to the United States and the way not left open for the encroachment of Communism and Fascism.

Virginia's press perceived the 1941 settlement on compensation and United States-Mexican defense agreements as vindication of the Good Neighbor policy.[53]

In its December 5, 1933, editorial, the Richmond Times-Dispatch recognized the importance of the Montevideo conference in planting the seeds of increased trade and good-will among the nations of the Western Hemisphere. Nearly three years later, the paper credited that conference for having "greatly improved and advanced the 'good neighbor' policy of the Administration." Central to that meeting was the reciprocal trade program of Secretary Hull. Newspapers throughout the state extolled the virtues of that policy and encouraged the State Department to conclude reciprocal trade agreements with the Latin American republics. Editorial opinion believed Hull's program would lower tariff barriers, expand markets, increase exports, eliminate Latin American dependence on European trade (especially German), check Nazi-fascist subversion of the Americas, improve relations between the United States and Latin America, and promote good-will and prosperity throughout the Western Hemisphere. The Daily Progress's (Charlottesville) September 3, 1936, editorial concluded:

> The building of international good will, principally through reciprocal trade agreements . . . has been an outstanding and constructive achievement of the Roosevelt administration which may well take historical rating as a diplomatic triumph.[54]

---

[53] Richmond Times-Dispatch, September 3, 1938, p. 6; Daily Progress (Charlottesville), October 31, 1938, p. 4, February 17, 1941, p. 4, February 25, 1941, p. 4, April 4, 1941, p. 4; Danville Register, April 12, 1938, p. 4, March 31, 1940, p. 6; Roanoke Times, December 3, 1940, p. 6; Richmond News-Leader, January 17, 1941, p. 10, March 5, 1941, p. 10; Norfolk Ledger-Dispatch, November 21, 1941, p. 10.

[54] Richmond Times-Dispatch, December 5, 1933, p. 6, June 8, 1934, p. 12, October 5, 1936, p. 6, December 24, 1936, p. 6, March 11, 1939, p. 8, February 7, 1940, p. 8, March 30, 1940, p. 10, April 7, 1940, p. 2, December

Three years after the Montevideo meeting, Virginia's newspapers supported Roosevelt's call for another Pan American peace conference. In December, 1936, editors throughout the state congratulated the president and Ambassador Weddell for their successful efforts to promote understanding, cooperation, harmony, unity, and peace at Buenos Aires. They described Roosevelt's good-will trip to the Argentine capital in glowing terms. The Daily Progress's (Charlottesville) December 3, 1936, editorial concluded that "Not since the establishment of the Monroe Doctrine 113 years ago has American statesmanship achieved such notable progress to insure the security of all the Americas as that effected by President Roosevelt." In its December 2, 1936, editorial, the Danville Register maintained that Roosevelt "brought a spirit of good-will that will advance the cause of peace." The Richmond News-Leader labeled the Buenos Aires agreement "a triumph for a 'Good Neighbor policy.'"[65]

In 1938, Virginia's leading newspapers praised the Declaration of Lima's forging of a united front against foreign aggression. The Richmond Times-Dispatch's December 27, 1938, editorial gave Hull most of the credit for the declaration's provisions on continental solidarity. That statement warned against all "foreign interventions or activity" that may threaten the "continental solidarity" of the twenty-one American republics and the "principles upon which said solidarity is based." The paper concluded that the declaration was achieved in "a spirit of good will and mutual understanding." The Alexandria Gazette's reaction to the Lima conference was more in line with that of the 1936 Republican presidential candidate, Alf Landon. In a radio broadcast the former Kansas governor said that neither Democrats nor

---

25, 1940, p. 10, July 31, 1941, p. 10, October 3, 1941, p. 20, October 13, 1941, p. 6; Richmond News-Leader, February 22, 1939, p. 10, March 10, 1939, p. 10, April 7, 1939, p. 10; Norfolk Ledger-Dispatch, August 30, 1933, p. 8, August 27, 1934, p. 6, March 11, 1939, p. 6, September 7, 1939, p. 10, January 15, 1940, March 28, 1940, p. 6; Alexandria Gazette, November 21, 1935, p. 4, October 27, 1937, p. 4, November 29, 1938, p. 4, April 7, 1939, p. 4, April 12, 1939, p. 4; Daily Progress (Charlottesville), November 9, 1939, p. 4, September 3, 1936, p. 4; Danville Register, February 18, 1936, p. 4.

[55] Richmond News-Leader, December 17, 1936, p. 8; Richmond Times-Dispatch, November 28, 1936, p. 6, December 2, 1936 p. 10, December 17, 1936, p. 10, December 22, 1936, p. 10, December 24, 1936, p. 6; Norfolk Ledger-Dispatch, November 18, 1936, p. 8; Daily Progress (Charlottesville), November 9, 1936, p. 4, December 3, 1936, p. 4, December 26, 1936, p. 4; Danville Register, February 18, 1936, p. 4, December 1, 1936, p. 4, December 2, 1936, p. 4, December 8, 1936, p. 4; Alexandria Gazette, April 28, 1936, p. 4, August 11, 1936, p. 4, December 14, 1936, p. 4, July 6, 1937, p. 4.

Republicans would tolerate "any foreign government gaining a foothold on this continent." As early as January, 1938, the Gazette asserted that the best defense for the entire Western Hemisphere rested with the Monroe Doctrine. The Good Neighbor policy, notwithstanding, the United States still bore the ultimate responsibility for protecting both North and South America against European domination or aggression.[56]

Just weeks after Hitler's invasion of Poland, Virginia's newspapers praised the Declaration of Panama's (1939) neutrality statement, but questioned the wisdom of the "safety zone" idea. The declaration warned belligerents that the American states would prohibit any acts of war in a "safety zone" off the coast of the Western Hemisphere, south of Canada. Nevertheless, they credited the foreign ministers of the American republics for building the foundation of closer hemispheric cooperation in light of the European war. They furthermore believed that the conference strengthened the call for closer trade relations and reaffirmed the Western Hemisphere's determination to protect its commerce, as well as its independence and neutrality, from the ravages of the European conflict. The Richmond Times-Dispatch's September 24, 1939, editorial encouraged the United States to purchase more Latin American goods than it had in the past.[57]

Even before the fall of France, Virginia's editors were cognizant of Latin America's military weakness and susceptibility to Axis subversion and aggression. They were most anxious for the United States to develop more definite means for common defense with other American states (e.g. Pan American economic sanctions against Latin America countries trading with the Axis powers, placing United States military and naval bases at strategic points in Latin America). The Alexandria Gazette reiterated its long-standing argument that the Monroe Doctrine required the United States to shoulder

---

[56]Roanoke Times, November 13, 1938, p. 6; Richmond News-Leader, December 26, 1938, p. 10; Norfolk Ledger-Dispatch, December 28, 1938, p. 10; Richmond Times-Dispatch, December 18, 1938, p. 2, December 27, 1938, p. 8, December 29, 1938, p. 8; Alexandria Gazette, January 14, 1938, p. 4, December 27, 1938, p. 4.

[57]Richmond Times-Dispatch, September 19, 1939, p. 8, September 24, 1939, p. 2, October 4, 1939, p. 8; Norfolk Ledger-Dispatch, September 27, 1939, p.6; Danville Register, January 17, 1940, p. 6.

the primary burden of protecting the Western Hemisphere from foreign subversion and attack.[58]

Those concerns were addressed, albeit not to every editor's satisfaction, at the July, 1940, Havana Conference. The press strongly endorsed Secretary Hull's "no-transfer" resolution, which was designed to strengthen Pan-American enforcement of the Monroe Doctrine. The Act of Havana authorized American seizure of any territory in the Western Hemisphere faced with the transfer of its sovereignty to another European power as a result of the war. All republics represented at the conference reaffirmed their democratic principles and pledged cooperation. Yet, eight of them attached reservations to the Act of Havana that weakened the "no-transfer" statement. Latin America's three largest states--Argentina, Brazil, and Chile--sent only functionary observers. That led the Richmond News-Leader's July 31, 1940, editorial to conclude that the United States suffered a "definite diplomatic defeat" at Havana. Virginia's editors also observed that the meeting demonstrated that United States-Latin American unity was not as strong as it should be. The Richmond Times-Dispatch's July 30, 1940, editorial argued that despite Roosevelt's request that Congress increase the Export-Import Bank's capital by one-half million dollars for the purpose of Latin American exports, the conference failed to adopt any definite plan for economic cooperation between the Americas. Neither had it "arrived at a satisfactory formula for hemispheric defense." The Alexandria Gazette, the Danville Register, and the Norfolk Ledger-Dispatch were more sanguine about the conference's achievements. In its July 30, 1940, editorial, the Ledger-Dispatch concluded that:

> the result of the Havana Conference is a triumph for the diplomacy of Secretary Hull and for the Good Neighbor policy of President Roosevelt. ... At the most, it is an augury of solidarity among the American states, great and small.[59]

The press' concern with Axis penetration of Latin America, the need for stronger hemispheric defense, and a more effective Pan-American Union

---

[58] Alexandria Gazette, May 10, 1939, p. 4, June 8, 1940, p. 4, June 12, 1940, p. 4, June 14, 1940, p. 4; Richmond Times-Dispatch, June 5, 1940, p. 10, June 22, 1940, p. 8; Danville Register, May 12, 1940, p. 6.

[59] Richmond News-Leader, July 29, 1940, p. 10, July 31, 1940, p. 12; Daily Progress (Charlottesville), July 30, 1940, p. 4; Richmond Times-Dispatch, July 30, 1940, p. 8, October 19, 1940, p. 6; Alexandria Gazette, July 31, 1940, p. 4, August 2, 1940, p. 4; Danville Register, July 2, 1940, p. 6, July 28, 1940, p. 6; Norfolk Ledger-Dispatch, July 23, 1940, p. 6, July 30, 1940, p. 6.

continued well into 1941. In its June 11, 1941, editorial, the Richmond Times-Dispatch maintained that in order to protect Latin America against Nazi invasion or further infiltration, "It may become necessary for the United States to establish bases along the east coast of South America." The paper also supported the 1941 lease-lend agreement between the United States and Brazil. It rejected Senator D. Worth Clark's suggestion that the United States "take over control" of Latin America and Canada and establish puppet governments there. The Times-Dispatch's July 31, 1941, editorial asserted:

> The best insurance against Nazi influence we have in South America . . . is the policy which President Roosevelt described as that of 'the neighbor who resolutely respects himself and because he does so, respects the rights of others--the neighbor who respects his obligations and respects the sanctity of his agreements in and with world neighbors.'"

The paper argued that since 1933, the Good Neighbor policy had been reenforced through "mutually advantageous" trade agreements and loans from the Export-Import Bank. The Roanoke Times and the Daily Progress (Charlottesville) cited the Pan-American highway as evidence of the Good Neighbor policy's success in strengthening hemispheric defense and drawing the Americas closer together.[60]

The Richmond newspapers were no less concerned with strengthening ties between the commonwealth and the Latin American republics. Both the Richmond News-Leader and the Richmond Times-Dispatch welcomed Latin American scholars and professionals during their February, 1941, visit to the capital. The News-Leader reminded its readers of the traditionally close commercial ties that existed between Richmond and Latin America. The capital sent flour to Latin America in exchange for its coffee. The paper also noted that General Robert E. Lee was one of the earliest advocates of cultural relations with Latin America. As president of Washington College (later known as Washington and Lee University), Lee was one of the first southern college presidents to support widespread instruction in Spanish. The News-Leader's February 13, 1941, editorial stated that "Our guests . . . are visiting a city whose hero was the advocate of the pleasant relationship exemplified." The Times-Dispatch admitted that Latin Americans understood the English language and American culture better than Americans knew theirs. In the interest of the Good Neighbor policy, the editorial encouraged American schools to teach their students Spanish and Portuguese. Students

---

[60] Richmond Times-Dispatch, July 7, 1940, p. 4, October 12, 1940, p. 8, June 11, 1941, p. 12, June 22, 1941, p. 6, July 31, 1941, p. 10, October 3, 1941, p. 20, October 20, 1941, p. 10; Roanoke Times, September 7, 1941, p. 6; Daily Progress (Charlottesville), July 24, 1936, p. 4.

at Richmond's John Marshall High School corresponded with more than 100 Argentinian students; 500 of them were studying Spanish. The paper's November 15, 1941, editorial praised the formation of the Inter-American Committee in Richmond. The committee worked in cooperation with the Washington-based Office of the Coordinator of Inter-American Affairs and served as hosts to Latin American scholars visiting Richmond. The Times-Dispatch encouraged Americans to continue studying Latin America, "if the good neighbors are to be understood." In its November 24, 1941, editorial, the paper applauded the Virginia Council of Administrative Women in Education's efforts to promote understanding between the United States and Latin America in the public school system. The Times-Dispatch believed their activities would encourage more North Americans to visit Latin America and study its history and culture.[61]

Virginia's colleges also were concerned with promoting better understanding between North and South America. In his July 24, 1940, speech to the Roanoke Kiwanis Club, Roanoke College president, Dr. Charles J. Smith argued that the United States must become a strong military power in order to draw Latin America into a closer relationship with it. From 1933 through 1938, the Institute of Public Affairs at the University of Virginia held round table meetings on United States-Latin American relations. Ambassadors and Latin American specialists from the State Department and colleges throughout the United States participated in those discussions. Most of the talks concentrated on the problem of trade barriers, reciprocal trade agreements, economic recovery, the doctrine of nonintervention, Pan-American cooperation, and the preservation of peace in the Western Hemisphere.[62]

Roman Catholic and Presbyterian editorial opinion favored Roosevelt's Good Neighbor policy. But the Catholic press criticized the president's tepid response to the leftist Mexican government's persecution of the Catholic Church. Lazaro Cardenas's regime took possession of church property, closed many churches, restricted the education and movement of priests, banished some clergy, removed religious education from the public schools, and even murdered many of its Catholic opponents. The editor of the Virginia Catholic, W. T. Winston, was especially critical of Josephus Daniels, the

---

[61] Richmond News-Leader, February 13, 1941, p. 10; Richmond Times-Dispatch, February 14, 1941, p. 10, November 15, 1941, p. 8, November 24, 1941, p. 10; James C. Harwood to Weddell, April 5, 1937, Weddell Papers.

[62] Roanoke World-News, July 24, 1940, p. 13; University of Virginia Newsletter, June 15, 1933, p. 1, June 1, 1934, p. 1, May 15, p. 1, May 15, 1936, p. 1, May 15, 1937, p. 1, May 15, 1938, p. 1.

American ambassador to Mexico. Daniels had praised the Mexican government's constitutionalism, educational system, and policy of social justice. Winston endorsed a congressional resolution that called for Daniels's retirement. The diocesan newspaper also castigated the press for condemning German anti-Semitism while remaining silent on Mexican persecution of the church. Bishop Peter L. Ireton of Richmond shared those sentiments.[63]

Virginia's leading black newspapers approved of Roosevelt's Good Neighbor policy and expressed contempt for the Monroe Doctrine and "Dollar Diplomacy." The Journal and Guide (Norfolk) characterized Hull's reciprocal trade program as a vehicle through which the "weeds" of "American prejudice" could be eliminated. It agreed with the National Association for the Advancement of Colored People's secretary, Walter White, that the United States could improve its political and economic relations with Latin America by eliminating racial discrimination and prejudice at home. It argued that the United States had lost untold commercial opportunities to Europe after dark-skinned Latin American businessmen visiting America had been insulted or denied access to public accommodations. The Journal encouraged black businessmen to partake of the fruits of the Good Neighbor policy through increased trade with the Central American and Caribbean states. In 1938, it condoned Mexico's expropriation of American oil properties. The paper considered Mexico's step toward "economic liberation" no worse than Europe's default on its war debts to the United States. It argued that Mexico should not be bound by a system of international law already abandoned by the rest of the world.[64]

---

[63] Most American Catholics supported Pan-Americanism and the Good Neighbor policy because they believed their church was the key to improving relations between the United States and Latin America. They also shared a common religious heritage with Latin Americans. Suspicious of Europe and trustful toward Latin America, American Catholics considered the Good Neighbor policy a form of isolationism, See Flynn, Roosevelt and Romanism, pp. 14-55; Virginia Catholic, November, 1934, p. 6, February, 1935, p. 7, March, 1935, pp. 9, 30, April, 1935, pp. 9, 13, 33, July, 1935, p. 7, August, 1935, p. 6, December, 1935, p. 6, January, 1936, pp. 6-7, March, 1936, p. 9, May, 1936, p. 12, August, 1936, p. 7, October, 1936, pp. 3, 9, January, 1937, p. 7, February, 1939, p. 7, January, 1941, p. 7; The Presbyterian of the South and the Presbyterian Standard, December 9, 1936, p. 5.

[64] Journal and Guide (Norfolk), May 15, 1937, p. 8, February 19, 1938, p. 8, April 2, 1938, p. 8, September 17, 1938, p. 8; Afro-American (Richmond), October 14, 1939, p. 13; Walter White to Nelson Rockefeller, April 22, 1941, General Office File, National Association for the Advancement of Colored People's Papers, Library of Congress, Washington, D.C.

Long before the Japanese attack on Pearl Harbor influential Virginians realized the benefits of cordial United States-Latin American relations in the event of war. By December 7, 1941, the United States' economic, political, military, even cultural and educational relations with Latin America had vastly improved. Those Virginians realized that reduced trade barriers, nonintervention, and cultural and educational exchanges were the sine qua non of increased prosperity, Pan-American cooperation, and effective hemispheric defense. Far removed from the Rio Grande, Virginians were convinced that the best way to insulate the Americas from European tyranny and subversion was through the policy of the "good neighbor." The state's political elite's favorable reaction to FDR's Latin American initiatives was further evidence of their support of his internationalist foreign policy.

PART II

VIRGINIA AND AMERICAN FOREIGN POLICY
BEFORE PEARL HARBOR

CHAPTER VI

WORLD WAR II: VIRGINIA'S CORNUCOPIA

The Second World War was an economic boon for the South, and especially Virginia. The war, not the New Deal, ended the depression in the state. America's war economy accelerated economic tendencies in operation throughout the commonwealth well before Pearl Harbor. During the years 1933-41, the Old Dominion experienced a dramatic increase in industrialization, modernization, population growth, urbanization, and prosperity. Hitler's European war closed many of Virginia's traditional markets; the state's tobacco and apple exporters were especially hit hard. But the conflict also brought billions of defense dollars into the state to compensate for those losses. Virginians were well aware of the economic and strategic importance of their state in America's national defense program and in the war against Hitler. The strategic Hampton Roads area, a vital shipbuilding, military, and naval center, was one of many localities to profit from government defense contracts worth billions of dollars. Virginia, home to more than fifty military and naval installations and numerous war plants, was a leading recipient of national defense expenditures.[1]

Economic considerations certainly affected Virginians' views on the direction of American foreign policy during the war. A majority of them realized that Roosevelt's "interventionist" foreign policy, including America's unprecedented defense buildup, would bring their state's factories, farms, and offices increased prosperity. Nevertheless, they did not want the United States to enter the war because it would benefit them economically. Virginians supported FDR's foreign policy because they believed Hitler's war threatened their European markets, American national security, and the survival of Western democracy and civilization. Along with that prosperity came short-lived problems: housing shortages, increased city traffic, and inadequate and overcrowded cities, public

---

[1]Governor James H. Price's January 10, 1940, address to the General Assembly of Virginia, Journal of the Senate of the Commonwealth of Virginia (Richmond: Division of Purchase and Printing, 1940) pp. 4-6; Interview with Virginius Dabney, Richmond, Virginia, November 28, 1986. See Wolfe, "Virginia in World War II," pp. 139-94, 196, for a detailed account of economic and social change in wartime Virginia. Also see Irish, "Foreign Policy and the South," pp. 308-15; Dabney's "The South Looks Abroad," pp. 172-76 and Below the Potomac, pp. 273-82; Seabury, The Waning of Southern 'Internationalism,' p. 15; Parke Rouse, Jr., "Newport News and Defense," The Commonwealth, June, 1941, pp. 11-15; Norfolk Ledger-Dispatch, September 10, 1940, p. 6.

transportation, health services, schools, and recreational facilities. Rationing, a shortage of goods, increased crime, venereal disease, promiscuity, juvenile delinquency, heightened racial tensions, a depopulation of the countryside, and severe shortages of agricultural labor also plagued the state. Despite those temporary inconveniences, however, Virginians were much better off by December, 1941, than they had been a decade earlier.[2]

During the First World War, the South also experienced an economic boom. But that prosperity was shortlived. Agricultural decline, drought, and depression followed within a little more than a decade of the 1918 armistice. World War II's economic good times, however, lasted far beyond the post-war era. What Roosevelt described in July, 1938, as "the Nation's No. 1 economic problem" had become a "development area" even before Pearl Harbor. During the early 1940s, northern industrialists came south in pursuit of vast natural resources, abundant cheap labor, weak trade unions, low taxes, fiscal conservatism, excellent transportation facilities, strategic location, and favorable climate. By the summer of 1940, capital invested in southern manufacturing since 1920 had increased by $3,136,000,000,or 31 percent, while the capital invested for the rest of the country during the same period increased by $5,719,000,000. While much of the South's industrial expansion (especially in shipyards, aircraft plants, and ordnance works) was temporary, the region remained more industrialized than ever before. During World War II, expansion increased the South's effective industrial capacity by approximately 40 percent. From 1939 to 1947, the number of manufacturing concerns rose from 26,516 to 42,739, the value added from $3,124,000,000 to $10,744,000,000, and from 12.7 to 14.4 percent of the national total. By November, 1943, the number of production workers grew from 1,349,000 to 2,835,000,and stood at 2,023,000 in 1947. After the return to a peacetime economy, the South had been able to retain almost one-half of the addition to its factory work force. Foreign trade provided jobs for southern farmers and factory workers at a higher percentage than in any other region of the country. From 1940 to 1943, the South lost 1,422,000 of its civilian population; however, 39 of 48 of its metropolitan areas increased in population (e.g. Norfolk grew 57%). Southern farm prices also steadily increased during the course of the war. Tobacco rose from 15.4 cents per pound in 1939 to 42.6 cents per pound in 1945. Cotton increased from 9.89 cents per pound to 22.52 cents per pound during that same period. Between 1938 and 1944, southern exports increased by 250%. Its imports rose by 150%. Norfolk and other southern cities shipped out petroleum, scrap metal, cotton, iron, steel, sulphur, phosphate, and other raw materials; they imported rubber, manganese, sugar, coffee, bananas, and cocoa from all parts of the world. By 1945, the South had more industrial and manufacturing workers, more unions, larger cities, fewer sharecroppers, and a higher standard of living. The Second World War transformed the South into a less conservative, less isolated, and less agrarian society. It had become more

___

[2]Rouse, "Newport News and Defense," pp. 11-15; Wolfe, "Virginia in World War II," pp. 139-94, 196; Norfolk Ledger-Dispatch, September 10, 1940, p. 6; Interview with Dabney, November 28, 1986.

like the rest of the nation.³

Between 1935 and 1940, Virginia experienced a rapid pace of industrialization and economic progress. During that period, 510 new manufacturing plants began operation. In 1939, only $78.5 million of new construction took place in the state. During 1940, the figure had more than doubled to $168.9 million; a year later the total was $250.3 million, and by 1942, it was $413 million. Those phenomenal increases were largely due to appropriations for war plants and defense workers' housing. During the war, Virginia consistently placed in the upper third among southern states in plant construction and employment gains. Its chemical industry (especially its synthetic fiber plants), textile mills, and furniture factories achieved rapid expansion. For the year ending September 30, 1941, the number of workers engaged in gainful occupations numbered over one million. Nearly 250,000 Virginians worked in the manufacturing and mechanical industries, including building construction. From 1939 to 1940, the number of wage earners employed in the manufacturing industries increased by 19,070, or 10.8%, while the number in shipbuilding and repairs increased by 10,074 or 57.9%. Those increases in the state's industrial work force were largely due to the rapid expansion of the shipbuilding industry and the accelerated production of war goods.⁴

The state's growing industrialization during the pre-Pearl Harbor period was accompanied by congressional enactment of the Wagner Labor Relations Act (1937), labor strikes (50 in 1937), labor union rivalries, and improved business conditions (notwithstanding the 1938 recession). Virginia's phenomenal industrial progress was largely due to the war, which accelerated already-existing economic trends. The commonwealth's rapid pace of industrialization would not have been possible, however, without its relative stability, favorable tax system, fiscal conservatism, adequate labor supply, low wage rates, abundant natural resources, moderate climate, and excellent transportation system.⁵

During World War II, the Old Dominion was an arsenal of democracy in miniature. War factories and shipyards essential for national defense were located throughout the state. They produced warships, weaponry, munitions, chemicals, clothing, and food on an

---

³Tindall, Emergence of the New South, pp. 599, 694-705, 710-11, 731; Seabury, The Waning of Southern 'Internationalism,' pp.21-22; Richmond Times-Dispatch, July 8, 1940, p. 8; Irish, "Foreign Policy and the South," p. 308.

⁴Dabney, Virginia, pp. 502-503; Raymond B. Bottom, "Virginia's Record of Economic Progress," The Commonwealth, March, 1940, pp. 7-10; Jean Gottman, Virginia in Our Century (Charlottesville: University Press of Virginia, 1969), pp. 405, 409; George T. Starnes, "State Reports: Virginia," Southern Economic Journal 8 (1942), p. 550; Wolfe, "Virginia in World War II," pp. 148, 154, 158-60, 230; Forty-fourth Annual Report of the Department of Labor and Industry of the State of Virginia, 1940 (Richmond, 1941), pp. 13-15; Richmond News-Leader, November 30, 1940, p. 17.

⁵Dabney, Virginia, pp. 502-503; Wolfe, "Virginia in World War II," p. 154.

unprecedented scale.⁶

The Norfolk-Newport News-Portsmouth area alone received $576,429,000 in war and navy department contracts between June 1 and October 31, 1940. Hampton Roads' award of $531,339,000 in shipbuilding contracts was exceeded only by the Boston area's award of $601,728,000. During the last six months of 1940, naval shipbuilding contracts alone amounted to $663,899,000;jobs previously assigned and under construction raised the total to more than $819,500,000. In November, 1940, $45 million was being spent to develop and expand military posts and naval stations in Virginia. By December, 1940, defense constituted the biggest industry in the state. Virginia was second only to Texas in the $1,244,711,000 of defense-related construction contracts awarded to the South for the eleven month period ending November 30, 1940. The state received more than $55 million for new plant construction and enlargement of existing factories to provide facilities for ordnance production. By the end of December, 1940, defense projects in Virginia amounted to more than one billion dollars. By the spring of 1941, the state received a larger share of defense awards than was represented by its proportion of the national population than any South Atlantic state. From June, 1940, to September, 1941, authorized defense projects in the state totaled $1,158,756,000. Shipbuilding contracts alone amounted to $916,325,000. In September, 1941, the Hampton Roads area was home to nineteen military and naval facilities; its defense-related contracts exceed $1 billion. By the end of 1941, Virginia ranked sixth nationally in the value of defense contracts awarded within the state. Five of the navy's seventeen battleships and four of its seven aircraft carriers were built in Virginia. Eight aircraft carriers and two battleships were in the process of completion at Hampton Roads when the Japanese struck at Pearl Harbor on December 7, 1941.⁷

The heart of Virginia's national defense establishment was the Hampton Roads area. Its great harbor, centrally-placed on the east coast, was a focal point of sea and rail transportation. Hampton Roads was a key training and staging area for convoys that carried American troops and supplies to Europe. The nearby Chesapeake Bay entrance provided access to Hampton Roads, Baltimore, and Washington, D.C. Appalachian coal

---

⁶Irish, "Foreign Policy and the South," p. 315.

⁷Richmond Times-Dispatch, June 14, 1940, p. 11, July 3, 1940, p. 3, July 11, 1940, p. 1, July 31, 1940, p. 5, September 5, 1940, p. 21, September 19, 1940, p. 6, September 29, 1940, p. 5, December 3, 1940, p. 19, December 14, 1940, p. 8, December 27, 1940, p. 5, January 30, 1941, p. 7, August 19, 1941, p. 6, September 5, 1941, p. 16, November 28, 1941, p. 9; Richmond News-Leader, October 25, 1940, p. 1; Times-Herald (Newport News), February 26, 1941, p. 1; Roanoke World-News, July 23, 1940, p. 3; Alexandria Gazette, October 26, 1940, p. 4; Clarence W. Newman, "Virginia in the National Defense," The Commonwealth, June, 1940, pp. 7-8; Ibid., August, 1940, p. 4; J. Harrison Hancock, "A Thousand Millions for Defense," The Commonwealth, November, 1940, p. 13; Ibid., December, 1940, p. 4, April, 1941, p. 4, December, 1941, p. 4; Governor James H. Price's January 14, 1942, address before the General Assembly, James H. Price Executive Papers, Virginia State Library, Richmond, Virginia.

and Midwestern wheat and manufactured products entered the Hampton Roads area via railroads en route to the Atlantic seaboard. The region was a crossroads for transportation lines linking the industrial Northeast with the developing South. As the principal Atlantic base of operations for the navy, Hampton Roads served as headquarters for the Fifth Naval District. The Naval Operating Base was located at Norfolk, just south of the entrance to Hampton Roads. The base comprised a major supply depot, as well as the Naval Training Station and the Naval Air Station. The Marine Hospital was also located at Norfolk. Portsmouth was home to the Norfolk Navy Yard and Norfolk Naval Hospital. The Naval Ammunition Depot was located at St. Juliens Creek, south of the Navy Yard. Fort Eustis, on the lower James River near Newport News, served as a wartime railway ordnance post. The Naval Mine Depot and minesweeper school were situated at Yorktown. Ft. Monroe, which commanded the lower Chesapeake and the entrance to Hampton Roads, was home to: the Submarine Mine Depot, the Third Coast Artillery District, nerve center of the country's entire coastal defense system, and site of the Coast Artillery School and Coast Artillery Board. The United States Army's General Headquarters (G.H.Q.) Air Force at Langley Field, near Hampton, was Virginia's largest military base. Langley Field was also headquarters for the Second Wing, one of G.H.Q. Army Air Force's three commands. The Nansemond Ordnance Depot was situated on the south shore of Hampton Roads. Camp Peary, just northwest of the Hampton Roads area, served as a base for the Seabees, an elite navy unit.[8]

Hampton Roads was the first part of Virginia to experience full economic recovery during the pre-Pearl Harbor period. The locus of that prosperity was the shipbuilding industry. As early as November, 1940, merchant ships under construction at Hampton Roads involved nearly $30 million. The Newport News Shipbuilding and Dry Dock Company at Newport News operated the largest private shipbuilding yard in the United States. Many of the navy's finest battleships and aircraft carriers were built at the Newport News shipyard. The yard also completed the first of the navy's new fleet of carriers specifically provisioned to convoy ships to Europe. The Newport News plant of the Dodge Boat and Plane Corporation also contributed to Hampton Roads' economic boom. The firm built two-engined "crash" boats for the army. Norfolk's Ford Motor Company plant also provided the army with mechanized military equipment. The defense buildup also affected, albeit to a lesser degree, Newport News' second largest industry, the Chesapeake and Ohio Railway's deep-water terminus. Due to the interruption of European coal exports, the C&O enjoyed a brisk foreign coal trade. Its passenger train travel increased threefold due to the great demand for troop train service during the reactivation and expansion of the state's military installations.[9]

---

[8] Alexandria Gazette, July 9, 1940, p. 4; The Commonwealth, April, 1939, pp. 7-9; Newman, "Virginia in the National Defense," pp. 7-11, 32; Rubin, Virginia, pp. 173-74; Rouse, "Newport News and Defense," p. 11; Dabney, Virginia, p. 513

[9] Wolfe, "Virginia in World War II," pp. 142-43; Newman, "Virginia in the National Defense," p. 32; Rouse, "Newport News and Defense," pp. 11-15; Hancock, "A Thousand Millions for Defense," p. 13.

The social and economic impact of the Second World War on the Hampton Roads area was unprecedented. As a result of the national defense program, the civilian population of the Hampton Roads-Peninsula Area increased 25% between 1940 and 1942, and 40.7% between 1940 and 1943. When the census was taken on April 1, 1940, the population was 408,624; in May, 1942, it was 510,884; on November 1, 1943, it was 576,075. Increases in Hampton Roads military population and shipyards' employment were accompanied by an almost three-fold increase in the volume of general business activity during the war years. From 1939 to 1945, the military population rose to nearly twenty times the 1939 average and shipbuilding employment to almost five times the pre-war level. Between 1940-44, the area's total labor force rose from 153,881 to 228,578. During that same period, employment increased from 91 to 99% of the labor force.[10]

As a result of the wartime boom, the total number of businesses in the Hampton Roads-Peninsula Area rose from 5,322 in September, 1939, to 5,759 in July, 1945, a 8.21% increase. Suburban shopping centers, new stores, and restaurants sprung up throughout the area. New hospitals, schools, roads, and bridges were constructed; civic improvements were made; a new airport in Norfolk was built. Wartime economic expansion helped produce substantial increases in both aggregate and per capita income. As early as July, 1940, it was estimated that in the Norfolk region the navy was paying out $3.5 million each month in salaries. Aggregate income payments and gross buying income for 1945 rose 153% and 171%, respectively, over 1940, as compared with only 130% and 163%, for the entire state. The war brought an enormous expansion in the volume of virtually all types of economic activity in the Hampton Roads-Peninsula Area. Most importantly, it brought permanent economic progress to the Hampton Roads-Peninsula Area despite the discontinuance of most war activities. Unlike World War I, many of the naval facilities and other military installations remained after the war.[11]

Northern Virginia experienced an economic revival nearly as spectacular as that of the Hampton Roads region. As a result of the defense buildup, Northern Virginia became one of the state's most populous urban areas. Government and military offices were located just across the Potomac. Thousands of civilian and military personnel and their families sought housing in Arlington, Alexandria, Fairfax County, and other residential suburbs in the metropolitan Washington, D.C. area. Several important military bases and ordnance factories were also located in Northern Virginia. The Third Cavalry and the First Battalion of the Sixteenth Field Artillery were located four miles southwest of Washington

---

[10]The Commonwealth, June, 1941, p. 37; Charles F. Marsh, The Hampton Roads Committee in World War II (Chapel Hill: The University of North Carolina Press, 1951), pp. 76-77, 145-46, 149-50.

[11]Ibid., pp. 151, 174, 178, 180, 314, 317; Norfolk Ledger-Dispatch, September 7, 1940, p. 6, September 10, 1940, p. 6, January 28, 1941, p. 8, July 12, 1941, p. 2, July 16, 1941, p. 16, September 18, 1941, pp. 1, 16; Times-Herald (Newport News), March 14, 1941, p. 2, March 29, 1941, p. 2, November 26, 1941, p. 6; Rouse, "Newport News and Defense," pp. 13-15; Marvin W. Schlegel, Conscripted City: Norfolk in World War II (Norfolk: Norfolk War History Commission, 1951), pp. 3-5, 11-14.

near Arlington Cemetery, at Fort Myer. Across the Potomac in Alexandria stood the World War I era Torpedo Station, one of the navy's two torpedo factories. Fourteen miles southwest of Alexandria stood Fort Belvoir, which headquartered the Army Engineer School and regular engineer troops. The most important installation was the Quantico Marine Base located on the Potomac thirty miles south of Washington. Quantico served as the east coast's major marine training base. Further down the Potomac near Fredericksburg the navy tested its weapons at the Dahlgren Proving Ground. The army's Remount Depot was situated sixty miles west of the capital at Front Royal.[12]

During the Second World War, Southwest Virginia became a major defense manufacturing center. The mountainous Southwest was ideal for munition and powder plants because of its location far from the coast and potential enemy air attacks. The region's numerous energy-producing rivers enjoyed proximity to the Tennessee Valley Authority's electric power. Southwest Virginia was only a few hours by rail from ports of embarkation in the Hampton Roads area. More than 20,000 people worked at Radford's New River Ordnance Works. The federal government leased operation of the war plant to Hercules Powder Company. The factory was one of the largest and most comprehensive facilities for powder manufacture in the United States. The Shenandoah Valley Defense Co-operative sought defense contracts for small machine shops throughout the valley. In September, 1940, Representative Clifton A. Woodrum, a powerful member of the House Appropriations Committee, persuaded the federal government to designate Woodrum Field, Roanoke's airport, a national defense project. By the end of 1941, the government spent nearly $560,000 to upgrade and expand the airport's existing facilities. The Roanoke Valley's economy benefitted from Woodrum Field's frequent military and civilian air traffic during the war.[13]

The Roanoke-based Norfolk and Western (N&W) Railway Company, an enthusiastic supporter of Roosevelt's foreign policy, played a significant role in the national defense program. The railroad was well aware of its critical function as transporter of war material, servicemen, and defense workers. The N&W mines produced nearly ten percent of all the bituminous coal (nearly fifty million tons in 1941 alone) mined in the United States. The railway company transported most of that coal to steel mills and other leading industries directly or indirectly involved in the manufacture of battleships, airplanes, tanks, guns, powder, and other defense products. In addition to hauling coal, the railroad helped the War Department and Hercules Powder Company select the site for the Radford Ordnance Works. The N&W also transported the materials, machinery, and men who built and operated the plant. During the war, the N&W underwent extensive modernization and expansion in order to meet the needs of increased coal and other freight, as well as

---

[12] Wolfe, "Virginia in World War II," p. 143; Rubin Virginia, p. 173; Newman, "Virginia in the National Defense," pp. 8, 11, 32; Whitton Morse, "Virginia Becomes an Armed Camp," Richmond Times Dispatch, December 15, 1940, p. 5.

[13] Wolfe, "Virginia in World War II," pp. 145-46; Rubin, Virginia, p. 174; Irish, "Foreign Policy and the South," p. 315; Richmond Times-Dispatch, May 26, 1941, pp. 1, 6, October 22, 1941, p. 14; Sargent, "Clifton A. Woodrum," pp. 359, 361-62, 364.

passenger traffic resulting from defense preparedness. From September, 1939, through December 1941, the railroad expended more than sixty million dollars for the construction and purchase of new cars and locomotives, expansion of terminals, and other improvements. Unlike a majority of their counterparts across the country, N&W executives were not isolationists resisting conversion to a war economy. They did not believe that the war would abridge their entrepreneurial liberty and lead them to economic ruin. Management maintained that the preservation of American freedom was well worth the staggering costs of war. Nearly a year before the United States entered the war, N&W president W. J. Jenks urged his employees to continue their hard work and sacrifice in the interest of the national defense effort. Jenks and other company officials believed that the railroads were in the "first line of defense." The war and the threat to America's national security provided--in their eyes--an opportunity for all N&W employees to serve their country in its hour of peril.[14]

The Second World War's defense buildup affected Richmond, the capital and commercial center of the commonwealth, to a somewhat lesser degree than was the case in Hampton Roads and Northern Virginia. The war did not dramatically alter the capital's population or diversified economic infrastructure. Nevertheless, Richmond prospered as a result of the war. The value of its manufactured goods (including war products) rose from $373,147,000 in 1939 to nearly $800 million in 1946. The product value of the American Tobacco Company's Richmond plants rose from $87,123,343 in 1940 to $173,323,846 in 1944, while the value of all manufactured tobacco fell from $30,429,000 in 1940 to $21,294,968 in 1944. Cigarette output rose from 71,638,976,000 in 1941 to 103,706,000,000 five years later. Despite the relatively few defense contracts its businesses held, Richmond ranked first in the South and fourteenth in the nation in the total value of its wartime industrial production. As a result of the war, manufacturers significantly increased their outputs or switched from old lines to war-related ones. Many factories doubled or trebled their number of employees. Aggregate retail sales increased from $108,306,000 in 1939 to nearly $258 million by the end of the war. A year after the war's end, department store sales were 171% higher than in 1940. Wholesale trade advanced from $208,066,000 in 1939 to an estimated one-half billion dollars by 1944. Total bank and trust company deposits reached an all-time high. By the end of 1941, aggregate savings in the capital's savings and loans equaled $7,363,086.55. Five years later, savings totaled $18,369,322.49. In 1941, there were 688 bankruptcy cases in Richmond; four years later, there were 95 cases; by 1946, only 80 cases. Nonetheless, inflation and the cost of living also rose during the war.[15]

---

[14] Norfolk and Western Magazine, December, 1940, p. 570, January, 1941, pp. 1, 12-13, September, 1941, pp. 387-92, October, 1941, pp. 444-52, 466-67, December, 1941, p. 582; Roland N. Stromberg, "American Business and the Approach of War, 1935-1941," Journal of Economic History 13(1953): 58-78; Polenberg, War and Society, pp. 8, 10.

[15] Wolfe, "Virginia in World War II," pp. 143-144, 174; Francis E. Lutz, Richmond in World War II (Richmond: The Dietz Press, Inc., 1951), pp. 34, 59-61, 66, 74.

Cities within a 25 mile radius of Richmond also benefitted from the national preparedness program. The army held maneuvers at Camp A. P. Hill, which was 15 miles north of the capital in Caroline County. The reopening and expansion of Camp Lee, a World War I army training base, enhanced Petersburg's economic recovery. Wartime demands had already increased the city's cigarette production. During the war, Petersburg became the headquarters for the United States Army Quartermaster's Corps. The war buildup brought economic revitalization to Hopewell, an industrial city located approximately 20 miles southeast of Richmond. The city's Solvay Process Company's nitrogen fixation plant augmented the country's supply of nitrogen products, which were essential for the manufacture of explosives. Hopewell's synthetic fiber-producing Rayon plants became increasingly important after Japan shut off America's Asian silk supply. The du Pont nylon plant at Martinsville, in southside Virginia, also provided a substitute for silk.[16]

Virginia profited more than any other state from its citizens working for the federal government. After 1939, federal service contributed more to personal income in Virginia than in the country at large. Between 1939 and 1942, per capita income in the state increased more rapidly than the national average. In 1940, realized income in Virginia totaled $1,093,000,000, a 12.3% increase over 1929. (That figure did not include the income of ever-increasing numbers of Virginians working in the District of Columbia.) National income totaled $71,900,000,000, which was 5.6% below the 1929 high. Federal government and defense industry employment were largely responsible for the significant increase in Virginians' income. Most importantly, the war augmented pre-war advances in personal income. During the years 1939-41, the total wages and salaries in Virginia increased in dollar volume from $614.3 million paid in 1938 to $987.6 million in 1941, a gain of 60.8%. The three major sources of wage income during that period were: manufacturing, $263.6 million; government, $211.3 million; and trade, $137.2 million, which represented an increase of 95.4%, 100.5%, and 39.4%, respectively. In 1941, contract construction produced $52 million in wages, an increase of 108.8% over the total wages that industry paid in 1938; it represented a higher percentage increase than any other sector of the state's economy. That same year, the shipbuilding program, the production of war material, and the creation of numerous military bases and facilities--which doubled the government payroll--accounted for 48% of the total amount of wages paid in Virginia. Between 1929-41, there was an 87.5% increase in total wages paid in the manufacturing industry. The largest percentage increase from a total volume of wages from any single source was the 147.4% in the government payroll for 1941 over 1929.[17]

---

[16] Newman, "Virginia in the National Defense," pp. 8, 32; Wolfe, "Virginia in World War II," pp. 144-45; The Commonwealth, December, 1941, p. 4; Hancock, "A Thousand Millions for Defense," p. 13; Dabney, Virginia, p. 513.

[17] Wolfe, "Virginia in World War II," pp. 148-49, 152, 160; Bottom, "Virginia's Record," p. 7; Forty-fifth Annual Report of the Department of Labor and Industry of the State of Virginia, 1941 (Richmond, 1942), pp. 13-14; Richmond Times-Dispatch, September 3, 1941, p. 10; The Commonwealth, December, 1940, p. 4, April, 1941, p. 4.

The war also stimulated business and enhanced consumer purchasing power throughout the state. Federal payrolls created an increased demand for all types of consumer goods from textile mills, chemical plants, and furniture factories. As early as November, 1939, consumption of electricity set an all-time record; employment rose sharply; gasoline sales were at new highs; tobacco manufacture went up 23%; business levels throughout the state's economy were up. In 1939, Virginia's bank debits to individual accounts were only 7% below that of 1929, but for the United States as a whole debits, as measured by bank returns in 140 financial centers excluding New York City, were 34% below that of 1929. Nineteen Thirty-Nine debits for 141 centers including New York, were 58% below the 1929 volume. In October, 1940, department store sales in the state exceeded those of September by 14% and were 13% above the sales of a year earlier. Also in October, 1940, a new record was set for automobile registration of new cars. October, 1940, contract awards for construction totaled $51,758,000, the second highest figure for any month in eleven years.[18]

Defense activity within the state accelerated the pre-war trend toward increased urbanization. The state's industrial work force was largely concentrated in the cities. Thousands of blacks and women flocked to the urban areas to fill jobs in defense plants and navy yards normally held by white males. Between 1940 and 1944, the number of women in Virginia's labor force doubled. The growing trade union movement also benefitted from the arms buildup. The Hampton Roads and Northern Virginia metropolitan areas experienced an average annual population increase of more than five percent. The Roanoke-Pulaski-Radford and Richmond-Petersburg-Williamsburg areas averaged an annual population increase of 2 to 4.9%. Between 1940 and 1947, the state as a whole saw an average annual population growth of 2.77%. In 1940, Virginia's population was 2,642,229; in 1943, it stood at 2,883,945; in 1945, the estimated population had reached 3,079,706.[19]

Virginia's farmers were far less sanguine about the war's economic impact on their livelihoods. The Danville Register's February 27, 1940, editorial argued that the war disrupted "ordinary trade." It asserted that the increased sale of American goods to the belligerents and Latin America would not bring prosperity to all Americans, much less Southerners. After all, the war had closed the South's lucrative European markets; tobacco exporters faced financial calamity. In its October, 1939, editorial, The Southern Planter,

---

[18] Ibid.; The Commonwealth, November, 1939, p. 4; Wolfe, "Virginia in World War II," p. 154; Richmond Times-Dispatch, August 7, 1940, p. 17, September 30, 1940, p. 9; Richmond News-Leader, November 30, 1940, p. 17.

[19] Wolfe, "Virginia in World War II," pp. 174-76; The Union News, September, 1941, pp. 2-3; James S. Wamsley and Anne M. Cooper, Idols, Victims, Pioneers: Virginia's Women from 1607 (Richmond: Virginia State Chamber of Commerce, 1976), pp. 281-82; Suzanne Lebsock, Virginia Women, 1600-1945: "A Share of Honour," (Richmond: Virginia State Library, 1987), pp. 128-29; "Resolution No. 5," Proceedings of the Forty-sixth Annual Convention of the Virginia State Federation of Labor, May 19-20, 1941, Norfolk, Virginia.

the state's leading agricultural journal, maintained that "wars are disastrous." They brought sudden inflation and ultimate deflation, falling prices, curtailed demand, bankruptcy, and farm foreclosures. The Planter cautioned its readers to avoid burdensome debt and keep livestock and staple crop production in line with visible demand. In December, 1940, the journal reiterated that warning and predicted that the following "war year" would bring "better markets at home, . . . somewhat higher prices, and . . . possibly the highest income since 1929." Farmers could also look forward to higher fertilizer, farm machinery, automobile, and building material costs, which would cut into their profits.[20] The Planter also maintained that due to the closing of their European markets, tobacco, cotton, wheat, and to a lesser extent, apple exporters, would face hard days ahead in 1941, and throughout the duration of the war. The journal held little hope that tobacco exports would find relief. The Planter did, however, believe that apple prices would rise in 1941--despite the loss of foreign markets--due to a smaller commercial crop the year before and increased domestic demand. The Richmond Times-Dispatch and the Danville Register shared the Planter's concern over the plight of Virginia's tobacco exports. The Dispatch also feared that if Germany won the war, tobacco growers might lose "virtually the entire European market, as well as that of England."[21]

The press' pessimistic outlook for Virginia agriculture was justified given the difficulties of the 1930s. Between 1929 and 1941, the relative importance of agriculture as a wage-producing source in Virginia declined. During that period, the total wages agriculture paid out decreased from $34.8 million to $25 million, a loss of $28.2%. Agriculture's entrepreneurial income declined $10 million, or 8.5% of the 1929 figure. During the Second World War, the state's agricultural sector did not flourish on the scale of manufacturing or federal service. Between 1940 and 1945, nearly 200,000 people left the farms for the armed forces or defense industry work. Virginia farmers faced shortages of fertilizer, machinery, and equipment.[22]

Nevertheless, during the war, the state's agricultural production rose dramatically; production per farm worker increased nearly 25%. From 1937 through 1941, there was a steady downward trend in combined acreage of grain and cultivated crops. After the United States entered the war, the combined acreage of principal crops was lower than it had been at any time since 1869. During the war years, however, nearly 58,000 acres were again brought under cultivation; crop yields per acre were considerably more than during the years 1937-41. Between 1941 and 1945, the combined acreage of small grains and

---

[20] Danville Register, February 27, 1940, p. 6; The Southern Planter, October, 1939, p. 6, December, 1940, pp. 8-9.

[21] The Southern Planter, December, 1940, pp. 8-9; Richmond Times-Dispatch, July 1, 1940, p. 10, October 17, 1941, p. 20; Danville Register, February 27, 1940, p. 6.

[22] Forty-fifth Annual Report, 1941, p. 13; Wolfe, "Virginia in World War II," 161-62; Harvey L. Price, Virginia Farmers at War: Essays on Agricultural Production in the Old Dominion During the Second World War (Blacksburg: The Virginia Agricultural Extension Service, Virginia Polytechnic Institute and State University, 1950), pp. 5-6.

cultivated crops averaged 4% less than during 1937-41. When the acreage of hay, which enjoyed the greatest increase of any other crop in the state was added, however, the harvested acreage of all major crops combined averaged 2% more during the war years than in the five-year period immediately before. From 1939 to 1940, the index of prices Virginia farmers received rose by only one point. The next year, however, the index of prices went up 25 points, or approximately 23%. A combination of higher prices and more units of production resulted in an increase of nearly $30 million from 1940 to 1941; that equaled a little less than 25% in the cash receipts of the state's farmers. In 1933, the total in cash receipts from farming was $79,387,000; six years later, it was $116,453,000; in 1941, it was $153,610,000, by 1945, it had reached $334,088,000. In 1942, the index of prices farmers received for their products rose fifty points or 38% from the previous year. Gross income was nearly 41% above that of 1941.[23]

World War II accelerated the pre-war trend towards increased modernization, mechanization, diversification, and rationalization of Virginia's agriculture. The initial fears of the state's farmers concerning the effects of the war on their livelihoods never materialized. Due to the demands of the war, Virginia's farmers increased production, obtained new markets, and received higher prices for their crops. They achieved the economic recovery and prosperity that had arrived much earlier for those Virginians employed in manufacturing, defense work, and federal service. Well before December 7, 1941, few Virginians were denied the fruits of their coveted "horn of plenty."[24]

---

[23] Price, Virginia Farmers, pp. 25-27, 84-85; Richmond Times-Dispatch, September 3, 1941, p. 10; Virginia Agriculture, 1900-1958: A Handbook of Information (Blacksburg: School of Agriculture, Virginia Polytechnic Institute and State University, 1960), p. 17.

[24] Wolfe, "Virginia in World War II," pp. 162-70.

CHAPTER VII

CAVALIER NEUTRALITY

During the pre-World War II Roosevelt era, a majority of Virginians supported American neutrality and greater presidential discretion over arms embargoes. Most of Virginia's "leadership elite" considered itself "internationalist," yet they opposed American involvement in European conflicts. Many Virginians were disillusioned with United States participation in the First World War. In 1917, Americans went to war to bring democracy and peace to Europe. Instead, poverty, disease, famine, economic ruin, utter devastation, lawlessness, immorality, revolution, civil war, communism, fascism, and Nazism swept the European continent. Consequently, between 1933 and 1939, anti-war sentiment was strong in the Old Dominion and throughout much of the United States. Like their fellow Americans, Virginians were bitter that their European "allies" had defaulted on their war debts to the United States. During the depths of the depression, Virginians were more concerned with their own economic survival than with rescuing Europe from its latest troubles. They believed that the United States should concentrate on economic recovery at home and avoid costly European entanglements. [1]

---

[1] George L. Grassmuck, Sectional Biases in Congress on Foreign Policy (Baltimore: The Johns Hopkins Press, 1951), p. 119. A November 17, 1935, Gallup Poll indicated that only 27% of Southerners (and 29% of all Americans) polled believed that the United States should join with other countries to end the aggression of one state against another. Public opinion revealed, however, that even before the Anschluss in 1937, a majority of Southerners believed that in the event of another major European war, the United States could or should not stay out of it. During the pre-World II period, Southerners were more interventionist than residents of any other region of the United States. According to the public opinion polls, a higher percentage of Southerners than any other sectional group supported revision of the Neutrality Act to permit the sale of arms to the Spanish Republicans (January, 1939) and the sale of war material to Britain and France in the event of war (March, July, and August, 1939), amendment of the Johnson Act so that Britain and France could borrow money from the United States government (May, 1939), and the use of American troops to aid the British and French in the event of war (April, May 1939). See Alfred O. Hero, Jr., The Southerner and World Affairs (Baton Rouge: Louisiana State University Press, 1965), pp. 91, 94-95. Also see George H. Gallup, The Gallup Poll: Public Opinion, 1935-1971, vol. I (New York: Random House, 1972), pp. 3,

Despite their sympathy for the Ethiopians, the Spanish Loyalists, and the Czechs, most Virginians wanted the United States to remain neutral during the Italian-Ethiopian conflict (1935-37), the Spanish Civil War (1936-39), and the Munich crisis (1938). Alexander W. Weddell articulated United States neutrality policy towards the end of the Spanish Civil War after becoming ambassador to Spain in May, 1939. Nevertheless, the state's black press opposed the Neutrality Act of 1935 because it banned the sale of weapons to Ethiopia during its struggle against Italian aggression. Black editors believed the United States government was hypocritical to prohibit arms sales to Ethiopia, while permitting the sale of oil and scrap iron to Italy. During the Spanish Civil War, Virginia's Catholics vigorously supported the arms embargo because it had the effect of aiding General Francisco Franco's Nationalist revolt against the leftist Republican government. Virginia's staunchly isolationist Catholic press persistently urged President Roosevelt not to lift the arms embargo. A number of Virginians endorsed the Ludlow Amendment of 1938, which would have required a national referendum on

---

137-38, 149, 152-54. Charles A. Beard, American Foreign Policy in the Making, 1932-1940: A Study of Responsibilities (New Haven: Yale University Press, 1946), pp. 43-44; John E. Wiltz, From Isolation to War, 1931-1941 (New York: Thomas Y. Crowell Company, 1968), pp. 16-17; Interview with Virginius Dabney, Richmond Virginia, November 28, 1986; Wayne S. Cole, Roosevelt and the Isolationists, 1932-45 (Lincoln, Nebraska, and London: University of Nebraska Press, 1983), pp. 8-9, 11; Robert A. Divine, The Illusion of Neutrality (Chicago: University of Chicago Press, 1962), pp. vii-ix; Donald F. Drummond, The Passing of American Neutrality, 1937-1941 (Ann Arbor: University of Michigan Press, 1955), p. 373; Robert A. Divine, "Franklin D. Roosevelt and Collective Security, 1933," Mississippi Valley Historical Review 48 (1961), p. 59; William E. Leuchtenburg, Franklin D. Roosevelt and the New Deal, 1932-1940 (New York: Harper & Row Publishers, 1963), p. 199. Robert Dallek argued that "Contrary to traditional belief, the 1930s were not a time of unrelieved isolationism in the United States." See Franklin D. Roosevelt and American Foreign Policy 1932-1945 (New York: Oxford University Press, 1979), pp. 78, 97, In The Challenge to Isolation, 1937-1940 (New York: Harper & Brothers Publishers, 1952; 1964), pp. 5-6, William L. Langer and S. Everett Gleason argued that Roosevelt overestimated isolationist strength and cohesion; according to public opinion polls taken before 1941, the public had been much less isolationist than many historians have maintained. Robert A. Divine agreed. See The Reluctant Belligerent: American Entry into World War II (New York: John Wiley & Sons, Inc., 1965; 1979). See also Divine's Roosevelt and World War II (Baltimore: Penguin Books, Inc., 1970); Manfred Jonas, Isolationism in America, 1935-1941 (Ithaca, N.Y.: Cornell University Press, 1966), pp. 24-26, 31.

a congressional declaration of war, except in case of invasion or threatened attack on the United States or its territories. Even the most vocal critics of British and French appeasement of Hitler urged American noninvolvement in the Munich crisis of 1938.

Most Virginians supported Roosevelt's pre-World War II internationalist foreign policy. The state's political elite provided the president with a "bedrock of support" for his discretionary neutrality position. A solid majority believed FDR was sincere in trying to keep the United States out of European wars. Few Virginians vigorously opposed the neutrality legislation of the 1930s, but many advocated greater executive discretion over arms embargoes. Most believed that the neutrality acts (despite their "flaws") and military preparedness would help prevent the United States from being dragged into another European war. Virginia's congressional delegation supported America's military buildup and overwhelmingly backed the Neutrality Acts of 1935, 1936, and 1937, despite their agreement with Roosevelt and Secretary of State Cordell Hull that greater presidential discretion over arms embargoes should be preserved. The state's elected representatives maintained that America's national security interests were best served if the president had the authority to discriminate against aggressor countries. Their constituents agreed.[2]

---

[2]Interview with Dabney, November 28, 1986; K. Richmond Temple, "Alexander Weddell: Virginian in Diplomatic Service," Virginia Cavalcade 24(1984), pp. 36-39. For a succinct summary of the meaning of neutrality and how countries have employed it from antiquity to the present, see Ruhl J. Bartlett, "Neutrality," in the Encyclopedia of American Foreign Policy ed. Alexander DeConde (New York: Charles Scribner's Sons, 1978), vol. 2, pp. 679-87. Bartlett wrote that "The term 'neutrality' is generally used to designate the legal status under international law of a sovereign state that wishes to avoid military involvement in a conflict between belligerent states and expects to enjoy its rights as well as to perform its duties as a neutral." (ibid., p. 679). For a discussion of the neutrality policy debate of the 1930s, see Edwin M. Borchard and William P. Lage, Neutrality for the United States (New Haven: Yale University Press, 1940; 1973). In The Illusion of Neutrality, Robert A. Divine traced the history of the neutrality legislation of the 1930s and examined its origins. He concluded that the enactment of congressional neutrality legislation marked the "high tide of American isolationism in the twentieth century." (ibid., p. vii). The American people's strong isolationist sentiments influenced FDR's decision to support a wartime arms embargo early in his administration. See Divine, "Roosevelt and Collective Security," pp. 43, 59. Roosevelt accepted congressional neutrality legislation, but he objected to those provisions that restricted his authority as president. See Divine, Roosevelt and World War II, pp. 5-6, 23. See

President Roosevelt later regretted signing the Neutrality Act of 1935, a temporary measure that limited his discretionary authority to decide whether or not to impose arms embargoes. Originally designed to preserve American neutrality in the Italian-Ethiopian conflict, the act called for a mandatory arms embargo, which was to be applied impartially to all belligerents; the president could not discriminate against the aggressor state when applying the embargo. The law also restricted American travel on belligerent ships and prohibited American vessels from carrying munitions to countries at war. It did not apply to raw materials that could be used for war (e.g. oil and scrap iron). Neither did it forbid loans and credits to belligerents. The act provided for a National Munitions Control Board-- under the secretary of state--to register and license munitions makers and shippers. In 1936, Roosevelt again acquiesced to the isolationist mood of Congress and the public and signed into law the Neutrality Act of 1936. That law extended the main provisions of the 1935 act (until May 1, 1937), included a loan ban, and provided the president with some discretion over implementation of its main provisions. The act did not include FDR's recommended restrictions on the abnormal export of nonmunition war materials to belligerents. Roosevelt also accepted the Neutrality Act of 1937, which retained many provisions of the 1935 and 1936 laws. It prohibited the arming of American merchant ships trading with belligerents and the use of American vessels for transporting munitions to belligerents. Most importantly,

---

Leuchtenburg, Roosevelt and the New Deal, pp. 199, 210-11, 218-20, 222; Dallek, Roosevelt and American Foreign Policy, pp. 102, 108, 140; Stuart L. Weiss, "American Foreign Policy and Presidential Power: The Neutrality Act of 1935," Journal of Politics 30 (1968): 672-95; Cole, Roosevelt and the Isolationists, pp. 163-65, 170-73, 176-79, 183-84, 186, 233; Drummond, Passing of American Neutrality, p. 373. A Gallup Poll taken on February 14, 1937, revealed that 53% of Southerners (and 66% of all Americans) polled expressed either neutrality or no opinion on which side they supported in the Spanish Civil War. According to Gallup Polls taken in November, 1935, and September, 1936, a majority (albeit the lowest percentage in the country) of Southerners polled believed that Congress should be required to obtain public approval (by means of a national vote) in order to declare war. A December 29, 1935, Gallup Poll showed that only 49% of Southerners supported an increase in army appropriations, while 57% supported greater navy appropriations, and 73% wanted increases in air force appropriations. By October, 1938, a solid majority of Southerners wanted the United States to build a larger army and a larger navy. According to an October 10, 1937, Gallup Poll, a higher percentage of Southerners (37%) than Americans as a whole (31%), believed that greater presidential discretion, rather than stricter neutrality laws, was the best way for the United States to keep out of war. See Gallup, The Gallup Poll, vol. I, pp. 3, 6-7, 35, 49-50, 71, 121-22.

the law permitted the sale of nonembargoed goods to belligerents on a cash-and-carry basis and applied to civil wars as well as wars between states.[3]

Between 1933 and 1941, on legislative matters pertaining to neutrality and "isolation," Southerners in Congress voted the least "isolationist." Virginia's elected representatives stood squarely behind FDR's "discretionary" neutrality policies and efforts to maintain world peace. Senators Carter Glass and Harry F. Byrd supported most of the neutrality legislation of the 1930s. Byrd did not, however, support the Johnson Amendment (1934), which prohibited non-government loans to countries that had defaulted on their war debts to the United States. He believed that the act, a precursor to the neutrality acts, would tie the president's hands in the negotiations at the Geneva Disarmament Conference. Roosevelt did not publicly support or oppose the bill. On February 2, 1934, the Senate passed the amendment without debate, without dissent, and without record vote. The House of Representatives gave two-thirds approval of the bill on April 4, 1934, without a roll-call vote. On January 10, 1938, the entire nine-man Virginia House delegation voted with the majority in rejecting a discharge resolution to allow consideration, debate, or vote on the Ludlow Amendment (1938), which would have required public consent for foreign wars. The amendment was a clear manifestation of isolationist and pacifist strength throughout the United States. The fact that it was never formally debated or voted on in the House, however, symbolized FDR's growing strength vis-a-vis the isolationists.[4]

No one in Virginia's congressional delegation cast votes against the Neutrality Acts of 1935, 1936, and 1937. On August 21, 1935, the Senate

---

[3]Cole, Roosevelt and the Isolationists, pp. 163, 165, 171, 176, 178-79, 183-84, 231, 233.

[4]Robert A. Dahl, Congress and Foreign Policy (New York: Harcourt, Brace & Company, 1950), pp. 191-93; Carter Glass to Francis J. Byrne, January 18, 1939, Carter Glass Papers, University of Virginia Library, Charlottesville, Virginia; Harry F. Byrd to Douglas S. Freeman, June 6, 1933, Douglas S. Freeman Papers, Library of Congress, Washington, D.C.; Cole, Roosevelt and the Isolationists, pp. 89-92, 94, 253, 259-61; Congressional Record, 73d Congress, 2d sess., 1934, 78: 1822-24, 6048-57; Ibid., 75th Congress, 3d sess., 1938, 83: 282-83. The best account of the Ludlow Amendment can be found in Ernest C. Bolt, Jr.'s Ballots Before Bullets: The War Referendum Approach to Peace in America, 1914-1941 (Charlottesville: University Press of Virginia, 1977), pp. 152-85. According to public opinion polls conducted from late 1935 through 1937, a majority of Americans and Southerners supported a war referendum. See Gallup, Gallup Poll, vol. I, pp. 3, 35, 71.

passed the Neutrality Act of 1935 (S.J. Res. 173) without debate, without objection, and without record vote. Two days later, the House adopted unanimously S.J. Res. 173 with minor changes in munitions control provisions and without a record vote. The following day, the Senate approved the House amendments to the resolution by a 79 to 2 vote; fifteen senators did not vote. Senator Glass voted with the majority. Byrd was detained from the Senate and was announced for the amendments. President Roosevelt signed S.J. Res. 173 into law on August 31, 1935.[5]

On February 17, 1936, the House passed the Neutrality Act of 1936 (H.J. Res. 491) by a 353 to 27 vote; fifty representatives did not vote. Virginia's congressman voted with the majority. Representative Andrew Jackson Montague did not vote, but was in a general pair with Congressman Ekwall, who also did not vote. The Senate adopted the House bill without a record vote. On February 29, 1936, Roosevelt signed the resolution into law.[6]

Nearly a year later, on March 3, 1937, the Senate passed the Neutrality Act of 1937 (S.J. Res. 51) by a 63 to 6 vote. Senator Glass was detained due to illness and was paired with Senator Henrik Shipstead, who also did not vote. Byrd was announced for the resolution. The House passed a similar measure allowing greater presidential discretion, especially on cash-and-carry, by a 376 to 12 vote. On April 29, 1937, both the Senate and House adopted the conference report to S.J. Res. 51. The Senate vote was 41 to 15 in favor, with 39 not voting. Senator Glass was again detained by an illness in his family and did not vote; he was paired with Senator Shipstead. Byrd was absent, attending ex-Governor John G. Pollard's funeral; however, he was paired for adoption of the conference report. Roosevelt signed the "permanent" Neutrality Act of 1937 into law on May 1, 1937.[7]

---

[5]Congressional Record, 74th Congress, 1st sess., 1935, 79: 13951-56; Ibid., 74th Congress, 1st sess., 1935, 79:14283-84, 14430-34; Entire Voting Record of Senator Harry F. Byrd By Subject From March 4, 1933, to October 13, 1962, p. 381, Box 349, Harry F. Byrd Papers, University of Virginia Library, Charlottesville, Virginia; Cole, Roosevelt and the Isolationists, pp. 163-86.

[6]Congressional Record, 74th Congress, 2d sess., 1936, 80:2253; Ibid., 74th Congress, 2d sess., 1936, 80:2291-2306; Cole, Roosevelt and the Isolationists, pp. 182-86.

[7]Congressional Record, 75th Congress, 1st sess., 1937, 81:1798-1807; Ibid., 75th Congress, 1st sess., 1937, 81:3961-62; Entire Voting Record of Senator Harry F. Byrd, p. 382, Box 349, Byrd Papers; Cole, Roosevelt and the Isolationists, pp. 223-38.

Third district Representative Andrew Jackson Montague, a trustee of the Carnegie Endowment for International Peace, was an outspoken internationalist and peace advocate. From 1920 to 1924, he served as president of the American Peace Society. Montague also served as American delegate to the Third Conference of American Republics at Rio de Janeiro (1906), delegate to the Third International Conference on Maritime Law at Brussels (1909-10), president of the American Society for Judicial Settlement of International Disputes (1917), president of the American Group of Interparliamentary Union (1930-35), and vice-president of the union (1936). The congressman believed that the bulk of the neutrality legislation of the 1930s was consistent with the cause of world peace. Nevertheless, he opposed the Ludlow Amendment as impractical. Montague, a member of the House Committee on the Judiciary that considered the amendment, was in favor of holding a public hearing on the bill. In his March 27, 1935, letter to Representative Louis Ludlow, Montague wrote:

> No one deplores war more than I do, and no one is more earnestly in favor of means to lessen wars than myself. But I doubt the practicability of your amendment. If other nations would adopt your plan I would be heartily for it. But will they do so? I appreciate that you exclude the operation of a referendum in the event of an invasion of the United States, but much valuable time would be lost by us in taking a referendum of the people before actual invasion may have occurred.

(Montague was no longer sitting in the House when it rejected a discharge resolution on the Ludlow Amendment on January 10, 1938.)[8]

Throughout his congressional career, Representative Clifton A. Woodrum of the sixth district maintained that a strong national defense and military preparedness were the best ways to guarantee American neutrality and world peace. As early as 1927, when the United States enjoyed peace and prosperity, the Roanoke congressman urged his House colleagues to support appropriations for the construction of additional battle cruisers for the

---

[8]James Brown Scott to Andrew Jackson Montague, October 21, 1930, Scott to Montague, November 5, 1930, "Congressman Andrew Jackson Montague, The People's Choice," (1936 election pamphlet), Philip Allen Swartz to Montague, August 22, 1935, Montague to Swartz, August 23, 1935, Francis P. Gaines to Montague, March 19, 1935, Montague to Gaines, March 20, 1935, Louis Ludlow to Montague, March 26, 1935, Montague to Ludlow, March 27, 1935, Andrew Jackson Montague Papers, Virginia State Library, Richmond Virginia; Congressional Record, 75th Congress, 3d sess., 1938, 83:282-83.

navy. Woodrum assured his fellow representatives that he was "not a militarist." He declared that he "abhor[ed] war" and "would not knowingly lend" his support or vote to any program that espoused American militarism. Nevertheless, he said he was "unwilling that we [the House] should deliberately and unreasonably weaken out [America's] national defense on the seas, on the land, or in the air." To repeated applause Woodrum asserted:

> Until such time as all nations of the earth can meet and agree upon some plan to reduce naval and military strength, I want to see America go froward with a steady, orderly, and progressive strengthening of her Military Establishment on the seas, on land, and in the air, so that at all times she may not only be willing but ready and able to defend her traditions and protect her citizens and their property.[9]

In October, 1937, Woodrum reiterated that message in an address before the Roanoke Rotary Club. He also voiced support for Roosevelt's international negotiations for peace and maintained that "America can be spared the wasteful effects of another war" through its advocacy of world peace, freedom of the seas for all, and a public declaration that it would protect itself. Woodrum declared that the United States could best guarantee noninvolvement in "European entanglements" though military preparedness. After his close 1938 re-election campaign, he continued to argue that defense spending needed to be increased in light of fascist aggression in Europe and Japanese expansion in Asia. On June 22, 1939, Woodrum joined his fellow Virginians in the House in opposing an amendment to the Army Appropriations Bill for 1940, which proposed to reduce by 1,283 the number of new airplanes to be purchased for the army. Earlier that year--on February 23--Woodrum and the rest of the Virginia House delegation, with the exception of the seventh district's A. Willis Robertson, opposed an amendment to the Guam Naval Base Bill, which deleted a navy appropriation of $5 million for harbor improvements.[10]

Despite his differences with Roosevelt over domestic policy, Woodrum--a fiscal conservative--continued to support the president's foreign policy. In

---

[9] "National Defense and Preparedness," Addresses and Speeches of Clifton A. Woodrum, Clifton A. Woodrum Papers, Roanoke Public Library, Roanoke, Virginia.

[10] Ibid.; Roanoke World-News, October 15, 1937, p. 1; The New Republic, May 18, 1942, pp. 699, 701-702; James E. Sargent, "Woodrum's Economy Bloc: The Attack on Roosevelt's WPA, 1937-1939," Virginia Magazine of History and Biography 92 (1985), pp. 181-85, 203; Roanoke Times, November 20, 1938, p. 1.

July, 1939, he maintained:

> Whatever may be the difference of opinion relative to some of the economic policies of the president, in my judgment the overwhelming majority of our citizens are in accord with the foreign policy of the administration as carried out by the president and the state department.

Woodrum supported FDR's neutrality policies and asserted that probably no critical issue that had emerged during his administration had "found such unanimity of opinion behind the president." He argued that the American people wanted peace and noninvolvement in European problems. Woodrum concluded that Americans "realize[d] that the best way to peace is to have sane and sensible foreign policy and to avoid taking a position which would not be in accord with our traditional policy."[11]

The highest ranking and most influential Virginian among Roosevelt's foreign policy advisers was Judge R. Walton Moore. As assistant secretary of state, Moore helped draft much of the administration's neutrality legislation during the 1930s. He also assumed the leading State Department role in the evolution of the Johnson Act (1934), which signified American disillusionment with Europe after the First World War. Moore maintained that Roosevelt supported the act--with amendments--despite the fact that he did not publicly express his opinion on it.[12]

In April, 1934, Secretary of State Cordell Hull asked Moore and other high-ranking State Department officials to study and make recommendations on neutrality policies. Due to administration, State Department, congressional, and public divisiveness on that issue, Moore advised Hull in February, 1935, that Roosevelt should delay recommending any neutrality legislation. On July 10, 1935, Moore and Hull testified before the Foreign Relations Committee in opposition to the Nye-Clark neutrality resolutions, which would have severely restricted American shipping and commerce during wartime and sharply curtailed presidential discretion over arms embargoes. Moore supported neutrality legislation, but opposed the mandatory arms embargoes that would have applied to all belligerents.[13]

---

[11] Roanoke Times, July 23, 1939, p. 1.

[12] Cole, Roosevelt and the Isolationist, pp. 92-94.

[13] Ibid., pp. 165-66, 170-83; R. Walton Moore to Douglas S. Freeman, April 19, 1935, Freeman Papers.

Three days before Roosevelt signed the Neutrality Act of 1935 into law, Moore enclosed in a letter to the president an August 27 memo on neutrality in which he criticized "The unwisdom of the mandatory embargo proposition" because it precluded American ordnance assistance to its friends during wartime. He wrote:

> no other nation has yet placed itself under a mandate to prevent the exportation of munitions of war, and ... it would be highly undesirable for our Government to announce to the world in advance of all that may possibly occur hereafter that we are under such a mandate.

Moore argued that it was "certainly not a time, when the future is so unpredictable, to tie our hands in advance instead of leaving a discretion to the President, who is primarily responsible for our international affairs." The assistant secretary also expressed opposition to Senate resolutions that would prevent Americans during wartime from shipping things other than munitions of war and even from shipping anything that any belligerent might consider contraband. Moore asserted:

> It would seem unthinkable that should two countries engage in a war, we will accord to either one of them the right to say to this Government that it shall make no shipment to either belligerent of any of the articles that are commonly exported, whether industrial or agricultural, and in that way subject ourselves absolutely to the will of another nation, whether powerful or insignificant.

He also disputed the view that presidential discretion over arms embargoes would give the president an opportunity to embroil the United States in war through the application of an embargo to one belligerent and not its adversary. Moore argued that presidential discretion would give the president no more power than he already enjoyed to involve the United States in war; as commander-in-chief of the armed forces he could attack and invade other countries in conducting American foreign policy.[14]

As assistant secretary of state, Moore also influenced the final form of the 1936 Neutrality Act. On December 31, 1935, he met with Roosevelt, Secretary Hull, Senator Key Pittman, Congressman Sam McReynolds, and Congressman John O'Connor at the White House to decide on the key provisions of the administration's revised neutrality legislation. During the evolution of that legislation, Moore even provided legal advice to Senator

---

[14]Edgar B. Nixon, ed. Franklin D. Roosevelt and Foreign Affairs, vol. 2 (Cambridge: The Belknap Press of Harvard University Press, 1969), pp. 623-28.

Hiram Johnson, an isolationist opponent of greater presidential discretion over arms embargoes. Johnson led the opposition in the Senate Foreign Relations Committee to the administration's neutrality proposal, which would have given the president discretionary power to limit the export to belligerents of nonembargoed war materials (excluding food, medical supplies, and clothing) to normal peacetime levels. The senator's state of California produced oil and cotton (i.e. raw materials essential for war), the export of which could have been limited under the administration's proposal. Both Moore and Johnson objected to the mandatory Nye-Clark resolution (that would have included nonmunition materials) and the administration's discretionary proposal.[15]

Moore agreed with Roosevelt that the arms embargo should be applied to civil wars. At a December 30, 1936, meeting with the president, Pittman, McReynolds, and others, then Acting Secretary of State Moore supported legislation to ban arms shipments to Spain during its civil war. Another meeting on January 5, 1937, determined that Pittman would introduce emergency legislation in the Senate calling for an embargo on the shipment of arms and munitions to Spain and McReynolds would sponsor similar legislation in the House. On January 6, Congress approved a ban on the sale and export of all arms, munitions, and implements of war to both the Loyalists and the Nationalists. It also prohibited the sale of munitions to neutrals for transshipment to Spain. Two days later, FDR signed the bill into law without reservation. A week later, Moore and Green H. Hackworth, a State Department legal advisor, represented the department at a Senate Foreign Relations Committee executive session. Moore urged the senators to support more discretionary neutrality legislation. He cautioned them against "legislation which will induce all the other nations of the world to channel their trade to other markets than the American markets." Moore concluded that the Pittman resolution was adequate, despite the fact that it fell short of providing as much presidential discretion as the administration wanted. After the Senate adopted Pittman's bill on March 3, Moore wrote the president that it was "a fairly liberal measure and the best that anyone knowing the situation could expect the Senate to pass."[16]

Like their co-religionists throughout the country, most of Virginia's Roman Catholics (less than 1 percent of the total population) were stalwart isolationists. Distrustful of European entanglements and anxious to keep America out of war, they vigorously supported the neutrality legislation of the 1930s, including the rejected Ludlow Amendment. Catholics throughout the

---

[15] Cole, Roosevelt and the Isolationists, pp. 182-84.

[16] Ibid., pp. 225-27, 231-33.

Old Dominion strongly believed that the Neutrality Acts of 1935, 1936, and 1937, were the best guarantees to prevent the United States from being dragged into another European war. They maintained that adherence to America's traditional isolationist policy was in the best interests of the country's national security. Isolationism, they argued, was also in the interests of world peace and domestic economic recovery. Nearly four years after President Roosevelt signed the 1935 Neutrality Act into law, the Virginia Catholic asserted that "the United States has simply no business meddling in European quarrels. Meddling will lead us straight into a war in which we will have no proper interest, for which we are unprepared and out of which we can gain only loss."[17]

Virginia's Catholic press, clergy, and lay leaders urged American neutrality during the Spanish Civil War. Staunchly anti-Communist and sympathetic to Franco's Nationalist rebellion, they pressured President Roosevelt not to lift the arms embargo. The Catholic press regularly lambasted the secular press for ignoring Republican atrocities against the church in Spain. The Virginia Catholic bitterly castigated "liberal" editors and columnists who praised the Loyalist regime. In its March, 1939, editorial, the official diocesan paper criticized a Richmond Times-Dispatch editorial that had warned Catholics sympathetic to the Nationalists that a Franco victory might encourage his Nazi allies to further their persecution of German Catholics. The Catholic maintained that it was "at least as likely that a victorious Franco will be able to exert on Herr Hitler considerable influence against German religious persecution." The paper asserted that Catholic sympathy for Franco was based on spiritual, not political factors. The Spanish Civil War, it argued, was a struggle between Christ and the Antichrist. Any outcome of the war "short of complete victory for General Franco," it concluded, "would mean the extirpation of the Faith in Spain."[18]

---

[17] George Q. Flynn, Roosevelt and Romanism: Catholics and American Diplomacy, 1937-1945 (Westport, Conn. and London: Greenwood Press, 1976), pp. 17-19, 22, 51-55, 64; Howard Odum, Southern Regions of the United States (Chapel Hill: The University of North Carolina Press, 1936), pp. 140-42; Virginia Catholic, October, 1935, p. 7, April, 1936, p. 10, December, 1936, p. 7, February, 1938, p. 10, December, 1938, p. 12, March, 1939, p. 12, May, 1939, p. 6, June, 1939, p. 18, September, 1939, p. 6.

[18] Flynn, Roosevelt and Romanism, pp. 19, 33-36, 51-55. For a succinct account of Catholic pressure on FDR to keep the arms embargo, see Wilson D. Miscamble, "Catholics and American Foreign Policy from McKinley to McCarthy: A Historiographical Survey," Diplomatic History 4(1980): 223-40. Also see J. David Valaik, "Catholics, Neutrality and the Spanish Embargo, 1937-39," Journal of American History, 54 (1967) pp.84-85; Virginia Catholic,

Protestant opinion was equally opposed to American involvement in European conflicts and wars. Anti-war feeling was strong among Baptist, Methodist, Presbyterian, Brethren, and Quaker clergy and leadership elites. Support for neutrality legislation was generally accepted. Brethren and Quaker representatives urged Senator Glass to support strong neutrality legislation. Justification for defensive wars and the Ludlow Amendment lacked a consensus. A number of protestant clergy disapproved of the growing arms race at home and abroad. Prominent protestant editors believed that America's military buildup during the mid-1930s was unnecessary and did nothing to promote world peace.[19]

When Senator Gerald P. Nye's Munitions Investigating Committee heard its last witness on February 20, 1936, the peace movement in the United States had reached its peak of influence. Despite its failure to prove that munitions makers and Wall Street had been responsible for pushing the United States into the First World War, the Nye committee, nevertheless, succeeded in promoting anti-war and isolationist sentiment throughout the

---

July, 1936, p. 10, September, 1936, p. 9, October, 1936, p. 5, July, 1937, p. 7, 12, 41-42, August, 1937, p. 7, January, 1939, pp. 3, 32, February, 1939, p. 22, March, 1939, p. 7; membership of the Edward Douglass White Council, No. 2473, Knights of Columbus, Arlington, Virginia, to Carter Glass, February 2, 1939, January 25, 1939, telegram from the Very Reverend F. Joseph Magri, Dean (representing Tidewater, Virginia Catholic Churches) to Glass, Francis J. Byrne, managing editor, The Catholic Virginian Press, Inc., Richmond, Virginia, to Glass, January 17, 1939, Estelle L. Raukin (representing the Virginia organization of the Catholic Daughters of America) to Glass, January 10, 1939, Glass Papers.

[19]Religious Herald, November 16, 1933, pp. 8-9, March 1, 1934, pp. 5-6, May 10, 1934, p. 10, April 25, 1935, pp. 8-9, 16, May 30, 1935, p. 10, September 12, 1935, p. 10, November 19, 1936, pp. 16-17, December 3, 1936, p. 6, May 20, 1937, p. 10, December 16, 1937, p. 10, December 30, 1937, pp. 10-11, February 24, 1938, p. 10, March 3, 1938, p. 11, September 22, 1938, pp. 10, 19, October 6, 1938, p. 10; Richmond Christian Advocate, April 29, 1937, pp. 3-4, September 16, 1937, p. 4, December 23, 1937, p. 2, May 18, 1939, pp. 10-11, August 31, 1939, p. 14; Presbyterian of the South and the Presbyterian Standard, September 20, 1933, p. 6, May 8, 1935, p. 2, November 6, 1935, pp. 3-5, June 10, 1936, pp. 3-4, May 19, 1937, pp. 2-3, November 3, 1937, pp. 2-3; Rev. Foster M. Bittinger to Glass, March 2, 1937, Rev. M. E. Clingenpeel to Glass, February 10, 1937, Mrs. Paul E. Hoover to Glass, February 2, 1937, Lucille Long to Glass, February 1, 1937, J. M. Foster to Glass, January 29, 1937, March 3, 1937, telegram from Mary L. Babb (representing Sedley, Virginia Friends) to Glass, Glass Papers.

country. Most importantly, it helped lay the foundation for the neutrality legislation of the 1930s. The Richmond Peace Council, the state's most influential anti-war (albeit internationalist) organization, was one of many such groups throughout the United States somewhat influenced by the Nye committee's assault on the country's nascent military-industrial complex.[20]

The Richmond Peace Council's membership consisted almost entirely of prominent citizens from the Richmond area. Despite its influence in the community, it did not have a large membership. The council was essentially a group of peace elites with internationalist views. Few of its members were pacifists. It held its first meeting on March 6, 1933, at St. Paul's (Episcopal) Parish House across the street from the state capitol. The founding members of the council, originally called the "Committee Named to Compose a Permanent Council on Peace," discussed future plans for their essentially educational organization. Three weeks later, the council held its second meeting--again at St. Paul's--and elected officers. Governor John G. Pollard was elected honorary chairman; Judge J. Hoge Ricks was chosen chairman; the Rev. G. Edwin Osborn, pastor of the Hanover Avenue Christian Church, was elected 1st vice-chairman; May Moore was selected 2nd vice-chairman; Rabbi Joseph E. Raffaeli was named treasurer; and Dr. Emily Gardner was elected secretary. The members also adopted the following policy:

> The purpose of the Richmond Peace Council shall be to promote World Peace and to further the outlaw and abolition of war through International Cooperation by means of education or otherwise, working through existing organizations as far as possible.

(By mid-October, 1936, the council's opposition to war extended to "resolutely" refusing "to approve of or participate in ANY war," "Except in case of an actual, unprovoked, armed invasion of continental United States by a foreign foe.") The organization held its third meeting in June, 1933, at which time it was decided to draft a resolution requesting that conscientious objectors not be denied American citizenship. The council intended to present the resolution to other organizations for their endorsement before sending it to Secretary of Labor Frances Perkins.[21]

---

[20] See Cole, Roosevelt and the Isolationists, pp. 141-62, for a superb account of the Nye committee's investigation of the munitions industry between 1934-36. Wiltz, From Isolationism to War, pp. 15-17.

[21] Minutes of the March 6, 1933, meeting of the Richmond Peace Council, minutes of the March 27, 1933, meeting of the council, minutes of the June, 1933, meeting of the council, Elsie F. Greentree to Emily Gardner, April 24, 1934, J. Shelton Horsley to Rev. R. T. Marsh, October 14, 1936, Richmond

In 1934, the council sponsored speakers and organized a peace essay contest for Richmond's public and private schools. All but one school-- McGuires--participated. At its April 6 meeting, the group went on record favoring the World Court treaties. Earlier in the year, council members voiced concern over budgetary increases in arms production throughout the world, including the United States. At its April 30 meeting, the council agreed to send a telegram to President Roosevelt protesting the national naval building program.[22]

During the following year, the peace council expanded its influence throughout the community. Some council members urged Senators Glass and Byrd to support Senator Nye's resolution calling for a Senate appropriation of $100,000 for continuation of the Senate Munitions Investigation Committee. (In 1936, Glass opposed giving the Nye committee additional funds; he led the attack that helped end the Nye investigation.) The organization unanimously agreed to cooperate with the Richmond Forum in securing Senator Nye as a speaker at a large meeting. The council also continued to sponsor its peace essay contest in Richmond's schools. During the course of the year, nearly 1,000 essays were written and prizes awarded. In his March 30, 1936, letter addressed "To the Friends of Peace," Dr. Edward N. Calisch, rabbi of Congregation Beth Ahabah and chairman of the essay committee, wrote: "The Richmond Peace Council has devoted itself to this task" to "educate our own youth concerning the causes and horrors of War and inculcate in their minds the spirit of Peace."[23]

In his March 30, 1935, letter to fellow members, the Rev. Osborn, past chairman of the council, wrote that the group should register a "vigorous protest" against the arms buildup. He urged council members to indicate their displeasure over "ever-increasing appropriations for military and naval

---

Peace Council Papers, James Branch Cabell Library, Virginia Commonwealth University, Richmond, Virginia.

[22] Greentree to Gardner, April 24, 1934, minutes of the January 12, 1934, meeting of the council, minutes of the April 6, 1934, meeting of the council, minutes of the April 30, 1934, meeting of the council, Richmond Peace Council Papers.

[23] Rev. G. Edwin Osborn to Mrs. J. L. Buck, May 15, 1935, Rabbi Edward N. Calisch to fellow members of the Richmond Peace Council, n.d., Box 13, minutes of the January 8, 1935, meeting of the council, Calisch, et al., "To the Friends of Peace," March 30, 1936, Richmond Peace Council Papers; Osborn to Glass, January 30, 1936, Glass Papers; Cole, <u>Roosevelt and the Isolationists</u>, pp. 157-58.

purposes" in letters to the president and their congressmen. Later that year, the council discussed American neutrality during the Italian-Ethiopian war. Members considered how the United States could best serve the cause of peace during that conflict. Osborn branded Italy the aggressor in his January 30, 1936, letter to Senator Glass. He urged the United States to "do everything in its power to cooperate with the League of Nations in bringing all reasonable pressure to stop this unjust and cruel war."[24]

During the fall of 1936, the council participated in a series of local meetings under the auspices of various churches, schools, and service organizations. The council organized two mass meetings and other activities in conjunction with the Philadelphia-based Emergency Peace Campaign, a member of the National Peace Conference. That organization's internationalist, anti-war agenda included support for passage of the "widest and tightest possible mandatory neutrality legislation, including embargoes on munitions, essential raw materials, loans, and credits," "reduction of our [American] military and naval forces to the minimum for defense from actual invasion of Continental America, as a first step toward total and universal disarmament," "the Ludlow Resolution or similar legislation calling for a referendum of all people in case of war," passage of the Nye-Kvale Bills to amend the National Defense Act (to limit its application in case of civil institutions to those offering elective course in military training), and "passage of the [Pope] Resolution authorizing membership of the United States in the League [of Nations], recognizing the Pact of Paris as the guiding principle of the League Covenant, and specifically exempting the United States from using armed force for the League."[25]

The Emergency Peace Campaign organized mass meetings in 500 towns and cities throughout the country during its campaign to keep the United States out of war. It set up organizations in Richmond, Norfolk, Hampton, Petersburg, Danville, Roanoke, and Lynchburg. The organization arranged for fifty pigeons carrying a peace message from First Lady Eleanor Roosevelt to arrive in Richmond on April 22, 1936. A week later, Dr. McNeill Poteat, Jr., a prominent Southern Baptist minister from Raleigh, North Carolina,

---

[24] Osborn to fellow members of the Richmond Peace Council, March 30, 1935, synopsis of minutes of the October 31, 1935, meeting of the council, Richmond Peace Council Papers; Osborn to Glass, January 30, 1936, Glass Papers.

[25] Minutes of the June 9, 1936, meeting of the Richmond Peace Council, Horsley to Virginius Dabney, October 9, 1936, Robert W. Ehrman to Jane Dickey, June 26, 1936, "Emergency Peace Campaign Legislative Program," Box 13, Richmond Peace Council Papers.

spoke on peace issues--under the sponsorship of both the Emergency Peace Campaign and the Richmond Peace Council--to the First Baptist Church and the Rotary Club in Richmond.[26]

On the eve of its Armistice Day, 1936, anti-war rally at the Mosque Theatre in Richmond, the peace council presented an "Interviews for Peace" program on WRVA radio. Three of the organization's most prominent members were interviewed: Dr. J. Shelton Horsley, attending surgeon at St. Elizabeth's Hospital and council chairman, Dr. Beverly D. Tucker, rector of St. Paul's Episcopal Church, and Dr. Edward N. Calisch, past chairman of the council and its executive committee. Calisch emphasized the need for "stricter and more inclusive neutrality legislation as proposed by President Roosevelt recently." Horsley cited secret alliances, militarism, nationalism, economic imperialism, and propaganda as the underlying causes of the First World War. Tucker indicated his support for the League of Nations, the World Court, and the need for "stronger neutrality legislation providing for mandatory embargoes on munitions, loans, credits, and essential materials of warfare to belligerents" during wartime. He also endorsed the use of American military power for defensive purposes only, reciprocal trade agreements, international cooperation to insure currency stabilization and access to raw materials and markets for all nations, taxation of wars profits, nationalization of the munitions industry, and "international cooperation for the settlement of disputes by peaceful means in accordance with the principles of the Kellogg-Pact including adherence to the new world court."[27]

From August 6 to November 9, 1936, council chairman Horsley received nearly thirty letters of support and/or requests for tickets to the November 11, 1936, peace rally at the Richmond Mosque, from diverse

---

[26]The University of Richmond's Peace Council was affiliated with the Emergency Peace Campaign. Samuel T. Schroetter, Jr., and Louise Eisen to W. W. Savage, September 28, 1938, James H. Price Executive Papers, Virginia State Library, Richmond, Virginia; Constance Rumbough to Dabney, February 2, 1937, Horsley to Marsh, October 14, 1936, minutes of the April 7, 1936, meeting of the Richmond Peace Council, John Dillingham to Emergency Peace Campaign staff and local peace council chairman, n.d., Box 13, Richmond Peace Council's news release of April 20 and April 22, 1936, "Dr. Poteat's Address," Box 13, Richmond Peace Council Papers.

[27]Edith Lindeman Calisch, "Edward Nathan Calisch: A Biography," in Three Score and Twenty (Richmond: Old Dominion Press, 1945), p. 19; Dickey to Osborn, March 4, 1936, transcript of Richmond Peace Council's radio address, "Interviews for Peace," over WRVA, November 10, 1936, pp. 1-9, Richmond Peace Council Papers.

religious, service, social, educational, professional, business, labor, patriotic, and veterans' organizations across the state. They ranged from the American Legion to the president of Bridgewater College, a Church of the Brethren (pacifist) institution. Despite considerable effort, council chairman Horsley was unable to get Admiral Richard E. Byrd to give the keynote address. Byrd, a friend of President Roosevelt and Antarctic/Arctic explorer, navigator, and aviator, was also an outspoken peace advocate. He proposed that the English-speaking countries support a six-month moratorium on war. (The admiral discussed his peace activities with First Lady Eleanor Roosevelt). In his July 3, 1936, letter to Horsley, Byrd explained that a previous commitment (i.e. radio broadcast) precluded his accepting the council's invitation to speak at the rally. The admiral wrote: "I want you to know that I am deeply interested in the work of the Richmond Peace Council and I have a very friendly and enthusiastic feeling towards what you are trying to do and all the members of the Council [sic]." Byrd assured Horsley that he would follow the council's work "with great interest." He also expressed disappointment that he was unable to come to Richmond and wished the council "good luck" with its "splendid efforts." He agreed, however, to send an address to be ready at the rally. (On April 6, 1937, Byrd launched his "No-Foreign-War Crusade" with a nation-wide radio broadcast. The admiral was honorary chairman of the "crusade," which was designed to "increase and make articulate the determination of the American people not to be drawn into a war in Europe and Asia." The "crusade" maintained that American military power should be restricted to the defense of the country and not be used to protect commercial investments abroad. Byrd also served as chairman of the Emergency Peace Campaign in 1937).[28]

Dr. S. C. Mitchell, a University of Richmond professor, read Admiral Byrd's address at the November 11 mass meeting. Dr. Horsley read a page from Byrd's diary, which described his conversion to the cause of peace. The rally also included: an invocation by Dr. Churchill Gibson, rector of St. James's Episcopal Church, a prayer for peace by Dr. Calisch, a benediction

---

[28] See Richard E. Byrd to Eleanor Roosevelt, July 6, 1937, Byrd to Franklin D. Roosevelt, July 6, 1937, Roosevelt to Byrd, August 16, 1937, Byrd to Roosevelt, July 31, 1939, Roosevelt to Byrd, August 2, 1939, President's Personal File 201, Franklin D. Roosevelt Papers, Franklin D. Roosevelt Library, Hyde Park, N.Y.; Box 13, Horsley to Dabney, June 22, 1936, Dabney to Horsley, June 24, 1936, Byrd to Horsley, July 3, 1936, Horsley to Byrd, July 8, 1936, Dabney to Horsley, July 9, 1936, Horsley to Dabney, July 20, 1936. "Let's Keep Out of War!" pamphlet of the Emergency Peace Campaign, Box 13, Richmond Peace Council Papers; Richmond Times-Dispatch, April 22, 1937, p. 12; Alexandria Gazette, April 17, 1937, p. 4; Frank Freidel Franklin D. Roosevelt, vol. 3 (Boston Little, Brown & Co., 1952-1973), p. 214.

from Bishop Peter L. Ireton of the Roman Catholic Diocese of Richmond, introductory remarks by Dr. Horsley, introduction of the guest speaker by J. Fulmer Bright, mayor of Richmond, and the keynote speech by Dr. Francis P. Gaines, president of Washington and Lee University. In his letter inviting Gaines to speak (in place of Byrd), Horsley wrote that he knew "of no more pressing national need at present than public instruction of the uselessness of war."[29]

Four months prior to the Mosque rally, the Richmond Peace Council was--in the words of its chairman, Dr. Horsley--"as yet not a very strong group." Less than two months after the rally, however, the council felt strong enough to "approve in principle" the placement of a regional office of the Emergency Peace Campaign in Richmond. When Dr. Beverly Tucker assumed the presidency of the council in May, 1937, a number of the city's leading citizens were still active members: Virginius Dabney, Dr. Douglas S. Freeman, Dr. Edward N. Calisch, Judge James H. Ricks, Dr. J. Shelton Horsley, Dr. S. C. Mitchell, Rabbi Sydney M. Lefkowitz, and Dr. F. W. Boatwright, president of the University of Richmond. As late as December, 1937, the council's executive committee discussed the possibility of reorganization, expansion of membership, and establishment of an area office in Richmond to accelerate peace activities in Virginia and North Carolina. Nevertheless, by 1938, interest in the organization began to taper off as pacifist influence nationwide started to wane. As early as October, 1937, the Emergency Peace Campaign was quite concerned about unpaid pledges among its Richmond followers.[30]

A somewhat similar anti-war group existed in the city of Petersburg. The Peace Council of Petersburg described itself as "a local and independent peace society" dedicated to "organizing and educating the people of our city and district in the means for developing peaceful and secure relationships between nations." The organization opposed militarism and entanglements

---

[29] "Mass Meeting At the Mosque, November 11, 1936, 8 p.m." (Armistice Day Rally program sponsored by the Richmond Peace Council), Box 13, Horsley to Francis P. Gaines, July 20, 1936, Richmond Peace Council Papers.

[30] Horsley to Richard E. Byrd, July 8, 1936, minutes of the December 29, 1936, executive committee meeting of the Richmond Peace Council, F. W. Boatwright to Jane K. Dickey, April 24, 1936, minutes of the May 19, 1937, meeting of the council, Richmond Peace Council membership list (as of May 24, 1937), Box 13, minutes of the December 8, 1937, executive committee meeting of the council, Horsley to Dickey, August 9, 1937, E. A. Schaal to Dabney, October 18, 1937, Dabney to Schaal, October 19, 1937, Richmond Peace Council Papers; Wiltz, From Isolation to War, p. 16.

that could lead to foreign wars. It supported the Kellogg-Briand Pact and strong, permanent, mandatory neutrality legislation. The council lobbied members of Congress and sponsored nationally-known guest speakers. In collaboration with the Emergency Peace Campaign, it invited John Nevin Sayre, president of the National Peace Conference and chairman of the Fellowship of Reconciliation, to speak to two of its meetings; Sayre also preached on peace in two of Petersburg's leading churches. The Peace Council of Petersburg cooperated with the Emergency Peace Campaign on other occasions and also worked closely with area churches. It held mass meetings in schools and churches where hundreds of people met to discuss peace issues. On February 2, 1937, a large group of citizens met at Petersburg High School and unanimously adopted a council resolution urging the president and congress to:

> replace the present temporary neutrality legislation by permanent mandatory legislation laying embargoes on the export to belligerents of arms, munitions, and materials essential for war purposes, forbidding loans and credits, and ensuring that all other trade with belligerents shall be upon a cash-and-carry basis, limited in extent to peace-time quotas.

In his February 5, 1937, letter to Senator Glass, John M. Duncan, chairman of the council, enclosed the resolution and asked him to support stronger neutrality legislation.[31]

The issues of peace and neutrality were of no less concern for Virginia's colleges and secondary schools. In the December, 1933, issue of the Virginia Journal of Education, Robert S. Garnett of Richmond urged teachers to promote peace via the classroom and their local, state, national, and international organizations. He also encouraged his fellow educators to initiate legislative committees committed to world-wide public referendums on declarations of war and active American cooperation in the creation and maintenance of a "world-wide political organization for the prevention of war." The educator concluded that "The splendid body of American teachers are peculiarly fitted" for the task of leading the peace movement. "The Problem of Neutrality as Sub-Topic" was included in the July 5-18, 1936, session of the Institute of Public Affairs' round table at the University of Virginia. The

---

[31] W. Poole Dryer, "The Peace Council of Petersburg," (April, 1937), Box 13, Richmond Peace Council Papers; John M. Duncan to Glass, February 5, 1937, "Resolution presented by the Committee of the Peace Council of Petersburg to the mass meeting of citizens held in Petersburg High School auditorium on February 2, 1937, and adopted unanimously," Box 358, Glass Papers.

issue of American neutrality was also discussed at the July 3-15, 1939, session of the institute. In her February 9, 1937, telegram to Senator Glass, Cherry Nottingham, president of the Norfolk-Portsmouth branch of the American Association of University Women, stated that her organization favored passage of a "strict neutrality law." Nearly two years later, Mary Clay Hines, president of the Farmville branch of the same organization, sent a signed petition to Senator Glass, President Roosevelt, and Secretary Hull, urging revision of the neutrality law to enable the president to distinguish between victim and aggressor.[32]

Labor unions were also anxious to reduce the probability of war; although trade unionists were more concerned with economic issues than with foreign policy. At its fortieth annual convention on May 20-21, 1935, in Portsmouth, the Virginia State Federation of Labor adopted a resolution calling for government ownership of the munitions industry. Resolution No. 10 stated:

> When the manufacture of the munitions of war is in the hands of private interests, the sole object is private gain and not the proper defense and safety of the country, . . . such private interests may be active in fomenting wars between foreign countries, and even in drawing our own country into war; . . . be it RESOLVED, That this convention . . . do everything possible to have our Federal Government take over and operate all factories for the manufacture of arms and munitions of war, and all equipment for the defense of this nation.[33]

Virginia's leading editors were in the forefront of the public debate over American neutrality during the 1930s. Douglas S. Freeman supported neutrality legislation and resolutely opposed American involvement in another European war. He was especially alarmed over what he considered the emotional appeal of interventionists who urged the United States to take action against Nazi Germany during the late 1930s. Nevertheless, he rejected the Johnson Amendment because it hampered the president's negotiating

---

[32] University of Virginia Newsletter, May 15, 1936, p. 1, June 15, 1939, p. 1; February 9, 1937, telegram from Cherry Nottingham to Glass, January 10, 1939, telegram from Mary Clay Hines and Mary S. Wilson to Glass, Roosevelt, and Hull, Glass Papers; Robert S. Garnett, "World-Wide Education for World-Wide Peace," Virginia Journal of Education (December, 1933), pp. 143-45.

[33] "Resolution No. 10," Proceedings of the Fortieth Annual Convention of the Virginia State Federation of Labor, May 20-21, 1935, Portsmouth, Virginia.

stance at the World Disarmament Conference in Geneva. The editor held strong internationalist views and affiliations, loathed totalitarianism, and sympathized with the Western democracies. Freeman, an enthusiastic member of the Richmond Peace Council, also urged American neutrality during the Munich crisis. At the same time, he served on the American Committee for Relief in Czechoslovakia, which helped provide relief and resettlement for Sudeten refugees. Freeman also served on the Committee of the American Friends of Czecho-Slovakia. Czech President and Mrs. Eduard Benes stayed with the Freeman's during their visit to Richmond in April, 1939. The Richmond News-Leader editor was deeply apprehensive over Hitler's growing power in Europe and the threat of war. He shared his concern with Assistant Secretaries of State A. Walton Moore and George S. Messersmith. Freeman asked Moore to send him "for confidential perusal such part of the memorandum on neutrality" as he thought "proper." He sent News-Leader editorials on Hitler to Messersmith, who assured him that the State Department followed his "editorial comment . . . with much interest." Cognizant of Freeman's knowledge of world affairs, Senator Byrd sought his advice on foreign policy matters (e.g. neutrality revision legislation) that came before the Senate.[34]

Freeman's editorial stance clearly reflected his strongly-held views on America's position vis-a-vis the European crisis. Fellow members of the Richmond Peace Council profusely praised his "peace editorials" and the generous publicity his newspaper provided both their organization and the Emergency Peace Campaign. Throughout the pre-World War II period, the Richmond News-Leader supported American neutrality and unconditionally

---

[34] Douglas S. Freeman to Harry F. Byrd, June 5, 1933, Byrd to Freeman, June 6, 1933, Freeman's June 9, 1936, commencement address at the University of Virginia, Freeman Diary, August 23, 1939, December 13, 1937, telegram from Nicholas Murray Butler to Freeman, Freeman to Butler, September 16, 1938, Butler to Freeman, September 20, 1938, Freeman to George S. Messersmith, February 22, 1938, Messersmith to Freeman, February 23, 1938, Freeman to R. Walton Moore, April 5, 1935, Freeman Papers; Richmond News-Leader, September 15, 1938, p. 10, September 28, 1938, p. 10; October 21, 1938, telegram from Freeman to Butler, Freeman to Isaiah Bowman, November 4, 1938, Murat Williams to Freeman, May 5, 1939, Freeman to Williams, May 12, 1939, Freeman to William Jay Schieffelin, July 15, 1939, Schieffelin to Freeman, July 17, 1939, Freeman Diary, April 13, 1939, Norman Mentlik to Freeman, April 15, 1939, Freeman to Mentlik, April 17, 1939. The best account of Freeman's growing concern over the European crisis can be found in his diary entries from August 23 to August 31, 1939. Byrd to Freeman, April 11, 1939, Freeman to Byrd, April 20, 1939, Byrd to Freeman, April 22, 1939, Freeman Papers.

opposed involvement in European wars and conflicts. As early as October 17, 1933, it concluded:

> If Europe is mad enough to renew the war, the United States must be wise enough to remain neutral. In case western civilization is overthrown by a wilder repetition of what happened in 1914-1918, America owes it to the world to keep democratic institutions alive in at least one part of the globe. That would be a larger service than intervention could possibly be.

The paper argued that the traditional doctrine of freedom of the seas was an anachronism; it recommended trade restrictions and even embargoes against belligerents rather than risk American involvement in another war.[35]

Even before the start of the Italian-Ethiopian conflict, the News-Leader urged American neutrality. It agreed with President Roosevelt who said that the United States "would be a good neighbor but would not interfere in quarrels which did not concern her directly." After undeclared war broke out in October, 1935, the paper supported FDR's neutrality proclamation, which banned American exports of direct contraband of war and declared that United States citizens who traveled on belligerent ships did so at their own risk. The News-Leader's October 8 editorial asserted:

> Whatever defects the present neutrality program of the United States may disclose, it is basically sound. . . . If the world goes mad, America must try, at the least, to save the wreck of Western civilization. Neutrality may be the only refuge.

The paper urged Americans to heed Roosevelt's moral appeal not to sell war materials (e.g. oil, scrap iron, cotton, wheat) to either Rome or Addis Ababa.[36]

The News-Leader supported the Neutrality Act of 1935, despite what it considered its limitations: the absence of loan and credit bans to belligerents, failure to prohibit embargoes on raw materials to warring states,

---

[35] Minutes of the April 30, 1934, meeting of the Richmond Peace Council, minutes of the April 23, 1936 meeting of the council, minutes of the June 9, 1936, meeting of the council, Freeman to Horsley, October 10, 1936, Richmond Peace Council Papers; Richmond News-Leader, October 17, 1933, p. 8, March 18, 1935, p. 8, March 19, 1935, p. 8, March 27, 1935, p. 8.

[36] Richmond News-Leader, July 29, 1935, p. 8, October 8, 1935, p. 8, October 21, 1935, p. 8, October 31, 1935, p. 8, November 7, 1935, p. 10.

and failure to prohibit Americans from traveling in war zones. The paper was more satisfied with the 1937 Neutrality Act, which prohibited the arming of American merchant ships in war zones, forbade Americans from traveling to belligerent countries, and banned loans to belligerents. The News-Leader argued that "cash-and-carry" neutrality was the "best insurance against involvement in wars that are not of our making." During the Spanish Civil War, the paper urged its readers not to develop partisan feelings for either side. It maintained that partisanship was the surest way to create a state of mind that might lead the United States towards involvement in the next European war. In 1938, the News-Leader opposed repeal of the Spanish arms embargo, citing the need for American noninvolvement in the Spanish conflict. Despite its strong noninterventionist position, the paper opposed the Ludlow Amendment. It maintained that no device could prevent war if the "mob mind" of the country were aroused. Its sympathy for the beleaguered Czechs, notwithstanding, the News-Leader urged American neutrality and a peaceful settlement during the Munich crisis of September, 1938. Roosevelt's threat to use America's economic resources against the aggressor states in April, 1939, did not please Freeman's newspaper; nevertheless, it did not believe that the president wanted war. As Europe moved closer to war in late August, 1939, the News-Leader exhorted the United States government to "Be Neutral and Build Ships."[67]

Throughout much of the mid-1930s, Virginius Dabney's editorials in the Richmond Times-Dispatch maintained that the United States should avoid being dragged into European conflicts. He believed that America should look after its own affairs and let Europe fight its own wars. Dabney's editorial support for the Richmond Peace Council and the Emergency Peace Campaign pleased those organizations. Despite his demanding editorial duties, he served as 1st vice-president of the council in 1936 and interim president in the fall of 1937. In his October 19, 1936, editorial, Dabney wrote that "the nationwide peace campaign . . . should demonstrate that the people of the United States are desirous above almost everything of staying out of the next war, if and when it comes and that they want whatever laws are needed to achieve that result." He concluded that "The Richmond Peace Council should have the cooperation of all peace-loving Richmonders in its effort to impress the President and Congress with the country's horror of war." Dabney's February 9, 1937, editorial asserted that the council deserved the support of "intelligent citizens." In April, 1937, Dabney encouraged Richmonders to

---

[37]Ibid., January 6, 1936, p. 10, February 19, 1936, p. 8, February 24, 1936, p. 8, September 22, 1936, p. 8, February 23, 1937, p. 10, March 19, 1937, p. 10, April 30, 1937, p. 8, September 30, 1937, p. 8, January 10, 1938, p. 8, January 11, 1938, p. 8, May 4, 1938, p. 12, May 9, 1938, p. 10, September 15, 1938, p. 10, September 28, 1938, p. 10, April 14, 1939, p. 10, August 24, 1939, p. 10.

"turn out en masse" for the April 22 Richmond Peace Council/Emergency Peace Campaign-sponsored peace rally at the Mosque. The featured speakers were Sherwood Eddy and Senator James P. Pope of Idaho. Dabney asserted that such a show of support would "signify this city's determination that the United States shall not become embroiled in the quarrels of Europe or Asia." "This country can and should," he argued,

> use its vast influence to promote international amity, but it ought likewise to see that peace is preserved in the Western Hemisphere and that if a conflagaration breaks out beyond the Atlantic or the Pacific, despite all that we can do, the United States will under no circumstances participate. [38]

Despite its sympathy for the Ethiopians and Spanish Republicans, the Richmond Times-Dispatch advocated American neutrality during both the Italian-Ethiopian conflict and the Spanish Civil War. In 1935, the paper did, however, support a "moral embargo" on credits and war goods ("implements of war") to Italy. It agreed with the News-Leader that more stringent neutrality legislation, including a ban on raw materials used for war, was necessary to curb aggression, eliminate war profiteering, and reduce the risks of American involvement. The paper supported greater presidential discretionary authority over the sale of nonembargoed goods to belligerents on a cash-and-carry basis. By January, 1939, it advocated lifting the arms embargo so that the Spanish Loyalists could buy arms, planes, and ammunition from the United States. The paper argued that a Loyalist defeat would be tantamount to a victory for Nazi Germany and Fascist Italy. In November, 1937, the Times-Dispatch expressed sympathy for the LaFollette Amendment, which was similar to the Ludlow Resolution. In its March 3, 1939, editorial, however, it rejected the Ludlow Amendment as impractical

---

[38] Interview with Dabney, November 28, 1986; minutes of the April 23, 1936, meeting of the Richmond Peace Council, Dabney to Horsley, June 24, 1936, Horsley to Dabney, July 8, 1936, Horsley to Dabney, September 28, 1936, Horsley to Dabney, October 9, 1936, Dabney to Horsley, October 12, 1936, Horsley to Dabney, October 19, 1936, Dabney to Horsley, October 20, 1936, Horsley to Dabney, December 17, 1936, Fred A. Moore to Dabney, December 18, 1936, Dabney to Moore, December 22, 1936, H. Conrad Blackwell to Dabney, February 9, 1937, Horsley to Dickey, August 9, 1937, Horsley to Dabney, August 31, 1937, Dabney to Horsley, September 1, 1937, Richmond Peace Council Papers; Richmond Times-Dispatch, October 19, 1936, p. 6, February 9, 1937, p. 8, April 22, 1937, p. 12.

and contrary to representative government.[39]

During the Munich crisis of September, 1938, Dabney denounced the British/French capitulation to Hitler. His celebrated and prescient September 20, 1938, editorial, "The Sell-Out to Hitler," received the greatest response of any editorial he ever wrote and was more favorably received than any single editorial the paper had published in decades. The editor contended:

> war should be avoided whenever that can be done with justice and honor. But in the present instance, we do not think it has been avoided with justice or with honor, and neither are we convinced that it has been avoided permanently.

Dabney argued that the "sell-out" to Hitler would strengthen isolationism in the United States. He asserted that after Munich, many Americans believed that Britain and France were no longer worth helping in the event of another European war. London and Paris had retreated before in the face of the dictators and in "the most crucial test of all, they have retreated again." Dabney concluded:

> War is terrible, but there are some things in the world worth fighting for. Liberty is one of those things. If Chamberlain and Daladier and the other so-called 'realists' aren't willing to put a battle for the preservation of liberty in those parts of the world which thus far have escaped the blight of Fascism, and prefer, instead, to sign agreements with medieval fanatics who admit openly that they break such agreements whenever they can get away with it, they need not count on any help from this side of the water. They have made their bed. Now let them lie in it.[40]

---

[39] Richmond Times-Dispatch, August 22, 1935, p. 8, September 29, 1935, p. 2, October 11, 1935, p. 14, November 1, 1935, p. 18, November 26, 1935, p. 18, January 20, 1936, p. 8, February 18, 1936, p. 8, September 1, 1936, p. 6, September 15, 1936, p. 8, March 1, 1937, p. 8, March 15, 1937, p. 10, March 22, 1937, p. 6, May 1, 1937, p. 6, November 19, 1937, p. 14, December 17, 1937, p. 16, January 20, 1939, p. 14, March 3, 1939, p. 12, March 21, 1939, p. 8, April 10, 1939, p. 6, May 3, 1939, p. 10, May 30, 1939, p. 6.

[40] Richmond Times-Dispatch, September 20, 1938, p. 6; "The European War and the Role of America," (Virginius Dabney's World War II Era Editorials), Box 6, Virginius Dabney Papers, University of Virginia Library, Charlottesville, Virginia; Dabney's December 7, 1986, letter to the author. (Letter is in the author's possession); Interview with Dabney, November 28, 1986.

Dabney believed that the United States also shared some of the responsibility for Czechoslovakia's unhappy fate. In 1919, at Versailles, Woodrow Wilson was instrumental in the creation of the Czech republic. Yet America washed its hands of any accountability for Czech (and European) affairs by failing to join the League of Nations. Dabney also asserted that the Johnson Act and the neutrality acts served notice to the British and French that they could expect no help from the United States if they went to war to defend Western democracy. He maintained that "The United States has followed policies in the past 18 years which have not only helped to make the rise of the dictators inevitable, but which have made resistance by Britain and France to the dictators more difficult." Dabney concluded

> Since the United States intends, and rightly, to exert every effort to stay out, if and when war begins, citizens of this country are in a difficult position, when they comment upon the course followed in this crisis by England and France.

Nearly six months after the Munich tragedy, the Times-Dispatch reiterated its position that the United States must keep out of any European war. The paper also urged the United States to continue its rapid rearmament and sell raw materials and planes to the British and French on a cash-and-carry basis. It maintained that a "blanket cash-and-carry clause on all shipments of arms, ammunition, war materials and food to belligerents" was in the national interest because it would reduce the risks of American involvement in any European war.[41]

The major dailies in the state agreed with the News-Leader and Times-Dispatch's views on American neutrality and rearmament. None of those newspapers maintained that the United States should involve itself in the Italian-Ethiopian conflict, the Spanish Civil War, the Munich affair, or any European quarrel or war. Virginia's press was critical of "imperfections" in the neutrality legislation of the 1930s. Nevertheless, all of the state's major papers accepted the Neutrality Acts of 1935, 1936, and 1937, as essential for maintaining American noninvolvement in European conflicts. Most papers supported greater presidential discretionary authority over the sale of noncontraband goods to belligerents. There were, however, some differences over the degree of presidential discretionary power over the arms embargo, the use of "moral embargoes" against aggressor states (e.g. Italy), and the Ludlow Amendment. Still, only a few papers wanted to limit presidential discretion to extend the arms embargo, sell oil, cotton, or scrap iron to Italy,

---

[41] Richmond Times-Dispatch, September 26, 1938, p. 8, September 29, 1938, p. 12, March 17, 1939, p. 18, April 11, 1939, p. 6, July 11, 1939, p. 6, July 12, 1939, p. 8, July 16, 1939, p. 2, July 20, 1939, p. 10.

or hold a public referendum on America's entry into a foreign war.[42]

Black editors also opposed American involvement in European conflicts, except in the case of the Italian-Ethiopian war. The Richmond Planet and the Journal and Guide (Norfolk) vigorously trumpeted the Ethiopian cause and criticized American neutrality during that undeclared war. Both papers supported embargoes on war goods to Italy. The Planet denounced the "Imperialist" American government's "cowardice and hypocrisy." It also attacked the "studied indifference of the Roosevelt administration" to Italian aggression. The paper argued that the American policy of neutrality was "particeps criminis" to the "rape of Ethiopia" and "served only to strengthen the arm of the rapist Mussolini." In its October 12,

---

[42] Norfolk Ledger-Dispatch, August 22, 1935, p. 8, August 31, 1935, p. 6, September 28, 1935, p. 6, October 3, 1935, p. 8, October 8, 1935, p. 10, November 18, 1935, p. 8, November 23, 1935, p. 6, November 24, 1935, p. 8, August 24, 1935, p. 6, February 19, 1936, p. 6, August 21, 1936, p. 10, November 9, 1936, p. 6, October 15, 1938, p. 6, November 17, 1938, p. 10, December 26, 1938, p. 10, January 12, 1939, p. 6, March 2, 1939, p. 6, December 30, 1936, p. 6, May 1, 1937, p. 6, September 23, 1938, p. 6, October 3, 1938, p. 10, April 24, 1939, p. 6; Daily Progress (Charlottesville), July 9, 1935, p. 4, August 22, 1935, p. 4, October 4, 1935, p. 4, October 9, 1935, p. 4, October 18, 1935, p. 4, October 15, 1935, p. 4, November 25, 1935, p. 4, January 29, 1936, p. 4, July 6, 1936, p. 4, August 13, 1936, p. 4, August 14, 1936, p. 4, December 22, 1936, p. 4, December 31, 1936, p. 4, February 5, 1937, p. 4, May 5, 1937, p. 4, June 1, 1937, p. 4, September 28, p. 4, May 29, 1939, p. 4, July 17, 1939, p. 4, November 18, 1938, p. 4, May 4, 1939, p. 4; Danville Register, January 10, 1934, p. 4, August 22, 1935, p. 4, August 25, 1935, p. 6, September 3, 1935, p. 4, October 8, 1935, p. 4, October 12, 1935, p. 4, November 15, 1935, p. 4, November 27, 1935, p. 4, December 28, 1935, p. 4, August 18, 1936, p. 4, July 10, 1937, p. 4, December 30, 1937, p. 4, August 21, 1938, p. 6, September 20, 1938, p. 4, October 2, 1938, p. 4, October 5, 1938, p. 4, October 12, 1938, p. 4, November 9, 1938, p. 4, February 19, 1939, p. 6, March 19, 1939, p. 6; Roanoke Times, October 18, 1933, p. 6, April 2, 1935, p. 6, September 27, 1935, p. 6, November 19, 1935, p. 6, December 18, 1937, p.6, May 14, 1939, p. 6, September 21, 1938, p. 6, December 15, 1938, p. 6, March 27, 1939, p. 6, April 10, 1939, p. 6, April 11, 1939, p. 6; Alexandria Gazette, January 24, 1934, p. 4, August 2, 1935, p. 4, August 24, 1935, p. 4, August 26, 1935, p. 4, August 28, 1935, p. 4, October 9, 1935, p. 4, November 12, 1935, p.4, March 5, 1936, p. 4, March 17, 1936, p. 4, March 31, 1936, p. 4, August 14, 1936, p. 4, December 21, 1936, p. 4, January 7, 1937, p. 4, January 25, 1937, p. 4, April 7, 1937, p. 4, April 23, 1937, p. 4, October 13, 1937, p. 4, September 30, 1938, p. 4, October 5, 1938, p. 4, May 9, 1939, p. 4.

1935, editorial, the paper asserted that "The neutrality which places the strong and aggressive nation and the weak and outraged nation on the same footing entrenches might and sacrifices right." The Planet strongly advocated the sale of American arms and munitions to Ethiopia. Donald Burke's December 14, 1935, column in the Planet also castigated the United States' "hypocritical" attitude on neutrality. He wrote: "While banning munitions shipments to both nations, it [America] is allowing Italy to buy oil, scrap, and all other raw materials essential for the conduct of war, not classed as munitions." The columnist urged fellow Richmonders to "join in the demand that the United States join in League of Nations sanctions against Italy, . . . and at the same time work to force the League of Nations to shut down completely on all supplies to Italy, and render direct aid to Ethiopia." Burke, a self-proclaimed Communist, praised the Soviet Union's efforts to defend Ethiopian sovereignty against "all imperialist war and banditry."[43]

Throughout the rest of the decade, the editorial position of the Planet remained anti-war; it continued to oppose sending American troops to European wars. Nevertheless, by February, 1939, it supported the sale of planes to Britain and France. The paper also expressed unhappiness that so few blacks were given the opportunity to train at the military academies and in ROTC units. Its leading columnist, Donald Burke, however, ran as the Communist party's candidate for Senate against Carter Glass in 1936. His columns followed the party's "internationalist" line: support for the Spanish Loyalists, the Soviet Union, and collective security; opposition to Nazi Germany, Fascist Italy, militarist Japan, the 1936 billion dollar defense budget, and the 1937 Neutrality Act (which banned the sale of arms to both the Ethiopians and the Spanish Republicans). Burke urged workers to form anti-war committees in the interest of "peace." He also exhorted the Planet's readers to contribute financially to the Spanish Republican cause.[44]

The Journal and Guide (Norfolk) argued that most Americans were

---

[43] Richmond Planet, July 13, 1935, p. 12, October 12, 1935, p. 12, December 14, 1935, p. 12, April 18, 1936, p. 12, May 9, 1936, p. 12, March 13, 1937, p. 4; Journal and Guide (Norfolk), July 13, 1935, p. 8, October 16, 1937, p. 8, April 23, 1938, p. 8, July 9, 1938, p. 8, April 29, 1939, p. 10, May 27, 1939, p. 10.

[44] Richmond Planet, March 14, 1936, p. 12, April 18, 1936, p. 12, September 5, 1936, p. 12, September 12, 1936, p. 12, March 13, 1937, p. 4, December 11, 1937, p. 4, March 26, 1938, p. 4; The Afro-American and The Richmond Planet, February 25, 1939, p. 4. (The Richmond Planet changed its name several times during the 1930s; by May 27, 1939, it was known as The Richmond Afro-American.)

concerned with economic survival, not European quarrels. It supported the Ludlow Amendment as consistent with America's democratic traditions. In its January 1, 1938, editorial, it rejected the role of the United States as "International Chief-of-Police for a world gone mad." The paper maintained that the American people were "unalterably opposed to any ambitious scheme to send Americans to their death to save the investments of Wall Street, or the prestige of Great Britain when involved in foreign entanglements." The Journal concluded:

> An overwhelming vote by the workers, housewives, mothers, and peace-loving neighbors of America against plunging our country into war--except in event of invasion--is highly necessary to save it from becoming an eternal battlefield as Europe and Asia have been for centuries.

Despite its disgust with British and French appeasement of Hitler at Munich, the Journal did not advocate American involvement. Just six months before the German invasion of Poland, the paper concluded that America's neutrality was a "mirage." It asserted that because of its national security interests, the United States was "compelled to play a leading role in dictating the course of world affairs." The Journal argued that "Americans endorse the [Roosevelt] administration's foreign policy because their sympathies lie with the democratic nations; because they prefer the blunderings of democracy to the barbarism of Fascism."[45]

As war clouds gathered over Europe on the eve of the Second World War, the hearts of most Virginians lay with the Western democracies. Hatred and mistrust of Hitler and Mussolini were manifest throughout the state. But vivid memories of the carnage of 1914-1918 remained too strong to push the people of the Old Dominion towards full-blown interventionism. Few Virginians believed that the neutrality laws permanently guaranteed American noninvolvement in any future European war. Nevertheless, most Virginians believed that President Roosevelt sincerely wanted to keep America out of war. Only a minority had trouble accepting his brand of discretionary neutrality.

---

[45] Journal and Guide (Norfolk), January 1, 1938, p. 8, March 19, 1938, p. 8, June 18, 1938, p. 8, October 1, 1938, p. 8, October 8, 1938, p. 8, October 15, 1938, p. 8, October 29, 1938, p. 8, November 12, 1938, p. 8, March 4, 1939, p. 8, June 24, 1939, p. 8.

CHAPTER VIII
VIRGINIA'S ROAD TO PEARL HARBOR:
THE TRIUMPH OF INTERNATIONALISM

After the Second World War erupted in September, 1939, a solid majority of Americans, Southerners, and Virginians sympathized with Britain, France, and the other Western democracies. Nonetheless, they firmly opposed United States participation in that conflict. Many Virginians believed that Britain and France had forfeited a right to American military intervention (i.e. troops) on their behalf after having sold out the Czechs at Munich through their appeasement of Hitler. Nevertheless, a growing number of Americans no longer considered themselves isolationists.

Just three weeks after war broke out in Europe, 57 percent of all Americans polled favored repeal of the arms embargo and reenactment of cash-and-carry so that Britain and France could buy arms and war material from the United States. According to numerous public opinion polls, most Southerners, including Virginians, were more interventionist, pro-British, and bellicose than other Americans. An October 4, 1939, Gallup Poll revealed that 77% of Southerners (and 62% of all Americans) polled supported congressional revision of the neutrality laws. Most Virginians were convinced that President Roosevelt was sincere in trying to keep the United States out of war. An overwhelming majority of Virginians and their elected representatives supported the president's unprecedented rearmament program and aid-short-of-war policies. They believed that American military assistance to the Western democracies was the best way for the United States to protect its national security and stay out of the war. On September 12, 1939, the Richmond Times-Dispatch reported that its own poll on neutrality revision showed that by a 21 to 6 margin, Richmonders favored the sale of arms to Britain and France under the cash-and-carry provisions. Virginians were determined to play an active role in saving their "Mother Country" from Nazi conquest. Local chapters of "Bundles for Britain," the British War Relief Society, and other groups that sent money and clothing to England organized throughout the state. Even before September, 1939, many leading Virginians maintained that the Roosevelt administration's call for repeal of the arms embargo and extension of cash-and-carry would discourage further German aggression and lessen the chances of world war. After Congress enacted those revisions in November of that year in the Neutrality Act of 1939, most Virginians believed that the new law--which they and most Americans strongly backed--would bolster FDR's aid-short-of-war policy. (The revised neutrality law enabled Britain and France to purchase arms and other war material from the United States on a cash-and-carry basis.) Most importantly, they believed that the 1939 neutrality act would keep the United State out of the

European war as well.[1]

---

[1]For a good summary of the world-wide events between September 1, 1939, and the Japanese attack on Pearl Harbor on December 7, 1941, see Waldo Heinrichs, Threshold of War: Franklin D. Roosevelt and American Entry into World War II (New York and Oxford: Oxford University Press, 1988), pp. 8-12, 208-220. Interview with Virginius Dabney, Richmond, Virginia, November 28, 1986; Richmond Times-Dispatch, September 20, 1938, p.6, September 11, 1939, p.6, September 12, 1939, p.5, September 22, 1939, p. 14, September 24, 1939, p. 3, September 28, 1939, p. 10; According to the public opinion polls, Southerners were more supportive of Roosevelt's pro-British, aid-short-of-war policies and revision of the neutrality acts during the pre-Pearl Harbor period than any other regional group. See George H. Gallup, The Gallup Poll: Public Opinion, 1935-1971, vol. I (New York: Random House, 1972), pp. 178, 183. A September 3, 1939, AIPO (American Institute of Public Opinion) Poll also indicated that 60% of Southerners (and only 50% of all Americans) polled believed that Congress should change the neutrality law so that America could sell war materials to England and France. A Fortune poll of November, 1939, revealed that 79.8% of Southeasterners (and 69.2% of all Americans) polled approved of Roosevelt's policies "with regard to the European situation up to now." See the "AIPO and Fortune polls," Public Opinion Quarterly 4(1940), p. 105; Wayne S. Cole, Roosevelt and the Isolationists, 1932-45 (Lincoln, Nebraska and London: University of Nebraska Press, 1983), pp. 310, 324, 327, 329. Also see Alfred O. Hero, Jr., The Southerner and World Affairs (Baton Rouge: Louisiana State University Press, 1965), pp. 5-6, 91-92, 94-97, 103. V.O. Key, Jr., Southern Politics in State and Nation (New York: Vintage Books, 1949), pp. 353-54; Robert Dallek, Franklin D. Roosevelt and American Foreign Policy, 1932-1945 (New York: Oxford University Press, 1979), pp. 183-84, 188, 199, 201, 204, 256; Robert A. Divine, The Illusion of Neutrality (Chicago: University of Chicago Press, 1962), pp. 334-35; Manfred Jonas, Isolationism in America, 1935-1941 (Ithaca, N.Y.: Cornell University Press, 1966), pp. 31, 216-17, 221. A January 17, 1941, Richmond News-Leader editorial attributed southern belligerency and pro-British attitude to: its coastal position exposed to invasion, its maritime trade, strong British racial heritage, paucity of anti-British elements (i.e. Americans of Irish and German descent), and martial tradition. See the Richmond News-Leader, January 17, 1941, p. 10. Francis E. Lutz, Richmond in World War II (Richmond: The Dietz Press, Inc. 1951), pp. 5, 7-20, 23; Marvin W. Schlegel, Conscripted City: Norfolk in World War II (Norfolk: Norfolk War History Commission, 1951), pp. 9-10, 41, 44, 47, 48, 113-15; W. Edwin Hemphill, ed. Pursuits of War: The People of Charlottesville and Albermarle County, Virginia, in the Second World War (Charlottesville: Albermarle County Historical Society, 1948), pp. 5, 9, 159, 160-64, 185. Roanoke Times, May 15, 1941, p.6.

The public opinion polls conducted between the fall of 1940 and the eve of American entry into World War II reflected continued support for Roosevelt's aid-short-of-war policy and a growing belligerency among the American people (and especially Southerners, including Virginians). According to a November 17, 1940, AIPO Poll and a November 18, 1940, Gallup Poll, 94% of Southerners (and 90% of all Americans) polled believed that the United States should provide Britain with more food and war material if it appeared that it would lose the war to the Axis powers. A December 20, 1940, Gallup Poll indicated that 69% of Southerners (and 55% of all Americans) polled favored revising the Johnson Act to enable Britain to borrow money from the American government. A Gallup Poll of September 23, 1940, revealed that only 30% of Southerners (and 48% of all Americans) polled thought it was more important for the United States to keep out of the European war than to help Britain win at the risk of getting into the war. On January 10, 1941, only 24% of Southerners (and 40% of all Americans) polled felt that way. An October 5, 1941, Gallup Poll showed that only 12% of Southerners (and 30% of all Americans) polled believed it was more important for the United States to keep out of war than for Germany to be defeated. Public opinion polls also revealed that the overwhelming majority of Americans opposed a declaration of war against Germany, although more Southerners than other Americans supported a war declaration. A March 21, 1941, Gallup Poll indicated that only 20% of Southerners (and 17% of all Americans) polled supported a war declaration against Germany (versus 24% of Southerners and 17% of all Americans polled in October, 1940). According to a May 16, 1941, Gallup Poll, 28% of Virginians (and 21% of all Americans) polled supported American entry into the war. The final tabulation of the July, 1941, Richmond Times-Dispatch War Poll revealed that three Virginians in eight (37.5% vs. 62.5%) favored America's immediate entry in a "shooting war" against Germany. (According to Gallup Polls, only 21% of all Americans polled supported war.) A Richmond Times-Dispatch poll of June 17, 1940, showed that a large majority of Richmonders strongly favored providing all-out aid to the Allies, but they firmly opposed sending American troops into war. Fifty-one out of 57 opposed American entry into the war, and 52 of 57 supported giving the Allies all the material assistance they required.

By the autumn of 1940, after the fall of France and during the Battle of Britain, when England seemed on the verge of defeat, the sentiments of many Virginians became considerably more militant. Despite their opposition to an American declaration of war against Nazi Germany, most Virginians supported aid-to-Britain "even at the risk of war." A higher percentage of Southerners, including Virginians, than other Americans believed that it was more important to defeat Hitler than for the United States to stay out of the war. What determined the interventionist sentiments of Virginians more than anything else was their antipathy for Hitler, their aversion to totalitarian aggression, their economic interests, and their strong Anglo-Saxon heritage. Virginians perceived Hitler as a mortal threat to Western civilization, Christianity, democracy, world peace, as well as American neutrality, national security, freedom of the seas, commerce, and overseas markets. They believed that Hitler had to be stopped in Europe--preferably by the British--before he had the opportunity to attack the United States.[2]

---

[2]Hero, Southerner and World Affairs, pp. 14, 91, 93-102; Richmond Times-Dispatch, June 17, 1940, p. 5. A Gallup Poll of October 8, 1941, revealed that 25% of Southerners (and 16% of all Americans) polled thought FDR had not gone far enough in his aid-to-Britain policies. See Gallup, Gallup Poll, vol, I, pp. 231, 243, 245, 250, 254, 256, 259, 270, 280, 300-301; Public Opinion Quarterly 5 (1941), pp. 158-59; Richmond Times-Dispatch, October 13, 1940, p. 7, April 6, 1941, p. 7, August 3, 1941, p. 1; Cole, Roosevelt and the Isolationists, pp. 448-49; Interview with Dabney, November 28, 1986; Peter Calvocoressi and Guy Wint, Total War The Story of World War II (New York: Pantheon Books, 1972), pp. 192, 195-96; Dallek, Franklin D. Roosevelt and American Foreign Policy, pp. 256-57, 289. The overwhelming majority of Southerners (including Virginians) were native-born white protestants of Anglo-Saxon and Scotch-Irish heritage. Strong racial ties with the British Isles were a major factor in the pro-British interventionist position of that majority group during the pre-Pearl Harbor period. Unlike the Midwest, the South (and Virginia) lacked significant numbers of German, Irish, and Italian-Americans. In 1940, less than 10,000 residents of Virginia spoke German or Italian as their mother tongue. See Oscar Handlin, The American People in the Twentieth Century (Cambridge: Harvard University Press, 1954), pp. 83-84; Howard Odum and Harry E. Moore, American Regionalism: A Cultural-Historical Approach to National Integration (New York: Henry Holt and Company, 1938), pp. 520, 535-536; Howard Odum Southern Regions of the United States (Chapel Hill: The University of North Carolina Press, 1936), p. 91; Rupert B. Vance, in collaboration with Nadia Danilevsky, All These People: The Nation's Human Resources in the South (Chapel Hill: The University of North Carolina Press, 1945), pp. 14-17; Virginius Dabney, "The South Looks Abroad," Foreign Affairs 19 (1940), p. 177; John Temple Graves, "The Fighting South," Virginia Quarterly Review 18 (1942), p. 63; Paul Seabury, The Waning of Southern 'Internationalism,' (Princeton, N.J.: Center of International Studies, 1957), p.6; Alexander De Conde, "The South and Isolationism," Journal of Southern History 24 (1958), pp. 344-45; George C. Herring and Gary R. Hess, "Regionalism and Foreign Policy: The Dying Myth of Southern Internationalism," Southern Studies Fall (1981), p. 250; Ralph B. Levering, The Public and American Foreign Policy, 1918-1978 (New York: William Morrow and Company, Inc., 1978), p. 28; Lutz, Richmond in World War II, pp. 10, 30; Samuel Lubell, The Future of

According to the public opinion polls, a larger percentage of Southerners than other Americans supported the draft (and its extension), the Destroyer Deal, Lend-Lease, the occupation of Iceland, the shoot-on-sight policy, convoying, and the Neutrality Act of 1941. In June, 1940, a Gallup Poll indicated that 68% of Southerners (and 64% of all Americans) polled supported the military draft. An August 6, 1941, Gallup Poll showed that 63% of Southerners (and 50% of all Americans) polled thought that drafted men should be kept in active service for longer than one year. In February, 1941, 77 percent of Southerners (and 54% of all Americans) polled believed that Congress should pass the Lend-Lease bill. According to the Gallup Poll of June 15, 1941, 75% of Southerners (and 55% of all Americans) polled believed that the United States navy should be used to guard ships carrying war material to Britain. An October 3, 1941, Gallup Poll revealed that 78% of Southerners (and 62% of all Americans) polled approved of American navy vessels shooting at German submarines and warships on sight. The South was the only section of the country where a majority of those with opinions favored revision of the neutrality law so that American ships could transport war material to Britain. A January, 1941, Gallup Poll showed that 58% of Southerners (and 42% of all Americans) polled believed that supplies should be sent to Britain on American ships. An August 9, 1940, AIPO Poll revealed that 68% of Southerners (versus only 56% of Northeasterners) approved of the Destroyer-Deal. According to a Richmond Times-Dispatch poll of June 17, 1940, 35 out of 57 Richmonders supported the military draft. Virginians were proud of their noble martial tradition. Few questioned the need for the United States to rearm after Hitler's aggressive designs on Western Europe became all too apparent. They believed that the United States should be fully prepared to fight. Thousands of the Old Dominion's sons voluntarily enlisted in the armed forces. During World War II, more than 300,000 Virginians served in the armed forces; nearly 9,000 died for their country. Ten Virginians received the Congressional Medal of Honor. A majority of Virginians supported executive and congressional measures that paved the way for American entry into the war: the Destroyer Deal, the Burke-Wadsworth Selective Service Act (and its extension), Lend-Lease, the American occupation of Greenland and Iceland, the shoot-on-sight policy, and convoying. They also supported the Neutrality Act of 1941, which rescinded

American Politics, 2nd edit., rev. (Garden City, N.Y.: Doubleday and Company, Inc., 1956), p. 141; Leroy N. Rieselbach, The Roots of Isolationism: Congressional Voting and Presidential Leadership in Foreign Policy (Indianapolis: Bobbs-Merrill Co., 1966), p. 18; Robert E. Osgood Ideals and Self-Interest in America's Foreign Relations: The Great Transformation of the Twentieth Century (Chicago and London: The University of Chicago Press, 1953), pp. 417, 421, 425.

the restrictive clauses of the 1939 neutrality law and allowed United States merchant ships to arm themselves and carry war material through war zones enroute to belligerent ports. Virginians agreed with President Roosevelt that those were the best ways to aid Britain and still keep the United States out of the war.[3]

During the 1940 election, Virginians of diverse economic, ethnic, religious, and occupational backgrounds voted for Roosevelt's re-election. The 235,961 votes FDR received constituted the largest vote any candidate with major party opposition ever received in the state of Virginia. Wendell Willkie, the Republican candidate, received 109,363 votes. Support for the president came from all parts of the state. Roosevelt carried 92 of 100 counties. Carroll, Grayson, Floyd, Highland, Page, Rockingham, Shenandoah, and Scott counties--all located west of the Blue Ridge Mountains--voted Republican. All twenty-four "independent cities" of the commonwealth went for Roosevelt. Foreign policy issues were prominent during the campaign. Virginians critical of the president accused him of not doing enough to speed up arms production. Many were concerned that his administration had failed to take strong action against strikes in defense plants. Few Virginians accused FDR of leading the country into war. Nevertheless, some prominent Virginians (e.g. Senator Byrd) expressed displeasure that Roosevelt was

---

[3]Interview with Dabney, November 28, 1986; Louis D. Rubin, Jr., Virginia: A History (New York, London: W.W. Norton & Co., 1984), p. 174; W. Edwin Hemphill, ed., Gold Star Honor Roll of Virginians in the Second World War (Charlottesville: Virginia World War II History Commission, 1947), p. xxi; Richmond Times-Dispatch, June 17, 1940, p. 5, June 23, 1940, p. 5; Richmond News-Leader, September 4, 1940, p. 1, January 17, 1941, p. 10. In its September 24, 1940, editorial, the Richmond News-Leader attributed the South's nearly universal support for conscription to its coastal position, martial tradition, and Anglo-Saxon heritage. It noted that only three Southern Congressmen opposed the draft. The paper pointed out that nearly all of the South's representatives were "of British stock," and were strongly pro-British in their views. Gallup, Gallup Poll, vol. I, pp. 229, 252-53, 263, 284, 291-92, 299-300; Hero, Southerner and World Affairs, pp. 97-102. Dallek, Franklin D. Roosevelt and American Foreign Policy, pp. 243-49, 255, 258, 260-61, 288, 291-92; Arthur M. Schlesinger, Jr., The Imperial Presidency (Boston: Houghton Mifflin Co., 1973), pp. 105, 107-114; Warren F. Kimball, The Most Unsordid Act: Lend-Lease, 1939-1941 (Baltimore: Johns Hopkins Press, 1969), pp. v-vi, 231-32, 241; T.R. Fehrenbach, F.D.R.'s Undeclared War, 1939-41 (New York: David McKay Company, Inc., 1967), pp. 323-25; Cole, Roosevelt and the Isolationists, p. 454.

seeking a third term and privately wished Willkie success.[4]

---

[4]For excellent summaries of the role foreign policy issues played in the 1940 election campaign, see Cole, Roosevelt and the Isolationists, pp. 383-405; Robert A. Divine, Foreign Policy and U.S. Presidential Elections, 1940-1948 (New York: New Viewpoints, A Division of Franklin Watts, Inc., 1974) pp. ix-xi, 3-89; Dallek, Franklin D. Roosevelt and American Foreign Policy, pp. 250-51; Rexford G. Tugwell, The Democratic Roosevelt: A Biography of Franklin D. Roosevelt (Garden City, N.Y.: Doubleday and Co., Inc., 1957), p. 540; Jonas, Isolationism, pp. 19-21; Samuel Lubell, "Who Votes Isolationist and Why,"Harper's, April (1951), p. 30. Richmond News-Leader, November 26, 1940, p.2; Ralph Eisenberg, Virginia Votes, 1924-1968 (Charlottesville: Governmental and Administrative Research Division, Institute of Government, University of Virginia, 1971), pp. 117-20; Report of the Secretary of the Commonwealth To The Governor and General Assembly of Virginia for the Year Ending June 30, 1941 (Richmond: Division of Purchase and Printing, 1941), pp. 363. A March 24, 1941, Gallup Poll showed that only 21% of Southerners (and 30% of all Americans), polled thought that America's production of arms, airplanes, and other war material was "going ahead fast enough." See Gallup, Gallup Poll, vol. I, p. 270. Hero, Southern and World Affairs, pp. 101. The most recent comprehensive account of American entry into the Second World War is Waldo Heinrichs, Threshold of War: Franklin D. Roosevelt and American Entry into World War II (New York, Oxford: Oxford University Press, 1988). Also see Waldo Heinrichs, "President Franklin D. Roosevelt's Intervention in the Battle of the Atlantic, 1941,"Diplomatic History 10 (1986): 311-32. For other accounts of American entry see Robert A. Divine, The Reluctant Belligerent: American Entry Into World War II, 2nd edit. (New York: John Wiley & Sons, Inc., 1979), pp. ix-x; Donald F. Drummond, The Passing of American Neutrality, 1937-1941 (Ann Arbor: University of Michigan Press, 1955), pp. 370, 380-81; William L. Langer and S. Everett Gleason, The Challenge to Isolation, 1937-40 (New York: Harper & Brothers Publishers, 1952; 1964), pp. 5-6, 471-72; Charles A. Beard, President Roosevelt and the Coming of the War, 1941: A Study In Appearance and Realities (New Haven: Yale University Press, 1948); Richard N. Current, Secretary Stimson: A Study in Statecraft (New Brunswick, N.J.: Rutgers University Press, 1954); Bazel Rauch, Roosevelt from Munich to Pearl Harbor: A Study in the Creation of a Foreign Policy (New York: Creative Age Press, 1950), pp. 27, 70-73; Arnold A. Offner, "Appeasement Revisited: The United States, Great Britain, and Germany, 1933-1940," Journal of American History 64 (1977): 373-93; Dallek, Franklin D. Roosevelt and American Foreign Policy, pp. 241, 261, 269-313, 529-32. Barbara Trigg Brown (also known as Mrs. D. Tucker Brown) to A. Liddon Graham, June 26, 1941, Fight for Freedom Committee Papers, Princeton University Library,

Isolationists such as Charles A. Lindbergh enjoyed little support in the South and in the Old Dominion. According to a September 22, 1941, Gallup Poll, only 9% of Southerners (and 16% of all Americans) polled said that they would vote for the candidate of a "keep-out-of-war" party organized by Lindbergh, Wheeler, Nye, and others in the next congressional elections. The leading noninterventionist organization--the America First Committee--gained few members in Virginia. Its organization was weak and ineffective. Most Virginians agreed with the aid-short-of-war position of the Committee to Defend America by Aiding the Allies (White Committee). A noisy minority of prominent Virginians led by Senator Glass supported a declaration of war against Germany. The militant Fight for Freedom Committee was very active in the state. Influential Virginians such as Glass and Francis P. Miller held high positions within its ranks.[5]

From September, 1939, through December 7, 1941, President Roosevelt's aid-short-of-war policies enjoyed the overwhelming support of southern Democratic congressmen. Only two members of Virginia's eleven-man, Democratic congressional delegation, Senator Harry F. Byrd and Representative Howard W. Smith of Alexandria--both solid interventionists--ever voted against a major administration-backed aid-to-Britain bill. (That dissent was aimed primarily at the administration's failure to end strikes in defense plants, which hindered American rearmament and aid-to-Britain.) Those Virginia congressmen who provided a bedrock of support for FDR's foreign policy included: Senators Glass and Byrd; Schuyler Otis Bland of the 1st congressional district, which stretched from the Eastern Shore to Tidewater and north to Fredericksburg; Colgate W. Darden, Jr., of the 2nd congressional district in the Tidewater area, which included Norfolk and Portsmouth; Dave E. Satterfield, Jr., of the 3rd district, which included the capital of Richmond in Central-Southside Virginia and historic Williamsburg in Tidewater; Patrick Henry Drewry of the 4th congressional district, also located in Central-Southside and home to the industrial towns of Petersburg and Hopewell and more rural areas to the southwest. Other representatives included: Thomas G. Burch, of the 5th district, which included Danville, a major textile and tobacco center in Southside; it stretched westward to Grayson County beyond the Blue Ridge Mountains; Clifton A. Woodrum of the 6th district, also west of the Blue Ridge, in Southwest Virginia, which was nestled in the beautiful Shenandoah Valley, home to Roanoke, a railroad center, and Lynchburg, a manufacturing city; A. Willis Robertson of the 7th district, also in the "Valley of Virginia;" it ran from Frederick County in the

Princeton, New Jersey.

[5]See Gallup, Gallup Poll, Vol. I, pp. 298-99; Hero, Southerner and World Affairs, pp. 102-103; Richmond Times-Dispatch, July 4, 1940, p. 8.

north to Amherst in the southwest; Howard W. Smith, of the 8th district in Northern Virginia; it included Alexandria, Arlington, Fairfax, and other Washington, D.C. suburbs and ran southward to Charlottesville in Albermarle County and beyond to Goochland in Central-Southside; and avid New Dealer John W. Flannagan, Jr., of Bristol, situated in the "Fighting Ninth", a mountainous coal mining district in the Highlands, which he had "redeemed" from Republican control in the 1930 election.[6]

On October 27, 1939, the Senate passed the Neutrality Act of 1939 (H.R. 306) by a 63-30 vote. Senator Byrd voted for the bill. Senator Glass was detained from the Senate on account of illness and did not vote. He was in a general pair with Senator Henrik Shipstead. Glass would have voted with the majority, however, had he been present. Less than one week later, on November 2, the House of Representatives approved H.R. 306 by a 243 to 181 vote. The entire Virginia House delegation supported the bill. Representative Howard W. Smith was ill, but would have voted with the majority had he been present. The following day, the House-Senate conference committee submitted its report. The Senate approved the report by a 55 to 24 vote. Byrd voted with the majority. Glass was still ill and did not vote, but was in a pair with Shipstead and would have voted with the majority had he been present. The House approved the report by a 243 to 172 vote. Again, Virginia's representatives went with the majority. Smith remained ill and did not vote, but had he been present would have supported the report. President Roosevelt signed H.R. 306 into law on November 4, 1939. The Neutrality Act of 1939 was an early cornerstone of FDR's aid-short-of-war policy. It repealed the arms embargo and reenacted the cash-and-carry provisions that had expired six months earlier. Britain and France could finally buy arms and other war material from the United States on a cash-and-carry basis (i.e. they would pay for supplies and arms in advance in cash and transport them back to their own country in their own ships, thus

---

[6]George L. Grassmuck, Selectional Biases In Congress On Foreign Policy (Baltimore: The Johns Hopkins Press, 1951), pp. 15, 40-42, 99-100, 111, 122, 124, 125, 130-132, 152-154; Robert A. Dahl, Congress and Foreign Policy (New York: Harcourt, Brace and Co., 1950), pp. 192-93; The New Republic, May 18, 1942, pp. 699-703, 705; Richmond Times-Dispatch, September 5, 1939, p. 10, September 14, 1939, p. 17, September 22, 1939, p. 7, October 22, 1939, p. 2, January 7, 1941, p. 3; Report of the Secretary of the Commonwealth 1941, pp. 365-67; Virginius Dabney, Virginia: The New Dominion: A History From 1607 to the Present (Charlottesville: University Press of Virginia, 1971), pp. 502, 510. Congressional Directory, 76th Congress, 1st session, January 3, 1939 - 77th Congress, 2nd session, January 3, 1942, p. 141.

eliminating the danger of American lives and vessels carrying contraband being lost in the war zones enroute to belligerent ports).⁷

Less than one year later, on August 28, 1940, the Senate passed the Burke-Wadsworth Selective Service Act (S. 4164) by a 58 to 31 vote. Byrd and Glass voted for the measure. On September 7, 1940, the House approved the bill, as amended, by a 263 to 149 vote. One week later, the Senate approved the conference report by a 47 to 25 vote. Byrd voted with the majority. Glass was absent and did not vote, but would have voted for the report, had he been present. The House approved the report by a 233 to 124 vote. All of Virginia's House members supported the report. Representative Drewry did not vote, but was paired for it with William Lemke, who opposed it. President Roosevelt signed the Burke-Wadsworth Act into law on September 16, 1940. The selective service act required all male citizens and aliens between the ages of 21 and 36 years old, living in the United States, to register for the draft. Those inducted into the armed forces were required to spend twelve months in service.⁸

On February 8, 1941, the House passed the Lend-Lease Act (H.R. 1776), with amendments, by a 260 to 165 vote. The entire Virginia House delegation voted for the measure. Exactly one month later, on March 8, after impassioned debate, the Senate passed H.R. 1776 by a 60 to 31 vote. Byrd and Glass voted with the majority on that momentous piece of legislation. On March 11, Roosevelt signed the Lend-Lease bill into law. The act allowed the president to "sell, transfer title to, exchange, lease, lend, or otherwise dispose of" any "defense article" to "the government of any country whose defense the President deems vital to the defense of the United States."⁹

Exactly one month before the Japanese attack on Pearl Harbor, the

---

⁷Congressional Record, 76th Congress, 2nd sess., 1939, 85: 1024, 1344-45, 1356, 1389; Entire Voting Record of Senator Harry F. Byrd By Subject From March 4, 1933, to October 13, 1962, p. 384, Box 349, Harry F. Byrd Papers, University of Virginia Library, Charlottesville, Virginia; Cole, Roosevelt and the Isolationists, pp. 310-330.

⁸Congressional Record, 76th Congress, 3rd sess., 1940, 86: 11142, 11754-55, 12160-61, 12227, 12290; Entire Voting Record of Senator Harry F. Byrd, p. 221, Box 349, Byrd Papers; Cole, Roosevelt and the Isolationists, pp. 378-79.

⁹Congressional Record. 77th Congress, 1st sess., 1941, 87: 815, 2097; Entire Voting Record of Senator Harry F. Byrd, pp. 377-79, Box 349, Byrd Papers; Cole, Roosevelt and the Isolationists, pp. 419, 421-22.

Senate approved major revisions of the neutrality act. On November 7, 1941, the Senate passed the Neutrality Act of 1941 (H.J. Res. 237) by a 50 to 37 vote. Senator Glass voted with the majority. Senator Byrd opposed the bill. On November 13, the House voted 212 to 194 in favor of revision of the neutrality law. Seven of Virginia's House members voted for the revised neutrality act, including the 2nd district's Winder R. Harris who had replaced Darden, the recently elected governor. Representative Smith joined Byrd in opposition. Satterfield did not vote, but was in general pair with Congressman Scrugham, who also did not vote. The Richmond congressman would have supported revision, had he been present. President Roosevelt signed the Neutrality Act of 1941 into law on November 17, 1941. The new law permitted American merchant ships to arm themselves, pass through war zones, and carry goods to belligerent ports.[10]

Carter Glass, an avowed foe of Hitler and Nazism, was the most militant and outspoken interventionist in Virginia's congressional delegation. The senior senator believed that the defeat of Hitler was in the "best interests of America and civilization." He was "in favor of doing anything that would beat hell out of Hitler." After his reconciliation with Roosevelt in the fall of 1939, Glass became one of the president's staunchest allies in his efforts to rearm the United States and save Britain from Nazi conquest, regardless of the cost or risk. In May of 1940, the senator wrote one of his constituents that while he was "not in favor sending an expeditionary force to France at the present time," he believed that both America's "economic welfare" and its "democratic institutions" were "in mortal peril" and could "only be saved by quick and immediate aid to those hard pressed forces which are now defending both our [America's] welfare and our institutions and everything that we hold dear." Glass opposed a third term for FDR. He even nominated Postmaster General James A. Farley for president at the 1940 Democratic national convention. The senator did not take an active role in the election campaign. Nonetheless, Roosevelt supported his appointment to the Senate Foreign Relations Committee in January, 1941. The president quite rightly realized how indispensable the crusty old Virginian would be on the committee's treatment of crucial aid-to-Britain measures. Unlike many of his colleagues, Glass complained not that Roosevelt's policies were too

---

[10] Congressional Record, 77th Congress, 1st sess., 1941, 87: 8680, 8891; Entire Voting Record of Senator Harry F. Byrd, pp. 384-85, Box 349, Byrd Papers; Cole, Roosevelt and the Isolationists, pp. 452-53; Congressional Directory, 77th Congress, 2nd sess., (January 3,) 1942, p. 141. Richmond Times-Dispatch, November 8, 1941, pp. 1-2, November 14, 1941, p. 1, 4, November 16, 1941, p. 10.

bellicose, but that they were too cautious.[11]

Glass was an early advocate of repeal of the arms embargo. He firmly rejected the idea that neutrality revision or President Roosevelt himself would lead the United States into war. In the summer of 1940, Glass was a champion of conscription; he even rebuked some of his Senate colleagues for delaying passage of the Burke-Wadsworth bill. He was unwilling to preclude the possibility of sending American soldiers overseas to defeat Hitler. The senator was also a staunch advocate of Lend-Lease. (In February, 1941, he assured the state's tobacco interests that he would "cooperate with Senator Byrd and other representatives of tobacco growing states in fully protecting tobacco interests in any proper way in consideration of the Lend-Lease bill.") In 1941, Glass suspended his opposition to excessive federal spending and opposed congressional efforts to slash the $7 billion Roosevelt asked for in his Lend-Lease proposal.[12]

As early as May, 1940, Glass called for repeal of both the 1939 neutrality act and the Johnson Act in order to provide the Allies "every possible assistance in their struggle against a barbarian nation [i.e. Nazi Germany]." In October, 1941, the senator called the neutrality act "a craven piece of poltroonery." Earlier that year, in January, Glass complained that the United States was "not moving fast enough" against Hitler. He declared that the United States navy should be sent "over to blast hell out of

---

[11] Interview with Dabney, November 28, 1986; Alfred C. Koeniger, "'Unreconstructed Rebel': The Political Thought and Senate Career of Carter Glass, 1929-1936" (Ph.D. diss., Vanderbilt University, 1980), pp. 229-232; Kimball, Unsordid Act, pp. 145-46. See Box 241, James R. Garfield to Carter Glass, October 24, 1940, Glass to Garfield, October 30, 1940, Glass to Elizabeth W. Baker, May 24, 1940, Glass to Charles S. Webb, n.d., Glass to Robert S. Orr, May 15, 1941, Glass to W. Hallam Tuck, June 9, 1941, Carter Glass Papers, University of Virginia Library, Charlottesville, Virginia; Richmond Times-Dispatch, December 27, 1940, pp. 1-2, January 5, 1941, p. 1, January 7, 1941, p. 3, November 15, 1941, p.1; Glass to Franklin D. Roosevelt, January 30, 1941, Roosevelt to Glass, February 3, 1941, Roosevelt to Glass, June 20, 1940, President's Personal File 687, Franklin D. Roosevelt Papers, Franklin D. Roosevelt Library, Hyde Park, N.Y.

[12] Glass's secretary to Julian A.S. Meyer, September 15, 1939, Glass to Matthew F. Woodward, May 25, 1940, Glass to Mr. DeJarnette, February 18, 1941, Glass to Mary S. Porter, March 6, 1941, Glass to John W. Watson, March 6, 1941, Glass Papers; Richmond Times-Dispatch, September 22, 1939, pp. 1, 7, October 30, 1939, pp. 1. 4, August 11, 1940, p. 1; Koeniger, "'Unreconstructed Rebel'," pp. 230-32

Germany." In February, Glass was the only senator openly to support a declaration of war against Germany. The following month, he publicly supported armed convoys. On November 14, 1941, Glass told a meeting of the Virginia commissioners of revenue that his only disagreement with Roosevelt on foreign policy was that he "didn't think he [FDR] shoots quick enough or effectively enough."[13]

In April of 1941, Glass became the honorary chairman of the New York City-based Fight for Freedom Committee, the most militant interventionist pressure group. Most of that organization's leadership had belonged to the Century Club and the Council on Foreign Relations. Members of those two New York City-based organizations were eastern establishment elitists with impeccable internationalist credentials. Fight for Freedom was committed "to do whatever is necessary to insure a Hitler defeat." It supported a declaration of war against Germany and waged its own relentlessly vicious battles at home against the noninterventionist America First Committee and its leaders. In his April 17, 1941, telegram to the Rt. Rev. Henry W. Hobson, Bishop of the Episcopal Diocese of Southern Ohio and national chairman of the Fight for Freedom Committee, Glass explained why he supported the group:

> Since the Fight for Freedom Committee is dedicated to the great principle that human liberty may only be won and kept by those who are willing to fight for it and since the pathway of history the past two years is literally strewn with the wreckage of hitherto proud and independent nations who went down one by one because they ignored this great principle until it was too late, I am proud to lend my name and whatever strength I may have to the committee's efforts for bold and resolute measures to save this nation, at this late hour and in this critical military situation, from complete encirclement and probable destruction. In the midst of a contemptible, organized campaign to instill fear and promote cowardice, let us at least raise a standard to which all brave and liberty loving Americans may repair.

---

[13] Glass to W.A. Knight, May 15, 1940, Glass to Wallace N. Tiffany, n.d., Glass to G.A. Reynolds, May 17, 1940, Glass to William Rowland, May 17, 1940, Glass to John L. Crist, May 20, 1940, Glass to Walter E. Batterson, July 21, 1941, Glass Papers; June 11, 1940, telegram from Glass to Roosevelt, Roosevelt to Glass, June 20, 1940, President's Personal File 687, Roosevelt Papers; Richmond Times-Dispatch, January 5, 1941, p. 1, October 19, 1941, p. 1, November 15, 1941, p. 1; Kimball, Unsordid Act, p. 179; Allan Nevins, The New Deal and World Affairs: A Chronical of International Affairs, 1933-1945 (New Haven: Yale University Press, 1950), p. 225.

The following month, the senator telegramed Mrs. D. Tucker Brown, secretary of the Virginia Fight for Freedom Committee: "Virginia has always been a leader in the vanguard of the fight for freedom. She has never pursued a policy of appeasement or expediency. She has stood fast for principles. She is ready today as in the past to give virile leadership not craven council to the nation. I commend and felicitate those of you who have met to implement her courage." Unlike the junior senator from Virginia, Glass held little admiration for Charles A. Lindbergh. In his June 9, 1941, letter to Admiral Richard E. Byrd, Glass wrote: "The truth is if Lindbergh has ever done anything for this country except to fly across the Atlantic Ocean, I do not know what it is. Yet he seems to be making some sort of impression with a class of emotional people".[14]

The Fight for Freedom Committee was most pleased that Glass, the fiscally-conservative chairman of the Senate Appropriations Committee, had accepted the honorary chairmanship of their organization. In his April 26, 1941, letter to Glass, Bishop Hobson, the great-grandson of Henry A. Wise, a former governor of Virginia, wrote:

> Not only have I greatly admired you, and the courageous leadership you have always been ready to give in every issue that comes up, but I also have been happy to think of you as a fellow Virginian.... In joining you on the Fight For Freedom Committee I feel that it gives me an opportunity to express some of that Virginia spirit which refuses to bow before aggression or compromise on moral issues.

Nevertheless, the senator had to remind the committee's leadership occasionally that due to the exigencies of the times, he had take the position against his "better judgement" and "considered practice of a lifetime" and would not play an active or aggressive role in its activities. Glass believed that senators should address themselves to their constituencies and country from the Senate and not through "a propaganda organization." Despite his conservative views on racial matters (which alienated some potential black members), the committee realized that Glass's militant oratory in the Senate chamber and solid conservative credentials would benefit their organization. In July, 1941, Fight for Freedom news releases repeated Glass's statement that the neutrality act had been "passed because a lot of people were afraid

---

[14] Daily Advance (Lynchburg), April 21, 1941, p. 9; Cole, Roosevelt and the Isolationists, pp. 427-28; Glass to Richard E. Byrd, June 9, 1941, April 17, 1941, telegram from Glass to the Rt. Rev. Henry W. Hobson, May 16, 1941, telegram from Glass to Mrs. D. Tucker Brown, Glass Papers; Mark L. Chadwin, The Warhawks: American Interventionists Before Pearl Harbor (New York: W.W. Norton & Co., Inc., 1968; 1970), pp. 164-65.

of Hitler" and that it was time to "tell him now that we are not afraid." Glass's October, 1941, address to the Fight for Freedom-sponsored "Continental Congress for Freedom" held in the nation's capital, helped bring the organization national publicity. The committee widely quoted the senator's statement that the United States navy "ought to . . . shoot hell out every U-boat."[15]

Senator Harry F. Byrd was considerably more anxious to keep the United States out of the European war than was his senior colleague. His antipathy for Roosevelt and the New Deal, notwithstanding, Byrd was by no means an isolationist. Despite his friendship with Charles A. Lindbergh, the leading spokesman for the American First Committee, he--more often than not--supported to FDR's rearmament and aid-short-of-war policies as the surest ways to keep the United States out of a foreign war. Byrd argued that while the United States should provide Britain with military assistance, it should not enter any war until it was militarily strong enough to do so. Just a month before America entered the war, the senator withheld further support of the president's legislative initiatives to aid Britain, due to his administration's failure to end strikes in the defense industry and make the defense program more efficient.[16]

According to Lindbergh's wartime diary, between May, 1939, and April, 1941, he and Senator Byrd met on numerous occasions to discuss the pre-war situation in Europe, the course of action the United States should take in the event of a European war, and the war itself. They also talked about American neutrality, neutrality legislation, Roosevelt's policies vis-a-vis the war, the 1940 election, and the necessity of American nonparticipation in the conflict. Both men shared a lack of confidence in Roosevelt and opposed his re-election in 1940. Senator Byrd played no part in FDR's re-election campaign. He preferred Wendell Willkie. Despite his sentiments, Byrd told Lindbergh that he had to vote for the president because senatorial candidates in Virginia had to promise to vote for their party's presidential nominee.

---

[15] Daily Advance (Lynchburg), April 21, 1941, p. 9; April 17, 1941, telegram from Glass to Hobson. See Glass to Hobson, May 16, 1941, Hobson to Glass, April 26, 1941, Barbara Trigg Brown to Glass, June 26, 1941, Glass to Brown, June 27, 1941, Glass to Sidney Homer, Jr., August 15, 1941, J.W. Rixey Smith (Glass's secretary) to Ulric Bell, August 19, 1941, Glass Papers; Chadwin, The Warhawks pp. 67, 164-65, 229, 238-39.

[16] Interview with Dabney, November, 28, 1986; Alden Hatch, The Byrds of Virginia (New York: Holt, Rinehart and Winston, 1969), p. 467-68; Richmond Times-Dispatch, November 2, 1941, pp 6, 11.

Lindbergh and Byrd also vigorously opposed American entry into the war. In his September 5, 1940, diary entry, Lindbergh wrote: "Byrd is definitely opposed to our entering the war. He told me that the way he now feels, he would rather resign his seat in the Senate than vote for war." Unlike Lindbergh, however, Byrd did not believe that FDR wanted to lead the country into war. And Byrd did not oppose repeal of the arms embargo and aid-to-Britain.[17]

In August, 1939, Byrd told a convention of the American Legion meeting in Richmond that he had: "supported the foreign policies of the present administration" and "supported and strongly favor[ed] adequate national defense." He also pledged his support for "neutrality legislation that will best keep us neutral in fact and in practice. The cash and carry principle may best do this." Byrd also said:

> the fight must be continued to keep all dangerous foreign influences [fascism, Nazism, Communism, and militarism] out of democracy. . . . In both Fascist and Bolshevist ideologies the state stands supreme over the individual. There the individual exists only for the state. Any totalitarian government is repugnant to American ideals and destructive of American progress.[18]

Nearly three weeks after war broke out in Europe, Byrd issued a statement that said:

> The President's presentation of the administration's neutrality plan was admirable and furnishes the basis for a non-partisan and unprejudiced discussion in Congress of the neutrality legislation. America is united in the determination to keep out of this war....The essence. . . is to keep American ships and American citizens out of war-danger zones. In the present circumstances, the strictest sort of cash and carry policy, vigorously enforced, is . . . our best safeguard.

Byrd's amendment on cash-and-carry was defeated; he did, however, vote for

---

[17] Wayne S. Cole, <u>Charles A. Lindbergh and the Battle Against American Intervention in World War II</u> (New York and London: Harcourt Brace Jovanovich, 1974), pp. 70, 75, 104, 172; Charles A. Lindbergh, <u>The Wartime Journals of Charles A. Lindbergh</u> (New York: Harcourt Brace Jovanovich, Inc., 1970), pp. 201-202, 217-18, 261, 263, 265, 273, 275, 327-29, 382-83, 453, 474, Rubin, <u>Virginia</u>, p. 171.

[18] Harry F. Byrd's August 28, 1939, speech before the American Legion, Richmond, Virginia, Byrd Papers.

the president's amendment, which was enacted. On October 16, 1939, the senator issued a lengthy statement to the people of Virginia concerning pending neutrality legislation designed to keep the United State out of the war. Byrd reiterated his support for a strong national defense, "a strict cash and carry plan of commerce with belligerent nations and the main essentials of the administration's neutrality proposals," national unity, American neutrality, and America's nonparticipation in the conflict. He asserted that while he had "differed with the President on important domestic policies," he "wholeheartedly" gave him his "support in the essentials of his present foreign policies." Byrd maintained that Roosevelt was "eminently right in urging repeal of the existing law and substituting the cash and carry plan with the prohibition of American ships trading with belligerent nations and keeping American citizens out of combat areas".[19]

Throughout 1940, Senator Byrd continued to advocate national preparedness, keeping America out of foreign wars, support for Roosevelt's foreign policies, greater government efficiency, and fiscal restraint. In his February 1, 1940, speech at Portsmouth for the keel-laying of the battleship Alabama, Byrd, a member of the Naval Affairs Committee, said:

> I take a deep interest in the United States Navy and in the operation of the Norfolk Navy Yard. . . . America, I pray God, will never again enter a foreign war, yet we must not forget that in this day of ruthless dictators and uncurbed ambitions the best insurance for peace is national preparedness. Our Navy will ever remain our front line of defense.... The present Naval building program in America is not for aggression or to conquer new territory but is to defend this nation from any attack, no matter from whence it comes.

In his remarks at the reopening of the Portsmouth-Norfolk Bridge in Portsmouth on that same day, Byrd emphatically declared that the United States must keep out of foreign wars. He asserted that America could remain at peace "if we keep our heads cool and . . . not allow our emotions to run away with our convictions." Byrd provided his audience with a litany of the "appalling effects of war": death, destruction, depression, debt, trade stagnation, industrial stoppages, and unemployment. The senator also

---

[19]Byrd's September 21, 1939, statement to the press, Byrd's October 16, 1939, statement to the people of Virginia, Byrd Papers; Richmond Times-Dispatch, September 22, 1939, p. 7; Hatch, Byrds, p. 467; In his November 10, 1939, letter to President Roosevelt, R. Walton Moore wrote that "Senator Harry F. Byrd takes every opportunity to state how strongly he favored the neutrality legislation." Official File 208-z, Roosevelt Papers.

reminded his listeners that America's domestic problems remained unsolved and cautioned them not to be "deceived by the temporary war boom with its inevitable post-war depression." He argued that the government "must eliminate waste and extravagance in the administration of . . .public affairs, reduce ... expenditures so far as possible, and restore our country to fiscal sanity and security."[20]

During the spring and summer of 1940, Byrd continued to support FDR's national defense program, including his request for additional emergency defense appropriations, despite his past opposition to the president's deficit financing and spending policies. On May 15, he asserted: "Expenditures sufficient for adequate national defense must be authorized immediately, so our military preparedness can be made effective. But, we must remember that financial preparedness is just as important as military preparedness." In August, Byrd urged immediate action on the universal military training bill. (Two weeks before the Senate approved the first peacetime draft in American history, the War Department assured Senator Byrd that Camp Lee would be utilized in the event the selective service legislation passed.) On August 28, he voted for the draft act of 1940 (S. 4164). Nearly ten months later, on June 12, 1941, he voted for his own amendment to the first draft act of 1941 (S. 1524), which declared: "Strikes or lockouts in industry that impede or delay the national defense effort are contrary to sound public policy and . . . are hereby condemned." The measure was adopted. In August, 1941, Byrd also voted for extension of the one year period of training under the selective service act.[21]

Byrd joined his colleague, Senator Glass in supporting aid to the Allies. In his January 15, 1940, speech at the Jackson Day Dinner in Richmond, the senator urged his fellow Americans to make the country strong enough to repel any attack and "to continue to give unstinted aid in greater and greater

---

[20] Byrd's February 1, 1940, speech at Portsmouth for the keel-laying of the battleship <u>Alabama</u>, Byrd's February 1, 1940, remarks at the re-opening of the Portsmouth-Norfolk Bridge in Portsmouth, Byrd's notes for his March 13, 1940, speech to the Danville Women's Club, Byrd's March 28, 1940, comments to a joint meeting of the civic clubs of Roanoke, Byrd Papers.

[21] Hatch, <u>Byrds</u>, p. 468; Byrd's May 15, 1940, statement for the press, Byrd's May 22, 1940, speech to the Senate, Byrd's June 11, 1940, commencement address at Benedictine High School, Richmond, Byrd's August 14, 1940, statement for the Associated Press, Byrd's August 2, 1940, statement for the press, Byrd's August 25, 1940, statement, <u>Entire Voting Record of Senator Harry F. Byrd</u>, pp. 221-24, Box 349, Byrd Papers; <u>Richmond Times-Dispatch</u>, June 2, 1940, p. 8, June 12, 1940, p.7.

amounts to the gallant nation across the seas [i.e. Britain] which is today fighting for its very existence and for the preservation of American ideals." On June 1, 1940, he told the annual convention of the Virginia Association of Insurance Agents: "I do not favor our nation getting into this war but I favor every possible aid to France and England short of war." He also reminded his audience of his continued support for the president's foreign policy and his record of having supported every defense appropriation during the previous seven years. Nearly a fortnight later, Byrd promised fellow Democrats at their state convention in Roanoke that he would "do all in my power short of war to send material aid to the democratic nations France and Great Britain in their mighty struggle to preserve their very existence." He also expressed hope that the United States would "remain at peace; that we will not send millions of American boys to fight and die on foreign soil." Byrd asserted: "The cost of adequate national preparedness and the annual maintenance of a greatly enlarged military establishment will require a sacrifice in the payment of increased taxes on the one hand and a reduction in non-defense spending on the other." In late July, Byrd reiterated his support for FDR's aid-to-Britain policies in a speech to the Young Democrats in Alexandria. [22]

As early as January, 1940, Byrd urged the United States government to "take firm and stern measures to prevent strikes in vital defense industries." The senator complained: "When England is fighting with her back to the wall we in this country are interrupting vital defense projects by strikes for . . . trivial reasons." He strongly asserted that Americans "must forget all political considerations and act to save and preserve our Republic." In late May, 1941, Byrd urged Congress to declare by formal resolutions that strikes "in industries that affect the national defense effort are contrary to sound public policy and they are hereby condemned." The senator maintained that while he wanted "all justice done to labor . . . new and continuing strikes are dangerously retarding aid to England and our own defense preparations." Byrd protested that neither the president nor any administration leaders had taken or even recommended to Congress any "effective action" to "curb this

---

[22] Byrd's January 15, 1940, Jackson Day dinner speech, Richmond, Byrd's June 1, 1940, speech to the annual convention of the Virginia Association of Insurance Agents in Virginia Beach, Byrd's June 14, 1940, speech before the Democratic State Convention in Roanoke, Byrd's July 27, 1940, speech before the Young Democrats in Alexandria, Byrd Papers: Norfolk Ledger-Dispatch, June 1, 1940, p.2.

menace."[23]

In late August of 1940, Senator Byrd expressed grave concern over the slow pace of defense production, the "alarming delay" in placing orders for "vital" military equipment (especially airplanes), and the "lack of coordination and effective cooperation between the different agencies of government in military preparations." The senator threatened to introduce legislation calling for a congressional investigation unless a "promptly forthcoming and satisfactory" explanation was provided from "those in authority." Byrd was manifestly unhappy with the administration's explanation concerning the number of combat planes contracted for and the threat "lagging" defense deliveries posed to America's national security. On August 26, he introduced a resolution calling for a Senate Committee on National Defense, which would closely monitor the progress of defense production and delivery and "take steps that may be necessary to expedite it when unreasonable delays occur."[24]

During the following two months, Byrd successfully urged Congress to meet its constitutional responsibilities by remaining in session. He maintained that it was imperative that Congress be able to deal with any new emergencies that might arise due to the world crisis. The senator argued that if Congress adjourned it could not constitutionally reconvene itself until January 3, 1941, during which time it would not be able to deal with aid-to-Britain and military preparedness matters, as well as keep the United States out of war.[25]

Throughout the remainder of the pre-Pearl Harbor period, Byrd remained deeply apprehensive over what he considered the unsatisfactory progress of the national defense program. In late December, 1940, he

---

[23] Byrd's January 15, 1940, Jackson Day dinner speech, Byrd's May 26, 1941, Senate speech, Byrd Papers; Richmond Times-Dispatch, May 27, 1941, pp. 1, 3, November 2, 1941, p. 11; Hatch, Byrds, p. 471.

[24] Hatch, Byrds, p. 471; For the senator's opinions on the progress of defense production, see Byrd's August 25, 1940, statement, Byrd's August 26, 1940, statement, and the text of Byrd's August 26, 1940, resolution calling for a Congressional National Defense Committee, Byrd Papers; Franklin D. Roosevelt, The Public Papers and Addresses of Franklin D. Roosevelt, 9: 347-48, 354-55.

[25] For the senator's views on congressional adjournment, see Byrd's September 25, 1940, statement, Byrd's October 7, 1940, statement, and Byrd's October 9, 1940, Senate remarks, Byrd Papers.

welcomed the appointment of William S. Knudsen as chairman of the Emergency National Defense Management. He also lamented the fact that his selection was so long overdue. Byrd asserted:

> No one who knows the facts can deny that our national defense program has bogged down to such an extent as to constitute a menace to our national security, and seriously interfere with our effective aid to Great Britain. We have been floundering along in haphazard fashion during the critical days when the map of Europe was reshaped by Hitler's conquests. And only now, sixteen months after the beginning of the European war, we appear to have awakened to the fact that, notwithstanding the enormous appropriations made by Congress, our production of essential military equipment is in very meager amounts.

He once again exhorted the American people to make sacrifices during the national emergency. Byrd also urged industrial cooperation, government efficiency, and administration straightforwardness to the American people as to the present state of the country's military preparedness. As late as November, 1941, Byrd considered the national defense program a "failure." He concluded that the country was "not producing sufficient war material to arm ourselves adequately." "We are not," he warned, "supplying Great Britain with the armaments she needs. Worst of all, the American people are not being told the whole truth about our failure."[26]

In March, 1941, despite his unhappiness with the administration's

---

[26] Byrd's December 2, 1940, statement on the appointment of William S. Knudson as chairman of the Emergency National Defense Management, to the Associated Press and Baltimore Sun, Byrd Papers; Richmond Times-Dispatch, December 22, 1940, pp. 1, 8; Congressional Record, 77th Congress, 1st sess., 1941, 87: 7371-73. The Roosevelt administration disputed as "completely wrong," Senator Byrd's figures on America's defense production and military strength. See Undersecretary of War Robert P. Patterson's August 21, 1941, memo to Roosevelt, President's Personal File 2834, and "Memo For the President" for use at his August 22, 1941, press conference, President's Personal File 2834, Roosevelt Papers; Roosevelt, Public Papers and Addresses of Franklin D. Roosevelt, 10: 337-41; Harry F. Bryd, "The Failure of Our National Defense Program," The Readers Digest, November, 1941, pp. 16-25; Bryd sought Douglas S. Freeman's advice on whether or not to make public certain information concerning America's "desperate" "lack of preparedness." See Bryd to Douglas S. Freeman, December 27, 1940, Freeman to Byrd, December 30, 1940, Freeman Papers.

handling of the national defense program, Byrd voted for the president's Lend-Lease proposal. He also supported amendments to the bill, however, which weakened FDR's discretion over use of congressional appropriations. Byrd wanted all foreign aid to be taken out of an appropriation specifically passed for that purpose. His own amendment was--to a degree--more limiting than the Byrnes Amendment, which he also supported. It limited Lend-Lease to those items purchased under a specific Lend-Lease appropriation or congressionally approved contract (i.e. military appropriations would be spent only on United States armed forces). Both the Senate and House passed the bill with the Byrnes amendment and the president signed it.[27]

One month before America entered the war, Senator Byrd voted against amendments to the neutrality act, which allowed merchant ships carrying Lend-Lease supplies to arm themselves and travel through combat zones to belligerent ports. Unlike most isolationist opponents of neutrality revision, however, Byrd's opposition was not due to his disapproval of such measures. The senator maintained that he would not vote for further aid-short-of-war measures until the administration took appropriate steps to end defense industry strikes, improved the national rearmament program, and suspended New Deal social programs that interfered with the defense program.[28]

Representative Clifton A. Woodrum, a fiscal conservative and longtime advocate of military preparedness, played a major role in guiding Roosevelt's defense and aid-to-Britain measures through Congress. In September, 1940, after FDR failed to back him for the House Democratic majority leadership position, Woodrum, nonetheless, continued to support defense preparedness and the president's handling of foreign policy. From 1939 through 1941, Woodrum, an influential and ranking Democratic member of the House Appropriations Committee, "floor-managed" nearly $23 billion of essential defense appropriations legislation through the House. That included the Lend-Lease Act of March, 1941. Nevertheless, the Roanoke congressman (chairman of the Deficiency Subcommittee) remained an adamant foe of government waste, inefficiency, and excessive spending.[29]

---

[27] Kimball, Unsordid Act, pp. 211-14, 219-220; Hatch, Byrds, pp. 470-71.

[28] Richmond Times-Dispatch, November 2, 1941, p. 11, November 8, 1941, p. 1; Hatch, Byrds, p. 472; Cole, Roosevelt and the Isolationists, pp. 446-55.

[29] James E. Sargent, "Clifton A. Woodrum of Virginia: A Southern Progressive in Congress, 1923-1945," Virginia Magazine of History and Biography 89 (1981), pp. 341, 358-59, 363; James E. Sargent, "Woodrum's Economy Bloc: The Attack on Roosevelt's WPA, 1937-1939, " Virginia

In July, 1939, Woodrum urged Congress to take "definite action on neutrality" before its adjournment. He asserted that probably no important issue which had developed during the Roosevelt administration had "found such unanimity of opinion behind the president [as his neutrality legislation]." After the war got underway, Woodrum urged the United States to keep out of the conflict. The congressman argued that it was "of the very utmost importance" that Congress revise the neutrality law in accordance with Roosevelt's wishes. In his September 18, 1939, radio address over WDBJ, Woodrum expressed strong support for repeal of the arms embargo and the extension of cash-and-carry. He declared: "Our present so-called neutrality which denies these democracies the right to buy our supplies, is a most flagrant and unjust discrimination against those democracies. . . and in favor of the aggressor in this sorry business. It just doesn't make sense!" Woodrum also continued to support Roosevelt's foreign policy and defended the president from charges that he was leading the country into war.[30]

The following month, Woodrum proposed a congressional investigation of the "purposes and activities" of the "National Committee to Keep America Out of Foreign Wars." That organization was headed by Representative Hamilton Fish, the isolationist Republican from Roosevelt's home district in Dutchess County, New York. The Roanoke congressman gained national attention after having made public what he said were duplicate copies of letters written on Fish's congressional stationery soliciting funds for the committee's "propaganda" campaign, which was designed to influence congressional action on repeal of the arms embargo.[31]

Magazine of History and Biography 92 (1985), pp. 204-206; Roanoke Times, March 18, 1941, p. 6, May 13, 1942, p. 16; "National Defense and Preparedness," Addresses and Speeches of Clifton A. Woodrum, Clifton A. Woodrum Papers, Roanoke Public Library, Roanoke, Virginia.

[30] Roanoke Times, July 23, 1939, p. 1, September 19, 1939, p. 1, October 10, 1939, p.1; Roanoke World-News, September 4, 1939, p. 1; Woodrum's September 18, 1939, radio address over WDBJ, Woodrum Papers; Richmond Times-Dispatch, September 5, 1939, p. 10, September 14, 1939, p. 7, September 19, 1939, p. 5, September 22, 1939, p.7.

[31] "Woodrum Exposed Activities of National Committee to Keep America Out of Foreign Wars," Addresses and Speeches of Clifton A. Woodrum, "A Selection of Editorial and News Comments Upon the Occasion When Clifton A. Woodrum Announced His Intention of Retiring from Congress," Woodrum Papers; Roanoke World-News, October 9, 1939, p. 1, October 10, 1939, p.6.

Throughout 1940-1941, Woodrum continued to support Roosevelt's requests for additional national defense appropriations and aid-short-of-war policies. On December 15, 1940, he told a Richmond audience that the United States must increase its aid-to-Britain and yet stay out of the war. The congressman argued that while

> The valiant armies fighting for democracy and their homeland must have more ships, more planes, more ammunition, more tanks, . . . no good, sound reason can be suggested to show that our active entry into the war or any entangling alliance with any other country would be of any real assistance in this conflict.

Woodrum reiterated those sentiments in his May 19, 1941, speech to a college student audience in St. Paul, Minnesota. He asserted: "We must deliver our goods to England, even if it requires naval convoys and shooting, but we should not let ourselves be aroused to the pitch of a declaration of war." In December, 1941, he sharply criticized those opposed to American participation in the war, who were "unwilling to make an economic contribution" to stop the Axis forces "before they get here [to America]."[32]

During that same period of time, however, Woodrum argued that defense items would not be exempt from budget cuts. In early December, 1940, as Congress began consideration of new appropriation bills, the "Economy Bloc" leader maintained: "Congress already has over-appropriated in almost every instance for national defense." He said that there were indications that the army and navy had not been able to spend their appropriations as fast as they had originally planned. Woodrum concluded: "Now is the time for a sort of post-audit. It may be that a lot of money already appropriated and not yet used can be diverted to what the generals

---

[32] "America Prepares for Peace," Woodrum's January 11, 1940, House speech on the Emergency Supplemental Appropriations Bill (H.R. 7805), Addresses and Speeches of Clifton A. Woodrum, Woodrum Papers; Roanoke Times, May 11, 1940, p. 1; Roanoke World-News, June 14, 1940, p. 4; Richmond Times-Dispatch, June 13, 1940, p. 4, December 6, 1940, p. 1, December 15, 1940, p. 5, March 2, 1941, p. 8; clipping from the Saint Paul Pioneer Press, May 20, 1941, p. 1, Box 77, Ulric Bell to Woodrum, June 16, 1941. In June, 1941, Bell, executive chairman of the Fight for Freedom Committee, congratulated the congressman on his May 20, 1941, pro-aid-to-Britain speech in Milwaukee. He also praised Woodrum for his past efforts on behalf of Britain and asked him to join the committee and give speeches for it. (ibid.) Fight for Freedom Committee Papers, Princeton University Library, Princeton, New Jersey. Clipping from the St. Paul Dispatch, May 19, 1941, p. 1, Woodrum Papers.

and admirals now think is the greatest necessity."³³

Woodrum was equally concerned with the injurious effects of defense industry strikes on war production. In his June 10, 1941, address at the University of Virginia, the congressman said that he was prepared to "vote for such legislation as may be necessary" to keep defense plants "in full operation." Woodrum maintained that "disputes, disagreements and misunderstandings must be taken up promptly and considered on their merits and in the meantime we must keep at work for our enemy never sleeps." Just three days before the United States entered the war, Woodrum once again told his House colleagues that strikes in the defense industry must be ended in order to get vital war material to Britain. He argued: "If we can go forward with our industrial production Adolph Hitler will continue to go the downward path and we shall be spared the ravages of war."¹⁸⁴

Despite his opposition to many New Deal programs, Congressman A. Willis Robertson, a fiscal conservative, supported the president's foreign policies. He strongly backed neutrality revision, conscription, rearmament, and aid-short-of-war. On October 19, 1940, at a Democratic rally in Harrisonburg, Robertson lashed out at Republican (i.e. isolationist) criticism of Roosevelt's handling of the national defense program. He also asserted: "We must stand alone with England and we must give her all the assistance possible short of war." In his May 27, 1941, letter to FDR, Robertson wrote: "I campaigned my District from one end to the other last fall in behalf of your foreign policies and I have not turned back. Please enroll me as a volunteer, enlisted for the duration of the war."¹⁸⁵

---

³³ Roanoke World-News, December 9, 1940, p. 1.

³⁴ "National Defense and Preparedness, "Addresses and Speeches of Clifton A. Woodrum, Woodrum Papers; Congressional Record, 77th Congress, 1st sess., 87: 9484-85.

³⁵ Cordell Hull to A. Willis Robertson, June 14, 1939, Robertson to Hull, June 16, 1939, Robertson to Hull, September 27, 1939, Hull to Robertson, October 2, 1939, Robertson's June 2, 1940, commencement address, Robertson to Hull, June 12, 1940, Hull to Robertson, June 17, 1940, A. Willis Robertson Papers, Earl Gregg Swem Library, College of William and Mary, Williamsburg, Virginia; Robertson to Douglas S. Freeman, August 28, 1940, Robertson to Freeman, April 10, 1941, Robertson to Freeman, July 7, 1941, Freeman to Robertson, July 8, 1941, Douglas S. Freeman Papers, Library of Congress, Washington, D.C.; Richmond Times-Dispatch, October 20, 1940, p. 16, January 7, 1941, p. 3; Robertson to Roosevelt, May 27, 1941, Roosevelt

Representative Colgate W. Darden, Jr., of Norfolk, a member of the House Naval Affairs Committee, and expert on national defense, strongly endorsed Roosevelt's interventionist policies. He ardently believed that the United States could stay out of the war by building a national defense second to none and by providing Britain with all the aid it needed. On October 23, 1940, he told the Richmond Lodge of Elks that his recent inspection tour of American naval bases in the Pacific convinced him that in order for the United States to remain a free country, it must have a two-ocean navy as a barrier through which no potential enemy could break. He added that America's survival depended upon its ability to meet any adversary with overwhelming armed force, chiefly in the air and on sea. Darden asserted: "Power is the only doctrine the dictators can understand, and we must prepare, without delay, to speak to them in the only language they can comprehend." The congressman maintained that only the United States possessed the industrial capacity to defend the freedom of the Western world. Two days later, Darden told the Eastern States Conference of the National Junior Chamber of Commerce that the only hope for America to stay out of the war was to create an armed force no nation would dare oppose. He argued:

> We have no hope of escaping this cataclysm unless we can convince any one trespassing on the Western World that he will do so at the risk of meeting the world's greatest armed force. It is behind a great fleet that we must prepare to face any invasion of the Western Hemisphere. We must have a sea defense line so strong that we in this hemisphere will feel secure. ... There is no surer method of guaranteeing peace than to have overwhelming military power.[36]

Throughout 1941, Darden continued to give talks throughout the state on the necessity of strengthening America's national defense and aiding Britain. In early January, 1941, he warned that failure to provide Britain with immediate and unreserved aid would place "the ultimate security and the safety of the American people in the gravest jeopardy." Darden asserted that the Axis powers were "bent ultimately on world empire." He said it would be "fatal for us to assume that, having succeeded in Europe and the East, they will be content to leave unmolested the continents of the Americas." Darden

---

to Robertson, May 25, 1941, President's Personal File 7565, Roosevelt Papers; Robertson's December 6, 1940, address to Norfolk and Western Railway Company employees in Roanoke, Norfolk and Western Magazine, January, 1941, p. 12.

[36] Richmond Times-Dispatch, September 14, 1939, p. 7, October 24, 1940, p. 9, October 26, 1940, p. 4; Roanoke Times, October 5, 1939, p. 6.

concluded: "The survival of Great Britain offers the only opportunity to a long period of peace. . . . We can insure that survival by pressing forward with all possible speed in the production of those materials which she so desperately needs." On January 23, the congressman told the Bristol Bar Association: "America faces the gravest moment in its history." He urged national unity on rearmament and aid-to-Britain and asserted:

> President Roosevelt is dead right on his foreign policy. Clearer than any other American he has apprehended the trend of events abroad and this nation must back him and the Congress in the determination to support England and hold the would-be world conquerors from our doors.[37]

During his campaign for governor in 1941, Darden, a conservative backed by all factions of the state's Democratic organization, emphasized national defense and Virginia's role in it. He also stressed his continued support for FDR's interventionist foreign policy. On March 18, he reiterated the need to aid Britain in a speech to an "Americanism" meeting sponsored by the Hampton Roads post no. 31 of the American Legion. He argued that with "sufficient" American aid, Britain could defeat Germany. Darden declared that the American people "must not be so stupid as to let the only real force standing between Hitler and his objective go down to defeat because of a lack of supplies."[38]

Richmond's representative in Congress held equally interventionist sentiments. In June, 1940, Dave E. Satterfield told a hometown audience that the "fiction" of preserving peace through isolation was "destroyed forever." The congressman helped Woodrum steer defense appropriation bills through the House Appropriations Committee. In his May 8, 1941, address to Congress, Satterfield argued: "We cannot stand in the middle of the road all summer engaging in halfway measures We can no longer afford to stand another hour vacillating, wondering, doubting the future." He urged his colleagues to support the use of convoys to insure delivery of American aid

---

[37] Guy Friddell, Colgate Darden: Conversations with Guy Friddell (Charlottesville: University Press of Virginia, 1978), p. 74: Richmond Times-Dispatch, January 5, 1941, p. 2, January 7, 1941, p. 3, January 24, 1941, p. 11.

[38] Times-Herald (Newport News), March 19, 1941, p. 13; Jonathan J. Wolfe, "Virginia in World War II," (Ph.D. diss., University of Virginia, 1971), pp. 35, 38-40.

to Britain.³⁹

Virginia's other congressmen were no less committed to FDR's aid short-of-war policies. Representatives Winder R. Harris, Schuyler O. Bland, Thomas G. Burch, Patrick H. Drewry, and John W. Flannagan, Jr., stood squarely behind the president's efforts to rearm the country and save Britain from Nazi conquest. In early January, 1941, Flannagan declared:

> What Great Britain needs is action--immediate action and not talk-- and I am in favor of assisting her in every way possible short of sending our boys over. The place to stop the Hitlers is over there, and not over here. The way to do this is to assist Great Britain to the limit.⁴⁰

Howard W. Smith, the long-serving (1931-1966), arch-conservative, anti-New Deal congressman from Northern Virginia's 8th district, shared Senator Byrd's interventionist views and opposition to strikes in the defense industry. In January, 1941, he introduced a bill that prohibited "acts of sabotage with respect to the performance of national-defense contracts." The House rejected Smith's proposal to bar appropriations to defense contractors (under union pressure) who required new workers to become union members (i.e. ran a "closed shop"). In the spring of 1941, the congressman sponsored another anti-strike bill aimed at the defense industry, which the House passed, but the Senate rejected. On November 12, 1941, Smith reminded his House colleagues that he had-- without exception--supported the president's defense program and foreign policies. He went on to inform them that while he supported the arming of merchant ships, he could not accept the Senate's "vastly different proposal," which authorized those vessels' entry into belligerent ports. Smith considered that tantamount to a "declaration of war." He asserted that the United States was "ill-equipped, ill-trained, and ill-prepared" to enter into undeclared naval war with the Axis powers in order to protect those American merchant ships. Smith argued that he was

> unwilling to vote to plunge this country into the horrors and uncertainties of war until we have first set our own house in order, and quelled the labor insurrection [i.e. defense industry strikes], with its violence and bloodshed, that is occurring daily in our midst, or until the President and his administration are ready to take a firm stand in

---

³⁹ Norfolk Ledger-Dispatch, June 17, 1940, p. 18; Richmond Times-Dispatch, June 17, 1940, p. 5, March 2, 1941, p. 8, May 9, 1941, pp. 1, 8, May 10, 1941, p. 8.

⁴⁰ Richmond Times-Dispatch, September 22, 1939, p. 7, August 31, 1940, p. 4, January 7, 1941, p. 3; Virginian-Pilot (Norfolk), May 25, 1941, pp. 1,7.

behalf of the great masses of American people and recommend measures that will put a stop to the labor dictatorship that has been sabotaging our defense effort from the moment of its inception.

Smith kept his word and voted against revision of the neutrality act the following day.[41]

Virginia's state officials and elected representatives from both parties were no less supportive of Roosevelt's foreign policy. In his Armistice Day, 1939, address at the Virginia Military Institute, Governor James H. Price expressed confidence in the president's "clear-headed and courageous determination to avoid involvement in the foreign conflict [i.e. the European war]." In the fall of 1939, Price believed that the war was a European concern and would not directly affect most Virginians. When the General Assembly met in January, 1940, it was slow to react to the urgency of national defense and the European war. It did, however, authorize the transfer of state lands to the federal government for military or naval purposes. In his February 17, 1940, address to the legislature, which met in the Hall of the House of Burgesses in the restored capital of Williamsburg, Governor Price emphasized the close ties that bound the Old Dominion to Great Britain. He then introduced the Marquess of Lothian, Britain's ambassador to the United States, who spoke to the General Assembly on the historic links and common political values that bound his country to its oldest American colony.[42]

---

[41] Bruce J. Dierenfield, Keeper of the Rules: Congressman Howard W. Smith of Virginia (Charlottesville: University Press of Virginia, 1987), pp. 49, 52, 54, 74, 95-96; Congressional Record, 77th Congress, 1st sess., 1941, 87: 8995-97; "Neutrality Act Repeal Speech of November 12, 1941," Box 191, Howard W. Smith Papers, University of Virginia Library, Charlottesville, Virginia; Richmond Times-Dispatch, November 14, 1941, p. 1, November 16, 1941, p. 10.

[42] James H. Price's November 11, 1939, Armistice Day Address at the Virginia Military Institute, Lexington, James H. Price Executive Papers, Virginia State Library, Richmond, Virginia; Price's February 17, 1940, address to the General Assembly, Williamsburg, Marquess of Lothian, British Ambassador to the United States' February 17, 1940, address to the General Assembly, Williamsburg, Journal of the House of Delegates (Richmond: Division of Purchase and Printing, 1940), pp 18-25; Francis H. Heller, Virginia's State Government During the Second World War: Its Constitutional, Legislative, and Administrative Adaptations, 1942-1945 (Richmond: Virginia State Library, 1949), pp. 45-46; Richmond Times-Dispatch, October 15, 1941, p. 8; Alvin L. Hall, "James H. Price and Virginia

By the summer of 1940, when the Battle of Britain was well underway, Governor Price and a majority of this fellow Virginians had become convinced that the United States must help rescue their English cousins even at the risk of war. After the close of the 1940 General Assembly, Price used his executive authority to help prepare the commonwealth for the war. In a series of Roosevelt-style "fireside" chats over state-wide radio, he discussed the obligation of all Virginians to help defend American democracy from totalitarian aggression. On May 30, 1940, the governor established the Virginia Defense Council, the first state council in the country, and named Douglas S. Freeman chairman. His action came only one day after FDR appointed the National Advisory Commission on Defense and one year before the president established the national Office of Civilian Defense. Both the state council and the national commission were designed to help coordinate the national defense effort. Governor Price also set-up regional councils to deal with transportation, public health, communications, civil protection, public recreation, and housing problems, especially those concerning workers at major defense installations throughout the state. Price was the first governor in the country to contend that blacks be given equal opportunity to participate in the national defense program. He insisted that at least one black be appointed to each local draft board, especially in areas where there was a significant black population. The governor appointed the president of St. Paul's Polytechnic Institute, an all-black college affiliated with the Episcopal Church, to the State Defense Council. In December, 1940, Price developed a six-year capital improvement budget for the state in order to prevent post-war economic dislocations.[43]

Politics, 1878 to 1943" (Ph.D. diss., University of Virginia, 1970), pp. 310-11.

[43] Heller, Virginia's State Government, pp. 45-46; Alvin L. Hall, "James Hubert Price: New Dealer in the Old Dominion," in The Governors of Virginia, 1860-1978, eds. Edward Younger and James T. Moore (Charlottesville: University Press of Virginia, 1982), pp. 287-88; The Virginia Defense Council supervised the state's civilian police mobilization, the aircraft warning and air raid services, and helped mobilized Virginia's military, industrial, and moral resources on behalf of the national defense effort. See Marvin W. Schlegel, Virginia on Guard: Civilian Defense and the State Militia in the Second World War (Richmond: Virginia State Library, 1949), pp. 1-2, 35; Lutz, Richmond in World War II, p. 8; Dabney, Virginia, p. 509; Governor Price's May 30, 1940, announcement concerning the appointment of the Virginia Defense Council, Price's October 14, 1940, radio address, "Report on the Progress of the Defense Program in Virginia," organization-Program-Activities of Virginia Defense Council, Richmond, September, 1941,"Price Papers; The Commonwealth, September, 1940, p. 6; Hall, "James H. Price and Virginia Politics," p. 311.

Throughout the pre-Pearl Harbor period, Governor Price continued to provide FDR--a man whom he described as America's "greatest leader"--with steadfast moral support. In February, 1941, Price was among eight southern governors who sent a telegram to Senator Walter George, chairman of the Foreign Relations Committee, endorsing the Lend-Lease bill in the interests of American national security. In his July 22, 1941, statewide radio address, Governor Price told his fellow Virginians:

> Every loyal American in this hour of unlimited national emergency assumes the primary duty of full and complete support of the President in carrying out the preparedness program for the defense of the United States. When the time for action and sacrifice comes, the President can count on the people of Virginia.

On September, 20, 1941, he told a Lansing, Michigan audience:

> Perpetuation of the American Way of Life can be assured only if we are willing to fight for it at any time, anywhere, against all who would challenge us as a Nation and attempt to bar our free passage on the highways of the world. There was no appeasement in the establishment of American liberty, and there can be none in its preservation. We can assure our national safety now only with discipline, spirit, and loyalty on the part of our citizens as a united and immitigable people inspired with the common purpose of defending our country and our form of government against all aggressors.[44]

As early as June, 1940, Colonel LeRoy Hodges, chairman of the State Compensation Board and state comptroller, joined with Francis P. Miller, a House of Delegates member from Fairfax County, in support of a declaration of war against Germany and continued military assistance for Britain. On January 24, 1941, Hodges, a lieutenant colonel in the Virginia National Guard, told an American Legion audience that the United States must be willing to fight for its liberties, including freedom of the seas. He asserted: "To stop the Nazi scourge is our fight." In his June, 1940, keynote address at

---

[44] December 29, 1940, telegram from Price to Franklin D. Roosevelt, Roosevelt to Price, January 3, 1941, May 27, 1941, telegram from Price to Roosevelt, Roosevelt to Price, June 4, 1941, President's Personal File 3743, Roosevelt Papers; n.d. telegram from southern governors to Senator Walter George endorsing the Lend-Lease bill, Box 67, Fight for Freedom Committee Papers; Price's July 22, 1941, radio address, "National Defense and State Progress," Price's September 20, 1941, speech on "National Unity" in Lansing, Michigan, Price's October 10, 1941, speech in Tyler, Texas, Price Papers.

the Democratic state convention, State Senator John W. Carter of Danville urged the United States to arm "to the teeth" and warned his fellow Democrats: "If England and France fall victims. . . we are next on the list." Judge Leon Bazile, a state legislator from Hanover County (and future member of the executive committee of the Virginia Fight for Freedom Committee), told a veterans' group in early December, 1940, that the United States should send its air force and navy to the aid of Britain, who he maintained, was fighting America's battle as well as its own.[45]

Benjamin Muse, a liberal Republican state legislator from Petersburg and unsuccessful gubernatorial candidate in 1941, also embraced Roosevelt's aid-to-Britain policies. In his May 16, 1940, speech to the Lynchburg Republican Club, he urged rapid rearmament and lamented the "crippled" state of American industry under New Deal rule. On October 22, 1941, Muse, chairman of the Petersburg Defense Council, assured Wendell L. Willkie: "I am working at all times for national unity, for aid to Britian [sic] and, generally speaking, for the furtherance of your policies." In his November 3, 1941, press release, Muse urged national unity and pledged his support to the national defense program. Admitting that the country was already "at war," he encouraged all Virginians, Democrats and Republicans, "to uphold, and cooperate with, our national government in the measures which it has taken and the program which it has laid down to make our nation safe." He also maintained: "In the matter of national defense we are none of us Democrats, we are none of us Republicans. We are just 130 million Americans standing shoulder to shoulder."[46]

The state organization of both the Democratic and Republican parties wholeheartedly endorsed aid-to-Britain. At its state convention in Roanoke on June 14, 1940, the Democratic party adopted a foreign policy plank in its platform which stated:

Believing that the United States should lend its moral and economic

---

[45] Richmond Times-Dispatch, June 10, 1940, pp. 1, 5, December 10, 1940, p. 1, December 27, 1940, pp 1, 2, January 25, 1941, p. 5; Norfolk Ledger-Dispatch, June 14, 1940, p. 1; Dabney, Virginia, p. 508.

[46] Dabney, Virginia, p. 510; Benjamin Muse's May 16, 1940, speech to the Lynchburg Republican Club, Benjamin Muse Papers, University of Virginia Library, Charlottesville, Virginia; Muse to Franklyn Waltman, August 29, 1941, October 20, 1941, telegram from Wendell L. Willkie to Muse, Muse to Willkie, October 22, 1941, Muse's November 3, 1941, press release on "National Unity," Benjamin Muse Papers, Duke University Library, Durham, North Carolina.

support to those nations whose regard for treaties and concept of liberty are the same as ours, we put the Democratic party of Virginia on record as favoring speedy aid to the Allies, to the fullest extent of our resources.

The resolution also urged the Roosevelt administration "to take the initiative in drawing together the English-speaking peoples of the world and their Allies into a unity adequate to maintain their freedom, to preserve their culture and to perpetuate their representative forms of government." In early September, 1940, L. Preston Collins, state Democratic campaign manager, publicly praised the Destroyer Deal. On May 18, 1940, Virginia's minuscule Republican party decided at its state convention--also in Roanoke--to support Roosevelt's national defense policies, but attacked his New Deal policies as well.[47]

Virginians in federal service stood squarely behind FDR's foreign policy. R. Walton Moore, trusted Roosevelt ally and counselor to the State Department, held pro-British sentiments. He supported repeal of the arms embargo and stoutly defended FDR's decision to run for a third term. As early as the summer of 1935, Secretary of the Navy Claude A. Swanson favored FDR's naval buildup. In the spring of 1938, he supported a large navy bill. During Swanson's tenure as navy secretary (1933-1939), a "two ocean navy" became a reality. The navy's fleet increased from 155 vessels in March, 1933, when Swanson entered the administration, to 272 ships when the authorized program of ship construction had been completed. The Atlantic squadron was reactivated and received fleet status in November, 1938.[48]

---

[47] "Plank on Foreign Policy in the Platform Adopted by the Virginia State Democratic Convention, Roanoke, Virginia, June 14, 1940," Francis P. Miller Papers, University of Virginia Library, Charlottesville, Virginia; Richmond Times-Dispatch, June 15, 1940, pp. 1, 5, September 5, 1940, p. 4; New York Times, May 19, 1940, p. 3; Virginia's even smaller Socialist party vigorously opposed any American involvement in the European war. On June 18, 1940, Samuel Kocen withdrew as the Socialist party's candidate for Congress from the 3rd district and resigned from the party in protest against its unyielding isolationist position. Kocen maintained that the war was a battle for democracy. See the Richmond Times-Dispatch, September 8, 1939, p. 12, September 19, 1939, p. 6, June 19, 1940, p. 4.

[48] See R. Walton Moore to Roosevelt, November 27, 1936, in Edgar B. Nixon, ed., Franklin D. Roosevelt and Foreign Affairs, vol. 3 (Cambridge: The Belknap Press of Harvard University Press, 1969), p. 512; Roosevelt to Moore, September 11, 1939, Franklin D. Roosevelt, F.D.R.: His Personal Letters, 1928-1945, 2: 918-919; Moore to Roosevelt, July 22, 1940, Roosevelt

Throughout the Roosevelt administration, Alexander W. Weddell remained a steadfast admirer of the president and ally in his efforts to aid Britain. An Anglophile, he enjoyed impressive pro-British credentials. He was a member of the prestigious, internationalist-oriented Council on Foreign Relations. After his retirement from the foreign service in March, 1942, he became a chief financial supporter of the American and British Commonwealth Association (of the United States) and held the positions of director of the English-Speaking Union's national organization and president of its Richmond, Virginia branch. Weddell never doubted the righteousness of the British cause. In his April 17, 1941, letter to John Stewart Bryan, he wrote: "I agree with all my heart that England and the United States and the countries associated with them have an enormous moral advantage over the barbarians [i.e. Germans]." The ambassador also criticized Charles A. Lindbergh for failing to recognize the moral superiority of the British and the subjected people of Europe over the Nazis. In May, 1941, Weddell made a "token" financial contribution to the Committee to Defend America by Aiding the Allies to symbolize his "deep and continuing interest" in the organization. Despite his support for the White Committee, Weddell's sentiments were considerably more militant. In his May 7, 1941, letter to T. Garnett Tabb, treasurer of the Richmond chapter of the White Committee, Weddell wrote:

> Since it is our war that is being waged we should be prepared to accept the necessary and inescapable implications and do all in our power including measures not 'short of war' but 'up to and beyond war' to scotch this hideous Thing which is lose [sic] in the world.

Nearly six months later, he wrote a Richmond friend that he considered the "Prussian" element in German life as a "race apart and must be looked on as a world menace." Weddell also wrote:

> I find myself equally out of patience with those who would not 'send our boys abroad to fight.' For the life of me I cannot see why a person would not prefer to have a fight across the street in another's man

---

to Moore, August 3, 1940, November 25, 1940, telegram from Moore to Roosevelt, Roosevelt to Moore, November 25, 1940, Moore to Roosevelt, January 27, 1941, Roosevelt to Moore, January 29, 1941, President's Personal File 2605, Roosevelt Papers. See FDR's confidential memorandum of July 2, 1935, to Swanson, Nixon, Roosevelt and Foreign Affairs, 2: 546; Henry C. Ferrell, Jr., Claude A. Swanson of Virginia: A Political Biography (Lexington: University Press of Kentucky, 1985), pp. 217-18.

home rather than in his own drawing room.[49]

On May 3, 1939, Weddell, former ambassador to Argentina, assumed his new post as United States ambassador to civil war-torn Spain. As ambassador, Weddell articulated American neutrality in the Spanish Civil War and made it clear to Madrid that the United States considered the survival of British and French power essential to its national security. He correctly argued that while General Franco did not intend to enter the European war--unless certain demands were met--he might--in desperation--ask Hitler for help if conditions in his country continued to deteriorate. Weddell believed that the United States could keep Spain out of the Axis coalition and out of the war by providing it with humanitarian and economic assistance. (Sir Samuel Hoare, Britain's ambassador to Spain, with whom Weddell had been in close and continuous contact with for months, agreed.) The State Department, cognizant of public opposition to aiding a fascist-dominated, pro-Axis country, rejected Weddell's proposal. It remained convinced that Madrid would join the Axis states at any time. Despite his frustration over failure to obtain American aid for Spain and his uneasy relationship with its foreign minister, Ramón Serrano Suñer (who denied Weddell access to Franco for months), Weddell--according to FDR--served his country "with great distinction." Most importantly, he had helped achieve the official United States goal of keeping strategically-placed Spain out of the war and in doing so rendered inestimable service to the British war effort.[50]

---

[49] Virginia Magazine of History and Biography, April, 1948, p. 124; January 22, 1937, telegram from Alexander W. Weddell to Franklin D. Roosevelt, Roosevelt to Weddell, January 25, 1937, President's Personal File 7482, Roosevelt Papers; "Biographical Sketch of Alexander Wilbourne Weddell," Description and Guide Index to Selected Manuscript Accessions Since 1981 (Richmond: Virginia Historical Society, 1985), pp. 1-3, Alexander W. Weddell to Walter H. Mallory, January 2, 1935, Weddell to S. Pinkney Tuck, January 19, 1939, Weddell to Helen F. Draper, October 4, 1940, Weddell to Roosevelt, December 30, 1940, Weddell to John Stewart Bryan, April 17, 1941, Weddell to Douglas S. Freeman, April 21, 1941, Weddell to T. Garnett Tabb, May 7, 1941, Weddell to Mrs. Henry Baskerville, October 30, 1941, Alexander Wilbourne Weddell Papers, Virginia Historical Society, Richmond, Virginia.

[50] "Biographical Sketch of . . . Weddell," Description, p. 1, Weddell to Roosevelt, August 28, 1940, Roosevelt to Weddell, September 24, 1940, Weddell to Helen F. Draper, October 4, 1940, Weddell to Sumner Welles, November 23, 1940, Weddell to Draper, November 26, 1940, Weddell to John Stewart Byran, January 29, 1941, Roosevelt to Weddell, February 6, 1941,

Chief of Staff and General of the Army, George Catlett Marshall, the highest-ranking Virginian to serve in the armed forces during the Second World War, was a strong advocate of military preparedness (especially airplane production), selective service, and aid-short-of-war. He maintained that the Selective Training and Service Act and legislation authorizing the federalization of reserve forces were vital for the national defense and "constituted a reversal of the historic and almost tragic policy that the United States would prepare for war only after becoming involved in war." Marshall welcomed increased British purchases of American weapons and munitions and was particularly pleased that Congress passed FDR's Lend-Lease bill. The general supported a greater American military presence in the Atlantic, which would benefit Britain, strengthen hemispheric security, and lay a solid foundation for Anglo-American collaboration in the event of American entry into the war. Despite his pro-British sympathies, Marshall always placed American military needs (e.g. with regard to the shipment of war material to Britain) first.[51]

Following the eruption of war in September, 1939, Rear Admiral Richard E. Byrd, commanding officer of the United States Antarctic Service and staff member of the navy department's Bureau of Aeronautics, abandoned his anti-war stance and firmly embraced FDR's interventionist policies. From 1939-41, Byrd lobbied members of Congress to support the president's neutrality revision legislation, destroyers-for-bases deal, Lend-Lease proposal, and other aid-to-Britain policies. The admiral publicly refuted the allegations of Charles Lindbergh and the America First Committee that the president

---

Weddell to Roosevelt, March 28, 1942, Roosevelt to Weddell, April 1, 1942, Weddell Papers; K. Richmond Temple, "Alexander Weddell: Virginian in Diplomatic Service," Virginia Cavalcade 34 (1984), pp. 36-39; Charles R. Halstead, "Diligent Diplomat: Alexander W. Weddell as American Ambassador to Spain, 1939-1942," Virginia Magazine of History and Biography 82(1974): 3-38; Drummond, Passing of American Neutrality, pp. 163, 231, 325; United States Department of State, Foreign Relations of the United States: Diplomatic Papers, 1940, 2: 824-31.

[51] Forrest C. Pogue, George C. Marshall: Ordeal and Hope, 1939-1942, vol. II (New York: Viking, 1966), pp. 5, 6, 56-63, 68-71, 121-122, 126-127, 135-36, 144-145, 148-154; George C. Marshall's February 16, 1940, radio broadcast to the Reserve Officers Association, from Washington, D.C., Marshall's August 5, 1940, NBC broadcast on the Selective Service Act, Marshall's September 15, 1941, speech to the American Legion convention in Milwaukee, Wisconsin, George C. Marshall Papers, George C. Marshall Research Library, Lexington, Virginia; Douglas S. Freeman to Marshall, August 5, 1940, Marshall to Freeman, August 16, 1940, Freeman Papers.

was leading the country into war. On August 19, 1941, Byrd told 15,000 people at a Madison Square Garden rally sponsored by the New York City-based, interventionist Council for Democracy that Roosevelt was trying to preserve American democracy, not push America into the European war. He defended the president's foreign policy and accused some politicians (with Senator Burton K. Wheeler in mind) of playing politics at the expense of national defense. The admiral declared: "This is the age-old struggle between democracy and tyranny, between freedom and slavery, between good and evil. This is everybody's war."[62]

On October 8, 1941, Byrd delivered another assault on the isolationists via a radio address over WABC and the Columbia Broadcasting Service. In his Council for Democracy-sponsored address, the admiral declared that Hitler threatened to destroy American democracy. He warned his fellow Americans against disunity, which could lead to an invasion of the "Nazi idea from within." Byrd predicted that in the event of a British defeat, Germany could threaten Latin America and even the United States. The admiral asserted that those who recognized the danger of the Nazi threat were not "warmongers." The real "warmongers," he argued, included Hitler and those

---

[52] Hatch, Byrds, pp. 362-63; "Biographical Sketch of Admiral Richard E. Byrd," Richard E. Byrd to Franklin D. Roosevelt, n.d., Roosevelt to Byrd, July 12, 1939, September 20, 1939, telegram from Byrd to Roosevelt, Roosevelt to Byrd, September 22, 1939, President's Personal File 201, Byrd to Roosevelt, September 27, 1939, Byrd to Roosevelt, September 30, 1939, President's Official File 1561, Byrd to Roosevelt, October 26,1939, Roosevelt to Byrd, November 2, 1939, Byrd to Roosevelt, August 28, 1940, September 4, 1940, telegram from Byrd to Roosevelt, Roosevelt to Byrd, September 5, 1940, November 5, 1940, telephone message from Byrd to Roosevelt, November 6, 1940, telegram from Byrd to Roosevelt, Roosevelt to Byrd, November 12, 1940, December 30, 1940, telegram from Byrd to Roosevelt, Roosevelt to Byrd, December 31, 1940, President's Personal File 201, Byrd to Roosevelt (via Grace G. Tully), February 7, 1941, FDR's secretary to Byrd, February 13, 1941, President's Official File 4193, Byrd to Roosevelt, March 18, 1941, Byrd to Roosevelt, June 10, 1941, Tully (on behalf of FDR) to Byrd, June 17, 1941, August 18, 1941, telegram from Byrd to Tully, clipping from the New York Times, August 20, 1941, pp. 1, 4F, 4, Edwin M. Watson (FDR's secretary) to Byrd, August 21, 1941, Byrd to Watson, August 22, 1941, Roosevelt to Byrd, September 24, 1941, President's Personal File 201, Roosevelt Papers; "First Annual Report of the Council for Democracy," (October 20, 1941), Box I, "Council for Democracy," (pamphlet), 1941, (objectives), Box I, Virginius Dabney Papers, University of Virginia Library, Charlottesville, Virginia.

Americans preaching national disunity.[53]

During the weeks leading up to the Pearl Harbor attack, Byrd warned his fellow Americans that labor strikes were doing irreparable harm to national security. In October, 1941, he predicted that if current strikes continued, Hitler would win without the necessity of a physical invasion. The admiral called for an armistice between industry and labor and pleaded with his trade unionist friends to end the strikes. In his "statement to the American people," Byrd declared: "It is a matter of life or death to this Republic that strikes be stopped, that an armistice be declared immediately between industry and labor." The following month, Byrd sent a telegram to Philip Murray, president of the Congress of Industrial Organizations (CIO), which congratulated the union for passing a "national unity" resolution at its recent convention. (Murray read Byrd's message to the convention.) The admiral expressed sympathy for labor and urged the union to continue its support for national unity in order to avoid economic collapse and invasion of the "Nazi idea." To do otherwise, he argued, would weaken democracy, result in the loss of those gains labor had made, and antagonize fellow citizens who viewed the strikes as a threat to the national defense effort. Byrd also reminded Murray that Roosevelt was labor's friend and trade unionists needed to rally behind him. In his November 25, 1941, letter to Byrd, President Roosevelt expressed his appreciation for the admiral's communications with labor and his efforts on behalf of national unity.[54]

Editorial opinion in Virginia stood solidly behind Roosevelt's interventionist foreign policy. Some editors were considerably more militant than their fellow Virginians. As of August, 1941, seven daily (albeit minor) newspapers favored America's immediate entry into the war. The Old Dominion's most influential newspaper publisher, John Stewart Bryan, president of the College of William and Mary, was a staunch advocate of aid-

---

[53] October 7, 1941, telegram from Byrd to Tully, text of Byrd's October 8, 1941, radio broadcast, "Disunity The Warmonger," over WABC and the Columbia Broadcasting Service, Tully to Byrd, October 10, 1941, Byrd to Roosevelt, October 11, 1941, President's Personal File 201, Roosevelt Papers; "First Annual Report of the Council for Democracy," (October 20, 1941), Box I, Dabney Papers.

[54] Byrd to Roosevelt, October 29, 1941, Byrd to Tully, October 30, 1941, clipping form the New York Times, n.d., Roosevelt to Byrd, November 7, 1941, Roosevelt to Byrd, November 14, 1941, November 20, 1941, telegram from Byrd to Philip Murray, Byrd to Roosevelt, November 22, 1941, Roosevelt to Byrd, November 25, 1941, President's Personal File 201, Roosevelt Papers.

to-Britain. He was a member of both the White Committee and the Fight for Freedom Committee. Bryan was deeply concerned over the plight of England and was convinced that America's national security depended on British domination of the Atlantic. Virginia's three leading editors--Douglas S. Freeman (Richmond News-Leader), Virginus Dabney (Richmond Times-Dispatch), and Louis I. Jaffe (Norfolk Virginian-Pilot), a member of the White Committee, shared Bryan's support for aid-short-of war. In late December, 1940, Bryan, Dabney, and Freeman (albeit reluctantly) were among 169 Americans who sent Roosevelt a telegram, "A Statement of Urgency," which urged him to do "everything [short-of-war] that may be necessary to insure the defeat of the Axis powers." The message called for "industrial mobilization," greater defense preparation, and continued aid-to-Britain. [55]

Douglas S. Freeman shared his publisher's distress over the outbreak of war in September, 1939, and Nazi Germany's domination of Western Europe. The editor strongly advocated American neutrality and supported most of Roosevelt's rearmament and aid-short-of-war policies. He did not, however, approve of Roosevelt's Destroyer Deal or re-election to a third term. Neither did he share what he considered Bryan's "frantic" and "bellicose" attitude. Despite his pro-British sympathies, Freeman regularly expressed dismay over "war hysteria" and criticized those who advocated immediate American entry into the war. He did not think it wise for the United States to rush into the war--either by provocative action or war declaration--until it was militarily prepared. Unlike most influential Virginians, Freeman was convinced that FDR was "maneuvering to make

---

[55] Interview with Dabney, November 28, 1986; Douglas S. Freeman, John Stewart Bryan: A Biography (New York: Charles Scribner's Sons, 1947), p. 39, not published for sale, Douglas S. Freeman Papers, Virginia Historical Society, Richmond, Virginia; John Stewart Bryan to Francis P. Miller, June 8, 1940, Louis I. Jaffe to Miller, June 6, 1940, Francis P. Miller Papers, University of Virginia Library, Charlottesville, Virginia; "List of Signers, May 7, 1941," Box 130, Bryan to Miller, August 5, 1940, Bryan to Ulric Bell, July 28, 1941, Fight for Freedom Committee Papers; Bryan to Alexander W. Weddell, October 28, 1940, Bryan to Weddell, December 16, 1940, Bryan to Weddell, October 28, 1941, Weddell Papers; White Committee membership list as of May 29, 1940, Box 13, White Papers; "What Is The Fight For Freedom," p. 13, Box 403, Glass Papers; Barbara Trigg Brown to Dabney, July 13, 1941, Dabney Papers; Richmond Times-Dispatch, October 10, 1939, p. 9, June 11, 1940, p. 8, December 27, 1940, pp. 1-2, August 3, 1941, p. 14,; David J. Winton to Bryan, December 17, 1940, Freeman to Bryan, December 20, 1940, Freeman Papers.

Germany strike the first blow" against the United States. Nevertheless, his editorials argued otherwise. As early as January, 1939, the editor advocated repeal of the arms embargo and adoption of cash-and-carry provisions applicable to all exports during wartime. In July of that year, Freeman sent Roosevelt--via the president's secretary, Stephen Early--his News-Leader editorials on neutrality revision legislation. Throughout the early stages of the war, Freeman, a highly-regarded military strategist, sent his daily editorials on the war situation and military operations, to the White House. On September 19, 1939, he journeyed to Washington to discuss the European war situation with various military officials, including General Marshall and the General Staff.[56]

On November 20, 1941, John W. Wheeler-Bennett of the New York City - based British Information Services, invited Freeman, on behalf of Brendan Bracken, Minister of Information and close personal friend of Prime Minister Winston S. Churchill, to "pay an early visit to England." Wheeler-Bennett wrote that Bracken believed that considering Freeman's "wide knowledge of general strategic problems, and the history of the war, and . . . close study of the present war operations," he "would be interested in seeing Britain under war-time conditions." Wheeler-Bennett also indicated that

---

[56] See Freeman's diary entries from September 1, 1939-December 4, 1941, for a revealing account of his unhappiness and preoccupation with Germany's blitzkrieg through Western Europe. Freeman also spent a good deal of his time discharging his duties as permanent chairman of the Virginia Defense Council. See Freeman's diary entries for June 5, 1940-December 4, 1941, and the minutes of the council's first meeting on June 5, 1940. Freeman to Harry F. Byrd, April 20, 1939, Freeman to Stephen Early (FDR's secretary), July 6, 1939, Early to Freeman, July 7, 1939, Freeman to Early, July 10, 1939, Freeman to Early, July 19, 1939, Early to Freeman, July 20, 1939, Freeman diary, September 5, 1939, Freeman to Early, September 8 ,1939, Early to Freeman, September 11, 1939, Murat Williams to Freeman, October 13, 1939, Freeman diary, May 19, 1940, Freeman diary, May 20, 1940, Freeman diary, July 17, 1940, excerpts form Freeman's "Prepare for Economic War!" address at the ABA Graduate School of Banking, see The Bankers Magazine, August, 1940, Freeman to George C. Marshall, August 5, 1940, Marshall to Freeman, August 16, 1940, Freeman diary, September 3, 1940, Freeman diary, September 27, 1940, Freeman's "An Appraisal for Mr. John Stewart Bryan of the [European war] Situation, September 28, 1940," Box 35, Freeman diary, October 14, 1940, Freeman to Bryan, June 24, 1941, A. Willis Robertson to Freeman, July 7, 1941, Freeman to Robertson, July 8, 1941, Freeman to Lord Halifax, July 28, 1941, Lord Halifax to Freeman, August 8, 1941, Freeman diary, September 19, 1939, Freeman Papers; Richmond Times-Dispatch, September 28, 1940, p. 6; Richmond News-Leader, January 4, 1939, p.10.

Bracken "would appreciate the benefit of your [Freeman's] views." Freeman confided in Eugene Meyer, publisher of the Washington Post, that he would not go to England to be "pumped full of propaganda," but would go if he "had any information of real value to the allied cause." In early December, 1941, Freeman decided it would be "unwise to attempt to go to England."[57]

Nearly nine months before the outbreak of war in Europe, the Richmond News-Leader supported repeal of the arms embargo and the application of cash-and-carry for all exports to belligerents as the "surest way to keep out of a European war." After September 1, 1939, its pro-British sentiments, notwithstanding, the paper supported American neutrality and cautioned Americans to "avoid partisan feeling." Throughout most of the pre-Pearl Harbor period, the News-Leader supported rapid rearmament (especially of ships) and warned against actual American involvement in the war until the country was militarily prepared. It did not believe that FDR wanted to take the United States into war. The paper enthusiastically backed conscription as patriotic and compatible with democracy. Despite its support for the sale of war material to the Allies, the News-Leader opposed the Destroyer Deal. It argued that the executive agreement annulled American neutrality and constituted "an act of war" and [unconstitutional] "executive dictatorship."[58]

In September, 1940, the News-Leader endorsed Roosevelt for a third-term, despite its differences with him on economic and fiscal policy (and Freeman's personal objections). Its September 26, 1940, editorial acknowledged the danger of any president serving a third term; nonetheless,

---

[57] John W. Wheeler-Bennett to Freeman, November 20, 1941, Freeman diary, November 21, 1941, Freeman to Wheeler-Bennett, November 29, 1941, Freeman to Eugene Meyer, December 6, 1941, Freeman to Meyer, December 9, 1941, Freeman Papers.

[58] Richmond News-Leader, January 4, 1939, p. 10, February 20, 1939, p. 10, March 8, 1939, p. 10, April 7, 1939, p. 10, April 10, 1939, p. 10, April 11, 1939, p. 10, April 14, 1939, p. 10, May 1, 1939, p. 10, June 21, 1939, p. 10, July 10, 1939, p. 10, August 24, 1939, p. 10, August 25, 1939, p. 10, September 1, 1939, p. 10, September 22, 1939, p. 10, October 3, 1939, p. 10, October 27, 1939, p. 10, November 3, 1939, p. 10, November 24, 1939, p. 10, May 23, 1940, p. 10, June 3, 1940, p. 10, June 11, 1940, p. 10, June 13, 1940, p. 10, June 14, 1940, p. 10, June 17, 1940, p. 10, June 21, 1940, p. 10, June 25, 1940, p. 10, August 6, 1940, p. 10, August 26, 1940, p. 10, August 29, 1940, p. 10, September 3, 1940, p. 10, September 4, 1940, September 9, 1940, p. 10, September 17, 1940, p. 10, October 24, 1940, p. 10, October 31, 1940, p. 10.

it supported FDR because of his social ideals, experience in foreign policy, and ability to protect the United States from foreign enemies. The News-Leader also continued to support rapid rearmament and additional aid to Britain, including Lend-Lease. By early October, 1941, it embraced repeal of the neutrality act. In its July 7, 1941, editorial, the News-Leader abandoned its long-held advocacy of neutrality and its argument that the United States should avoid participation in the war until its national defense was strong enough to defeat any adversary. It asserted that the United States should enter the war whenever the president and Congress decide is the appropriate time. Three days later, the paper criticized Charles A. Lindbergh's isolationist views and declared that Hitler had to be destroyed. The News-Leader concluded: "Ours is the choice between the noblest and the beast, between a fight for a free world and a solitary, perhaps futile, struggle for an isolated and insulated America."[59]

In December of 1940, while the Battle of Britain still raged, Virginius Dabney abandoned his long-held position that the United States should have nothing to do with European wars. The Richmond Times-Dispatch editor argued that the Munich "sell-out" to Hitler, notwithstanding, the United States faced a grave danger from abroad. It could not afford-- he asserted-- to remain aloof from the European conflict and allow Britain to lose the war. Nevertheless, he did not advocate America's entry into the war. He turned down Francis P. Miller's invitation to sign the "Summons To Speak Out," which called for a declaration of war against Germany. In his May 18, 1940, letter to William Allen White, Dabney expressed appreciation for the editor's invitation to serve on his committee. He wrote:

> I think we ought to do everything we possibly can to help the Allies, provided we are not drawn into the war ourselves. I believe that if we become belligerents, we run a grave risk of losing our democracy permanently, even though our side is the nominal 'winner' in the war. If we should go in as active participants on the side of the Allies, and should pile up a national debt totaling around one billion dollars, I think our fiscal structure would collapse, and that we would be in serious danger of a dictatorship here. . . . I am tremendously interested

---

[59] Ibid., September 26, 1940, p. 10, October 1, 1940, p. 10, December 5, 1940, p. 10, December 11, 1940, p. 10, January 10, 1941, p. 10, January 31, 1941, p. 10, February 1, 1941, p. 8, February 8, 1941, p. 8, March 10, 1941, p. 10, April 25, 1941, p. 10, April 29, 1941, p. 10, May 9, 1941, p. 10, June 13, 1941, p. 10, June 14, 1941, p. 8, June 23, 1941, p. 10, July 7, 1941, p. 6, July 10, 1941, p. 10, August 7, 1941, p. 10, September 1, 1941, p. 6, October 6, 1941, p. 10, October 8, 1941, p. 10, October 10, 1941, p. 10, October 31, 1941, p. 10.

in the success of the Allies, but not sufficiently interested to do anything which seems to me gravely to imperil our own democratic way of life.

Dabney believed that his reluctance to see the United States--already burdened with a $45 billion national debt--make "every economic effort to help the Allies" (i.e. provide them with billions of dollars) made him "ineligible to serve" on White's committee. Nevertheless, he did join the committee. Less than a month later, however, he reluctantly resigned from it. In his June 14, 1940, letter to White, he wrote:

> The situation of the Allies has deteriorated so very rapidly in the past week, that I am becoming more and more convinced of the very danger that we shall get into the war too late to save them, and just in time to absorb the full load of carrying the battle on. I can think of nothing more certain to wreck this country if that should happen.[60]

Dabney did, however, join other interventionist organizations. At the invitation of Henry R. Luce, owner and publisher of Time magazine, and Col. William Donovan, father of the Office of Strategic Services (OSS), he served on the board of directors of the Council for Democracy. The council defended and promoted democracy as "the best way of life," advocated national unity, and supported Roosevelt's aid-short-of-war policies. Dabney was a founding member of the "United Americans," a similar, non-partisan organization also dedicated to democracy, national unity, and Roosevelt's foreign policy. (In April, 1941, the "United Americans" became part of the White Committee.) Dabney also served as a special advisor to the National

---

[60] Interview with Dabney, November 28, 1986; Dabney's December 7, 1986, letter to the author. (Letter is in author's possession.); Virginius Dabney to Francis P. Miller, June 6, 1940, Miller Papers; Dabney to William Allen White, May 18, 1940, White to Dabney, May 24, 1940, White to Dabney, May 31, 1940, Dabney to White, June 14, 1940, White to Dabney, June 19, 1940, William Allen White Papers, Library of Congress, Washington D.C.; Dabney to Miller, August 12, 1940, Fight for Freedom Committee Papers. See Dabney's celebrated December 1, 1940, Richmond Times-Dispatch editorial entitled "The Hour Strikes for America," which reflected his changed view as to American involvement in the European conflict and the necessity to save Britain.

Defense Advisory Commission, which published DEFENSE. [61]

During the 1940 presidential election campaign, before his views on the war had changed, Dabney agreed with what he considered Republican candidate Wendell L. Willkie's "noninterventionist" foreign policy views. In the spring of 1941, Dabney turned down an invitation from Mrs. D. Tucker Brown (also known as Barbara Trigg Brown), secretary-treasurer of the militant Virginia Fight for Freedom Committee, to join its executive committee. The editor subscribed to the group's "general objectives" and wished it well, but was unwilling to support its "dogmatic" "demands" (e.g. a declaration of war against Germany). Nevertheless, Brown frequently congratulated Dabney on his pro-interventionist editorials in the Times-Dispatch and considered him "a great help to the Fight for Freedom Committee." [62]

When war broke out in September, 1939, the Richmond Times-Dispatch advocated both American noninvolvement and revision of the neutrality act. It argued that American participation in the European war would jeopardize its democracy and invite economic ruin. The paper maintained that American entry into the war could lead to economic collapse and either a communist or fascist dictatorship in Washington. It concluded that repeal of the arms embargo and reenactment of cash-and-carry would

---

[61] Henry R. Luce, Col. William Donovan, et al., to Dabney, September 18, 1940, September 23, 1940, telegram from Dabney to the Council for Democracy, Raymond Gram Swing and C.D. Jackson to Dabney, October 4, 1940, "Council for Democracy," Pamphlet, 1941, (objectives), Box I, Dabney to Jackson, October 17, 1940, Jackson to Dabney, March 10, 1941, "Council for Democracy: A Brief Statement of Aims and Activities," Pamphlet, n.d., Box I, "First Annual Report of the Council for Democracy," (October 20, 1941), Box I, February 3, 1941, telegram from William Allen Neilson, Frank Hogan, et al., to Dabney, n.d. telegram from Dabney to Edward Hart, O. McPherson to Dabney, April 18, 1941, Dabney's December 16, 1940, expense account statement for the National Defense Advisory Commission, Box I, Frank Bane to Dabney, December 7, 1940, Dabney to Bane, December 9, 1940, Dabney Papers.

[62] Interview with Dabney, November 28, 1986; Wendell L. Willkie to Dabney, February 19, 1941, Dabney to Francis P. Miller, April 28, 1941, Mrs. D. Tucker Brown to Dabney, May 8, 1941, Dabney to Brown, May 9, 1941, Brown to Dabney, July 7, 1941, Dabney to Brown, July 8, 1941, Brown to Dabney, July 13, 1941, Brown to Dabney, September 26, 1941, Dabney to Brown, August 15, 1941, Dabney to Brown, September 27, 1941, Dabney to Brown, December 13, 1941, Dabney Papers.

provide invaluable assistance to the Allies and reduce the chances of American involvement in the conflict. The Times-Dispatch stood steadfastly behind the president's foreign policy and believed he sincerely wanted to keep the country out of the war. It strongly favored his rearmament program. On occasion, however, it criticized FDR for making "unneutral" public statements. [63]

Throughout 1940, the Times-Dispatch continued to support the president's aid-short-of-war policies, including the provision of additional assistance to the Allies (especially airplanes), the selective service act, and the strengthening of American defense. Nevertheless, it criticized FDR's "provocative" and "inflammatory" commencement address at the University of Virginia on June 10. (Roosevelt declared that American policy had changed from "neutrality" to "non-belligerency," i.e. the United States would openly support the Allies without itself going to war.) The paper was slow to condone the destroyers-for-bases deal, which it argued drew the United States closer to war. It was not until September of 1940 that the Times-Dispatch finally gave its blessing to that controversial decision. The paper concluded that the agreement was in the country's national security interests because it would save England from defeat and strengthen America's position in the Western Hemisphere. Later that month, the paper endorsed FDR for re-election, despite its disapproval of a third term and its unhappiness with many of the president's methods and policies. It argued that Roosevelt was infinitely better qualified and more experienced to handle the country's foreign policy during those turbulent times. The Times-Dispatch's editorial of December 1, 1940, reflected Virginius Dabney's changed view as to what America's attitude should be towards the war. It argued that the United States could not permit a German victory over Britain, notwithstanding the latter's "sell-out to Hitler" in 1938. The paper urged the government to use every means, short of war to save England, regardless of the risks of

---

[63] Richmond Times-Dispatch, September 2, 1939, p. 8, September 4, 1939, p. 10, September 7, 1939, p. 12, September 10, 1939, p. 2, September 13, 1939, p. 8, September 14, 1939, p. 10, September 15, 1939, p. 14, September 16, 1939, p. 6, September 20, 1939, p. 8, September 21, 1939, p. 12, September 22, 1939, p. 14, September 23, 1939, p. 8, September 27, 1939, p. 8, October 6, 1939, p. 16, October 7, 1939, p. 8, October 22, 1939, p. 2, October 29, 1939, p. 2, November 3, 1939, p. 14, December 10, 1939. p. 2, December 14, 1939, p. 10.

American involvement.[64]

During the months leading up to America's entry into the war, the Times-Dispatch defended Roosevelt's increasingly interventionist policies. It "enthusiastically" supported his Lend-Lease proposal, the extension of the draft, and criticized the "isolationist" opinions of Lindbergh and the American First Committee. The Times-Dispatch went so far as to accuse Lindbergh of being "pro-Nazi." The paper also urged the president to end strikes in the defense industry, which it maintained, impeded the country's national defense program. As early as the spring of 1941, the paper asserted that in the event of a British defeat, the United States would be Hitler's next victim. Once again, it reiterated its advocacy of "more comprehensive and effective aid to England." It also called for convoying war material to that beleaguered country. In September, 1941, the paper endorsed FDR's "shoot-on-sight" policy in the Atlantic, and urged Congress to repeal the neutrality act because the United States had long since abandoned neutrality and its commitment to a British victory required "a far more effective American war effort."[65]

---

[64] Ibid., May 14, 1940, p. 10, May 17, 1940, p. 14, May 19, 1940, p. 4, May 21, 1940, p. 10, June 1, 1940, p. 8, June 4, 1940, p. 8, June 7, 1940, p. 16, June 8, 1940, p. 10, June 9, 1940, p. 4, June 11, 1940, p. 12, June 12, 1940, p. 10, June 14, 1940, p. 16, June 15, 1940, p. 8, June 16, 1940, p. 4, June 18, 1940, p. 10, June 23, 1940, p. 4, June 26, 1940, p. 8, July 4, 1940, p. 8, July 11, 1940, p. 8, July 16, 1940, p. 6, July 27, 1940, p. 6, August 1, 1940, p. 8, August 6, 1940, p. 8, August 8, 1940, p. 10, August 18, 1940, p. 6, August 30, 1940, p. 16, September 4, 1940, p. 10, September 5, 1940, p. 10, September 14, 1940, p.8, September 26, 1940, p. 10, September 27, 1940, p. 18, October 8, 1940, p. 8, October 13, 1940, p. 6, October 14, 1940, p.10, October 17, 1940, p. 12, October 31, 1940, p. 10, November 4, 1940, p. 10, November 26, 1940, p. 8, December 1, 1940, p. 8, December 5, 1940, p. 12, December 10, 1940, p. 8, December 22, 1940, p. 6, December 29, 1940, p. 4, December 27, 1940, p. 10, December 28, 1940, p. 6, December 30, 1940, p. 10, Dabney's December 7, 1986, letter to the author.

[65] Ibid., January 4, 1941, p. 6, January 23, 1941, p. 10, January 29, 1941, p. 10, February 1, 1941, p. 10, February 6, 1941, p. 10, February 9, 1941, p. 6, February 24, 1941, p. 6, February 26, 1941, p. 8, February 29, 1941, p. 16, March 5, 1941, p. 12, March 7, 1941, p. 18, March 9, 1941, p. 6, March 12, 1941, p. 12, March 19, 1941, p. 10, March 24, 1941, p. 10, March 26, 1941, p. 10, April 12, 1941, p. 10, April 22, 1941, p. 10, April 24, 1941, p. 14, April 27, 1941, p. 6, April 29, 1941, p. 10, May 8, 1941, p. 14, May 10, 1941, p. 8, May 23, 1941, p. 18, May 28, 1941, p. 12, May 29, 1941, p. 18, June 23, 1941, p. 8, June 24, 1941, p. 8, July 5, 1941, p. 6, July 8, 1941, p. 8, July 10, 1941, p. 8, August 2, 1941, p. 6, August 13, 1941, p. 10, August 15, 1941, p. 18,

None of the state's other major daily newspapers defended Lindbergh's attacks on Roosevelt's foreign policy. Not one espoused "isolationist" editorial positions. Most of those dailies were convinced that the president's aid-short-of-war policies--which they supported--would keep America out of the war. They also believed that Roosevelt sincerely wanted to keep the country out of the conflict. All of them supported the president's rearmament and aid-to-Britain policies. The press maintained that the survival of Britain, a country bound by blood, language, government, and markets to America, was in the national interest. Virginia's editors believed that Hitler was an enemy of liberty, democracy, freedom of the seas, and world peace. They argued that he must be stopped in Europe--via aid-to-Britain--before he could attack the United States. There were, however, minor differences of opinion as to the extent of that assistance (e.g. "convoying" vs. "patrolling"). Despite their opposition to a third-term and many of his domestic policies, all of the state's major papers endorsed FDR's re-election in 1940. They believed Roosevelt was the only available candidate capable of handling the country's foreign affairs. Seven of the state's minor dailies supported a declaration of war against Germany. Those included the Staunton News-Leader and the Lynchburg News. Most of the press argued that Roosevelt should accelerate the country's defense program-- which they considered inadequate--and end strikes in the defense plants, which hurt America's war production and jeopardized the flow of invaluable war material to Britain.[66]

September 10, 1941, p. 10, September 12, 1941, p. 18, September 14, 1941, p. 6, September 16, 1941, p. 10, September 24, 1941, p. 12, September 28, 1941, p. 6, October 5, 1941, p. 6, October 10, 1941, p. 18, October 21, 1941, p. 14, October 31, 1941, p. 18, November 1, 1941, p. 8, November 2, 1941, p. 6, November 7, 1941, p. 18, November 14, 1941, p. 22.

[66] Norfolk Ledger-Dispatch, February 18, 1939, p. 6, March 9, 1939, p. 6, March 21, 1939, p. 10, April 5, 1939, p. 10, April 7, 1939, p. 6, April 24, 1939, p. 6, July 1, 1939, p. 6, July 3, 1939, p. 6, July 12, 1939, p. 6, July 13, 1939, p. 10, July 20, 1939, p. 10, September 4, 1939, p. 6, September 13, 1939, p. 6, September 14, 1939, p. 10, September 22, 1939, p. 10, September 27, 1939, p. 6, October 10, 1939, p. 6, October 28, 1939, p. 6, October 31, 1939, p. 6, November 3, 1939, p. 12, November 4, 1939, p. 6, November 11, 1939, p. 6, January 4, 1940, p. 6, February 27, 1940, p. 10, March 27, 1940, p. 6, May 13, 1940, p. 6, May 17, 1940, p. 10, May 21, 1940, p. 10, May 30, 1940, p. 10, June 8, 1940, p. 6, June 11, 1940, p. 10, June 12, 1940, p. 6, June 14, 1940, p. 10, June 15, 1940, p. 6, June 18, 1940, p. 10, June 19, 1940, p. 10, June 20, 1940, p. 10, July 11, 1940, p. 10, July 12, 1940, p. 10, July 18, 1940, p. 6, August 2, 1940, p. 10, August 3, 1940, p. 6, August 6, 1940, p. 6, August 15, 1940, p. 10, August 21 1940, p. 6, August 27, 1940, p. 6, September 4, 1940, p. 6,

September 14, 1940, p. 6, September 16, 1940, p. 6, November 28, 1940, p. 10, November 30, 1940, December 6, 1940, p. 10, December 12, 1940, p. 10, December 30, 1940, p. 6, January 7, 1941, p. 6, January 9, 1941, p. 6, January 10, 1941, p. 8, January 11, 1941, p. 6, January 17, 1941, p. 8, January 25, 1941, p. 6, February 1, 1941, p. 6, February 8, 1941, p. 6, February 15, 1941, p. 6, February 26, 1941, p. 6, March 10, 1941, p. 6, April 9, 1941, p. 6, April 11, 1941, p. 10, April 15, 1941, p. 6, April 26, 1941, p. 6, May 1, 1941, p. 10, May 7, 1941, p. 8, May 24, 1941, p. 6, June 16, 1941, p. 6, June 17, 1941, p. 10, June 20, 1941, p. 8, June 25, 1941, p. 6, July 18, 1941, p. 8, July 19, 1941, p. 6, July 22, 1941, p. 10, August 15, 1941, p. 8, September 5, 1941, p. 8, September 12, 1941, p. 8, September 16, 1941, p. 10, September 24, 1941, p. 6, October 4, 1941, p. 6, October 10, 1941, p. 8, October 22, 1941, p. 6; Daily Progress (Charlottesville), March 26, 1938, p. 4, March 30, 1939, p. 4, April 4, 1939, p. 4, May 4, 1939, p. 4, May 9, 1939, p. 4, May 29, 1939, p. 4, July 17, 1939, p. 4, September 6, 1939, p. 4, September 13, 1939, p. 4, September 14, 1939, p. 4, September 15, 1939, p. 4, September 21, 1939, p. 4, September 22, 1939, p. 4, September 28, 1939, p. 4, September 29, 1939, p. 4, October 3, 1939, p. 4, October 4, 1939, p. 4, October 17, 1939, p. 4, October 28, 1939, p. 4, November 6, 1939, p. 4, November 10, 1939, p. 4, May 17, 1940, p. 4, May 18, 1940, p. 4, June 14, 1940, p. 4, July 10, 1940, p. 4, July 11, 1940, p. 4, August 1, 1940, p. 4, August 23, 1940, p. 4, September 4, 1940, p. 4, September 13, 1940, p. 4, December 30, 1940, p. 4, February 7, 1941, p. 4, March 10, 1941, p. 4, March 20, 1941, p. 4, April 12, 1941, p. 4, April 26, 1941, p. 4, April 29, 1941, p. 4, June 19, 1941, p. 4, June 28, 1941, p. 4, July 8, 1941, p. 4, July 18, 1941, p. 4, August 15, 1941, p. 4, August 18, 1941, p. 4, August 23, 1941, p. 4, September 12, 1941, p. 4, September 25, 1941, p. 4, September 27, 1941, p. 4, October 16, 1941, p. 4, November 3, 1941, p. 4, December 3, 1941, p. 4; Danville Register, July 17, 1938, p. 6, November 9, 1938, p. 4, March 24, 1939, p. 4, September 12, 1939, p. 4, September 23, 1939, p. 6, October 4, 1939, p. 4, October 12, 1939, p. 4, October 13, 1939, p. 4, October 15, 1939, p. 6, October 17, 1939, p. 4, November 5, 1939, p. 4, January 24, 1940, p. 4, May 17, 1940, p. 4, May 18, 1940, p. 6, May 31, 1940, p. 6, June 9, 1940, p. 6, June 11, 1940, p. 4, August 1, 1940, p. 6, August 17, 1940, p. 4, October 10, 1940, p. 4, November 5, 1940, p. 4, November 6, 1940, p. 4, November 27, 1940, p. 6, January 5, 1941, p. 6, January 15, 1941, p. 4, January 24, 1941, p. 6, January 29, 1941, p. 4, March 26, 1941, p. 4, April 8, 1941, p. 4, April 22, 1941, p. 4, April 25, 1941, p. 6, May 11, 1941, p. 6, May 14, 1941, p. 6, May 22, 1941, p. 6, May 24, 1941, p. 4, May 27, 1941, p. 4, May 29, 1941, p. 4, June 14, 1941, p. 6, July 4, 1941, p. 4, July 8, 1941, p. 4, August 14, 1941, p. 6, August 15, 1941, p. 6, August 24, 1941, p. 4, September 12, 1941, p. 6, September 13, 1941, p. 4, September 14, 1941, p. 4, September 26, 1941, p. 4, September 30, 1941, p. 4, October 14, 1941, p. 4, October 18, 1941, p. 4, October 21, 1941, p. 4, October 22, 1941, p. 6, October 28, 1941, p. 4,

Black editorial opinion was considerably more militant than its white counterparts in September, 1939. Both of Virginia's leading black (statewide) newspapers, the Journal and Guide (Norfolk) and the Afro-American (Richmond), declared that American blacks were eager to fight for their country in the event it went to war against the totalitarian, racist, Axis powers. The black press asserted that no American should be denied the right--on account of color--to serve his country in any branch of the armed forces. Black newspapers were confident that unlike the First World War, the present conflict would afford blacks the opportunity to receive the same military

---

November 1, 1941, p. 4, November 8, 1941, p. 4, November 12, 1941, p. 4, November 14, 1941, p. 4; Roanoke Times, September 1, 1939, p. 6, September 3, 1939, p. 6, September 4, 1939, p. 6, September 14, 1939, p. 6, September 15, 1939, p. 6, October 22, 1939, p. 6, May 17, 1940, p. 6, May 19, 1940, p. 6, May 21, 1940, p. 6, May 22, 1940, p. 6, May 25, 1940, p. 6, June 8, 1940, p. 6, June 12, 1940, p. 6, June 14, 1940, p. 6, August 3, 1940, p. 6, August 18, 1940, p. 6, August 27, 1940, p. 6, August 28, 1940, p. 6, September 4, 1940, p. 6, September 5, 1940, p. 6, October 6, 1940, p. 6, October 15, 1940, p. 6, October 16, 1940, p. 6, November 5, 1940, p. 6, February 20, 1941, p. 6, March 11, 1941, p. 6, March 12, 1941, p. 6, March 18, 1941, p. 6, April 12, 1941, p. 6, April 23, 1941, p. 6, April 25, 1941, p. 6, April 26, 1941, p. 6, May 7, 1941, p. 6, May 9, 1941, p. 6, May 15, 1941, p. 6, May 18, 1941, p. 6, May 29, 1941, p. 6, June 2, 1941, p. 6, June 8, 1941, p. 6, June 17, 1941, p. 6, July 2, 1941, p. 6, July 9, 1941, p. 6, August 14, 1941, p. 6, August 15, 1941, p. 6, August 21, 1941, p. 6, September 9, 1941, p. 6, September 13, 1941, p. 6, September 29, 1941, p. 6, October 8, 1941, p. 6, October 10, 1941, p. 6, October 29, 1941, p. 6, November 1, 1941, p. 6, November 5, 1941, p. 6; Alexandria Gazette, March 2, 1939, p. 4, July 25, 1939, p. 6, August 31, 1939, p. 6, September 14, 1939, p. 6, September 21, 1939, p. 6, September 22, 1939, p. 6, October 29, 1939, p. 6, November 4, 1939, p. 6, November 18, 1939, p. 6, December 25, 1939, p. 6, March 12, 1940, p. 4, May 17, 1940, p. 4, May 27, 1940, p. 6, May 29, 1940, p. 4, June 19, 1940, p. 4, July 29, 1940, p. 4, August 1, 1940, p. 4, September 5, 1940, p. 4, September 9, 1940, p. 4, September 26, 1940, p. 4, October 12, 1940, p. 4, October 18, 1940, p. 4, November 16, 1940, p. 6, December 5, 1940, p. 4, December 20, 1940, p. 4, January 7, 1941, p. 4, January 30, 1941, p. 4, February 13, 1941, p. 4, March 8, 1941, p. 4, March 10, 1941, p. 4, April 16, 1941, p. 4, May 6, 1941, p. 4, May 8, 1941, p. 4, June 4, 1941, p. 4, June 24, 1941, p. 4, July 10, 1941, p. 4, August 15, 1941, p. 4, September 12, 1941, p. 4, October 6, 1941, p. 4, October 10, 1941, p. 4, October 23, 1941, p. 4, November 17, 1941, p. 4, November 20, 1941, p. 4; Richmond Times-Dispatch, December 15, 1940, p. 9; Walter P. McGuire, President and Editor of the Southside Virginia News (Petersburg) to William Allen White, July 27, 1940, White to McGuire, July 29, 1940, White Papers.

training and right to enter the officer corps as whites enjoyed. The editor of the Journal argued that despite the repeated repression his people had endured, blacks remained patriotic Americans eager to take up arms to protect their country and its democratic, albeit flawed, form of government from Nazi aggression. The Afro-American maintained that the war against Hitler was a struggle against oppression, intolerance, and inequality at home and abroad.[67]

Throughout the rest of the pre-Pearl Harbor period, the black press advocated military preparedness and enthusiastically supported Roosevelt's aid-to-Britain policies. The Journal and the Afro-American perceived Nazi Germany as a threat to American liberty and national security. The Journal rejected the idea of a "fortress America," and instead, argued that America's frontiers were "on the Thames." The paper also encouraged the United States to set up air bases in Liberia. The Afro-American urged the United States to trade war equipment for the strategically-placed British West Indies. Black editors continued to press the Roosevelt administration to integrate all sectors of the armed forces with enlisted black servicemen and admit more blacks to the service academies and officer training schools. The black newspapers also urged the government to ban discriminatory practices against skilled black workers who were being denied the opportunity to participate fully in the country's rearmament program. They argued that such discrimination slowed down the country's defense program. The Afro-American was considerably more critical of the Roosevelt administration's failure to quickly integrate the armed forces and prohibit discrimination than was the Journal. It also attacked the slow pace of the government's national defense program. In 1940, the Afro-American supported Wendell Willkie for president after endorsing Democrats for the past twelve years. It asserted that the Republican candidate's business background and leadership qualities would accelerate the country's lethargic defense program. The Afro was please with Willkie's pledge to abolish Jim Crow throughout the federal government and the armed forces. The paper also expressed opposition to a third-term and made clear its dissatisfaction with the Roosevelt administration's deficit spending, silence on the anti-lynching bill, and failure to end unemployment and extend social security to domestic and farm workers. It reiterated its unhappiness with the slow pace of integration in the armed forces and

---

[67] Journal and Guide (Norfolk), September 16, 1939, p. 8, September 30, 1939, p. 8; Afro-American (Richmond), September 2, 1939, p. 4, September 9, 1939, p. 4, September 16, 1939, p. 4.

defense industry. The Journal endorsed FDR for re-election.[68]

Virginia's blacks were more concerned with domestic issues than with foreign affairs. They did not so actively support Roosevelt's foreign policies as their fellow whites (or black editors). The Virginia branch of the National Association for the Advancement of Colored People (NAACP) concentrated on domestic concerns during most of the Roosevelt presidency. They were involved with voter registration, equal education, equal pay for black teachers, passage of the federal anti-lynching bill, and membership growth. In addition to its efforts to obtain racial equality, however, the NAACP advocated the hiring of more blacks at the Hercules Powder Plant in Radford. In July, 1940, a black chapter of the White Committee was formed in Richmond. On July 25, Oliver Sands, chairman of the Richmond branch of the committee, spoke to the first meeting of the black group at the Sharon Baptist Church in Richmond. During the 1940 presidential election, the overwhelming majority of blacks, including their leadership, supported Roosevelt. Willkie's past opposition to various New Deal programs gained him few black votes, the Afro-American, notwithstanding.[69]

---

[68] Journal and Guide (Norfolk), November 11, 1939, p. 10, November 18, 1939, p. 10, April 20, 1940, p. 8, May 25, 1940, p. 8, June 1, 1940, p. 8, June 8, 1940, p. 6, June 15, 1940, p. 8, September 21, 1940, p. 8, October 12, 1940, p. 8, November 2, 1940, p. 8, January 18, 1941, p. 8, March 8, 1941, p. 8, June 7, 1941, p. 8, July 5, 1941, p. 8, July 26, 1941, p. 8, August 2, 1941, p. 8, September 20, 1941, p. 10; Afro-American (Richmond), October 7, 1939, p. 4, October 21, 1939, p. 4, May 18, 1940, p. 4, June 1, 1940, p. 4, June 29, 1940, p. 4, July 6, 1940, p. 4, August 17, 1940, p. 12, September 14, 1940, p. 6, October 19, 1940, p. 4, December 14, 1940, p. 6, January 11, 1941, p. 4, January 18, 1941, p. 6, January 21, 1941, p. 4, June 21, 1941, p. 4, June 28, 1941, p. 4, July 5, 1941, p. 4, August 16, 1941, p. 4, August 23, 1941, p. 4, September 6, 1941, p. 4, September 27, 1941, p. 4, October 4, 1941, p. 4, October 11, 1941, p. 4. In August, 1940, Senator Glass voted against Senator Robert F. Wagner's amendment to Senate bill 4164, which provided for equal opportunity "regardless of race, creed, or color" for enlistment in the country's "land or naval forces." Senator Byrd did not vote on the measure. That was the only instance of united southern congressional opposition to a miliary measure during the pre-Pearl Harbor Roosevelt presidency. See Congressional Record, 76th Congress, 3rd sess., 1940, 86: 10892-10895, and Grassmuck, Sectional Biases, p. 41.

[69] Richard Polenberg, War and Society: The United States, 1941-1945 (Philadelphia: Lippicott, 1972), pp. 100-102; John Temple Graves, The Fighting South (New York: G.P. Putnam's Sons, 1943), pp. 120-21, 128;

With a few notable exceptions, a majority of the predominantly white, protestant religious leadership in Virginia opposed American entry into the European war. Religious leader were, however, vehemently anti-Nazi and very sympathetic to the Allies. Virtually all of the influential protestant newspaper editors and religious leaders supported American rearmament and aid-to-Britain. The Old Dominion's small Catholic population's "opinion-markers" were staunchly anti-Hitler and isolationist. Catholic editorial support for aid-to-Britain came begrudgingly in the late winter of 1941. It was based solely on America's national security interests (i.e. Hitler threatened the United States and it was in its national interest to support England). Nevertheless, many Virginians of German, Italian, and Irish ancestry openly supported aid-to-Britain and were ready to fight for America in the event it went to war against the Axis powers. Virginia's even smaller Jewish community was strongly interventionist and supportive of efforts to aid Britain even at the risk of American participation in the war.[70]

"NAACP Branch Files" (1933-41, Virginia), Boxes G206-212, Group I, "Annual Report of [NAACP] Branch Activities" (1941, Virginia), Boxes C277-278, Group II-C, Branch Files, National Association for the Advancement of Colored People's Papers, Library of Congress, Washington, D.C.; Interview with Dabney, November 28, 1986; Andrew Buni, The Negro in Virginia Politics, 1902-1965 (Charlottesville: University Press of Virginia, 1967), pp. 144-45; Richmond Times-Dispatch, June 23, 1940, p. 13, July 24, 1940, p. 6, July 28, 1940, p. 10; According to Alfred O. Hero, Jr., "Southern Negroes lowered the Southern averages favoring intervention and mutual security against the Axis--with but minor exceptions, they were less favorable to active support of the Allies than Southern whites and more inclined to feel that we should avoid international commitments and risks which might entail war or lesser personal sacrifices." See Hero, Southerner and World Affairs, p. 103.

[70] The Southeast was overwhelmingly protestant. Southern Baptists and Methodists easily outnumbered all other religious groups. According to the 1926 census, Virginia was home to nearly 1.5 million Baptists and Methodists. Only 27, 298 Catholics and 22, 414 Jews lived in the state. See Odum, Southern Regions, pp. 140-42. The classic work on the role public opinion (including ethnic and religious influence) has played in the formulation of American foreign policy is Thomas A. Bailey's The Man in the Street: The Impact of American Public Opinion on Foreign Policy (New York: The Macmillan Company, 1948). During the pre-Pearl Harbor period, the most internationalist-oriented religious group in America were Jews, the least interventionist-oriented were Catholics, and protestants fell in between. Episcopalians were solidly interventionist, while most Lutherans leaned toward isolationism. See Jonas, Isolationism, p. 253, Rieselbach, Roots of Isolationism, p. 19, George Q. Flynn, Roosevelt and Romanism: Catholics and

Virginia's Episcopal clergy and leadership ardently supported Roosevelt's aid-to-Britain policies. In October, 1939, the Rt. Rev. Robert C. Jett, Bishop of the Diocese of Southwestern Virginia and the Rev. W. E. Rollins, president of the Virginia Theological Seminary in Alexandria, were among the 100 southern leaders who endorsed FDR's proposal to repeal the arms embargo and extend cash-and-carry. Jett later joined the White Committee. Dr. A.C. Zabriskie, a professor at the Episcopal seminary, was a member of the executive committee of the Virginia Fight for Freedom Committee. According to a September, 1941, poll, a number of Richmond's leading Episcopal clergy, including the Rev. Beverly Boyd, rector of Grace and Holy Trinity Church, advocated immediate or ultimate American intervention in the war, "if it becomes necessary to the national defense." Boyd later became a member of the executive committee of the White Committee in Virginia. The Rt. Rev. Henry St. George Tucker, Bishop of Virginia and Presiding Bishop of the Protestant Episcopal Church, was a strong supporter of FDR's foreign and domestic policies. He directed the provision of church relief for victims of the war and also helped raise $300,000 for the hard-pressed Church of England's missionary work. In November, 1941, Tucker, co-chairman of the church section of the United Service Organizations (U.S.O.) urged fellow Episcopalians to cooperate with God in redeeming those evil days from the forces of evil (i.e. Axis powers). As editor-in-chief of the The Virginia Churchman, the diocesan publication, Tucker repeated that theme throughout the pre-Pearl Harbor period. In late 1940, the Diocese of Virginia strengthened its ties to its "Mother Church" and English "brethren" by sending over $6,700 to the British Missions Fund. Dr. Vincent C. Franks, rector of St. Paul's Episcopal Church, chaired a Richmond-based group that placed English refugee children in local homes. Franks was also a member of the executive committee of the White Committee. The girls of St. Catherine's, an Episcopal prep school in Richmond, sold Christmas cards and knitted sweaters, socks, scarfs, and

---

American Diplomacy, 1937-1945 (Westport, Conn.: Greenwood Press, 1976), pp. x, xvi, 6, 10-12, 17-22, 64, 68-69, 73, 76-83, 85-90, 142, 123, 174, and Alfred O. Hero, Jr., American Religious Groups View Foreign Policy: Trends in Rank-and-File Opinion, 1937-1969 (Durham, N.C.: Duke University Press, 1973), pp. 5-8, 12-13, 21-25. According to a questionnaire circulated in the summer of 1940 by the Layman's Magazine, a national Episcopal monthly, a higher percentage of Episcopal clergy than laity favored abandoning neutrality and supported military aid to Britain. See the Presbyterian of the South and the Presbyterian Standard, August 7, 1940, p. 10; Interview with Dabney, November 28, 1986; Richmond Times-Dispatch, June 11, 1940, p. 8, August 1, 1940, p. 4; Lutz, Richmond in World War II, p. 9.

blankets to raise money for the British War Relief and Red Cross.[71]

Presbyterian opinion also portrayed Nazism as a "pagan ideology" and mortal enemy of Christianity and world peace. As early as October, 1939, the Rev. Ben R. Lacy, Jr., president of the [Presbyterian] Union Theological Seminary in Richmond, supported Roosevelt's proposed neutrality revision. Lacy later joined the White Committee. According to a September, 1941, poll of Richmond clergy, Presbyterian ministers supported FDR's defense and foreign policies, including all possible aid-to-Britain. The Presbyterian of the South and the Presbyterian Standard, the leading Presbyterian weekly, was consistently anti-Hitler and pro-British. Its editorials supported FDR's aid-short-of-war policies. That support was based on America's national security interests and its concern for its beleaguered British cousins. The weekly emphasized the historical, religious, political, and language ties that bound American Presbyterians to the United Kingdom, and especially Scotland.[72]

Baptist opinion was considerably more divided on the issue of American interventionism. In September, 1941, the Baptist Ministers' Conference of Richmond and vicinity objected to a newspaper headline that indicated that a majority of Richmond's clergy favored American intervention in the war. Anti-war and anti-interventionist articles regularly appeared in the pages of the influential Baptist paper, The Religious Herald. Nevertheless, the prominent editor of that weekly, Reuben E. Alley, was an outspoken

---

[71] Richmond Times-Dispatch, October 10, 1939, p. 9, June 11, 1940, p. 8, July 8, 1940, p. 6, September 29, 1941, pp. 1-7; membership list of the White Committee as of May 29, 1940, Box B, White Papers; Virginia Churchman, July, 1940, p. 3, November, 1940, p. 5, December, 1940, pp. 4-5, 7, January, 1941, pp. 7, 11, February, 1941, p. 3, March, 1941, pp. 7, 12, April, 1941, pp. 11-12, June, 1941, p. 6, July, 1941, p. 16, November, 1941, pp. 1-3; Rt. Rev. Henry St. George Tucker to Franklin D. Roosevelt, January 1, 1941, Roosevelt to Tucker, January 8, 1941, President's Personal File 7211, Roosevelt Papers; Mrs. D. Tucker Brown to A. Liddon Graham, September 30, 1941, Fight for Freedom Committee Papers; Lutz, Richmond in World War II, p. 20.

[72] Richmond Times-Dispatch, October 10, 1939, June 11, 1940, p. 8, September 29, 1941, pp. 1, 7; Presbyterian of the South and the Presbyterian Standard, September 13, 1939, p. 2, November 1, 1939, p. 2, November 8, 1939, p. 2, April 17, 1940, p. 2, April 24, 1940, pp. 2, 16, July 3, 1940, pp. 3-5, July 24, 1940, p. 2, August 14, 1940, p. 2, September 11, 1940, p. 2, November 27, 1940, pp. 2, 16, April 30, 1941, pp. 2-3, May 7, 1941, p. 3, May 21, 1941, pp. 2-3, June 25, 1941, p. 2, July 30, 1941, p. 2, September 24, 1941, pp. 2-3, November 5, 1941, p. 2.

advocate of neutrality revision, conscription, rearmament, and aid-to-Britain. Alley and other Baptist intellectuals who wrote for the Herald argued that Hitler threatened both democracy and Christianity. They maintained that aid-short-of-war (and even American participation in the conflict) were preferable to living under totalitarian slavery. Alley forcefully argued that interventionism was not incompatible with his faith and hatred of war. He reminded his fellow Baptists of their historic ties to Britain. The editor, a member of the Richmond-headquartered Foreign Mission Board, supported the Southern Baptist Convention's program of financial assistance to the British Baptist Missionary Society.[73]

Virginia's Methodists--second only to Baptists in number-- overwhelmingly supported Roosevelt's rearmament and aid-short-of-war policies. After war broke out in September, 1939, the Richmond Christian Advocate asserted that the United States must remain neutral and stay out of the war. In June, 1940, the Virginia Methodist Advocate, which supplanted the Richmond Christian Advocate as the official organ of the Methodist Church in the state, advocated rapid American rearmament, non-belligerency, and aid-short-of-war. Nearly a year later, the Advocate argued that Hitler, the greatest threat to democracy, peace, and Christianity, must be defeated "by force if necessary." In March, 1941, the Virginia Conference of the Methodist Church pledged more than $33,000 to aid fellow Methodists in Britain. The most militant Methodist leader was Bishop James Cannon, Jr., of Richmond. In May of 1940, he sent an open letter to Secretary of State Hull calling for repeal of the "cowardly Neutrality Act." He urged Hull to use his "great influence with the President and Congress to declare war against Hitler and his fellow monsters." Cannon, a member of the Fight for Freedom Committee, argued that Hitler threatened liberty, religion, and American

---

[73] Richmond Times-Dispatch, September 29, 1941, pp. 1, 7, September 30, 1941, p. 6; Religious Herald, September 7, 1939, p. 10, October 19, 1939, pp. 1, 10, November 9, 1939, p. 10, November 16, 1939, p. 10, December 7, 1939, p. 10-11, December 21, 1939, p. 5, December 28, 1939, pp. 4-5, January 4, 1940, p. 10, May 16, 1940, p. 10, May 30, 1940, p. 10, June 20, 1940, pp. 10, 14, June 27, 1940, pp. 10-11, 19, July 11, 1940, p. 10, July 18, 1940, pp. 10, 12, August 1, 1940, p. 10, October 17, 1940, p. 10, October 24, 1940, p. 10, October 31, 1940, p. 10, December 12, 1940, p. 10, January 2, 1941, p. 10, February 27, 1941, p. 10, April 3, 1941, pp. 5, 20, June 5, 1941, pp. 3, 10, 19, June 19, 1941, p. 10, July 17, 1941, p. 4, August 7, 1941, p. 10, August 21, 1941, p. 10, October 9, 1941, pp. 4-5; Waynesboro News-Virginian, May 28, 1941, p. 2.

national security.[74]

Virginia's Lutherans did not articulate strong positions on the question of interventionism. In October, 1939, the Virginia Lutheran published an anti-war, pro-neutrality letter from F. H. Knubel, president of the United Lutheran Church in America, of which the Lutheran Synod of Virginia was a part. The president of the synod, the Rev. J.J. Scherer, Jr., pastor of Richmond's First English Evangelical Lutheran Church, was, however, a strong supporter of FDR's foreign policy and a member of the executive committee of the White Committee in Virginia. In September, 1941, he declared that the United States should have entered the war two months earlier.[75]

The strongest opponents of American involvement in the European war included Brethren, Quakers, and Roman Catholics. Throughout most of the pre-Pearl Harbor period, the Virginia Catholic urged the United States to rearm, remain neutral, and stay out of the war. Unlike its protestant and Jewish counterparts, its sympathies were not with Britain (nor with Nazi Germany, an enemy of the church). The official diocesan paper opposed revision of the neutrality laws and FDR's efforts to aid Britain. As late as November, 1941, (non-military) Catholic priests in the state overwhelmingly opposed American participation in a "shooting war outside the Western Hemisphere." Finally, in February, 1941, the Virginia Catholic joined many other Catholic publications nationwide in abandoning its rigid isolationist stance. Its conversion was largely due to its concern for America's national security, which it reluctantly concluded was tied to Britain's survival. The paper expressed concern that Germany might attack the United States. It asserted: "Our desire to aid England is not based on England's being a Democracy--England is . . . an oligarchy--but on England's being for us a

---

[74] Richmond Times-Dispatch, May 20, 1940, pp. 1, 5, June 8, 1940, p. 3, July 10, 1940, p. 24, July 25, 1940, p. 5, September 29, 1941, pp. 1, 7, October 17, 1941, p. 20; Richmond Christian Advocate, September 14, 1939, p. 14, October 12, 1939, p. 16; Virginia Methodist Advocate, June 6, 1940, pp. 10-11, June 20, 1940, p. 10, August 8, 1940, pp. 10-11, October 17, 1940, p. 10, January 16, 1941, p. 10, February 20, 1941, p. 11, March 20, 1941, p. 10, May 15, 1941, p. 10, July 31, 1941, p. 10, November 6, 1941, p. 10, October 30, 1941, pp. 10-11; Virginius Dabney, Dry Messiah: The Life of Bishop Cannon (Westport, Conn: Greenwood Press, 1970), p. 329; "What Is The Fight For Freedom?", p. 12, Box 403, Glass Papers.

[75] Richmond Times-Dispatch, July 8, 1940, p. 6, September 29, 1941, pp. 1, 7; Virginia Lutheran, October, 1939, p. 1.

bulwark against potential enemies (i.e. the Axis powers)."[76]

Virginia's Jews were deeply concerned with the plight of their persecuted brethren in Nazi-occupied Europe. Between 1934 and 1943, Richmond's Jewish community (which constituted only 3 percent of the population), the sixth oldest in America, welcomed 328 German-Jewish refugees. Nazi anti-Semitism drove most American and Virginian Jews into the interventionist camp. They supported aid-to-Britain, even at the risk of American involvement. The Richmond-based Southern Jewish World attacked German anti-Semitism, British/French appeasement of Hitler, Axis aggression, American isolationism, and Charles Lindbergh, whom it labeled a "Nazi mouthpiece." In its December, 1941, issue, the paper reiterated its support for American rearmament and "all-out aid" to Britain, America's "sister democracy." It argued that American freedom could be best defended through aid-to-Britain. Nonetheless, few Jews overtly urged the United States to enter the war. Richmond's Jewry shared their fellow citizens' patriotic fervor. An estimated seven hundred Jews from the Richmond area served in the armed forces during the war. Major Milton Joel of the army air corps, recipient of the Silver Star, the Distinguished Flying Cross, and the Air Medal, was among ten Richmond Jews who lost their lives in World War II. Morton Marks, Jr., another highly-decorated soldier, was awarded the Purple Heart. Richmond's Colonel Lewis I. Held, Jr., and Rear Admiral Lewis L. Strauss, future chairman of the Atomic Energy Commission, were among the highest ranking Jews to serve in the armed forces. In October, 1944, Sidney M. Lefkowitz, army chaplain, Bronze Star recipient, and former assistant rabbi at Congregation Beth Ahabah, conducted the first Jewish worship service on "liberated" German soil. Temple Beth-El's former rabbi, Morris Frank was one of the first Jewish chaplains to enlist in the armed services.[77]

---

[76] Richmond Times-Dispatch, September 29, 1941, pp. 1, 7; LaVerne Wellons (representing the Black Creek Monthly Meeting of Friends, Sedley, Virginia) to Carter Glass, September 8, 1939, Lavelle L. Koogler and Alice Hylton (representing the Women's Work Organization of the First Church of the Brethren, Roanoke) to Glass, July 19, 1940, Glass Papers; Virginia Catholic, July, 1939, p. 15, October, 1939, pp. 6-7, 12, November, 1939, p. 7, June, 1940, pp. 6-7, July, 1940, pp 6-7, August, 1940, p. 6, September, 1940, pp. 6-7, October, 1940, p. 18, February, 1941, pp 6-7, April, 1941, pp. 6-7, July, 1941, pp. 6-7, November, 1941, pp. 6-7.

[77] Jonas, Isolationism, p. 253; Interview with Dabney, November 28, 1986; Southern Jewish World, July 15, 1938, pp. 1, 4, September 23, 1938, p. 4, February, 1940, p. 4, March, 1940, pp. 1, 8, May, 1941, p. 8, July, 1941, p. 6, November, 1941, p. 8, December, 1941, p. 6; Myron Berman, Richmond's

210 VIRGINIA IN FOREIGN AFFAIRS

The most prominent Jewish advocate of aid-to-Britain in the state was Dr. Edward N. Calisch, the distinguished spiritual leader of Beth Ahabah, the sixth oldest congregation in America (including its merger with Beth Shalome). As early as April, 1933, the rabbi spoke out against German anti-Semitism. In his February, 1939, keynote address during "Brotherhood Week" at Richmond's First Baptist Church, he characterized the European conflict as a struggle between democracy and totalitarianism, freedom and slavery, good and evil. In October, 1939, the rabbi openly supported Roosevelt's proposed neutrality revisions. Calisch was a member of the Virginia Defense Council, the English-Speaking Union (president and treasurer), and the executive committees of the White Committee and the Fight for Freedom Committee in Virginia. In his September 16, 1941, letter to Mrs. D. Tucker Brown, executive secretary of Virginia Fight for Freedom Committee, the rabbi wrote:

> I believe it [the Fight for Freedom Committee] to be one of the finest influences in our country during these troubled times, and especially fine defense against the tactics of that group of people hiding under the name of [the] America First Committee.[78]

In September, 1939, Virginia businessmen voiced no objection to the anti-war positions of the country's two most powerful business organizations, the United States Chamber of Commerce and the National Association of

---

Jewry, 1769-1976: Shabbat in Shockoe (Charlottesville: University Press of Virginia, 1979), pp. 2, 288, 298-99, 312-13; Richmond Times-Dispatch, September 28, 1988, p. 13.

[78] Richmond Times-Dispatch, June 23, 1935, p. 1, October 10, 1939, p. 9, December 31, 1939, p. 1, July 8, 1940, p. 6, September 29, 1941, pp. 1, 7, January 8, 1946, p. 6; Daily Progress (Charlottesville), February 21, 1939, p. 4; Berman, Richmond's Jewry, p. 289; from the text of "Edward Nathan Calisch, An American Rabbi in the South, His Views on the 'Promised Land,'" a paper given by Dr. Myron Berman, at the 70th annual meeting of the American Jewish Historical Society, Richmond, May 5-7, 1972, pp. 23-24, 28, Mrs. C. Cotesworth Pinckney (on behalf of the board of directors of the Virginia branch of the English-Speaking Union) to Mrs. Edward N. Calisch, January 10, 1946, Edward N. Calisch Papers, Beth Ahabah Museum and Archives, Richmond, Virginia; Edith Lindeman Calisch, "Edward Nathan Calisch: A Biography," in Three Score and Twenty (Richmond: Old Dominion Press, 1945), pp. 121-22, 135-37, 149-54, 175; Edward N. Calisch to Mrs. D. Tucker Brown, September 16, 1941, Brown to A. Liddon Graham, September 19, 1941, Graham to Brown, September 25, 1941, Fight for Freedom Committee Papers.

Manufacturers. Throughout the pre-Pearl Harbor period, however, many business establishments and individuals expressed support for the president's national defense and aid-to-Britain policies. Some even called for a declaration of war against Germany. Homer L. Ferguson, chairman and president of the Newport-News Shipbuilding and Dry Dock Company, was a member of Fight for Freedom Committee. Prominent Richmond industrialist John Skelton Williams, Jr., was a member of the executive committee of the White Committee in the state. The Virginia State Chamber of Commerce and the Norfolk and Western Railway Company were particularly supportive of Roosevelt's interventionist foreign policies. They were quite aware of the state's vital role in industrial mobilization, national defense, and military and naval activities. In August, 1941, F.M. Rivinus, general counsel for the N&W, warned members of the 81st company of the Virginia Protective Force that Nazi Germany threatened their democratic way of life, which he argued, was inseparably linked to the survival of Great Britain. On October 10, 1941, he reiterated that warning to 550 N & W employees at the 22nd Annual Better Service Conference in Roanoke. Rivinus declared: "The thing at stake in the war that ravages Europe is no less than civilization itself--civil life as English-speaking peoples have created and developed it for centuries." The counsel urged his audience to support the president. He also criticized those congressmen who jeopardized "national safety" through their opposition to Lend-Lease and other aid-to-Britain policies.[79]

Virginia's trade unionists were no less supportive of Roosevelt's national preparedness and aid-short-of-war policies. Labor union leaders perceived Hitler as a mortal threat to democracy, free labor, and the United States. The Virginia State Federation of Labor (VSFL), a staunchly pro-Roosevelt, anti-totalitarian organization, advocated national unity, rapid rearmament, and a end to strikes in the defense plants. On May 19, 1941, at its forty-sixth annual convention in Norfolk, the union adopted a resolution (no. 9), which endorsed the American Federation of Labor's pledge of "wholehearted support of the national defense program, and . . . a 'no-strike' policy in defense industries." The resolution noted that many defense strikes

---

[79] Richmond Times-Dispatch, September 20, 1939, p. 8, September 21, 1939, p. 7, July 8, 1940, p. 6; Roanoke World-News, June 26, 1940, p. 4; Szanto to James H. Price, June 17, 1940, Szanto to Cordell Hull, June 17, 1940, Price Papers; Homer L. Ferguson to F.H. Peter Cusick, April 21, 1941, Fight for Freedom Committee Papers; John M. Miller, Jr., to Carter Glass, July 22, 1941, Glass Papers; The Commonwealth, June, 1940, p. 4, July 1940, p. 22; Norfolk and Western Magazine, December, 1940, p. 570, January, 1941, pp. 1, 12-13, 49, April, 1941, p. 157, September, 1941, pp. 387-93, 438-39, October, 1941, pp. 444-47, 450-52, 466-67, December, 1941, p. 582.

were communist-inspired and originated outside the American Federation of Labor.[80]

Farmers in the Old Dominion also rallied behind Roosevelt's interventionist policies. Tobacco farmers were particularly supportive of efforts to repeal the arms embargo and reenact cash-and-carry. They believed that such measures might result in the restoration of British purchases of American tobacco. In September, 1939, some influential farmers were convinced that the European war would result in an increased demand for their flue-cured tobacco crop. Others were anxious to see tobacco included in the Lend-Lease bill. Throughout the pre-Pearl Harbor era, Virginia farmers advocated rapid rearmament and all-out aid-to-Britain. They viewed Hitler as a menace to their world markets, liberties, and religious freedom. Farmers welcomed the opportunity to help save democracy and "Christian civilization" from "the Godless totalitarian" through "full-time week-in week-out effort[s] at producing abundance of food and fibre." In May, 1941, farm organizations throughout the state contributed money and seed to the American Seeds for British Soil fund. Virginia apple growers converted surplus apples into less perishable canned products, such as apple sauce, to send to their English cousins.[81]

Secondary and college-level educators throughout the commonwealth enthusiastically backed FDR's efforts to aid Great Britain. Despite their

---

[80] The Union News, May, 1940, pp. 56-57, November, 1940, p. 4, February, 1941, pp. 1, 25, 28, 30-31, 38, 44, September, 1941, p. 1; "Resolutions Nos. 7 and 8," Proceedings of the Forty-fifth Annual Convention of the Virginia State Federation of Labor, May 20-21, 1940, Danville, Virginia; "Resolutions Nos. 1, 2, 8, 9, and 22,""Report of the Chairman of the Legislative Committee, of the Virginia State Federation of Labor," (R.H. Wilton), Proceedings of the Forty-sixth Annual Convention of the Virginia State Federation of Labor, May 19-20, 1941, Norfolk, Virginia.

[81] Richmond Times-Dispatch, September 14, 1939, p. 1, September 20, 1939, p. 17, November 14, 1941, p. 32; February 18, 1941, telegram from Edward A. DeJarnette to Carter Glass, Glass to DeJarnette, February 18, 1941, February 18, 1941, telegram from Bernard Sneed to Glass, February 17, 1941, telegram from John R. Booth to Glass, February 17, telegram from R.O. Harrell to Glass, February 17, 1941, telegram from the Halifax County Board of Supervisors to Glass, Robert S. Orr to Glass, May 13, 1941, Glass to Orr, May 15, 1941, Glass Papers; The Virginia Farm Bureau News, April 15, 1941, pp. 1, 6-7, May 15, 1941, p. 3, June 15, 1941, p. 3, July 15, 1941, p. 2, September 15, 1941, p. 2; The Southern Planter, July, 1940, p. 10, May, 1941, pp. 4-6, July, 1941, pp 4, 31.

desire for peace, few academicians welcomed complete American isolation from the European conflict. Instead, many educators welcomed the chance to extol the virtues of democracy and the need for the United States to assume its "proper" responsibilities in a troubled world. Most teachers and professors characterized the war as a life or death struggle between tyranny and freedom, totalitarianism and democracy. In October, 1939, many college presidents like Washington and Lee College's Francis P. Gaines abandoned their rigid anti-war and pro-neutrality positions and urged revision of the neutrality law. The University of Richmond's highly-respected president, F.W. Boatwright maintained his support for the arms embargo. Nevertheless, his views were in the minority. As America drew closer to war, a number of Virginia educators publicly advocated increased aid-to-Britain, conscription, rearmament, repeal of the 1939 neutrality act, and even a declaration of war against Germany. The "cheers and rebel yells" of students and faculty that greeted "every reference" FDR made to American assistance to the Allies during his June 10, 1940, commencement address at the University of Virginia were indicative of academia's approval of his foreign policies.[82]

By the summer of 1940, noninterventionism found little support among veterans organizations and other fraternal/patriotic groups throughout the state. Organizations ranging from the American Legion and the Veterans of Foreign Wars to the Daughters of the American Revolution and the Virginia Society, Sons of the American Revolution, stood squarely behind FDR's aid-short-of-war policies. Their respective members maintained that neutrality revision, conscription, Lend-Lease, and "all-out aid" to Britain were essential to the preservation of democracy and the economic and national security

---

[82] Virginia Journal of Education, January, 1939, p. 163, December, 1939, p. 101, June, 1940, pp. 369-72, October, 1940, pp. 5-6, 9, November, 1940, p. 55, May, 1941, pp. 301-302, September, 1941, pp. 8, 29, December, 1941, p. 131; John C. Metcalf to Glass, May 27, 1940, J. Gamerweekep to Glass, December 5, 1940, Glass Papers; Lutz, Richmond in World War II, p. 7; Richmond Times-Dispatch, September 20, 1939, p. 7, September 23, 1939, p. 8, October 10, 1939, p. 9, June 10, 1940, pp. 1, 5, June 11, 1940, pp. 8, 12, November 19, 1940, p. 10, December 16, 1940, p. 8, July 11, 1941, p. 7, November 12, 1941, p. 6; Daily Progress (Charlottesville), September 17, 1940, p. 3; Roanoke World-News, January 28, 1941, p. 2; C. Carter Walker to Ulric Bell, October 4, 1941, A. Liddon Graham to Walker, October 7, 1941, n.d. declaration from the Southern Regional Conference to Franklin D. Roosevelt and the Congress, Box 67, Fight for Freedom Committee Papers.

interests of the United States.[83]

Interventionist pressure groups were active throughout Virginia. In January, 1941, a Lynchburg Advocates of Aid for Britain was formed. That local organization was not affiliated with any national British relief agency. Its announced objective was "to promote the prompt rendering of all aid to Britain necessary for the successful conclusion of her present struggle." In the course of only one week, 7,699 Lynchburgers joined the organization. On January 14, 1941, 9,684 citizens of that city signed an Advocates' petition to President Roosevelt pledging their support of his aid-to-Britain policies.[84]

Most Virginians' views on assistance to Britain were similar to those of the White Committee. It advocated American rearmament and aid-short-of-war. On June 12, 1940, more than 100 prominent Richmonders met at the exclusive Commonwealth Club to organize a Richmond chapter of the committee. The group elected Oliver J. Sands executive chairman and adopted a resolution endorsing Roosevelt's defense program. The resolution also called on Congress to provide every possible aid to the Allies. The Richmond committee went beyond the national organization's program and urged repeal of the Johnson Act and additional taxation to finance the national defense program. The group declared its readiness "to place on ourselves the burden of a conscription of manpower, labor and wealth." In addition to its announced purpose of defending democracy via military

---

[83] Jonas, Isolationism, pp. 218-219; L.T. Snell (representing Portsmouth Post No. 993, Veterans of Foreign Wars) to Glass, September 14, 1939, Glass's secretary to Snell, September 16, 1939, W. Glenn Elliott (representing the American Legion, Department of Virginia) to Glass, May 15, 1941, Glass to Elliott, May 16, 1941, Alfred P. Goddin (representing the Sons of the Revolution in the State of Virginia) to Glass, May 16, 1941, Glass to Goddin, May 19, 1941, Glass Papers; September 17, 1941, resolutions adopted by the Virginia Society, Sons of the American Revolution during its semi-annual meeting, Box 43, Price Papers; Greenlee D. Letcher to the National Fight for Freedom Committee, September 26, 1941, Fight for Freedom Committee Papers; Richmond Times-Dispatch, September 25, 1939, p. 5, June 15, 1940, p. 4, June 19, 1940, p. 4, August 21, 1940, p. 5, November 12, 1941, p. 6; Norfolk Ledger-Dispatch, June 7, 1940, p. 16, June 8, 1940, p. 3, June 14, 1940, p. 4; Times-Herald (Newport News), January 10, 1941, p. 16; Roanoke World-News, June 11, 1940, p. 9, June 18, 1940, p. 9; Evening Star (Winchester), June 18, 1940, p. 10; Herald Courier (Bristol) October 8, 1941, p. 2.

[84] Daily Advance (Lynchburg), January 3, 1941, p. 3, January 6, 1941, p. 3, January 13, 1941, p. 13, February 26, 1941, p. 3.

assistance to Britain, the organization's "Statement of Program" included support for rapid rearmament, the preservation of civil liberties, and the use of education to counteract defeatism and appeasement. Virginians from across the state contributed financially to the White Committee. Chapters were also organized in Arlington and Nelson County.[85]

Organized in May, 1941, the Virginia Fight for Freedom Committee was larger, more active, and better organized than the White Committee. Captain Greenlee D. Letcher, a World War I veteran, attorney, and Rockbridge County Defense Council chairman, served as state chairman of the organization. Letcher preached the Fight for Freedom gospel in a number of public speeches and through much correspondence with fellow Virginians. The individual most responsible for the committee's success was, however, its secretary-treasurer and organizer, Mrs. D. Tucker Brown of Lexington. She was a writer, lecturer, and political activist. From 1939 to 1940, Brown served as president of the Woman's National Democratic Club. In May, 1941, she organized the state executive committee and helped set up chapters in at least fourteen cities and counties throughout the state. In September, 1941, the committee signed up over 1,000 new members at its booth at the state fair. The Richmond branch's membership stood at 1,500. During the following month, Fight for Freedom began a successful advertising campaign with the eager cooperation of sixteen newspapers throughout the state. On October 24, Senator Claude Pepper spoke to a Fight for Freedom-sponsored rally at the Richmond Mosque. Active committee members spent most of their time trying to secure favorable editorial comment and newspaper coverage, attacking Lindbergh and the America First Committee,

---

[85] Interview with Dabney, November 28, 1986; See Walter Johnson's polemical, pro-interventionist study, The Battle Against Isolation (Chicago: University of Chicago Press, 1944) and William M. Tuttle, Jr.'s "Aid-to-the-Allies Short-of-War versus American Intervention, 1940: A Reappraisal of William Allen White's Leadership," Journal of American History 56 (1970): 840-58. White's committee was divided between those like himself who wanted to keep America out of the war and those who believed that the United States should do "whatever is needed to insure the defeat of the Axis." (ibid., pp. 841-42, 848, 857-58). W. M. Kemper to Oliver Sands, July 6, 1940, Harrison Mann to James H. Price, August 14, 1940, Kemper to Mann, August 15, 1940, Price Papers; White Committee membership list as of May 29, 1940, Box 1, list of White Committee's financial contributors as of July 3, 1940, Box 15, "Confidential Memorandum an Contributors to [the] National Organization," August 3, 1940, Box 13, White Papers; Richmond Times-Dispatch, June 11, 1940, p. 8, June 13, 1940, p. 8, July 8, 1940, pp. 3, 6; News-Virginian (Waynesboro), January 13, 1941, p. 6, January 17, 1941, p. 1.

and pressuring Congress to rearm rapidly, repeal the neutrality act, extend the draft, and declare war on Germany. They agreed with Bishop Hobson's characterization of the war as "a decisive battle between two enemy worlds, the world of dictatorship and the world of freedom.[86]

---

[86] Chadwin's Warhawks remains the best work on the Century Club and the Fight for Freedom Committee. Chadwin argued that despite their herculean efforts, neither group was able to persuade a majority of Americans to support a declaration of war against Germany. Neither were they responsible for getting the United States into the war; external events, he concluded, pushed the country towards internationalism and into the conflict. (ibid., pp. 261-62, 276-77). See also Cole, Roosevelt and the Isolationists, pp. 427-28; "What Is The Fight For Freedom? The Story of the First Six Months of the Fight For Freedom Committee," Box 403, Fight for Freedom Committee's "Statement of Purpose," Box 382, Glass Papers; Richmond Times-Dispatch, July 24, 1941, p. 6, August 5, 1941, p. 6, October 8, 1941, p. 6; "Virginia Fight For Freedom Committee: What Does It Stand For?" (advertisement), Box 130, biographical sketch of Mrs. D. Tucker Brown (also known as Barbara Trigg Brown), Box 130, May 7, 1941, telegram from Francis P. Miller to Ulric Bell, Mrs. D. Tucker Brown to Bell, May 9, 1941, H.M. Sutherland to Fight For Freedom Committee, (New York), May 20, 1941, A. Liddon Graham to Brown, May 29, 1941, Graham to James R. McKeldin, May 29, 1941, Graham to Sutherland, May 29, 1941, Graham to McKeldin, May 30, 1941, Brown to Graham, June 2, 1941, Brown to newspaper editors, n.d., Box 130, Graham to Brown, June 3, 1941, Eugenia H. Osbourn to F.H. Peter Cusick, June 3, 1941, McKeldin to Graham, June 4, 1941, Graham to Osbourn, June 5, 1941, Graham to Brown, June 17, 1941, Graham to Robert L. Campbell, June 17, 1941, Graham to Greenlee D. Letcher, June 18, 1941, Graham to McKeldin, June 18, 1941, Brown to Graham, June 21, 1941, Graham to Letcher, June 26, 1941, Brown to Graham, June 27, 1941, Letcher to the Fight for Freedom (New York), June 27, 1941, Brown to Graham, July 5, 1941, Brown to Graham, July 11, 1941, July 12, 1941, telegram from Brown to Graham, Brown to Graham, July 17, 1941, Graham to Brown, July 21, 1941, Brown to Graham, July 21, 1941, Graham to Brown, July 22, 1941, Brown to Graham, July 29, 1941, E.T. Enright to Graham, July 31, 1941, Graham to Leslie Jones, August 14, 1941, Osbourn to Cusick, August 15, 1941, Jones to Graham, August 28, 1941, Graham to Jones, August 29, 1941, Mrs. Douglas Murray to Graham, September 2, 1941, Graham to Murray, September 4, 1941, Murray to Graham, September 11, 1941, Graham to Irvine Guy, September 12, 1941, Graham to Murray, September 12, 1941, Brown to Graham, September 15, 1941, Gilbert Andrews to Brown, September 26, 1941, Jones to Graham, September 29, 1941, Brown to Graham, September 30, 1941, Graham to Letcher, September 30, 1941, Graham to Brown, October 1, 1941, Graham to Jones, October 2, 1941, Jones to Graham, October 5,

Despite its extensive organization in Virginia, the national organization was not completely satisfied with the results of Brown's efforts to organize, recruit new members, raise money, and distribute literature and supplies throughout the state. Arlington and Alexandria lacked chapters. Brown was only in the initial stages of starting a chapter in Norfolk when America finally entered the war. The big October Richmond rally had been postponed several times for lack of a nationally-known speaker. The state treasury was usually empty. Brown, a widow without independent means, almost resigned due to inadequate financial compensation. The secretary was equally frustrated over those unfulfilled objectives; she was also disappointed with the lack of "active work" in some chapters.[87]

1941, Brown to Graham, October 14, 1941, Graham to Claude Harrison, October 14, 1941, Brown to Cusick, October 16, 1941, Graham to Douglas S. Freeman, October 16, 1941, Graham to Brown, October 16, 1941, Graham to Osbourn, August 19, 1941, Graham to Murray, October 20, 1941, Graham to Jones, November 4, 1941, J.A. Osborne to Graham, November 15, 1941, E.E. Hurley to Osborne, November 22, 1941, Letcher to Fight for Freedom (New York), November 22, 1941, Graham to Letcher, November 25, 1941, Osbourn to Fight for Freedom (New York), December 8, 1941, Graham to Osbourn, December 9, 1941, Letcher to Bell, December 13, 1941, Fight for Freedom Committee Papers; Brown to Dabney, July 7, 1941, Brown to Dabney, July 13, 1941, Dabney to Brown, August 15, 1941, Brown to Dabney, September 26, 1941, Dabney to Brown, September 27, 1941, Dabney Papers; Brown to J.W. Rixey Smith, July 7, 1941, Brown to Smith, July 14, 1941, July 25,1941, telegram from "Richmond Committee, Fight for Freedom" to Franklin D. Roosevelt, Glass Papers.

[87]Brown to Graham, June 26, 1941, Graham to Brown, June 27, 1941, Brown to Graham, July 1, 1941, Brown to Graham, August 22, 1941, Graham to Brown, August 26, 1941, Graham to Brown, September 9, 1941, Brown to Graham, September 30, 1941, Brown to Bell, October 13, 1941, Brown to Graham, October 16, 1941, Graham to Brown, October 17, 1941, Graham to Brown, November 19, 1941, Graham to Brown, November 25, 1941, Graham to Brown, November 28, 1941, Brown to Graham, November 29, 1941, Brown to Graham, December 1, 1941, Graham to Brown, December 2, 1941, Graham to Brown, December 3, 1941, Brown to Graham, December 3, 1941, Graham to Brown, December 4, 1941, Graham, to Brown, December 5, 1941, Graham to Irving Winkler, December 5, 1941, Brown to Graham, December 5, 1941, Francis P. Miller to Bell, December 5, 1941, Fight for Freedom Committee Papers; Brown to Smith, June 12, 1941, Brown to Glass, June 26, 1941, Glass to Brown, June 27, 1941, Brown to Smith, July 14, 1941, Smith to Brown, August 19, 1941, Brown to Smith, August 21, 1941, Brown to Smith,

Francis P. Miller, prominent Presbyterian layman and liberal Democratic member of the House of Delegates from Fairfax, served as national vice-chairman of the Fight for Freedom Committee. Miller was a former Rhodes scholar, World War I veteran, and Anglophile. He held strong internationalist views and served as chairman of the World Student Christian Federation, executive director of the Century Group, and organization director for the Council on Foreign Relations. In early June, 1940, Miller helped draft "A Summons to Speak Out," which advocated a declaration of war against Germany. Nearly six and a half months later, he signed a "Statement of Urgency," which criticized the slow pace of the defense program. (In August, 1941, Miller castigated Senator Byrd, his long-time political foe, for his criticism of the administration's unsatisfactory efforts to increase defense production.) In early May of 1941, Miller persuaded Governor Price to present Roosevelt with an aid-to-Britain petition signed by prominent Virginians at the dedication of the Woodrow Wilson Shrine in Staunton. The petition declared that American "civilization" and the "democratic way of life" was "in mortal danger." It urged the president: "to declare a state of full national emergency," to use the armed forces of the United States "to establish control over the whole North Atlantic area," and to convoy supplies to British ports, to apprehend "fifth columnists and traitors," and to sever diplomatic relations with the Axis powers. Throughout 1941, Miller bitterly denounced Lindbergh and other members of the America First Committee. [88]

---

n.d., Glass Papers.

[88] Chadwin, Warhawks, pp. 45-48, 198; "Francis Pickens Miller: Democratic Nominee from Fairfax County for the House of Delegates," (political pamphlet), Box VII, February 14, 1941, telegram from Miller to Dabney, Miller to Dabney, April 26, 1941, May 4, 1941, petition to Roosevelt at the dedication of the Woodrow Wilson Shrine in Staunton, Box VII, Miller to Dabney, August 29, 1941, Dabney to Miller, September 2, 1941, Dabney Papers; The Commonwealth, February, 1939, p. 20; Miller to Bell, February 5, 1941, n.d. Fight for Freedom press release, Box 54, Fight for Freedom Committee Papers; Miller to Glass, August 13, 1941, Glass Papers; Richmond Times-Dispatch, June 24, 1940, pp. 8, 9, July 12, 1940, p. 14, September 18, 1940, p. 4; Miller to William Allen White, July 18, 1940, White Papers; "Francis Pickens Miller Profile: Chronology," pp. i-vii [Francis Pickens Miller]: Scope and Content, compiled by Martha D. Parthemos and Robin Wagner, Miller's June 3, 1940, draft letter concerning the "Summons To Speak Out," "A Summons To Speak Out," June 10, 1940, Box 26, "A Statement of Urgency," December 23, 1940, Box 27, outline of Century Club's January 9, 1941, dinner meeting, Box 25, Miller's draft, "A Petition To The President of the United States," May 4, 1941, Box 27, minutes of the June 17-18, 1941,

Miller was convinced that anything short of repeal of the neutrality act and a declaration of war would result in Hitler's conquest of Britain. He repeatedly argued that American national interests were tied to Britain's survival. Miller believed that Nazi Germany posed a mortal threat to Christianity, Western civilization, democracy, liberty, freedom of the seas, and America's national security and economic interests. The staunch Calvinist perceived the European war as a struggle between Christianity and the "giant forces of evil." In his September 17, 1940, address to the William Byrd chapter of the Daughters of the American Revolution in Montpelier, Miller declared:

> This is no ordinary war. This is no balance of power struggle. This is the supreme and ultimate conflict of a thousand years. The Beast [i.e. Hitler] has met the man. Hitler has met Mason and Washington and Madison. Man believes in government by consent. The Beast believes in government by force. The two cannot continue to inherent the earth together. . . . If free men wish to remain free, they must chain the Beast, or else the Beast will enslave them.[89]

Central to Miller's extreme interventionist position was what he considered the unique character of the North Atlantic area, "the cradle of our civilization." He believed that the survival of the "American Way of life" depended upon the survival of that civilization. That society, he maintained, was based on the dignity of man, representative government, and the Bill of Rights. Miller asserted that aid-to-Britain and American/British control of the North Atlantic ("the ocean of freedom") were essential to stopping Hitler and preserving American freedom and national security. He argued that German conquest of the British Isles and its hegemony over the Atlantic area would destroy the buffer between Europe and the United States, threaten American commerce, the Panama Canal, Latin America, and the Monroe Doctrine. Miller believed: "The battle for the control of the North Atlantic

---

meetings of the officers of the Fight for Freedom Committee, Miller Papers.

[89] Miller's September 17, 1940, address to the William Byrd chapter of the Daughters of the American Revolution in Montpelier, Miller, "America's Last Chance," Christianity And Crisis, July 1, 1941, Miller, "Repeal the Neutrality!" Christianity And Crisis, October 3, 1941, Miller, "Where Do I Stand?" The Student World, December 4, 1941, Miller Papers.

is not a British battle; it is our battle."[90]

During the pre-Pearl Harbor period, David K.E. Bruce, one of America's most distinguished diplomats, represented Charlotte County in the General Assembly and served as the American Red Cross delegate to Britain. Bruce was a strong advocate of the British cause. During his stay in London, he saw first-hand the devastation and death wrought by the Luftwaffe's "blitz" of the British capital. Bruce empathized with the embattled British and called them "an extraordinary gallant people." Most importantly, he supported both increased relief and military aid for Britain. (In June, 1941, Bruce sent a check for $2,000 to the Fight for Freedom Committee on behalf of his wife.) Bruce believed that America's national interests required rearmament and all-out aid to Britain, "regardless of the consequences." He agreed with Francis P. Miller that preservation of the "American Way of Life" required the defeat of Nazi Germany. Bruce maintained that Hitler threatened the survival of free enterprise, America's commerce, and American liberty. He argued: "There are things worse than war. There are ideals worth fighting for. There are causes worth dying for. The maintenance of human freedom is such a cause."[91]

---

[90] Miller "Shall We Convoy Supplies To Britain?" January 24, 1941, Box 25, Miller, "The Crisis," Christianity And Crisis, January 29, 1941, Miller's May 19, 1941, radio address over WINX, Washington, D.C., Miller, "The Atlantic Area," reprinted from Foreign Affairs, July, 1941, in pamphlet form, Miller Papers; Miller to Dabney, August 13, 1940, Miller's May 14, 1941, Boston speech, Box 54, Fight for Freedom Committee Papers.

[91] Between 1942-43, David K.E. Bruce headed Secret Intelligence (S.I.) within the European Office of Strategic Services (OSS) and OSS/London. He later served as United States ambassador to France, West Germany, Great Britain, and NATO. See Virginius C. Hall, Jr., "David Kirkpatrick Este Bruce, 1898-1977," in Portraits in the Collection of the Virginia Historical Society (Charlottesville: University Press of Virginia, 1981), pp. 35-36, and Robin W. Winks, Cloak & Gown: Scholars in the Secret War, 1939-1961 (New York: William Morrow and Co., 1987), p. 264. Bruce's October 17, 1940, talk over the Blue Network of the National Broadcasting Company, Washington, D.C., Bruce's April 24, 1941, address to the national convention of the American Red Cross in Washington, D.C., Bruce's June 26, 1941, remarks published in the Charlotte Gazette, n.d., Box 3, David K.E. Bruce Papers, Virginia Historical Society, Richmond, Virginia; Francis P. Miller to Bruce, April 30, 1941, Miller to Peter Cusick, April 30, 1941, Bruce to Pierre Jay, June 27, 1941, Ulric Bell to Mrs. David K.E. Bruce, June 30, 1941, July 22, 1941, telegram from Ward Cheney to Mr. & Mrs. Bruce, Fight for Freedom Committee Papers.

Noninterventionist sentiment was very weak throughout the South and especially in the Old Dominion. The America First Committee failed to enlist the support of even a significant minority of Virginians. Its leading spokesman, Charles A. Lindbergh, was very unpopular among Virginians; he was regularly vilified in the state press. There were, however, three small, largely ineffectual America First chapters in Richmond, Norfolk, and Roanoke. On September 12, 1941, fifteen America First members organized the Richmond branch. They named J. Stanley Collins temporary chairman and treasurer. Collins was also treasurer of the Republican Club of Virginia and a member of the Republican city committee. Robert W. Waitt, Jr., national regional director for the Young Republican Federation, was later named co-chairman. He was also state chairman of the Virginia Young Republicans and a member of the City Republican Committee. Elise Sweeney served as secretary. A week later, between 40 to 50 people attended the chapter's second meeting. Later that month, the group set up an America First booth at the state fair in Richmond and enlisted three new members. Only eighteen persons came to the October 17 meeting, at which time the group decided to continue placing advertisements in the Richmond Times-Dispatch. The chapter fully subscribed to the principles of the national organization: keep America out of foreign wars, build a strong national defense, preserve and extend democracy at home, no convoys, humanitarian aid for England and the occupied countries, and support for a national advisory referendum for the American people to express their opinions on the question of war or peace. Despite his sympathy for England and disavowal of anti-Semitic feelings, Collins received anonymous hate letters directed at his association with the America First Committee.[92]

---

[92] Interview with Dabney, November 28, 1986; Wayne S. Cole, America First: The Battle against Intervention, 1940-1941 (Madison: University of Wisconsin Press, 1953), p. 171; Wayne S. Cole, "America First and the South, 1940-1941," Journal of Southern History 22 (1956): 36-47; Leslie L. Jones to A. Liddon Graham, September 17, 1941, Mrs. D. Tucker Brown to Graham, September 18, 1941, Fight for Freedom Committee Papers; Richmond Times-Dispatch, September 13, 1941, p. 5, October 2, 1941, p. 4; Jerald A.F. Brannon to America First Committee (Washington bureau), May 27, 1941, John S. Broeksmit, Jr., to Brannon, July 28, 1941, J.S. Collins to Harry C. Schnibbe, August 1, 1941, Robert W. Waitt, Jr., to Schnibbe, August 4, 1941, Broeksmit to Waitt, August 27, 1941, Broeksmit to Collins, August 27, 1941, Waitt to America First Committee (Chicago headquarters), September 3, 1941, "Application To Establish A Chapter Of The America First Committee," (Richmond, Virginia), September 3, 1941, Schnibbe to Waitt, September 10, 1941, September 10, 1941, telegram from Robert E. Wood to Waitt, September 16, 1941, telegram from Waitt to Schnibbe, Collins to Schnibbe,

In August of 1941, the Greater Norfolk chapter of the America First Committee was formed. A.J. Dunning, Jr., state chairman of the Prohibition Party of Virginia, was named chairman. Other founding members of the chapter included two protestant ministers, a sunday school teacher, and the president of the Women's Christian Temperance Union. Dunning was unable to attract enough interested people to make his group viable. He attributed his difficulties to the "pro-administration sentiment" and large defense industry and military/naval presence in the Norfolk area. In September, the chapter was denied use of a local assembly hall for a meeting. The proprietors labeled the organization, "Un-American."[93]

Efforts to create an effective America First organization in Roanoke proved equally unsuccessful. On August 31, 1941, only thirteen people were present at the first informal meeting of Roanoke members of the committee. Ralph W. Shoaf, an investment broker, was elected temporary chairman. Mrs. R.F. Taylor, president of the William Watts chapter of the United Daughters of the Confederacy and active in church (Episcopal) and veterans' organizations, was chosen secretary. Other founding members were active leaders in the American Legion, the Veterans of Foreign Wars, and the Republican Party of Virginia. Fifty persons attended the group's first public organizational meeting on September 16. The Roanoke chapter opposed efforts to repeal the neutrality act. In late September, they sent a resolution to President Roosevelt informing him of the "slandering," "arbitrary, un-American and un-Democratic conduct" of the "so-called war party." The

---

September 17, 1941, Edna Reynolds to Waitt, September 18, 1941, Schnibbe to Collins, September 24, 1941, William S. Foulis to Waitt, September 27, 1941, James L. Fallon to Waitt, October 1, 1941, minutes of the October 17, 1941, meeting of the Richmond chapter of the America First Committee, Elise Sweeney to John J. Wicker, October 26, 1941, Wicker to Sweeney, October 28, 1941, Sweeney to Reynolds, November 3, 1941, America First Committee Papers, Hoover Library on War, Revolution and Peace, Stanford, California.

[93] Cole, "America First and the South," pp. 38, 46; A.J. Dunning, Jr., to America First Committee (Chicago), July 28, 1941, Schnibbe to Dunning, July 30, 1941, "Application To Establish A Chapter Of The America First Committee," (Greater Norfolk), August 13, 1941, Schnibbe to Dunning, August 16, 1941, August 16, 1941, telegram from Wood to Dunning, Dunning to America First Committee (Chicago), September 22, 1941, Foulis To Dunning, September 27, 1941, Fallon to Dunning, October 1, 1941, Schnibbe to Dunning, October 2, 1941, Dunning to America First Committee (Chicago), October 10, 1941, "Important Announcement . . .Birtcherd Dairy," Schnibbe to Dunning, October 24, 1941, America First Committee Papers.

resolution also asked the president to use his

> great office and influence. . . to bring about a cessation of this intimidation and defamatory attitude towards the great body of United States citizens, who support and pay the expenses of all moves inaugurated by your administration for preparedness and defense.[94]

Despite opposition from a majority of his constituents, Senator Glass's early support for a declaration of war against Germany did him little or no political harm. The same could be said for Senator Byrd's vote against repeal of the 1939 neutrality act. Those two instances of political independence undermine the view that foreign policy positions arise from the grass roots level (i.e. the "bottom up"). The overwhelming majority of Virginians were, nonetheless, united behind President Roosevelt's increasingly risky aid-to-Britain policies. Unlike the 1930's, they were ready to risk going to war again in order to save what they considered to be their most fundamental and cherished liberties. Hitler's assault on Americans' democracy, security, trade, and English brethren severed Virginians from their anti-war, pro-neutrality stance. Most importantly, his violent efforts to disfigure Western civilization

---

[94] Cole, "America First and the South," p. 37; Anne W. Parker (Mrs. Felix K. Parker) to Schnibbe, August 17, 1941, Broeksmit to Mrs. Felix K. Parker, August 26, 1941, George V. Kromerto Schnibbe, August 27, 1941, Parker to Broeksmit, September 1, 1941, (letter #1), Parker to Broeksmit, September 1, 1941, (letter #2), Parker to Broeksmit, September 1, 1941, (letter #3), "List of Sympathizers In Roanoke, Virginia," (September 1, 1941), Box 22, Broeksmit to Parker, September 3, 1941, Kromer to America First Committee (Chicago), September 3, 1941, Broeksmit to Parker, September 5, 1941, Parker to Broeksmit, September 5, 1941, Kromer to Schnibbe, September 5, 1941, Schnibbe to Kromer, September 9, 1941, "Application To Establish A Chapter Of The America First Committee," (Roanoke), September 9, 1941, Parker to M.R. Page Hufty, September 10, 1941, Kromer to Schnibbe, September 17, 1941, Schnibbe to Kromer, September 19, 1941, Kromer to Schnibbe, September 22, 1941, September 22, 1941, telegram from Wood to Ralph W. Shoaf, Schnibbe to Shoaf, September 22, 1941, Kromer to Schnibbe, September 24, 1941, Foulis to Shoaf, September 27, 1941, Kromer to Schnibbe, October 1, 1941, (with enclosed resolution of September 30, 1941, meeting of the Roanoke chapter of the America First Committee), Fallon to Shoaf, October 1, 1941, Schnibbe to Kromer, October 2, 1941, Fallon to Shoaf, October 3, 1941, October 7, 1941, telegram from Foulis to Henry T. Swann, Kromer to America First Committee (Chicago), October 13, 1941, Kromer to America First Committee (Chicago), October 2, 1941, November 12, 1941, telegram from Swann to Schnibbe, America First Committee Papers.

rekindled a martial spirit that most believed had died on the fields of France more than twenty years earlier.

CHAPTER IX

CONCLUSION

Virginia's response to the major foreign policy issues of the pre-Pearl Harbor Roosevelt era reenforce the crucial role ideas, economics, and blood ties have played in influencing public opinion throughout American history. Most Virginians were more than willing for the United States to abandon its traditional isolationism in order to promote the interests of international cooperation, multilateralism, world peace, hemispheric security, expanding markets, economic freedom, democracy, and other Western political values. They were no less concerned with the fate of the British Isles (their ancestral homeland) than American Jews are today with the modern state of Israel.

Only a small percentage of the commonwealth's political elite played a significant role in determining foreign policy positions. Nonetheless, "average" Virginians concurred with the foreign policy views of those "opinion-makers." Foreign policy opinion did not originate from the grass roots level. Neither did it flow from Washington (i.e. FDR-Hull). It came from the Glass-Byrd/Freeman-Dabney leadership elite. (If the old Dominion was a microcosm of the country, then surely America's foreign policy was formulated from forty-eight political elites throughout the states of the union between 1933 and 1941.) Consensus was the norm throughout most of the pre-Pearl Harbor period. It was based on shared values.

Despite their growing disenchantment with the New Deal's social and economic agenda, the overwhelming majority of Virginians continued to support Roosevelt. Between 1933 and 1941, they consistently provided the president with crucial support for his internationalist foreign policy. Virginians' foreign policy sentiments were based primarily on ideological, national security, economic, and cultural factors. They supported cooperation with the League of Nations and American membership in the World Court because of the Wilsonian legacy and their fervent belief in international cooperation and world peace. Virginians embraced economic reciprocity because it reflected their traditional preference for low tariffs, which they believed would open more world markets for the state's farm exports. The state's leadership elite recognized that the policy of the "good neighbor" with Latin America was essential to increased trade, expanding markets, a secure Western Hemisphere, a viable Monroe Doctrine, and American security during wartime.

Throughout much of the 1930s, Virginians agreed with their fellow Americans that the United States must remain neutral and avoid foreign military crusades. Nevertheless, they opposed isolationists' efforts to tie the president's hands in foreign affairs via mandatory arms embargoes. When Hitler threatened to destroy what was left of European democracy, Virginians advocated American rearmament (which benefitted them economically) and aid-to-Britain even at the risk of war. They believed that living in a world dominated by totalitarian slavery was a fate far worse than war. Few questioned the argument that there were things worth fighting for, namely, political liberty and religious and economic freedom. Virginians were convinced that in providing Britain with military assistance, the United States was fighting its own war. They recognized that Nazi Germany was the antithesis of Christianity and Western civilization. Most Virginians believed that Hitler's next victim--after Britain--was the United States. It was in America's economic and national security interests, they contended, to provide England, their mother country, with all-out aid, regardless of the consequences.

There were several reasons why Virginia, unlike a number of liberty-loving, noninterventionist midwestern states with populations of predominantly Anglo-Saxon heritage (e.g. Iowa), supported interventionism. Firstly, the people of the Old Dominion identified closely with the British and their political, legal, economic, social, and cultural institutions. They were quite familiar with the British origins of American history, language, religion, economics, law, government, and politics. Virginia, the most aristocratic and Anglophilic state of the union, was England's first American colony. Named in honor of the "virgin queen" Elizabeth, the commonwealth carefully preserved its historical monuments, landmarks, and artifacts, which linked her to the mother country. Proud of their "Cavalier" ancestors who helped build the republic, Virginians (including the black elite) patterned their way of life after their British cousins. (Indeed, quite a number of them believed they were America's version of the British aristocracy.)[1]

Many prominent Virginians were related to and socialized with members of the British aristocracy. When the Nazi blitz over London threatened the very survival of their ancient homeland, many of them felt as if their own family and heritage had been violated. After German U-boats were sighted off Norfolk, they realized that more than their tobacco exports were in jeopardy. With their coastline vulnerable to Nazi attack and the land of their ideological patrimony besieged, Virginians had little difficulty concluding that Britain's war was indeed theirs. Perhaps it was more than

---

[1] For the most convincing study of the British origins of American culture, see David Hackett Fischer, Albion's Seed: Four British Folkways in America (New York and Oxford: Oxford University Press, 1989).

CONCLUSION 227

coincidence that the only modern native-born American ever elected to Parliament was a Virginian (and not an Iowan) named Lady Astor.

One can only speculate that Virginians' foreign policy views would have been less interventionist if their state had been situated thousands of miles from the Atlantic and heavily populated with Roman Catholics of German, Irish, or Italian ancestry. One can safely conclude, however, that the people of the Old Dominion were imbued with a strong identity and sense of history. They knew that their distinguished forefathers had successfully waged guerilla warfare against the world's mightiest empire in order to preserve their most cherished liberties. Few had forgotten that many of the Founding Fathers of the first successful republic in modern history were Virginians. Not surprisingly, Virginians did not hesitate to risk sacrificing their lives and fortunes when the forces of barbarism threatened their most fundamental spiritual, political, economic, and cultural values in the fourth decade of the twentieth-century.

BIBLIOGRAPHY

Manuscript Collections

America First Committee Papers. Hoover Library on War, Revolution and Peace, Stanford, California.

Bruce, David K. E., Papers. Virginia Historical Society, Richmond, Virginia.

Bryan, John Stewart, Papers. Virginia Historical Society, Richmond, Virginia.

Byrd, Harry F., Papers. University of Virginia Library, Charlottesville, Virginia.

Calisch, Edward N., Papers. Beth Ahabah Museum and Archives, Richmond, Virginia.

Committee to Defend America Papers. Princeton University Library, Princeton, New Jersey.

Dabney, Virginius, Papers. University of Virginia Library, Charlottesville, Virginia.

Fight for Freedom Committee Papers. Princeton University Library, Princeton, New Jersey.

Freeman, Douglas S., Papers. Library of Congress, Washington, D.C.

Freeman, Douglas S., Papers. Virginia Historical Society, Richmond, Virginia.

Glass, Carter, Papers. University of Virginia Library, Charlottesville, Virginia.

Marshall, George C., Papers. George C. Marshall Research Library, Lexington, Virginia.

Miller, Francis P., Papers. University of Virginia Library, Charlottesville, Virginia.

Montague, Andrew Jackson, Papers. Virginia State Library, Richmond, Virginia.

Muse, Benjamin, Papers. Duke University Library, Durham, North Carolina.

Muse, Benjamin, Papers. University of Virginia Library, Charlottesville,

Virginia. National Association for the Advancement of Colored People Papers. Library of Congress, Washington, D.C.

Pollard, John G., Executive Papers. Virginia State Library, Richmond, Virginia.

Price, James, H., Executive Papers. Virginia State Library, Richmond, Virginia.

Richmond Peace Council Papers. James Branch Cabell Library, Virginia Commonwealth University, Richmond, Virginia.

Robertson, A. Willis, Papers. Earl Gregg Swem Library, College of William and Mary, Williamsburg, Virginia.

Roosevelt, Franklin D., Papers. Franklin D. Roosevelt Library, Hyde Park, New York.

Smith, Howard W., Papers, University of Virginia Library, Charlottesville, Virginia.

United States, State, Department of, Central Decimal File. National Archives, Washington, D.C.

Virginia State Federation of Labor Papers. American Federation of Labor-Congress of Industrial Organizations Library, Washington, D.C.

Weddell, Alexander Wilbourne, Papers. Virginia Historical Society, Richmond, Virginia.

White, William Allen, Papers. Library of Congress, Washington, D.C.

Woodrum, Clifton A., Papers. Roanoke Public Library, Roanoke, Virginia.

Interviews

Dabney, Virginius, Richmond, Virginia, November 28,1986.

United States Government Documents

Congressional Directory, 1933-41.

Congressional Record,, 1933-41.

United States, Department of State. Foreign Relations of the United States, 1933-41. Washington: Government Printing Office, 1946-70.

Virginia State Documents

Annual Reports of the Department of Labor and Industry, 1933-41.

Journal of the House of Delegates of Virginia, 1933-41.

Journal of the Senate of the Commonwealth of Virginia, 1933-41.

Report of the Secretary of the Commonwealth to the Governor and General Assembly of Virginia, 1933-41.

Published Letters, Journals, and Memoirs

Hull, Cordell. The Memoirs of Cordell Hull. 2 vols. New York: Macmillan Co., 1948.

Lindbergh, Charles A. The Wartime Journals of Charles A. Lindbergh. New York: Harcourt Brace Jovanovich, 1970.

Nixon, Edgar B., ed. Franklin D. Roosevelt and Foreign Affairs. 3 vols. Cambridge, Massachusetts: Belknap Press of Harvard University Press, 1969.

Roosevelt, Franklin D. F.D.R.: His Personal Letters, 1928-1945. Edited by Elliott Roosevelt and Joseph P. Lash. 2 vols. New York: Duell, Sloan and Pearce, 1950.

_____. The Public Papers and Addresses of Franklin D. Roosevelt. Edited by Samuel I. Rosenman. 13 vols. New York: Random House and Harper & Brothers, 1938- 50.

Tugwell, Rexford G. The Democratic Roosevelt: A Biography of Franklin D. Roosevelt Garden City, New York: Doubleday and Co., 1957.

Newspapers

Afro-American (Richmond)
Alexandria Gazette
Daily Advance (Lynchburg)
Daily Progress (Charlottesville)
Danville Register

Evening Star (Winchester)
Herald Courier (Bristol)
Journal and Guide (Norfolk)
New York Times
News-Virginian (Waynesboro)
Norfolk Ledger-Dispatch
Richmond News-Leader
Richmond Planet
Richmond Times-Dispatch
Roanoke World-News
Roanoke Times
The Afro-American and The Richmond Planet
Times-Herald (Newport News)
Virginian-Pilot (Norfolk)

Periodicals

Agricultural History
American Economic Review
American Historical Review
American Political Science Review
Diplomatic History
Foreign Affairs
Harper's Magazine
Journal of American History
Journal of Economic History
Journal of Politics
Journal of the History of Ideas
Journal of Southern History
Mississippi Valley Historical Review
Norfolk and Western Magazine
Quarterly Journal of Economics
Reader's Digest
Religious Herald
Richmond Christian Advocate
South Atlantic Quarterly
Southern Economic Journal
Southern Jewish World
Southern Studies
The Commonwealth
The Historian
The Nation
The New Republic
The Presbyterian of the South and the Presbyterian Standard
The Southern Planter

The Union News
The Virginia Farm Bureau News
University of Virginia Newsletter
Virginia Catholic
Virginia Cavalcade
Virginia Churchman
Virginia Journal of Education
Virginia Lutheran
Virginia Magazine of History and Biography
Virginia Methodist Advocate
Virginia Quarterly Review
Virginia Social Science Journal

Books, Articles, Dissertations, and Theses

Accinelli, Robert D. "The Roosevelt Administration and the World Court Defeat, 1935." Historian 40 (1978).

Adler, Selig. The Isolationist Impulse: Its Twentieth Century Reaction. New York: Abelard-Schuman, 1957.

_____. The Uncertain Giant, 1921-1941: American Foreign Policy between the Wars. New York: Macmillan, 1965.

Allen, William R. "International Trade Philosophy of Cordell Hull." American Economic Review 43 (1953): 101-110.

_____. "Cordell Hull and the Defense of the Trade Agreements Program, 1934-1940." in Alexander DeConde, ed. Isolation and Security: Ideas and Interests in Twentieth-Century American Foreign Policy. Durham, North Carolina: Duke University Press, 1957, 107-32.

Alaimo, Peter Anthony, Jr. "Internationalist and Isolationist Thought: 1935-1941." Unpublished Ph.D. dissertation, University of Virginia, 1978.

Andrews, Matthew Page. Virginia: The Old Dominion. Garden City, New York: Doubleday, Doran & Company, Inc., 1937.

Bailey, Thomas A. The Man in the Street: The Impact of American Public Opinion on Foreign Policy. New York: Macmillan, 1948.

Bartlett, Ruhl J. "Neutrality." in Alexander DeConde, ed. Encyclopedia of American Foreign Policy. New York: Charles Scribner's Sons, 1978.

Bartle, Barbara. "Virginius Dabney: Southern Liberal in the Era of

Roosevelt." Unpublished M.A. thesis, University of Virginia, 1968.

Bass, Jack and DeVries, Walter. The Transformation of Southern Politics: Social Change and Political Consequences Since 1945. New York: Basic Books, Inc., 1976.

Beard, Charles A. American Foreign Policy in the Making, 1932-1940: A Study in Responsibilities. New Haven, Conn.: Yale University Press, 1946.

_____. President Roosevelt and the Coming of the War, 1941: A Study in Appearances and Realities. New Haven, Conn.: Yale University Press, 1948.

Beckett, Grace L. "The Affect of the Reciprocal Trade Agreements upon the Foreign Trade of the United States." Quarterly Journal of Economics 54 (1940): 80-94.

_____. The Reciprocal Trade Agreement Program. New York: Columbia University Press, 1941; reprint 1972.

Berman, Myron. Richmond's Jewry, 1769-1976: Shabbat in Shockoe. Charlottesville: University Press of Virginia, 1979.

Borchard, Edwin M. and Lage, William P. Neutrality for the United States. New Haven, Conn.: Yale University Press, 1940; reprint 1973.

Braeman, John, Bremmer, Robert, and Brody, David, eds., The New Deal. 2 vols. Columbus, Ohio: Ohio State University Press, 1975.

Buni, Andrew. The Negro in Virginia Politics, 1902-1965. Charlottesville: University Press of Virginia, 1967.

Burns, Richard Dean, ed., Guide to American Foreign Relations Since 1700. Santa Barbara, Calif.: ABC Clio, 1983.

Burns, James MacGregor. Roosevelt: The Lion and the Fox. New York: Harcourt, Brace and Company, 1956.

Calisch, Edith Lindeman. "Edward Nathan Calisch: A Biography." in Three Score And Twenty. Richmond: Old Dominion Press, 1945.

Callcott, George H. Maryland and America, 1940 to 1980. Baltimore and London: The Johns Hopkins University Press, 1985.
Calvocoressi, Peter, and Wint, Guy. Total War: The Story of World War II.

New York: Pantheon, 1972.

Chadwin, Mark L. The Warhawks: American Interventionists Before Pearl Harbor. New York: W. W. Norton & Company, Inc., 1970.

Cole, Wayne S. American First: The Battle Against Intervention, 1940-1941. Madison: University of Wisconsin Press, 1953; reprint ed., New York: Octagon Books, 1971.

_____. "America First and the South, 1940-1941." The Journal of Southern History XXII (February 1956): 36- 47.

_____. Charles A. Lindbergh and the Battle against American Intervention in World War II. New York and London: Harcourt, Brace, Jovanovich, 1974.

_____. "Isolationism." in Otis L. Graham, Jr., and Megham Robinson Wander, eds., Franklin D. Roosevelt: His Life and Times, An Encyclopedic View. Boston: G.K. Hall & Co., 1985.

_____. Roosevelt & the Isolationists, 1932-45. Lincoln, Nebraska and London, England: University of Nebraska Press, 1983.

Conkin, Paul. The New Deal. New York: Harlan Davidson, 1967; 2d ed., 1975.

Crawley, William Bryan, Jr. Bill Tuck: A Political Life in Harry Byrd's Virginia. Charlottesville: The University Press of Virginia, 1978.

Crighton, John C. Missouri and World War One: A Study in Public Opinion. Columbia, Missouri: University of Missouri Studies, 1947.

Current, Richard N. "Consequences of the Kellogg Pact." in George L. Anderson, ed., Issues and Conflicts: Studies in 20th Century American Diplomacy. Lawrence: University of Kansas Press, 1959, 210-29.

_____. "The United States and 'Collective Security': Notes on the History of an Idea." in Alexander DeConde, ed., Isolation and Security Ideas and Interests in Twentieth-Century American Foreign Policy. Durham, N.C.: Duke University Press, 1957, 33-55.

_____. Secretary Stimson: A Study in Statecraft. New Brunswick, N.J.: Rutgers University Press, 1954.

Dabney, Virginius. Below the Potomac: A Book about the New South. Port

Washington, New York: Kennikat Press, 1969.

_____. "The South Looks Abroad." in Foreign Affairs, New York (October 1940): 171-78.

_____. Dry Messiah: The Life of Bishop Cannon. New York: Knopf, 1949.

_____. Virginia: The New Dominion: A History from 1607 to the Present. Charlottesville: University Press of Virginia, 1971.

Dahl, Robert A. Congress and Foreign Policy. New York: Harcourt, Brace & Co., 1950.

Dallek, Robert. Franklin D. Roosevelt and American Foreign Policy, 1932-1945. New York: Oxford University Press, 1979.

DeConde, Alexander. ed. Encyclopedia of American Foreign Policy: Studies of Principal Movements and Ideas. 3 vols., New York: Scribner's Sons, 1978.

_____. Herbert Hoover's Latin American Policy. Stanford, Calif.: Stanford University Press, 1951.

_____. ed. Isolation and Security: Ideas and Interests in Twentieth-Century American Foreign Policy. Durham, N.C.: Duke University Press, 1957.

_____. "The South and Isolationism." The Journal of Southern History. XXIV (August 1958): 332-346.

_____. "On Twentieth-Century Isolationism." in Alexander DeConde, ed., Isolation and Security: Ideas and Interests in Twentieth-Century American Foreign Policy. Durham, N.C.: Duke University Press, 1957, 3- 32.

Dierenfield, Bruce J. Keeper of the Rules: Congressman Howard W. Smith of Virginia. Charlottesville: University Press of Virginia, 1987.

Divine, Robert A. Foreign Policy and United States Presidential Elections 1940-1948. New York: New Viewpoints, 1974.

_____. "Franklin D. Roosevelt and Collective Security, 1933." Mississippi Valley Historical Review 48: (1961): 42-59.

_____. The Illusion of Neutrality. Chicago: University of Chicago

Press, 1962.

_____. The Reluctant Belligerent: American Entry into World War II. New York: Wiley, 1965.

_____. Roosevelt and World War II. Baltimore, Maryland: Penguin Books, Inc., 1970.

_____. Second Chance: The Triumph of Internationalism in America during World War II. New York: Antheneum, 1967.

Drummond, Donald F. "Cordell Hull." in Norman Graebner, ed. An Uncertain Tradition: American Secretaries of State in the Twentieth Century. New York: McGraw-Hill, 1961, 184-209.

_____. The Passing of American Neutrality, 1937-1941. Ann Arbor: University of Michigan Press, 1955.

Eisenberg, Ralph. Virginian Votes, 1924-1968. Charlottesville: University Press of Virginia, 1971.

Fehrenbach, T. R. F.D.R.'s Undeclared War, 1939-1941. New York: McKay, 1967.

Feis, Herbert. The Road to Pearl Harbor: The Coming of the War between the United States and Japan. Princeton, N.J.: Princeton University Press, 1950.

Ferrell, Henry C., Jr. "Claude A. Swanson of Virginia." Ph.D. dissertation, University of Virginia, 1964.

_____. Claude A. Swanson of Virginia: A Political Biography. Lexington: University of Kentucky Press, 1985.

Fischer, David Hackett. Albion's Seed: Four British Folkways in America. New York and Oxford: Oxford University Press, 1989.

Fleming, Denna F. The United States and the League of Nations, 1918-1920. New York: Putnam's, 1932.

_____. The U.S. and World Organizations, 1920-1933. New York: Columbia University Press, 1938; reprint, 1966.

_____. The U.S. and the World Court, 1920-1966. Revised edit., New

York: Russell & Russell, 1945; reprint, 1968.

Flynn, George Q. American Catholics & the Roosevelt Presidency, 1932-1936. Lexington: University of Kentucky Press, 1968.

_____. Roosevelt and Romanism: Catholics and American Diplomacy, 1937-1945. Westport, Conn., London: Greenwood Press, 1976.

Fowler, Harold L. "John Stewart Bryan." in Edward T. James, ed., Dictionary of American Biography, Supplement Three, 1941-1945. New York: Charles Scribner's Sons, 1973.

Friedel, Frank. Franklin D. Roosevelt. 4 vols. Boston: Little, Brown & Co., 1952-1973.

_____. Franklin D. Roosevelt and the South. Baton Rouge: Louisiana State University Press, 1965.

Friddell, Guy. Colgate Darden: Conversations with Guy Friddell. Charlottesville: University Press of Virginia, 1978.

Fry, Joseph A. "George C. Peery: Byrd Regular and Depression Governor." in The Governors of Virginia, 1860-1978. eds. Edward Younger and James T. Moore. Charlottesville: University Press of Virginia, 1982, 261-76.

_____. "The Organization in Control: G.C. Peery, Governor of Virginia, 1934-38." Virginia Magazine of History and Biography 82 (1974): 306-30.

_____. "George Campbell Peery: Conservative Son of Old Virginia," M.A. thesis, University of Virginia, 1970.

Gallup, George H. The Gallup Poll: Public Opinion, 1935-1971. 3 vols. New York: Random House, 1972.

Gellman, Irwin F. Good Neighbor Diplomacy: U.S. Policies in Latin America, 1933-1945. Baltimore: Johns Hopkins University Press, 1979.

Gibbs, Christopher C. The Great Silent Majority: Missouri's Resistance to World War I. Columbia: University of Missouri Press, 1988.

Gignilliat, John Lewis. "The Thought of Douglas Southall Freeman." Unpublished Ph.D. dissertation, University of Wisconsin, 1968.

Glass, Robert C., and Glass, Carter, Jr. Virginia Democracy. 3 vols. Springfield, Illinois: University of Illinois Press, 1937.

Gottman, Jean. Virginia in Our Century. Charlottesville: University Press of Virginia, 1969.

Graebner, Norman A. American as a World Power: A Realist Appraisal from Wilson to Reagan. Wilmington, Delaware: Scholarly Resources, Inc., 1984.

_____. ed. Ideas and Diplomacy: Readings in the Intellectual Tradition of American Foreign Policy. New York: Oxford University Press, 1964.

Grassmuck, George L. Sectional Biases in Congress on Foreign Policy. Baltimore: The Johns Hopkins Press, 1951.

Graves, John Temple. "The Fighting South." Virginia Quarterly Review XVIII (Winter 1942).

_____. The Fighting South. New York: G. P. Putnam's Sons, 1943.

Guerrant, Edward O. Roosevelt's Good Neighbor Policy. Albuquerque: University of New Mexico Press, 1950.

Guinsberg, Thomas N. The Pursuit of Isolationism in the United States Senate from Versailles to Pearl Harbor. New York: Garland Press, 1981.

Hall, Alvin LeRoy. "James H. Price and Virginia Politics, 1878 to 1943." Unpublished Ph.D. dissertation, University of Virginia, 1970.

_____. "Politics and Patronage: Virginia's Senators and the Roosevelt Purges of 1938." Virginia Magazine of History and Biography. 82(1974): 331-50.

Hall, Virginius Cornick, Jr. "David Kirkpatrick Este Bruce, 1898-1977." in Portraits in the Collection of the Virginia Historical Society. Charlottesville: University Press of Virginia, 1981.

Halstead, Charles R. "Diligent Diplomat: Alexander W. Weddell as American Ambassador to Spain, 1939-1942." Virginia Magazine of History and Biography. 82(1974): 3-38.

Hamby, Alonzo L. ed. The New Deal: Analysis and Interpretation 2d. ed., New York: Longman, 1981.

Handlin, Oscar. The American People in the Twentieth Century, Cambridge: Harvard University Press, 1954.

Hatch, Alden. The Byrds of Virginia. New York: Holt, Rinehart & Winston, 1969.

Hawkes, Robert Thomas, Jr. "The Career of Harry F. Byrd, Jr., to 1933." Unpublished Ph.D. dissertation, University of Virginia, 1975.

_____. "The Emergence of a Leader: Harry Flood Byrd, Governor of Virginia, 1926-1930." Virginia Magazine of History and Biography LBXXXII (1974): 259-81.

Heinemann, Ronald L. Depression and New Deal in Virginia: The Enduring Dominion. Charlottesville: University Press of Virginia, 1983.

_____. "Blue Eagle or Black Buzzard? The National Recovery Administration in Virginia." Virginia Magazine of History and Biography. 89(1981): 90-100.

_____. "Harry Byrd for President: The 1932 Campaign." Virginia Cavalcade 25 (Summer 1975): 28-37.

_____. "Virginia in the Twentieth Century: Recent Interpretations." Virginia Magazine of History and Biography XCIV (1986): 131-160.

Heinrichs, Waldo. Threshold of War: Franklin D. Roosevelt and American Entry into World War II. New York, Oxford: Oxford University Press, 1988.

Heller, Francis Howard. Virginia's State Government During the Second World War: Its Constitutional, Legislative, and Administrative Adaptations, 1942-1945. Richmond, Va.: Virginia State Library, 1949.

Hemphill, W. Edwin. Gold Star Honor Roll of Virginians in the Second World War. Charlottesville: University Press of Virginia, 1947.

_____. Pursuits of War. Charlottesville, University Press of Virginia, 1948.

Hero, Alfred O., Jr. American Religious Groups View Foreign Policy: Trends in Rank-and-File Opinion, 1937-1969. Durham, N.C.: Duke University Press, 1973.

_____. The Southerner and World Affairs. Baton Rouge: Louisiana

State University Press, 1966.

Herring, George C. and Hess, Gary R. "Regionalism and Foreign Policy; The Dying Myth of Southern Internationalism." Southern Studies (Fall 1981): 247-77.

Hopewell, John L. "An Outsider Looking In: John Garland Pollard and Machine Politics in 20th Century Virginia." Unpublished Ph.D. dissertation, University of Virginia, 1976.

_____. "John Garland Pollard: A Progressive in the Byrd Machine." in Edward Younger and James T. Moore, eds., The Governors of Virginia, 1860-1978. Charlottesville: University Press of Virginia, 1982.

Howard, Irving. "The Influence of Southern Senators on American Foreign Policy from 1939 to 1950." Unpublished Ph.D. dissertation, University of Wisconsin, 1955.

Hunter, Robert F. "Carter Glass, Harry Byrd, and the New Deal, 1932-1936." Virginia Social Science Journal 4 (November 1969): 91-103.

_____. "Virginia and the New Deal." in John Braeman, Robert H. Bremmer, and David Brody, eds. The New Deal: The State and Local Levels. Columbus, Ohio: Ohio State University Press, 1975.

Irish, Marion D. "Foreign Policy and the South." in Journal of Politics X (May 1948): 306-26.

Johnson, Walter. The Battle Against Isolation. Chicago: University of Chicago Press, 1944.

Jonas, Manfred. Isolationism in America, 1935-1941. Ithaca, New York: Cornell University Press, 1966.

_____. "Isolationism." in Alexander DeConde, ed., Encyclopedia of American Foreign Policy. New York: Scribner's, 1978.

_____. "The United States and the Failure of Collective Security in the 1930s." in John Braeman, Robert H. Bremmer, and David Brody, eds., Twentieth-Century American Foreign Policy. Columbus, Ohio: Ohio State University Press, 1971, 241-93.

Kahn, Gilbert N. "Presidential Passivity on a Nonsalient Issue: President Franklin D. Roosevelt and the 1935 World Court Fight." Diplomatic

History 4:2 (1980): 137-60.

Key, V. O., Jr. Southern Politics in State and Nation. New York: Vintage Books, 1949.

Kimball, Warren F. The Most Unsordid Act: Lend-Lease, 1939-1941. Baltimore: Johns Hopkins Press, 1969.

Koeniger, Alfred Cash. "Carter Glass and the National Recovery Administration." South Atlantic Quarterly 74 (1975): 349-64.

_____. "The New Deal and the States: Roosevelt versus the Byrd Organization in Virginia." Journal of American History (March 1982): 876-96.

_____. "The Politics of Independence: Carter Glass and the Election of 1936." South Atlantic Quarterly 80 (Winter 1981): 95-106.

_____. "Unreconstructed Rebel: The Political Thought and Senate Career of Carter Glass, 1929-1936." Unpublished Ph.D. dissertation, Vanderbilt University, 1980.

Kottman, Richard N. Reciprocity and the North Atlantic Triangle, 1932-1938. Ithaca, New York: Cornell University Press, 1968.

Kuehl, Warren F. "Internationalists." in Warren F. Kuehl, ed. Biographical Dictionary of Internationalists. Westport, Conn. and London, England: Greenwood Press, 1983.

_____. "Internationalism." in Alexander DeConde, ed. Encyclopedia of American Foreign Policy. New York: Scribner's 1978, vol. 2, 443-54.

_____. "Internationalism and Peace." in Otis L. Graham, Jr., and Megham Robinson Wander, eds., Franklin D. Roosevelt: His Life and Times, An Encyclopedic View. Boston: G. K. Hall & Co., 1985.

Landecker, Manfred. The President and Public Opinion: Leadership in Foreign Affairs. Washington, D.C.: Public Affairs Press, 1968.

Langer, William L. and Gleason S. Everett. The Challenge to Isolation, 1937-1940. New York: Harper & Brothers Publishers, 1952; 1964.

Lebsock, Suzanne. "A Share of Honour": Virginia Women, 1600-1945. Richmond: Virginia State Library and Archives, 1984.
Lerche, Charles O., Jr. The Uncertain South: Its Changing Patterns of

Politics in Foreign Policy. Chicago: Quadrangle Books, 1964.

Leuchtenburg, William E. Franklin D. Roosevelt and the New Deal 1932-1940. New York, Evanston, & London: Harper & Row, 1963.

Levering, Ralph. The Public and American Foriegn Policy, 1918-1978. New York: William Morrow and Company, 1978.

Lubell, Samuel. "Who Votes Isolationist and Why." Harper's Magazine (April 1951): 29-36.

_____. The Future of American Politics, 2nd edit., rev. Garden City, New York: Doubleday and Co., Inc. 1956.

Lutz, Frank E. Richmond in World War II. Richmond: The Dietz Press, Inc., 1951.

Lyle, John D. "The United States Senate Career of Carter Glass of Virginia, 1919-1935." Unpublished Ph.D. dissertation, University of South Carolina, 1974.

Marsh, Charles F., ed. The Hampton Roads Communities in World War II. Chapel Hill: University of North Carolina Press, 1951.

McHale, James M. "National Planning and Reciprocal Trade: The New Deal Origins of Government Guarantees for Private Exporters." Prologue 6:3 (1974): 189-200.

McWilliams, Tennants. The New South Faces the World: Foreign Affairs and the Southern Sense of Self, 1877- 1950. Baton Rouge: Louisiana State University Press, 1988.

Miscamble, Wilson D. "Catholics and American Foreign Policy from Mckinley to McCarthy: A Historiographical Survey." Diplomatic History 4:3 (1980): 223-40.

Moger, Allen W. "Virginia's Conservative Political Heritage." South Atlantic Quarterly 50 (1951): 318-29.

Nevins, Allan. The New Deal in World Affairs, 1933-1945. New Haven, Conn.: Yale University Press, 1950.

Newport News History Commission. Newport News in the Second World War. Richmond: 1948.

Odum, Howard. Southern Regions of the United States. Chapel Hill: The

University of North Carolina Press, 1936.

Odum, Howard and Moore, Harry E. American Regionalism: A Cultural-Historical Approach to National Integration. New York: Henry Holt and Co., 1938.

Offner, Arnold A. "Appeasement Revisited: The United States, Great Britain, and Germany, 1933-1940." Journal of American History 64 (1977): 373-93.

Osgood, Robert E. Ideals and Self-Interest in America's Foreign Relations: The Great Transformation of the Twentieth Century. Chicago: University of Chicago Press, 1953.

Ostrower, Gary B. Collective Insecurity: The United States and the League of Nations during the Early Thirties. Lewisburg, Pa.: Bucknell University Press, 1979.

Palmer, James E., Jr., Carter Glass: Unreconstructed Rebel. Roanoke, Va.: Institute of American Biography, 1938.

Patterson, James T. "The New Deal and the States." American Historical Review 73 (1967): 70-84.

_____. The New Deal and the States. Princeton, N.J.: Princeton University Press, 1964.

Paterson, Thomas G. "Isolationism Revisited." Nation 209 (1969): 166-69.

Perkins, Dexter. A History of the Monroe Doctrine. Revised edit. Boston: Houghton Mifflin, 1963.

Peterson, Harold F. "Alexander Wilbourne Weddell." in John A. Garraty and Edward T. James, eds., Dictionary of American Biography. New York: Charles Scribner's Sons, 1974.

Pogue, Forrest C. George C. Marshall: Ordeal and Hope, 1939-1942. vol. II, New York: Viking, 1966.

Poindexter, Harry E. "From Copy Desk to Congress: The Pre-Congressional Career of Carter Glass. " Unpublished Ph.D. dissertation, University of Virginia, 1966.

Polenberg, Richard. War and Society: The United States, 1941-1945. Philadelphia: Lippincott, 1972.

Pratt, Julius W. Cordell Hull, 1933-1944. 2 vols. New York: Cooper Square, 1964.

Price, Harvey L., Virginia Farmers at War: Essays on Agricultural Production in the Old Dominion During the Second World War. Blacksburg: The Virginia Agricultural Extension Service, Virginia Polytechnic Institute and State University, 1950.

Rauh, Bazel. Roosevelt from Munich to Pearl Harbor: A Study in the Creation of a Foreign Policy. New York: Creative Age Press, 1950.

Rieselbach, Leroy N. The Roots of Isolationism: Congressional Voting and Presidential Leadership in Foreign Policy. Indianapolis: Bobbs-Merrill Company, 1966.

Roberds, Elmo. "The South and United States Foreign Policy, 1933-1952." Unpublished Ph.D. dissertation, University of Chicago, 1955.

Rubin, Louis D., Jr. Virginia: A History. New York: W. W. Norton & Company, 1984.

Salmon, Emily, ed. A Hornbook of Virginia History. Richmond: Virginia State Library, 1983.

Sargent, James E. "Clifton A. Woodrum of Virginia: A Southern Progressive in Congress, 1923-1945." Virginia Magazine of History and Biography 89 (1981): 341-64.

_____. "Woodrum's Economy Bloc: The Attack on Roosevelt's WPA, 1937-1939." Virginia Magazine of History and Biography XCII (1985): 175-207.

Schatz, Arthur W. "The Anglo-American Trade Agreement and Cordell Hull's Search for Peace, 1936-1938." Journal of American History 57: (1970): 85-103.

_____. "The Reciprocal Trade Agreements Program and the 'Farm Vote,' 1934-1940." Agricultural History 46: (1972): 498-514.

Schlegel, Marvin W. Conscripted City: Norfolk in World War II. Norfolk: Norfolk War History Commission, 1951.

_____. Virginia on Guard. Richmond: Virginia State Library, 1949.

Schlesinger, Arthur M., Jr. The Coming of the New Deal. Boston:

Houghton-Mifflin Company, 1958.

_____. The Imperial Presidency. Boston: Houghton-Mifflin Co., 1973.

Seabury, Paul. The Waning of Southern 'Internationalism.' Princeton, N.J.: Center of International Studies, 1957.

Smith, C. Calvin. War and Wartime Changes: The Transformation of Arkansas, 1940-1945. Fayetteville, Ar.: University of Arkansas Press, 1986.

Smith, Rixey, and Beasley, Norman. Carter Glass: A Biography. New York: Longmans, Green and Co., 1939.

Smith, Robert F. "Reciprocity." in Alexander DeConde, ed. Encyclopedia of American Foreign Policy. New York: Charles Scribner's Sons, 1978.

Smuckler, Ralph H. "The Regions of Isolationism." American Political Science Review 47 (June 1953): 386-401.

Steward, Dick. Trade and Hemisphere: The Good Neighbor Policy and Reciprocal Trade. Columbia: University of Missouri Press, 1975.

Stewart, William J., comp. and annot. (with the assistance of Jeanne Schauble). The Era of Franklin D. Roosevelt: A Selected Bibliography of Periodical, Essay, and Dissertation Literature, 1945-1971. Hyde Park, N.Y.: Franklin D. Roosevelt Library, 1974.

Stromberg, Roland N. "American Business and the Approach to War, 1935-1941." Journal of Economic History 13:1 (1953): 58-78.

_____. Collective Security and American Foreign Policy: From the League of Nations to NATO. New York: Praeger, 1963.

_____. "The Idea of Collective Security." Journal of the History of Ideas 17 (1956): 250-63.

Sweeney, James R. "Harry Byrd: Vanished Policies and Enduring Principles." Virginia Quarterly Review LII (1976): 596-612.

Sweetser, Arthur. "The United States, the United Nations and the League of Nations." International Conciliation (1946): 51-59.

Syrett, John. "Ambiguous Politics: James Price's First Months as Governor of Virginia." Virginia Magazine of History and Biography 94 (1986): 454-76.

_____. "The Politics of Preservation: The Organization Destroys Governor James H. Price's Administration." Virginia Magazine of History and Biography 97(1989): 437-462.

Tarter, Brent. "A Flier on the National Scene: Byrd's Favorite Son Presidential Candidacy of 1932." Virginia Magazine of History and Biography LXXXII (1974): 282- 305.

Tarter, Joe B. "Freshman Senator Harry F. Byrd: 1933- 1934." Unpublished M.A. thesis, University of Virginia, 1972.

Tasca, Henry J, The Reciprocal Trade Policy of the United States: A Study in Trade Philosophy. Philadelphia: University of Pennsylvania Press, 1938.

Temple, K. Richmond. "Alexander Weddell: Virginian in Diplomatic Service." Virginia Cavalcade. 34(1984): 22-39.

Tindall, George B. The Emergence of the New South, 1913-1945. Baton Rouge: Louisiana State University Press, 1967.

Tuttle, William N., Jr. "Aid to the Allies Short-of-War versus American Intervention; 1940, A Reappraisal of William Allen White's Leadership." Journal of American History 56 (1970): 840-58.

Underwood, Eric. "The Late A.W. Weddell." Virginia Magazine of History and Biography. 56(1948): 124.

Valaik, J. David. "Catholics, Neutrality and the Spanish Embargo, 1937-39." Journal of American History. 54(1967):74-85.

Vance, Rupert B., in collaboration with Nadia Danilevsky. All These People: The Nation's Human Resources in the South. Chapel Hill: The University of North Carolina Press, 1945.

Vipperman, Carl J. "The Coattail Campaign: James H. Price and the Election of 1937 in Virginia." Essays in History (History Club, University of Virginia) 8(1962- 63): 47-61.

Virginia Agriculture, 1900-1958: Handbook of Information. Blacksburg, Virginia: Virginia Polytechnic Institute, School of Agriculture, 1960.

Wamsley, James S. and Cooper, Anne M. Idols, Victims, Pioneers: Virginia Women from 1607. Richmond: Virginia State Chamber of Commerce, 1976.

Wander, Megham Robinson, and Graham, Otis L.,Jr. Franklin D. Roosevelt: His Life and Times, An Encyclopedic View. Boston: G. K. Hall & Co., 1985.

Weddell, Alexander W. Introduction to Argentina. New York: The Greystone Press, 1939.

Weinberg, Albert K. "The Historical Meaning of the American Doctrine of Isolation." American Political Science Review 34 (1940): 539-47.

Weiss, Stuart L. "American Foreign Policy and Presidential Power: The Neutrality Act of 1935." Journal of Politics 30 (1968): 672-95.

White, William S. "Meet the Honorable Harry (the Rare) Byrd." Reader's Digest 82 (April 1963): 205-12.

Wilkinson, J. Harvie III. Harry Byrd and the Changing Face of Virginia Politics, 1945-1966. Charlottesville: University Press of Virginia, 1968.

Wilkinson, Joe R. Politics and Trade Policy. Washington, D.C.: Public Affairs Press, 1960.

Wiltz, John E. From Isolation to War, 1931-1941. New York: Thomas Y. Crowell Co., 1968.

Wolfe, Jonathan J. "Virginia in World War II." Unpublished Ph.D. dissertation, University of Virginia, 1971.

Wood, Bryce. The Making of the Good Neighbor Policy. New York: Columbia University Press, 1961.

Woodward, C. Vann. The Burden of Southern History. Revised edit. Baton Rouge and London: Louisiana State University Press, 1960; 1968.

_____. "The Irony of Southern History." Journal of Southern History XIX (February 1953): 3-19.

Younger, Edward and Moore, James Tice, eds. The Governors of Virginia, 1860-1978. Charlottesville: University Press of Virginia, 1982.

INDEX

Abyssinia. *See* Ethiopia
Act of Havana, 106
Afro-American (Richmond), 201-3
Agricultural Adjustment Act (AAA) 7,25
Aid-to-Britain. *See* Interventionism
Alexandria Gazette, 57, 75, 104-6
Alley, Reuben E., 206-7
America First Committee, 17, 160, 165, 167,188, 198, 210, 215, 218, 221-23
American and British Commonwealth Association, 186
American Committee for Relief in Czechoslovakia, 144
American Federation of Labor, 211
American Seeds for British Soil fund, 212
American Tobacco Company, 118
Anschluss, 123 n.1
Argentina, 83-94, 96-100,104
Army Engineer School, 117
Astor, Lady, 227
Axis aggression, ix, x n.5, 12
Baptists, 6, 59, 125, 204 n.70, 206-7
Battle of Britain, 1, 18, 155, 182, 194
Bazile, Leon, 184
Benes, Edward, 144
Blacks, 6, 19, 60-61, 109, 120, 124, 150-52, 201-3, 204 n. 69
Bland, Schuyler Otis, 27, 160, 180
Boatwright, F. W., 141, 213
Boyd, Beverly, 205
Bracken, Brendan, 192
Brethren, 59, 135, 208
Bright, J. Fulmer, 141

Bristol Herald-Courier, 28
British Baptist Missionary Society, 207
British Information Services, 192
British Missions Fund, 205
British War Relief, 206
British West Indies, 202
Brown, Barbara Trigg. *See* Brown, Mrs. D. Tucker
Brown, Mrs. D. Tucker, 166, 196, 210, 215, 217
Bruce, David K. E., 39, 220, 220 n. 91
Bryan, John Stewart, 29, 34, 47, 52-53, 94, 186, 190-91
Buenos Aires conference, 81, 86, 90-91, 104
Burch, Thomas G., 27, 72, 160, 180
Burke, Donald, 61, 151
Burke-Wadsworth Selective Service Act, 16, 157, 162, 164, 170, 197-98
Businessmen, 210-11
Byrd, Harry F.: and foreign affairs, 49-51, 53, 66-69, 72, 74, 83-84, 89, 96-98, 127-28, 137, 144, 160-64, 167-74, 218, 223, 225
Byrd, Harry F.: and Great Depression, 6, 22, 22 n.4
Byrd, Harry F.: and New Deal, 7, 25, 25 n. 15, 26-28, 31-34, 174
Byrd, Harry F.: and 1932 presidential bid, 23, 23 n. 8
Byrd, Harry F.: and Roosevelt, x, 23, 25, 49, 158-59
Byrd organization, viii n. 3, 23 n. 5, 27, 27 n. 21, 32-33
Byrd, Richard E., 140-41, 188-90
Calisch, Edward N., 137, 139, 140-41, 210

Callcott, George C., ix
Camp A. P. Hill, 119
Camp Lee, 119, 170
Camp Peary, 115
Canada, 71, 73, 77, 107
Cannon, James, Jr., 207-8
Cardenas, Lazaro, 108
Carter, John W., 184
Century Club, 165, 216 n. 86
Chaco War, 82, 86, 95
Chesapeake and Ohio Railway, 115
China, x
Churchill, Winston S., 192
Clark, D. Worth, 107
Clark Memorandum, 80
Coast Artillery Board, 115
Coast Artillery School, 115
Cole, Wayne S., ix-x n. 5, 8, 9 n. 13, 14 n. 22
Collective security, 41, 41 n. 1, 42 n. 1
Collins, Harry T., 85
Collins, J. Stanley, 221
Collins, L. Preston, 185
Combs, E. R., 33
Committee of the American Friends of Czecho-Slovakia, 144
Committee to Defend America by Aiding the Allies. *See* White Committee
Commodity Credit Corporation, 11
Congress of Industrial Organizations (CIO), 190
Coolidge, Calvin, 45, 80
Council for Democracy, 189, 195
Council on Foreign Relations, 165, 186, 218
Court-packing plan, 7, 36, 94
Cuba, 81, 102
Czechoslovakia, 1, 13, 56, 124, 149, 153
Dabney, Richard Heath, 54
Dabney, Virginius: and foreign affairs 13-14 n. 22, 18, 49, 52, 54, 141, 146-49, 191, 194-97, 225
Dabney, Virginius: and Great Depression, 21
Dabney, Virginius: and New Deal, 39 n. 59
Dahlgren Proving Ground, 117
Daily Progress (Charlottesville), 74-75, 103-4, 107
Daniels, Josephus, 108-9
Danville Register, 75, 104, 106, 120-21
Darden, Colgate W., Jr., ix n. 3, 27, 29, 34, 160, 163, 178-79
Davis, Westmoreland, 28
de Cespedes, Carlos Manuel, 102
Declaration of Lima, 81, 104
Declaration of Panama, 81, 105
DEFENSE, 196
Democratic Party, vii, 7, 10, 15, 24, 30, 33-34, 38-39, 45, 47, 65, 104, 163, 171, 179, 184-85, 202
Destroyer deal, 157, 193, 197
Dodge Boat and Plane Corporation, 115
"Dollar Diplomacy," 80, 99, 109
Donovan, William 195
Draft Extension Act, 16
Drewry, Patrick Henry, 27, 72, 160, 162, 180
Duncan, John M., 142
Dunning, A. J., Jr., 222
du Pont nylon plant (Martinsville), 119
Early, Stephen, 37, 192
Economy Bloc, 35-36, 176
Eddy, Sherwood, 147
Educators, 142-43, 212-13
Emergency Peace Campaign, 138-39, 141-42, 144, 146-47
English-Speaking Union, 186, 210
Episcopalians, 59, 204 n. 70, 205 n. 70, 205-6
Espil, Don Felipe A., 92-93
Ethiopia, 54-55, 60-61, 124, 138,

145, 147, 149-51
Farley, James A., 30, 84, 163
Farmers, 120-22, 212
Federal Emergency Relief Administration (FERA), 7
Fellowship of Reconcilation, 142
Ferguson, Homer L., 211
Fifth Naval District, 115
Fight for Freedom Committee, 17, 160, 165-67, 184, 191, 196, 205, 207, 210-11, 215-18, 216 n. 86, 220
Fish, Hamilton, 175
Flannagan, John W., Jr., 28, 35, 161, 180
Ford Motor Company, 115
Foreign Mission Board, 207
Foreign Relations Committee (Senate), 44-46, 50, 131, 133, 163, 183
Fort Belvoir, 117
Fort Eustis, 115
Fort Monroe, 115
Fort Myer, 117
France, ix, x n. 5, 1, 8, 13, 54, 56, 61, 68, 98, 105, 123 n. 1, 125, 148-49, 151-54, 171, 209, 224
Franco, Francisco, 124, 134, 187
Frank, Morris, 209
Franks, Vincent C., 205
Fraternal/patriotic groups, 213-14
Freeman, Douglas, S.: and foreign affairs, 46, 49, 52-54, 63, 71-74, 83, 90-91, 98, 100, 141, 143-44, 182, 191-93, 225
Freeman, Douglas S.: and New Deal, 29, 34, 37-38
Fry, Joseph A., 28
Gaines, Francis R., 141, 213
Gardner, Emily, 136
Garnett, Robert S., 142
Geneva Disarmament Conference, *See* World Disarmament Conference in Geneva
George, Walter, 183

Germany, x, 1, 54-55, 70, 121, 143, 147-48, 152-53, 155, 157, 164-65, 179, 183, 189, 191-92, 194, 196-97, 199, 202, 208-9, 211, 213, 218, 219-20, 223, 226
Gibson, Churchill, 140
Gimenez, Rafael, 98
Glass, Carter: and foreign affairs, 11, 15, 17, 38-39, 44, 47-49, 51, 53, 63, 65-66, 72, 74, 83, 89, 96, 127-28, 135, 137-38, 142-43, 151, 160-67, 170, 223, 225
Glass, Carter: and New Deal, 7, 25, 25 n. 13, 15, 26-27, 30-34, 37-39
Glass, Carter: and Roosevelt, x, 163-64
Good Neighbor policy, 1-2, 8, 12, *See also* Virginia: and Good Neighbor policy
Grady, Henry F., 71-72, 97
Graves, John T., 14
Great Britain, vii, ix, x n. 5, 1, 8, 11, 13, 56, 60-61, 67-69, 71-73, 75-77, 87, 97, 121, 123 n. 1, 125, 149, 151-52, 153-224, 226
Great Depression, 11-12
Greece, 68
Greenland: occupation of, 157
Guam Naval Base Bill, 130
Hackworth, Green H., 133
Haile Selassie, 60
Hamilton, Norman, 29, 34
Harkrader, Charles, 28
Harris, Winder R., 163, 180
Havana conference, 81, 106
Held, Lewis I., Jr., 209
Hercules Powder Company, 117, 203
Hitler, Adolf, x, 1, 12-13, 15, 19, 38, 55, 91, 105, 125, 134, 144, 148, 152-53, 155-57, 163-65, 167, 173, 177, 179, 189-90, 194, 198-99, 202, 204, 206-7, 209, 211-12, 219-20, 223, 226
Hoare-Laval proposal, 55, 60

INDEX

Hoare, Samuel, 187
Hobson, Henry W., 165, 216
Hodges, LeRoy, 183
Hoover, Herbert, vii, 12, 95, 80
Horsley, J. Shelton, 139-41
Hull, Cordell, 11, 50, 63-77, 81-82, 84-88, 90-91, 95, 97, 103, 125, 131-32, 143, 207, 225
Hutchinson, Martin, 28
Iceland: occupation of, 157
Inter-American Committee (Richmond), 108
Internationalism, vii, ix, x, x n. 5, 8
Interventionism, ix, x, 1, 8-9, 16
Introduction to Argentina (Weddell), 92
Ireton, Peter L., 109, 141
Isolationism, ix n. 5, 1, 8-10, 9 n. 13, 16, 42, 124 n. 1, 135-36, 153
Italo-Ethiopian War. See Italy; Ethiopia
Italy, 1, 54-55, 57, 59, 60-61, 124, 138, 145, 147, 149-51
Jaffe, Louis 1., 191
Japan, x, 1, 11, 55, 59, 151, 154 n. 1
Jenks, W. J., 118
Jett, Robert C., 205
Jews, 19, 204, 204 n. 70, 208-10, 225
Joel, Milton, 209
Johnson Act, 9, 56, 127, 131, 143, 149, 155, 164, 214
Johnson, Hiram, 133
Journal and Guide (Norfolk) 60-61, 109, 150-52, 201-3
Kellogg-Briand Pact, 142
Kemper, W. M., 98
Key, V. O., Jr., 15
Knubel, F. H., 208
Knudsen, William S., 173
Kocen, Samuel, 185 n. 47
Koeniger, Alfred C., 37
Kuehl, Warren F., 8
Lacy, Ben R., Jr., 206

LaFollette Amendment, 147
Landon, Alf, 104
Langley Field, 115
Latin America. See Good Neighbor policy
League of Nations, 8, 10, 41-42
Lee, Robert E., 107
Lefkowitz, Sidney M., 141, 209
Lemke, William, 162
Lend-Lease Act, 16, 157, 162, 164, 174, 183, 188, 194, 198, 211, 213
Letcher, Greenlee D., 215
Liberia, 202
Lima conference, 92, 98, 104
Lindbergh, Charles A., 160, 166-68, 186, 188, 194, 198-99, 209, 215, 218, 221
Lodge, Henry Cabot, 97
Lothian, Ambassador Lord, 181
Luce, Henry R., 195
Ludlow Amendment, 124, 127, 129, 133, 135, 138, 146-49, 152
Lutheran Synod of Virginia, 208
Lutherans, 204 n. 70, 208
Lynchburg Advocates of Aid for Britain, 214
Lynchburg News, 199
Machado, Gerado, 102
Marine Hospital, 115
Marks, Morton, Jr., 209
Marshall, George Catlett, 18, 96, 188, 192
McNary, Charles L., 71, 90
McReynolds, Sam, 132-33
McWilliams, Tennant S., 14 n. 22
Merrill, John L., 84-85
Messersmith, George S., 99-100, 144
Methodists, 6, 59, 135, 204 n. 70, 207-8
Mexico, 81, 102-3, 108-9
Meyer, Eugene, 193
Miller, Carroll, R., 68
Miller, Francis P., 160, 183, 194, 218-20

INDEX

Mitchell, S. C., 140-41
Moger, Allen, 26
Moley, Raymond, 64
Monroe Doctrine, 12, 79-81, 90, 100-2, 104-6, 109, 219, 225
Monroe Doctrine Act of 1940, 98
Montague, Andrew J., 27, 84, 128-29
Montevideo Conference, 81, 85, 94-95, 103-4
Moore, John Bassett, 45
Moore, May, 136
Moore, R. Walton, 28, 50-51, 66, 131-33, 144, 185
Munich conference, 1, 13, 56-57, 125, 144, 146, 148-49, 152-53, 194
Munitions Investigating Committee, 9, 135-37
Murray, Philip, 190
Muse, Benjamin, 94-95, 184
Mussolini, Benito, 55, 61, 150, 152
Nansemond Ordnance Depot, 115
National Advisory Commission on Defense, 182
National Association for the Advancement of Colored People (NAACP), 109, 203
National Association of Manufacturers, 210-11
National Committee to Keep America Out of Foreign Wars, 175
National Defense Act, 138
National Defense Advisory Commission, 195-96
National Industrial Recovery Act (NIRA), 7, 25, 25 n. 14
National Peace Conference, 138, 142
Naval Air Station, 115
Naval Ammunition Deport, 115
Naval Mine Depot 115
Naval Operating Base, 115

Naval Training Station, 115
Neutrality, 125 n. 2
Neutrality acts, 16, 42, 124-25, 125 n. 2, 126-28, 132-34, 138-39, 142-43, 145-46, 149, 151, 153, 155, 157-58, 161-65, 168-69, 174-77, 179-81, 188, 191-94, 196, 198-99, 207, 210, 212-13, 216, 218, 223, 226
New York Times, 86
Newport News Shipbuilding and Dry Dock Company, 115, 211
New River Ordnance Works, 117
Noninterventionism. *See* Isolationism
Norfolk and Western Magazine, 75
Norfolk and Western (N&W) Railway Company, 117-18, 211
Norfolk Ledger-Dispatch, 58, 101, 106
Norfolk Naval Hospital, 115
Norfolk Navy Yard, 115, 169
Norfolk Virginian-Pilot, 191
Northern Virginia Daily, 70
Nottingham, Cherry, 143
Nye, Gerald, P., 47, 135, 137, 160
Nye Committee. *See* Munitions Investigating Committee
Nye-Kvale Bills, 138
O'Conner, John, 132
Office of Civilian Defense, 182
Office of the Coordinator of Inter-American Affairs, 108
Office of Strategic Services (OSS), 195, 220 n. 91
Osborn, G. Edwin, 136-38
Pan-American Conference, 96
Pan-American Society, 84-85
Panama Canal, 101, 219
Patterson, James T., 27
Patton, George S., 18
Peace Council of Petersburg, 141-42
Peek, George, 64
Peery, George C., 27-28

INDEX

Pepper, Claude, 215
Perkins, Frances, 136
Petersburg Defense Council, 184
Phillips, William, 87
Pittman, Key, 46, 50, 90, 132-33
Platt Amendment, 81, 81 n. 5, 101-2
Poland, 152
Pollard, John G., 6,22, 23 n. 5, 25, 46, 48-49, 51-52, 128, 136
Pope, James P., 147
Pope Resolution, 138
Portsmouth Star, 29
Poteat, McNeill, 138
Presbyterian of the South and the Presbyterian Standard, 206
Presbyterians, 59, 108, 135, 206
Price, James H., viii, 28, 31-33, 98, 181-83, 218
Protestants, 6, 19, 59-60, 135, 204-8
Public Works Administration (PWA), 7
Quakers, 59, 135, 208
Quantico Marine Base, 117
Raffaeli, Joseph E., 136
Reciprocal trade agreements program, 63-77, 87, 95-96, 103, 109
Red Cross, 206, 220
Religious Herald, 206-7
Remount Depot, 117
Republican Party, 64, 75, 105, 177, 184-85, 202
Reynolds, Robert, 16
Rhineland, 55
Richmond Christian Advocate, 207
Richmond News-Leader, 29, 38, 52, 54, 56-67, 72-74, 91, 99, 104, 106-7, 144-47, 149, 191-94
Richmond Peace Council, 58, 58 n. 50, 136-41, 144, 146-47
Richmond Planet, 61, 150-51
Richmond Times-Dispatch, 18, 31, 52, 54, 55-57, 74, 103-8,
121, 134, 146-49, 153, 155, 157, 191, 194, 196-98, 221
Ricks, J. Hoge, 136, 141
Rivinus, F. M., 211
Roanoke Times, 107
Roberts, Floyd H., 33-34, 34 n. 44
Robertson, A. Willis, 27, 63, 69-73, 97-98, 100, 130, 160, 177
Robinson, Joseph T., 46
Rockbridge County Defense Council, 215
Rohlsen, George, 31
Rollins, W. E., 205
Roman Catholics, 60, 79, 81, 108-9, 124, 133-34, 134 n. 18, 204, 204 n. 70, 208-9, 227
Roosevelt, Eleanor, 138, 140
Roosevelt, Franklin D: and elections, 16, 23, 31-32, 158-59
Roosevelt, Franklin D.: and foreign affairs, ix nn. 3, 5 x, 1, 8-10, 12-13, 15-16, 42, 42 n. 2, 43 n. 2, 63, 69, 79-81, 83, 85, 87, 90, 93-95, 100, 103, 111, 125, 127, 153-226
Roosevelt, Franklin D: and New Deal 1, 7, 9, 23 n. 7, 24 n. 11, 36-38
Roosevelt Corollary, 80
Root Formula, 45, 45 n. 10
Saar controversy, 54
Saavedra Lamas, Foreign Minister Carlos, 92
Sands, Oliver, J., 203, 214
Satterfield, David E., Jr., 160, 163, 179-180
Sayre, Francis B., 50
Sayre, John Nevin, 142
Scherer, J. J., Jr., 208
Seabury, Paul, 13 n. 20, 15, 37 n. 55, 39 n. 59
Second Wing, Army Air Force, 115
Selective Training and Service Act, 188

INDEX 255

Serrano Suner, Ramon, 187
Shenandoah Valley Defense Cooperative, 117
Ship Seizure Bill, 16
Shipstead, Henrik, 161
Shoaf, Ralph W., 222
Shoot-on-sight policy, 157
Smith, Charles J., 108
Smith, Howard W., 27, 160-61, 163, 180-81
Smith, J. W. Rixey, 30
Smoot-Hawley tariff, 11, 56, 64-67, 71
Social Security Act, 26
Socialist Party, 185 n. 47
Solvay Process Company, 119
South: and Great Depression, 11
South: and internationalism, vii, vii n. 1, viii, xi, 13, 14 n. 22, 41, 153, 154 n. 1, 155, 156 n. 2, 157, 160
South: and interventionism, vii, 13, 14 n. 22, 15-16, 37 n. 55, 39 n. 59, 123 n. 1, 153, 154 n. 1, 155, 156 n. 2, 157, 160
South: and isolationism, 17, 17 n. 32, 127, 160
South: and League of Nations, 10, 41
South: and military defense, 126 n. 2, 159 n. 4
South: and neutrality, 123 n. 1, 126 n. 2, 127, 153
South: and reciprocal trade, 11, 63
South: and World Court, 10, 41-42
South: and World War I, vii, 112
South: and World War II, vii, 11-13, 111-12, 153, 154 n. 1, 155, 156 n. 2, 157, 160
Southern Baptist Convention, 207
Southern Council on International Relations, 12
Southern Jewish World, 209
Southern Planter, 75, 120-21

Soviet Union, x n. 5, 61, 151
Spain, 1, 55, 187
Spanish Civil War, 124, 126 n. 2, 133-34, 146-47, 149, 187
State, Department of, 66-68, 71-72, 81-82, 86, 97, 99-100, 131, 144, 187
Statement of Urgency, 218
Staunton News-Leader, 199
Stimson, Henry L., 45, 80
Strauss, Lewis L., 209
Submarine Mine Depot, 115
Summons to Speak Out, 218
Swanson, Claude A., 10, 28, 31, 43, 43 n. 4, 44-46, 44 n. 4, 51, 53, 84, 185
Sweeney, Elsie, 221
Tabb, T. Garnett, 186
Taylor, Mrs. R. F., 222
Third Coast Artillery District, 115
Time, 195
Tindall, George B., 14 n. 22, 15
Torpedo Station, 117
Trade unionists, 120, 143, 211-12
Tucker, Beverly D., 59-60, 139, 141
Tucker, Henry St. George, 205
Turkey, 68
United Americans, 195
United Service Organizations (U.S.O.), 205
United States Army, General Headquarters (G.H.Q.), 115
United States Army Quartermaster's Corps, 119
United States Chamber of Commerce, 210
Versailles treaty, 55-56
Virginia: and Anglo-Saxon heritage, vii, 6, 13, 19, 156, 156 n. 2, 206, 225-27, 226 n. 1
Virginia: and elections, 158
Virginia: and Good Neighbor policy, vii-viii, x, 1, 2, 79-110, 225

Virginia: and Great Depression, ix n. 3, x, 6, 21-39, 63
Virginia: and internationalism, vii-viii, 1, 7, 10, 13-14 n. 22, 41, 123, 136, 139, 144, 153-224, 225-227
Virginia: and interventionism, vii, x-xi, 1-2, 7, 12-13, 14 n. 22, 17-19, 38, 111, 143, 153-224, 225-227
Virginia: and isolationism, 1, 17-18, 134, 160, 198-99, 204, 206, 208, 213, 221-23, 225-26
Virginia: and League of Nations, vii, x, 1-2, 10, 41-62, 138-39, 149, 151, 225
Virginia: and military defense, 125, 137, 139-40, 149, 153-224, 226
Virginia: and neutrality, xi, 2, 9, 13, 123-152, 156, 194, 208, 225-26
Virginia: and New Deal, viii n. 3, x, 7, 17, 21-39, 111-13, 225
Virginia: and reciprocal trade, vii, x, 1-2, 63-77, 139, 225
Virginia: and Sino-Japanese War, x
Virginia: and United Nations, ix n. 3
Virginia: and World Court, vii, x, 2, 10, 41-62, 137, 139, 225
Virginia: and World War I, 123
Virginia: and World War II, viii, viii n. 3, ix n. 3, xi, 1-2, 8, 12-13, 111-22, 153-224
Virginia: and World War II era economy, 11-12, 111-22
Virginia Catholic, 60, 108, 134, 208-9
Virginia Churchman, 205
Virginia Conference of the Methodist Church, 207
Virginia Defense Council, 182, 210
Virginia Journal of Education, 142
Virginia Lutheran, 208
Virginia Methodist Advocate, 207
Virginia Military Institute (VMI), 18, 96, 181
Virginia Protective Force, 211
Virginia State Chamber of Commerce, 211
Virginia State Federation of Labor, 143, 211
Wagner Labor Relations Act, 113
Waitt, Robert W., Jr., 221
Washington Post, 193
Weddell, Alexander Wilbourne, 50, 82-94, 99, 104, 124, 186-87
Weddell, Virginia Chase Steedman, 83
Welles, Sumner, 66, 70, 88, 91, 97, 102
Wheeler, Burton K., 160, 189
Wheeler-Bennett, John W., 192
White, John W., 86
White, Walter, 109
White, William Allen, 194-95
White Committee, 17, 160, 186, 191, 195, 203, 205-6, 208, 210-11, 214-15
Williams, John Skelton, Jr., 211
Willkie, Wendell L., 16, 158-59, 167, 184, 196, 202-3
Wilson, Woodrow, 10, 41, 44, 44 n. 4, 47, 54-55, 61-62, 149, 225
Winston, W. T., 108-9
Women: and defense plant employment, 120
Woodrum, Clifton A., 28-29, 35-36, 76-77, 117, 129-31, 160, 174-77, 179
Woodrum Field, 117
Works Progress Administration (WPA), 7, 35-37
World Court, 8, 10, 41-42, 43 n. 2, 44, 46
World Disarmament Conference in Geneva, 45, 127, 144
Zabriskie, A. C., 205

Rorin M. Platt is Visiting Assistant Professor of History at The University of Tennessee at Chattanooga. A native of Roanoke, Virginia, he received his B.A. from the University of North Carolina at Chapel Hill (1976) and his Ph.D. from the University of Maryland at College Park (1989). Professor Platt has also taught at the University of North Carolina at Greensboro, The University of Tennessee at Knoxville, The University of Maryland, Baltimore County, and St. Stephen's School, Alexandria, Virginia.